Everybody Ought to Be Rich

Everybody Ought to Be Rich

The Life and Times of John J. Raskob, Capitalist

DAVID FARBER

OXFORD
UNIVERSITY PRESS

OXFORD
UNIVERSITY PRESS

Oxford University Press is a department of the University of Oxford.
It furthers the University's objective of excellence in research, scholarship,
and education by publishing worldwide.

Oxford   New York
Auckland   Cape Town   Dar es Salaam   Hong Kong   Karachi
Kuala Lumpur   Madrid   Melbourne   Mexico City   Nairobi
New Delhi   Shanghai   Taipei   Toronto

With offices in
Argentina   Austria   Brazil   Chile   Czech Republic   France   Greece
Guatemala   Hungary   Italy   Japan   Poland   Portugal   Singapore
South Korea   Switzerland   Thailand   Turkey   Ukraine   Vietnam

Oxford is a registered trade mark of Oxford University Press
in the UK and certain other countries.

Published in the United States of America by
Oxford University Press
198 Madison Avenue, New York, NY 10016

Library of Congress Cataloging-in-Publication Data
Farber, David R.
Everybody ought to be rich : the life and times of John J. Raskob, capitalist / David Farber.
        pages cm
Includes bibliographical references and index.
ISBN 978–0–19–973457–3 (acid-free paper)
1. Raskob, John J. (John Jakob), 1879–1950.   2. Capitalists and financiers—United States—Biography.
3. United States—History—20th century.   I. Title.
HG172.R37F37 2013
338.092—dc23
[B]
2012041760

9 8 7 6 5 4 3 2 1
Printed in the United States of America
on acid-free paper

In memory of Adolph H. Rosenthal (1902–1978)
who believed in hard work, family, and being a mensch

CONTENTS

ACKNOWLEDGMENTS

Researching this book gave me opportunities to meet and talk and work with hundreds of people who were in some way connected with John J. Raskob. I am indebted to them all. This history could not have been written without their help.

As always I am thankful to the librarians and archivists who allow historical research to march forward. My particular thanks to the professionals at the Library of Congress. Our national library is a gold mine, and I feel lucky to have worked its rich veins, guided by the men and women of the manuscripts division. Once again, I have also found gold at the Columbia Center for Oral History at Columbia University. Special thanks to the staffs at the Scharchburg Archives at Kettering University and at Zimmerman Library, University of New Mexico, my old stomping grounds, where I was thrilled to discover the Thomas Campbell Papers. I also benefited from manuscripts at the Franklin D. Roosevelt Presidential Library. Thanks as well to Jeri Vogelsang at the Palm Springs Historical Society for help with photos. Patrick Scalasi at *Columbia*, the magazine of the Knights of Columbus, found a profile of Raskob for me in his magazine's archive and sent it to me within minutes. My special thanks, as well, to Terri Waller at the Raskob Foundation for Catholic Activities who compiled and made available to me critical historical documents exploring the foundation's early days. My home library at Temple University was critically important to this book; the university library's dedication to funding key historical databases, book acquisitions, and reference collections made this project possible. Special thanks to David Murray whose dedication and expertise is an invaluable asset to all history researchers at Temple.

My utmost thanks go to the people who work at the Hagley Library, particularly in the manuscript and archival collection. The recently retired Marge McNinch shared her in-depth knowledge of the du Pont family with me and pointed me toward several fruitful areas of research. Richard James received the assignment to process the John. J. Raskob papers at roughly the same time as I began this book. He provided me with dozens of spectacularly useful documents, information he personally compiled, and ideas for research. Richard, a relative newcomer to the profession, is one of the very best with whom I have ever had the good fortune to work. For most of my research time at the Hagley I thought of deputy director for library administration Terry Snyder as my fairy godmother. Terry always made researching at the Hagley productive but just as important she made it fun. She has since moved up to become Librarian at Haverford Library—I need to find a research project that brings me to her new digs. Thanks as well to the many other members of the Hagley family for all their assistance over the many years I haunted the reading room at the Soda House. The du Pont family has done many extraordinary things over the last several centuries; their establishment and continued commitment to the Hagley Museum and Library is a marvelous gift to everyone who is interested in the history of industry and the private enterprise system. I know of no other place like it in the world.

Throughout the long process of working on this book, I have felt fortunate to be guided by my editor at Oxford University Press, Susan Ferber. Susan is a hands-on editor of the old school and I am grateful for her sharp eye and keen insights. Thanks, as well, to the entire production and marketing team at Oxford, a great and good publishing house.

This book would not have been possible without the help of the Raskob family. Over the years I have talked with dozens of members of the family who have been so generous in sharing their memories, good will, and a few research gems. They have cheered on this book from the beginning and have been patient—well, pretty patient—waiting for me to finish. They have done more than wish me well. The Raskob Foundation for Catholic Activities, the family foundation established by John and Helena Raskob in 1945, provided a large grant to the Hagley that facilitated the reprocessing of the Raskob collection that made my work possible. Through the administrative offices of the Hagley they also supported a family oral history project, led by Richard James, in which I participated. The Foundation also supplied me—administered through the Hagley—with a grant that helped defray research expenses, provided research assistance, and gave me two summer research stipends. These grants-in-aid came with no strings attached whatsoever. I am grateful for their arm's length commitment to the project.

I owe special thanks to John Raskob's grandson, Charles Raskob Robinson. Charlie had read my book on Alfred Sloan and contacted me out of the blue and asked me if I would not be interested in writing about his grandfather. I had earlier penciled in an account of JJR on my "maybe" list and was flabbergasted by his call. While Charlie is several inches taller than his grandfather and a much more dapper fellow, I quickly came to understand how John Raskob was able to accomplish so much. Charlie paddled his way solo up the Amazon as a teenager, became an investment banker, then decided to give that up to paint—his work hangs in museums around the country. He is always juggling about a hundred side projects while he keeps in close contact with half the world. My wife told me I should also note that he has the best manners of any man she has ever met. The fact that his wife Barbara Paul Robinson is at least as accomplished, energetic, and invested in the world makes the Robinson duo a terrific template for imagining just how JJR moved through the world. That writing about John Raskob allowed me to get to know Charlie and Barbara has been an extraordinary treat.

Singling out other members of the Raskob clan—there are hundreds—is a bit dangerous as so many were so generous in their support. But I want to note that John Harmon, who had done his own historical research on his grandfather, graciously read the manuscript and steered me right on several important points. I also want to thank Kerry Robinson, great granddaughter and the executive director of the National Leadership Roundtable on Church Management, for looking over my sections related to Catholicism and the Church. Similar thanks to Dana Robinson for catching a whopper before the book went to press. Chris Raskob provided me with a wealth of material on Pioneer Point. I had a really useful talk with Pete Raskob before he died. Pete was Minerva and John Junior's son and in talking honestly about his parents and their relationship with JJR he helped me gain insight into what JJR was like as a father—not easy—and as a father-in-law—a delight. I also learned a great deal from talking with Sister Pat Geuting, who had a lot of fun with her grandfather on their 1950 trip to Europe. So many other members of the Raskob family gave me encouragement, useful tips, and their always interesting perspectives on the project. That they did so knowing—because I warned them regularly—that I had been accused by prior subjects of harsh treatment ("You don't know what it was like!" the pacifist Dave Dellinger roared at me after he read my critical account of his role in the 1968 Chicago antiwar protests) is a testament to their generosity.

I also benefited from the help of many others. I received sage advice from Al Smith's biographer Chris Finan; his counsel saved me not just from factual errors but from errors of interpretation. While my interpretation of Smith's turn away from the New Deal and embrace of the Liberty League is not his, it is, I hope, at least better argued thanks to his weighty objections. Thanks as well to Doug Craig, who knows way more about the politics of the Democratic Party in the first third of the twentieth century than I do; his published work and our conversations made me think harder and hopefully better about the era and Raskob's political role. I am much obliged, as well, to Sid Milkis for his incisive comments on the paper I gave on Raskob as political operator at the policy history conference; I am grateful to Alan Loeb for sharing his research on the time a container of tetraethyl lead blew up John Raskob's garage (a story, alas, left on the cutting room floor) and to Neil Jumonville for his encouraging comments at the US intellectual history conference.

I am indebted to the Longwood Foundation, established by Pierre du Pont; it also provided me with a research grant administered through the Hagley Museum and Library. My home institution, Temple University, generously chipped in with a summer research grant that helped move the project along. At Temple, I am comfortably housed in the history department where I am lucky to work with Patricia Williams and Vangie Campbell; their help through the years I have spent on this project is much appreciated. Thanks to my Temple colleagues, especially Drew Isenberg, Petra Goedde, David Watt, Laura Levitt, Harvey Neptune, Jay Lockenour, Heather Thompson, Jon Wells, David Waldstreicher, Vlad Zubok, Ralph Young, and Bryant Simon. Richard Immerman, éminence grise at Temple and the Center for the Study of Force and Diplomacy, has, as usual, battered down the many impediments that might have blocked both my scholarly pursuits and appropriate levels of fun. Before he died in 2007 Alfred Chandler and I talked about Pierre du Pont and John Raskob; it was an honor and a delight to hear our greatest business historian hold forth on a subject he knew so well. I also had the opportunity to talk about Pierre du Pont with Irénée du Pont, Jr. Mr. du Pont graciously helped me see his uncle as more than words on a page. We really need a life and times biography of Pierre du Pont (and I am not nominating myself to write it). Roy Lopata, who wrote his dissertation on Raskob's political operations, read chapters and provided me with expert advice; and as cited in my notes, his dissertation was essential to my own work. I also benefited from the advice of Joe Melloy, an alumnus of Archmere Academy who has done so much to preserve the Patio, former home of JJR and his family. My thanks, in memoriam, to Alberta Melloy, Joe's dear wife, who shared stories with me of her youth when she visited Pioneer Point. Former graduate students Lincoln Bramwell, Kate Scott, and Ryan Edgington provided me with expert research assistance. My son Max chipped in with some first-rate work on my behalf at the Hagley, as well. Good on ya, mate.

For my wife Beth Bailey: L.B.B.W.S.B. who is also B.W. when she is O.T. As always Beth read every word and gave her polish to every piece of prose. I promise: no more monologues about debentures, wash sales, or equity instruments...for a while, at least. After I finish this sentence—or as soon after as is possible—we are off to Maui.

D.F.

Everybody Ought to Be Rich

Introduction

"The name Raskob does not seem to suggest romance" began an article in one of America's most popular magazines at the advent of the Jazz Age.[1] But by 1927, when Big Business ruled the land, John Jakob Raskob was widely celebrated as a heroic figure, "an artist, though one who deals in facts and figures rather than pigments or marble."[2] His reputation reached its apogee in 1929, when he declared in an article published in the *Ladies Home Journal* that "Everybody ought to be rich!" He would become infamous soon enough, when the path to riches he promoted—monthly investments in the stock market—proved spectacularly bad advice.

John Jakob Raskob was far more than those few ill-timed words of advice.[3] In his day, he embodied the American Dream. In the first decades of the twentieth century, he exemplified what it meant to be a man of humble and provincial beginnings who joined the highest reaches of the American elite. In a 1919 front-page profile, the venerable and conservative New York *Sun* explained Raskob's rise in a way that captured the meaning it had for the era's burgeoning middle class. The well-known New York City writer and bon vivant Ed Hill focused on Raskob's small-town upbringing. Raskob, he explained, had been born in the old and dying Erie Canal service town of Lockport. The people in Lockport, New York, Hill continued, did not expect "geniuses" to be born in their midst: "Country towns all over the United States are full of middle aged and elderly men who have never been able to beat this point of view—to tear loose from it. The hometown gets hold of them somehow and cramps them and clogs their feet and chills their ambition, and they give up finally and bog down for life. Not Raskob."[4] Raskob, born in 1879, would not "Go West" to find his opportunity as had a prior generation. He would instead find his main chance in the hard-edged new world of capital.

John Raskob was not exactly an "Alger boy." He did not go from rags to riches. His father ran a modestly successful, local cigar-making business. Still, Raskob did haul himself up from the provincial backwaters and reach the center of national politics, finance, and culture. He was a small-town boy who became a big-city tycoon. Raskob had innate talent and some uncanny skills. And he would be helped by a host of well-born men. But, in large part, what people in the early decades of the twentieth century admired about John Raskob was that in making his way to the top he displayed a remarkable amount of pluck. The word "pluck" is little used today but in the early years of modern America it was the preferred term for heroes and heroines who displayed a combination of resourcefulness, dash, and spirited courage in the face of life's travails and uncertainties. John Raskob had pluck in spades.[5]

Raskob was the real-life version of the characters F. Scott Fitzgerald and Sinclair Lewis created in their portraits of the money-making men of the Jazz Age. He began as a $5 a week stenographer at Holly Pump and Machine Shops. He became the financial helmsman of the DuPont Company and then General Motors. His stock pronouncements made headline news and moved the markets. He built the Empire State Building. Raskob was one of a small group of men who created the capitalist order of the modern United States. As the leading business journalist in the 1920s wrote: "John J. Raskob of Wilmington, Delaware is to-day the organizing genius of this country."[6]

Americans tend to measure their historical journey through the lives of their most prominent politicians and statesmen—Washington and Lincoln, Theodore Roosevelt and Franklin Roosevelt, Kennedy and Reagan—a reasonable and understandable approach for a democratic people. They trace their struggle for social justice and civil rights by memorializing the efforts of individuals such as Frederick Douglass, Susan B. Anthony, Jane Addams, Martin Luther King, Jr., and the millions who marched and sat-in, picketed, struck, and organized. But just as the United States was shaped by democratic politics and social struggle, it was also forged by capitalists and the free market system. Thus, the stories of its most successful capitalists—men such as Stephen Girard, Cornelius Vanderbilt, John D. Rockefeller, and Sam Walton—tell us something equally significant about the making and meaning of the United States.[7] From the age of industrialization through the Jazz Age and then into the economic abattoir of the Great Depression, John Raskob helped write chapter and verse of America's free market adventure.

Raskob was a doer: a corporate financier, a stock market mover, a builder, a political operator, a philanthropist, a fun lover, a family man, a man of faith, a promoter of capitalist risk-taking, and an ever-restless instigator. The amount of energy he poured into life was prodigious. For decades, he had a framed statement in his office: "Go ahead and do things, the bigger the better, if your fundamentals are sound. Avoid procrastination. Do not quibble for an hour over things which might be decided in minutes. However, if the issue at stake is large, stay as long as the next man, but go ahead and do things."[8] From the time he was a $5-a-week stenographer in 1900 to when he became one of the nation's wealthiest men on the eve of the stock market crash in 1929, Raskob followed his own advice.

The drive to "do things," lots of things, lay at the core of Raskob's character. Raskob's own family often wondered what made their *pater familias* tick. Like many of the great men of the second industrial revolution, including Andrew Carnegie and John D. Rockefeller, Raskob was driven not by greed or avarice, or by the desire for adulation and power. Raskob's drive, at least in its rawest form, seemed to be almost physical. He loved to be, literally, in motion, careening from place to place and from opportunity to opportunity. From childhood days, he looked for ways to speed through his daily life. When he was young, he ran when others walked. He pedaled like a madman when he rode his beloved first bicycle. Later, he would fly down unpaved roads in automobiles, picking up moving violations at an alarming rate. Even in his old age he took pride and pleasure in his ability to speed-walk his way along crowded mid-Manhattan sidewalks as he raced from his East Side apartment to his Empire State Building office. Motion kept Raskob calm; the faster he moved the better he felt. Where that need came from Raskob never said, and no recorded early childhood incident lends itself to psychological explanation. The desire seems to have always been there: to be in motion and to stay in motion and to never just sit and watch the world go by. While Raskob's passion for speed and motion and change would on more than one occasion move him in the wrong direction, bringing financial reversal and personal crisis, much more regularly his restless character and physical need for motion linked up with his talents to produce extraordinary outcomes.

Raskob was an architect of the capitalist system. He was fascinated by the flow of money, the workings of the credit markets, the processes by which value was given to company assets, real estate, and stock prices. Without formal education, he drilled down into company reports and made himself a master of bond divestures and equity offerings. His interests were anything but academic. In partnership with the great industrialists and financiers of his time he put his knowledge to work: buying up companies, leveraging investments, creating new pools of credit for both the rich investor and the middle-class consumer, reorganizing corporations, plotting hostile takeovers, financing skyscrapers, and channeling money into the political system. Raskob was one of a handful of men in the United States who created the credit revolution at both the elite and the mass level that fueled America's spectacular, world-leading economic growth.[9]

Raskob was not much interested in the making and marketing of goods or new products. In that sense, he was nothing like Henry Ford. He built platforms—in his case financial platforms—that allowed companies to grow and consumers to buy. Raskob focused his genius on devising new ways for credit to flow from banker to industrialist, from investor to entrepreneur, and from seller to consumer. Raskob worked at the interstices of industry, finance, and—by the late 1910s—the booming new marketplace for consumer goods, specifically autos.

Within the business world, Raskob was a celebrated figure. Every big banker and corporate titan knew him and sought his friendship and his advice. During the 1920s *Time* magazine, the *New York Times*, and the *Wall Street Journal* printed story after story on Raskob's daring business escapades and financial moves. When he threw himself into politics in the late 1920s as manager of Al Smith's presidential campaign and head of the Democratic National Committee, he made headlines across the United States.

Despite such publicity, much of what Raskob actually did was often mysterious to the American public. He never ran a major corporation. He never invented a noteworthy product. Even when he started up a new enterprise he almost never took public credit for his accomplishment. When he built the tallest skyscraper in the world—the Empire State Building—he did not name that building after himself, as his close friend and rival Walter Chrysler had done with his own venture. Raskob did not even name himself president of the corporation that owned and managed the building. He gave that honor to Al Smith, whose 1928 presidential bid Raskob had largely funded and who, in the aftermath of defeat, needed a noteworthy position as balm to his wounded pride (and his empty wallet). Raskob never sought the limelight; he was the anti-Trump of his time.

Raskob's indifference to publicity was partially a matter of character. His ego needed little reinforcement from the public-at-large; his close friends in America's corporate and financial elite gave him more than enough praise and respect to maintain his sense of self. And Raskob saw no benefit in seeking publicity given how many of his financial deals involved careful, even secretive maneuvering.

Perhaps Raskob's indifference—even hostility—to publicity helps to explain why Raskob faded from American memory. Given the abstract quality and often deliberately secretive nature of their work, capitalists and financiers like John Raskob have often remained at the periphery of the American story—unless scandal or criminality or a debacle of some kind brought them public disgrace. Raskob got such unwelcome attention when the stock market crashed and when some of his less savory stock market plays were very publicly investigated by New Deal congressional committees. He was slammed by politicians and journalists for his role in luring the unwary investor into the great Bull Market of the late 1920s and for exploiting lax financial regulations to avoid federal taxes. Given how little clarity Raskob had brought to his place in the American economy or how rarely Raskob had taken credit for his successful financial alchemy, perhaps it is not surprising that in the public mind his glaring failures overwhelmed his complicated achievements. As the New Deal era replaced the Jazz

Age, chroniclers reduced Raskob to a footnote: he was one of the Old Order who delivered America to the ravages of the Great Depression. Raskob's role in American history deserves more and Raskob himself—a compelling character—deserves better.

When Raskob was barely out of his teenage years he partnered with Pierre du Pont to create one of the world's greatest business corporations. In 1902, Raskob worked side-by-side with the young Pierre du Pont to engineer the leveraged buyout of the DuPont Company, then a mid-sized family-owned explosive powders company operating in an illegal industry-wide cartel. Pierre and two of his capable cousins bought the creaky family business from their moribund elders for just $2,100 in cash. John and Pierre figured out how to finance the other $14 million. Then the unlikely partners, one a self-taught, small-town Catholic boy and the other an MIT-educated scion of a storied and wealthy family, crafted and deployed a sophisticated array of debt instruments to raise millions more to take control of the explosives industry, invest in research and innovation, reorganize every aspect of the corporation's operations, and lay the groundwork for DuPont's industrial empire.

Raskob's total dedication to the DuPont Company won him Pierre's love; his consistently successful financial strategies earned him the trust and respect of the rest of the men who ran the nation's largest explosives company. So when Raskob decided in 1915 that the sputtering new General Motors Company represented the greatest financial opportunity he had ever seen, Pierre and the rest of the DuPont men agreed to do what John recommended. Over time, Raskob wagered tens of millions of DuPont money, representing a sizable portion of the extraordinary profits the company had accrued from selling its deadly wares during the Great War, to finance the General Motors Company. Without DuPont's massive infusion of capital, General Motors could not have survived. As the business press of the era reported, it was Raskob, and Raskob alone, who brought the DuPont millions to GM.

To safeguard those millions, Raskob left his position as the chief financial officer of the DuPont Company to take over GM's finances. Billy Durant, GM's founder, became Raskob's new partner in corporate adventure. Raskob found the capital Durant said he needed to grow the business. Quickly enough, Raskob discovered that his new partner could not have been more different than the old one. Pierre du Pont was a rock steady, by-the-numbers corporate strategist. Durant had risk-taking zest and dreamed of every American family owning one or even two gleaming cars. Together, he and Durant were building not just a company but a new industry, a new way of life.

Most Wall Street bankers believed Billy Durant was much too willing to let his fantastic dream of an auto nation get in the way of sound corporate strategy. Raskob ran interference for Durant, justifying his plans to investors and finding

Durant the money he needed to buy up competitors, acquire more companies, hire talented managers, and expand into new markets. Raskob and the other men who helped run GM—including Walter Chrysler and Alfred Sloan—did their best to make Durant's dream a workable reality. But each of those men, as they watched Durant spend millions without much care for organizational efficiency or rational disbursement of investment capital, lost faith. Raskob was one of the last to doubt Durant. But when he finally took one risk too many, Raskob, in association with the hardnosed men of the House of Morgan, shoved Durant out the door.

Raskob then talked Pierre du Pont into replacing Durant as GM president. In the early 1920s, they partnered with Alfred Sloan to rebuild General Motors. It was Raskob who figured out how to beat Henry Ford at his own game by betting on a consumer credit revolution and creating GM's installment buying arm, GMAC, which allowed car dealers to fill their showrooms and millions of people to afford GM's more expensive and stylish cars. Then, to motivate and maintain the loyalty of GM's extraordinary management team, most especially the irreplaceable Alfred Sloan, Raskob devised one of the first corporate stock option plans. The business press dubbed it Raskob's "millionaires' club." The press was not exaggerating; dozens of GM managers would accrue GM stock worth millions (including Raskob); Sloan, who took over as GM president in 1923, eventually made hundreds of millions of dollars. The business elite saw Raskob as a visionary who had figured out how to get managers of corporate America to act like owners; instead of working only for salary they were working for a share of the company's profits. Raskob's stock option plan for top managers became conventional wisdom in corporate America.

Raskob was, in his time, best known for his financial genius. Without the money and status he earned in the business world his other activities in politics, religion, and philanthropy would not have been possible. But Raskob was more than just a successful capitalist; he threw himself into the life of the nation. He worked with everyone from President Wilson to John Rockefeller in attempting to solve the bitter labor strife of the post-World War I years. He was toasted in the 1920s, at least by some, for promoting labor peace through shared prosperity. From his early days in the business world, motivated in part by his own rise from relative obscurity, he thought about ways in which economic opportunity could be widely expanded. At the DuPont Company and then at General Motors he created savings and stock option plans for both salaried employees and hourly workers. He desperately wanted to bridge class divides in American life, and his fondest hope was that he could create a way to share the wealth the American corporate system was fast producing.

In the late 1920s Raskob laid out a plan to operate the largest investment trust in the world. Working people, he announced, would be welcome investors in this massive trust; for just a small monthly payment they, too, could leverage their money and become shareholders in America's booming corporate economy. "Everybody," he said, "ought to be rich." Before Raskob could launch his investment trust for the masses, the stock market broke and then crashed. Luckily for Raskob he had not realized his dream of taking and investing the savings of millions of working Americans in the stock market; if he had he would have lost it all.

Although Raskob had not directly invested the public's money in the market, he was pilloried by pundits and politicians for having ballyhooed corporate shareholding just before the Crash came. In a few months' time, Raskob went from Jazz Age hero to villain of the Old Order. He never accepted any responsibility for contributing to the stock market bubble. Instead, he felt betrayed by those who refused to understand that risk was at the very heart of the capitalist system and that losses were a part of the game. Raskob was never much good at understanding that few people had his nerve and willingness to rebound from dramatic setbacks; he failed to grasp that most of his fellow countrymen wanted less risk and more security in their lives.

Raskob himself lost most of his personal fortune in the 1930s. That loss bothered him much less than did Americans' support for the New Deal which, he believed, punished capitalist risk-taking by redistributing wealth and restricting economic opportunities. In the 1930s, Raskob stopped dreaming of making "everybody rich" and threw himself into safeguarding his own wealthy class. As the founder and behind-the-scenes operator of the American Liberty League, Raskob directed capitalists' most direct attack on the New Deal. Raskob, alongside other wealthy men, laid the course for economic conservatives' decades-long struggle to rein in the liberal welfare state.

Raskob believed that the great majority of Americans best served their own interests by binding their economic future to America's job-creating and wealth-producing elite. Public policies, government interventions, and even good-hearted politicians that stood in the way of that free market productivity weakened the national fabric and reduced, he argued, all Americans' ability to prosper. Even after the stock market crash of 1929 and the Great Depression of the 1930s, Raskob rejected the need for any major role of the federal government in American economic life or in the safeguarding of individuals from the "creative destruction" of the capitalist system.

Raskob was never just a hard-hearted economic conservative or, to put the case hardest, a political reactionary. He knew that businessmen could be predatory, and he supported Progressive Era efforts to rein in and punish businessmen and industrialists who cheated their customers or deliberately caused harm to consumers or workers. In that sense he was like many other leaders of the giant corporations who rose to power in the first decades of the twentieth century. Raskob wanted a rational corporate order based on the rule of law. But he never accepted the premise that complex, punitive regulatory measures and large-scale public welfare policies were the best way to ensure income equity, social virtue, and economic fair play in the United States. He refused to believe that most Americans wanted the security the New Deal promised and not the opportunity a relatively unfettered free market offered.[10] Raskob spent a sizable chunk of his fortune and of his energy in the late 1920s and 1930s fighting for his political principles, beliefs a later generation would call conservative. Raskob believed that the free market, not the federal government, provided Americans with their best opportunity to prosper. That his own life proved that a man with enough drive and talent could overcome humble beginnings and achieve great wealth made it hard for him to see the world differently.

Raskob was not, despite his faith in the virtue of the free market, a one-dimensional economic creature. He was a devout Catholic at a time when only a tiny number of his fellow religionists had cracked the WASP elite circles that ran the nation's affairs. His religion was a defining feature of his public and private life. As one of the very richest Catholics in the United States, Raskob felt it his duty to give millions to the Church for every kind of philanthropic effort. He provided the money to build schools, hospitals, churches, and better lives for Catholic priests and nuns. In thanks, Pope Pius made him one of the first American Knights of Malta and gave him a relic of the "True Cross." As a leading Catholic layman living in a time of widespread anti-Catholic feeling, Raskob worked hard to make American Catholicism strong and respected. At the elite intellectual level, he became a major benefactor of *Commonweal* magazine, American Catholics' most influential lay journal of ideas and opinion. Quietly, within American Catholic circles Raskob fought to give laymen a greater role in their Church. Especially in the late 1920s when Raskob was at the peak of his financial power and influence, he expended great sums of money, as well as his precious time, attempting to reform the operational side of Church affairs, urging the American Church's leadership to recognize what Catholic businessmen and other professionals could bring to what he called the secular side of their parishes and archdioceses. More famously, in 1928, Raskob was named head of both the Democratic National Committee and the presidential campaign of the first Catholic presidential candidate, the "Happy Warrior," Governor Al Smith. While his reasons for supporting Smith were personal and complicated, in part he joined the campaign to fight for repeal of Prohibition, which he saw as a hysterical slap at America's Catholic immigrants by the Protestant majority (as well as a portentous case of state-sponsored destruction of an entire industry). Though with only limited success, Raskob used his time in the political limelight to fight anti-Catholic prejudice in the United States.

While Raskob's millions were not enough to put Smith into the White House, soon after the campaign, Smith and Raskob teamed up to build and manage the Empire State Building. While the Great Depression tested Raskob's massive investment in the building—most of his fortune went into it—in the end, the Empire State Building paid off. Not only did his skyscraper become one of the iconic architectural wonders of the world, in the 1950s it was the world's most valuable building. While few remember that John Jakob Raskob built the Empire State Building, in his last quiet years he knew what he had accomplished and he loved little more than going each day to his wood-paneled office suite on the 80th floor and looking out over the world he had changed.

Raskob slowed down in the 1940s. He stepped out of politics and began no major ventures. Instead he bought up gold mines in Mexico and massive swathes of land in the American West. When Raskob died in 1950, after ensuring that his ten surviving children and his wife would never want for anything, he left most of his fortune to the Raskob Foundation for Catholic Activities which, as Raskob wished, quietly continues to donate money to good works around the world.

Raskob is a rare figure in modern American capitalism. He kept copious records of his personal life, his deals, and his nearly ceaseless activities. His excursions into Big Business, politics, religion, real estate, and the social whirl of the American elite are all neatly documented. In doing so, he illuminates the world of America's corporate big-wigs and financial masterminds. Raskob's private life was as rich as his business affairs: he traveled by private railway across the United States, gamboling in the El Mirador in Palm Springs with starlets, playing high stakes blackjack at the fabled Beach Club in South Florida, rolling into New York to take the best seats at Broadway openings, and then celebrating afterwards in exclusive speakeasies like midtown Manhattan's Club Borgo. A man of relentless energy and curiosity, Raskob makes for an entertaining, as well as an informative, guide to American high life.

Raskob's overarching belief that the marketplace could produce prosperity and that giant corporations could create stability in the American economy still undergirds American life. The consumer credit revolution he helped to build changed American values as much as it reshaped the material conditions of America's households. His belief that Americans needed to tie their savings and their fortunes to the corporate business world has taken modern form in 401K plans, the lure of employee stock options, and every giant pension program that invests in equities. Raskob's legacy is all around us.

This account of Mr. Raskob is no hagiography. Even setting aside the broader implications of Americans' faith in the market, Raskob was far from a saint. Even his economic judgment was far from perfect. Many of his business decisions and investments did not turn out well; many people, including those closest to him, lost a great deal of money by following his advice. He could be a hard man, too. He had no patience for or empathy with people who could not seize opportunities and make the most of them. He never understood how or why so many people banked their lives on security, avoided risks, and allowed themselves to be

tied down by their family backgrounds or restrained by their fears and insecuri-
ties. His social vision, too, was occluded by most of the limits of his time; he rarely
noticed racial inequality or showed any concern about the very poor. Especially
as he became older, he often failed to understand how people could disagree with
him about fundamental issues of political economy unless they were venal and
corrupt, and he railed against those who did. Raskob saw himself as a loving family man but his relations with his children and with his wife were often troubled.
Raskob's longtime friend, president of General Motors Alfred P. Sloan, once
called himself a "narrow man," acknowledging that his laser-like focus on business
success had limited his social vision. By that definition Raskob, a man of broad
interests and adventurous spirit, was not at all narrow, but sometimes his inability
to see that few other people could or would live as he did, that very few people
had his combination of talent, intelligence, drive, and risk-taking personality, had
a similar effect. Raskob could be a difficult man, limited in his sympathies and
mercilessly hard on his political opponents, as well as on his friends and family.

Raskob did, however, also demonstrate all his life a generous ebullience and
visionary enthusiasm that swept people up into his orbit. He stayed ever true
to his oldest friends, the humble men with whom he had come of age at the
end of the nineteenth century in Lockport; he sent many of their children to
college and safeguarded their families against misfortune. His closest friend,
Pierre du Pont, said that he had never met a man he trusted so much. Raskob
had an exceptional talent for walking into a room and convincing hardnosed
men, whether they were bankers or industrialists or politicians, that he was the
harbinger of the next and most necessary step in the adventure upon which they
had been waiting to embark. Raskob lived his life with wit, intellectual curiosity,
and constant self-challenge to do more, to see more, and to experience more.
He was a protean man, unafraid to throw himself into new social realms and to
reinvent and retool himself to take on new adventures. The inner fire that fueled
him seemed to many in his generation a source of American greatness. Men and
women of all kinds relished his company.

Of course, Raskob was more than just an extraordinary and complicated
man. He was a member of a particular economic elite in American life that took
up an extraordinary opportunity to shape their society and the American future.
Thus, this biography of Raskob is also a story of America's corporate and financial elite and the world they made. Insomuch as capitalism stands nearly unchal-
lenged and the marketplace acts as a powerful arbiter of Americans' individual
and social worth in our own time, Raskob's life and his time, his successes and
his failures, reveals much about the moral economy not just of the past but of the
present and of the future.

1

Small Town Catholic Boy

Johnny, as friends and family first called him, was a Catholic boy, half-Irish and half-German. He was born in America. His parents were native-born, as well, though just barely. His mother's parents, Ellen O'Riley Moran and John Moran, were from County Roscommon, Ireland. They had made their way from the little village of French Park to America around 1850, in the midst of the potato famine. Johnny's mother, Anne Frances, the seventh of what would be nine children, was born very soon thereafter in 1851. The Morans were neither quite so poor nor desperate as most of their countrymen who fled Ireland during the Great Famine. But they were very much a part of that great wave of Irish immigration that changed the religious and ethnic composition of the United States so dramatically and so quickly in the mid-nineteenth century, giving rise to an angry and populist anti-Catholic nativist movement. Grandfather John Moran had come to America with some skills as a bookkeeper and had been drawn to the commercial bustle of Lockport, New York, and the well-established, if often rough community of Irish immigrants that populated the town. That he had come to Lockport with some commercially useful education and with his wife marked the Morans as a class apart from the great many single, unschooled Irish men who had first arrived in Lockport in the 1820s to work as unskilled laborers on the Erie Canal.

Johnny's paternal grandfather, Jakob Raskob, had also come to America in 1845 with some advantages. Like a good many of his mid-nineteenth-century German immigrant compatriots he had a bit of capital and a great deal of drive. His name indicated the family's likely roots in the Alsace region that had, until the Franco-Prussian War of 1870, been a predominately German-language speaking part of France. But according to his own account he had been born in southwest Prussia, in the village of Großlittgen. That is where he had been when he decided to make his way to the United States at the age of twenty-five. He began the journey as a single man. During the month-long voyage, he met Margaret. In 1847, after Jakob established himself, they married at the St. Louis Roman Catholic Church in Buffalo. Soon thereafter, Jakob set himself up as a saloon keeper, a lucrative business in nearby Lockport where thousands of thirsty men working the Erie Canal stopped off while their boats stacked up around the locks that had made Lockport famous. By 1865 he was a licensed distributor of liquor, and he paid a yearly federal fee to make cigars, a business that had just started to take off in the United States, helped by a high tariff that virtually eliminated competition from the world's leading cigar makers in Germany and Belgium.

In 1866, Jakob Raskob was listed on the federal tax rolls as already possessing $2,000 in finished cigars. He told the 1870 federal census takers that he was a property owner worth some $5,000, with his assets neatly divided between inventory and real estate, making him a man of means in his small town. Unlike many recent immigrants, he had also chosen to become a naturalized citizen of the United States. The Raskobs were Americans though they did maintain a strong connection to German culture and the German language. By the 1870s, handmade cigars—there was as yet no such thing as a machine-made cigar—had become the Raskobs' sole business. Jakob had almost certainly learned cigar making in Germany and began to train his oldest son, John, in the trade.

When John Jakob Raskob was born March 19, 1879, his father John was still working for grandfather Jakob. They were solidly middle-class people, making and selling cigars locally. The extended family lived together at 43 East Avenue in a cramped building his grandfather owned. The cigar business was in the same building. The odor of tobacco permeated the household.[1]

John Raskob had married Anna Frances Moran, crossing ethnic but not religious lines, on May 28, 1878, at the Roman Catholic Church in Indianapolis. Anna's parents had left Lockport years earlier, first to neighboring Niagara Falls, and then to Indianapolis. Somehow John and Anna found each other and maintained a long-distance courtship. John was, at least according to one of his cousins, "a stunning looking man."[2] They were both twenty-seven when they married, which was, then, about average for a man and a little old for a woman. Johnny arrived just over nine months later. Three more children, Gertrude, William, and Edith, quickly followed. Intense, happy memories of his boyhood years stayed with Johnny all his life. He believed he had an idyllic childhood. He loved Lockport.

In the early nineteenth century, Lockport had stood as a proud symbol of American ingenuity and material prowess. In 1821 just three white families had settled in the area. Since the great majority of the Iroquois people who had lived in the area had been driven out or slaughtered by the Continental army in the late eighteenth century, these American settlers felt as if they had discovered a virgin territory, dotted with towering oak and black walnut trees. Their only neighbors were a small number of Indians who lived nearby on the recently allotted Tuscarora Indian Reservation. Among the Tuscarora, the site that would become Lockport was best known for the multitude of rattlesnakes that sunned themselves on the many expanses of bare gray rock that marked the plateau of the Niagara escarpment.

By 1825, a visitor wrote, everything had changed. Where once there had been only rock and trees, there was now "the canal—the locks—stone and frame houses—log buildings—handsome farms—warehouses—grist mills—waterfalls—barbers' shops—bustle and activity—wagons, with ox-teams and horse teams—hotels—thousands of tree stumps, and people burning and destroying them—carding machines—tanneries—cloth works—tinplate fac-tories—taverns—churches." The awestruck writer concluded, "What a change in four short years from a state of wilderness."[3] At the end of 1825 over 3,000 people lived in the brand new town of Lockport, the site of the great locks that made possible the 363-mile long Erie Canal, the greatest technological and economic accomplishment of the day.

The locks, ingenuously devised by one of the Erie Canal's unschooled hero-engineers, Nathan B. Roberts, conquered the sudden rise of the Niagara escarpment rock ridge that interrupted the canal's steady westward movement to Lake Erie. These locks lifted boats in five stages up sixty feet. Lockport, as was much celebrated in early nineteenth-century America, was where the great canal builders had defeated nature, turning wilderness into commerce by allow-ing cargo and passengers to make their way by "artificial river" from the Atlantic Ocean via the Hudson River to Lake Erie and thus the great interior of the American continent.

The opening of the great locks in 1825 had brought many dignitaries to Lockport and one of the most illustrious was the great friend of the American Revolution, the Marquis de Lafayette. He charmed his audience by noting of their locks and of the nearby Niagara Falls: "Lockport and the County of Niagara contain the greatest natural and artificial wonders, second only to the wonders of freedom and equal rights."[4] A modern-day observer, the historian Carol Sheriff, makes a related if more telling claim. The Founding Fathers, she notes, were widely seen by their fellow Americans, as "establishing free institutions, the next generation of leaders had the luxury—as well as the imperative—to concentrate on spreading prosperity."[5]

New York Governor DeWitt Clinton, champion of the Canal, certainly saw himself that way, as a new kind of national hero, not a founder of political democracy and liberty but a promoter of commerce and economic uplift. The Erie Canal was, as much as any single phenomenon in Jacksonian America, the physical manifestation of the American Dream: the idea that in the United States individual economic opportunity was a right and economic success likely for anyone—white men, that is—willing to take their chances and make their play. The government, politicians like Governor Clinton believed, had a responsibility to help make those opportunities possible. That the Erie Canal, unlike the far less glorious, slave-built canals popping up at the same time below the Mason-Dixon line, was dug and blasted into existence by free men, almost all of them recent immigrants to the United States, hungry for opportunity, only underlined the dazzling symbolism and functional reality of the canal.

Some 1,200 men, nearly all of them newly arrived Irish immigrants, built the Lockport section of the canal. Most earned $12 a month plus "found" (meaning food and drink, including a daily half-pint of whisky), a good wage, then, but one that also undercut prevailing pay, infuriating the small number of American-born laborers who often brawled with the Irish. Despite extraordinarily dangerous working conditions, these men overcame the greatest brute physical challenge facing the canal builders. They carved a channel through the rocky plateau of the Niagara escarpment that extended westward toward Buffalo for three miles past the site of the locks. Under the orders of the self-taught canal engineers, these men used black powder to blast away the dolomite rock and millions of cubic yards of debris. Erratic charges blew up men, too, and sent rock storms pounding into the newly established town. Nonetheless, the Irish hard men soldiered on. Using newly devised mechanical cranes and wooden-wheeled ox wagons, the men piled up shattered rock and debris some seventy-feet high along the south side of the canal. The massive piles were still there when Jakob Raskob arrived mid-century in Lockport to sell liquor and cigars to the booming town's still fast-growing population, which thanks to the large number of early workmen who stayed on to settle there had a powerful Irish Catholic cast. At the advent of the Civil War, when Johnny's father was just a boy, Lockport was a well-known, prosperous town, filled with shops, groceries, grog houses, taverns, and hotels.

When Johnny was growing up in the 1880s and 1890s, travelers still came to see the mighty locks at work and the canal still dominated Lockport but not as it had once done. By the mid-nineteenth century, railroads had begun to compete with the Erie Canal. When Johnny's father was born in 1850, the Canal had already lost almost all of it passenger business to the railroads, which, in fits and starts, had begun to run parallel to the canal in 1830, just five years after it opened. The great 1853 merger that created the New York Central Railroad finalized the process; four trains a day ran all the way from Albany to Buffalo. They made the run in about fifteen hours. The one-way ticket cost $10, serious money then. The canal's packet boats charged far less, around $6.50, but it took them ten days to cover the same distance. Very few were willing to trade that much time for that amount of savings. Before 1850, passenger travel by packet boat had been a lucrative business, drawing a relatively high-class clientele of businessmen, traders, and tourists. Up to 120 passengers, with nighttime sleeping quarters for forty, floated comfortably on a seventy-eight by fourteen-and-a-half foot craft towed by mules down the canal; musicians serenaded them and fancy meals of roast beef and plum pudding, with plenty of liquor, were served. These passengers had sustained all sorts of businesses up and down the canal, most especially in Lockport, which was a natural stopping point due to the time it took boats to work their way along the queue lined up at the locks. But by the end of the 1850s the canal passenger business was finished. With the end of the service-oriented higher-end passenger trade, freight alone sustained the slow-moving, mule-towed canal boats and even they faced ever fiercer competition from the railroads. As a result of close profit margins, the canal boat crews were increasingly made up of poorly paid, hard-worked, rough single men who had few other opportunities.

By the time Johnny was a boy, living just a few blocks from the waterway, the canal had long lost its allure. Freight tonnage had peaked in 1880, despite fervent attempts by the canal's supporters and beneficiaries to retool the canal to make it a more cost-effective carrier. The men who worked as boat crew, as well as the boys, some no older than Johnny, who led the slow-stepping mules that still towed the freight boats were often tough customers, sometimes on the run from the law or family troubles. Few talked about their past lives. Usually known only by monikers such as Oswego Dutch, Rhode Island Red, Bohemian Dutch, Squirrel Wheeler, Shivery Newman, and Monkey Joe, many stole fruits and vegetables growing along the towpath, as well as the occasional chicken. They were a hard-drinking bunch. The son of one of the boat captains, who grew up alongside these men and boys, remembered them fondly but he readily admitted that "they were a footloose breed of men."[6]

For Johnny, the canal did not represent Governor De Witt Clinton's dream of American prosperity or of technological mastery. The canal was the local swimming hole. Johnny's parents and the parents of his friends let the boys play there, but Johnny knew that the rheumy-eyed men who worked the canal boats were to be avoided. The canal never figured in his dreams for the future; he grew up knowing that the best years of the Erie Canal were behind it. Young Johnny Raskob was growing up in a town that directly witnessed what the European émigré economist Joseph Schumpeter described so brilliantly in his characterization of a market-based capitalist society: its economic progress—America's economic progress—depended on a process of "creative destruction" that continually upended whole industries and social relations and produced turmoil so that new, more efficient, and more profitable uses of capital could form and so replace the old, outdated, and less efficient. As Johnny Raskob was finishing grammar school, Lockport's greatest days as the site of national and even international renown for technological mastery and canal-based economic vibrancy were behind it.

By the end of the nineteenth century, Lockport was just a provincial little town that serviced an economically marginal, old-fashioned artificial waterway.

Not many years later, though long after Johnny Raskob had made his way far from upstate New York, F. Scott Fitzgerald would use Lockport as a marker of failure. In *Tender Is the Night*, Fitzgerald casts out his tragic hero Dick Diver from the glamour of the French Riviera and places him at novel's end, destitute, alcoholic, and hopeless, in Lockport on a journey to oblivion.

As a boy, Johnny Raskob did not see Lockport that way, and as a young man he never wanted to, even as its desultory job market put a ceiling on his ambitions. He would always remember his small town as a warm-hearted community where everyone, Protestant and Catholic alike, got along. For young Johnny, Lockport was like a contemporary Currier and Ives print come to life. The lithographs of horse-drawn sleighs running through fields of snow, passing by clapboard houses, so popular in Victorian American middle-class homes, could have been sketched from everyday life in wintertime Lockport.

Johnny loved the curtains of snow that fell on Lockport every year, burying the town in a white blanket. He never forgot the great blizzard of 1893 that left snow drifts ten-feet high. Bursting with energy and always avid for exercise, Johnny, at a young age, took charge of shoveling the mounds of snow that covered the sidewalks at the corner of East Avenue and Charles Street where his family lived and the family's cigar-making business was housed. When the canal froze over, forcing the freight boats to quit for the winter months, Raskob and his friends skated on the hard ice. As a teenager, he rode in horse-drawn sleighs, racing along and flirting with girls. Raskob came of age at the end of the nineteenth century in a small-town America that he and others like him, soon enough, would make obsolete in the twentieth century. Even as his fame and his wealth accrued, even at the very end, a part of him yearned to go back to his small town, a recurring dream for so many of the men and women who left provincial pleasures and security at the cusp of the twentieth century to build the juggernaut of modern American mass society.

Johnny worked part-time from an early age. When he could, he picked fruits and vegetables for local farmers and at harvest time he guarded area vineyards from the pilfering hands of the canal boat workers, though he later admitted that he and his friends were a greater danger to the grapes than the boys who walked the canal tow path. But his first steady job came in 1891 when he was twelve.

In Lockport, every boy wanted a paper route. Few got one. Almost any kid ten or older could be a "newsie," selling papers on the corner or to the boat men who lined up at the locks waiting their turn to move up and down the Erie Canal. But hawking newspapers was a precarious game; a paper route was a sure thing, money in the bank and high status in Johnny's circle of friends. Johnny set his sights on winning a prized route. Although Johnny was smaller than most boys his age, in 1891 he talked the circulation manager at the *Lockport Daily Journal* into giving him not one but two paper routes.

Johnny had an advantage in pursuit of his first vocational challenge. His parents had provided their first-born son with a bicycle and not one of the penny-farthing big-wheeled novelty contraptions. Raskob was one of the first boys in town to have a relatively expensive pneumatic tire "safety" bike—a steel-stamped, lugged frame bicycle that floated along on two wood-rimmed, ball-bearing equipped wheels of the same size. He loved the bike, and it made the two paper routes circuit possible. Still, Johnny had to convince the manager of his riding prowess and his dedication to the newspaper delivery business. And he had to want to work not just one route but two, despite the fact that his family was economically secure and by no means needed Johnny's small wages. From the beginning, Johnny liked to work and to work hard; his father took evident pride in his son's enterprising spirit and in the evening they would talk about business. Johnny's success left his friends jealous.

Johnny's paper routes gave him the run of the town. One route was near his house in lower-town, the fading industrial district. The other route took him past the mighty five-stage canal lock, one-time technological wonder of the North American continent, and into the slightly posher environs of Lockport's upper-town. Johnny rode from bottom to top in Lockport, delivering his papers and collecting the weekly subscription fees. Johnny, even then, a careful observer of the world around him, noted how a wide spectrum of Lockport families lived.

Indicative of his life to come, Johnny kept scrupulous accounts. Once, memorably, he got into a fist fight with his closest friend who was helping him with collections after Johnny had spotted a discrepancy of two cents. Johnny flew through the town, racing the clock, a ball of energy, focused on his missions. Only a few years earlier, his second grade teacher at the Washburn Street School had been struck by Johnny's almost uncanny discipline and his warm, steady brown eyes, which always returned her gaze. He was slim, she remembered, and not an outstandingly handsome boy, but he had "a face one would remember."[7]

As Johnny's bike-riding prowess indicated, he was an avid athlete. He found an outlet for his restless physical energy at the Lockport YMCA. Basketball had been invented at the Springfield Massachusetts YMCA Training School in 1891 and almost immediately made its way to the Lockport Y where Johnny, despite topping out at around 5'6", relished the game. Johnny also took to the gymnasium exercise routines that the Y first made widely available to American youths—he was particularly good at rope climbing and was not shy about demonstrating his skill, especially if girls were in view.

The YMCA was one of many organizations in the late nineteenth century that were nationalizing culture in the United States, breaking down traditional regional and ethnic ways of life. At the Y national culture meant, in part, playing brand new games, such as basketball, as well as volleyball, and following the games' standardized rules. Not only were young Americans increasingly playing the same games, whether an Anglo-Saxon Protestant boy in Springfield, Massachusetts, a Jewish kid in Chicago, or a half-Irish and half-German Catholic teenager in Lockport, but they also were changing the culture simply by *playing*. Johnny was part of that generation of American young people who came of age thinking that recreation and fun and a certain amount of frivolity were part of a good, healthy, and respectable life.[8]

That Johnny was a member of the Y, as were so many of his friends, says a good deal about his family and the relatively unusual, easygoing relationship between Catholics and Protestants in Lockport. Catholic boys were not supposed to join the YMCA. The Y had begun in London in 1844, at least in part, as a place to train boys and young men in Protestant beliefs. At a meeting of New York state YMCA leaders in 1892 the proselytizing mission was reaffirmed: "No association is satisfied...until the man is grounded spiritually and has a being active in the Lord Jesus."[9] The Catholic Church hierarchy understood that this version of Christian "spirituality" was not meant to be supportive of theirs. A Catholic priest in nearby Connecticut explicitly warned his parishioners that the YMCA was an "anti-Catholic institution" and insisted that a canon of the Church forbade Catholics from joining the Y or even attending YMCA activities.[10]

Word of this canon had either not made its way to upstate New York or more likely no one, including the local priests, paid attention to it, a spirit of nonconformity not unusual in American Catholicism at that time. Although there had been plenty of troubles between Protestant "native" Americans and Irish Catholic immigrants in the early and mid-nineteenth century, by the end of the nineteenth century relations between Catholics and Protestants in Lockport were remarkably amicable. Johnny had no idea growing up that in much of the United States many Protestants had religious contempt for Catholicism and viewed Catholics—"Papists"—with grave suspicion, fearing that the Pope commanded them in ways incompatible with American democracy.

In Lockport, Johnny had Protestant and Catholic friends and never seems to have thought much about it, just as his parents felt no concern about his membership in the "Protestant" YMCA. For Johnny, and perhaps his parents, the Y was a place of middle-class respectability, not a covert form of Protestant proselytizing. Likewise, as a little boy he went to the nearby public school and not a Catholic one.

At the same time, the Raskobs were very much a religiously observant Catholic family. Johnny had been baptized at St. Mary's, the German-dominated Roman Catholic Church that had been established in 1859 as an alternative to the Irish-oriented St. John the Baptist Parish. When Johnny was older, he left the public school to attend the new Catholic school established at St. Mary's.

Johnny's father was a committed member of the local chapter of the Catholic Men's Benevolent Association, an affiliate of the Catholic Central Union that had been founded by upstate New York German-American parishes in 1855 in nearby Buffalo "for the promotion of Catholic interests, temporal and spiritual, and the zealous practice in common of Christian virtue and works of charity."[11] As a boy and young man Johnny regularly attended Mass and practiced his faith. He mournfully wrote a friend at one point that he had attended a rollicking party with plenty of good-looking girls, but he could not ask any of them for a dance; he had given up dancing for Lent. Johnny held his faith dear, but he did not grow up in an all-Catholic or ethnic community or neighborhood. Unlike many Americans who came of age at the end of the nineteenth century, Johnny was and would remain all his life at his ease among people of different faiths and ethnicities.

Johnny's teenage years were happy ones. Indicative of his middle-class status, he went on to high school, a relatively rare undertaking for Americans in the 1890s. He admitted later in life that he had been an indifferent student. Far more of his energies went into his social life. Johnny was unendingly and vocally infatuated with girls. He and his friends spent countless hours talking about lower-town girls and upper-town girls and girls who were pretty and girls who were sweet and who had interests in whom. His admiration for and interest in attractive women would be another life-long constant.

Sometime in his mid-to-late teens, Johnny began working part-time on the New York Central passenger trains on the Lockport to Buffalo route. He was a "candy butcher," walking up and down the aisles selling candy, as well as newspapers and books, to the passengers. It was a good job for a teenager with wit and energy; Thomas Alva Edison had gotten his start in life working on the trains as a candy butcher, too. Selling on the trains put Johnny for the first time in the commercial whirl of the national marketplace. His customers, the men who filled the passenger cars, were often drummers or traveling salesmen, a field that had exploded onto the American scene in the decades after the Civil War. Often representing big companies out of New York and Philadelphia, the urbane drummers tended to be a fast talking, sharply dressed breed of men, far different than the kind of people who populated Lockport. Successful sales representatives could earn several thousand dollars a year, big money then.

Johnny was not a complete rube. He had, by this time, visited New York City with his parents (he had an aunt who lived in Brooklyn), a family visit unusual enough to be reported by the *Lockport Daily Union*. But walking the aisles of the New York Central, pitching his wares to the savvy, smart-talking men aboard the New York Central was a direct education into the ways of the world that lay outside the cultural bounds of Lockport.[12]

Another teenage candy butcher working around the same time as Johnny Raskob tells an instructive story about his own introduction to the ways of the marketplace by an older salesman. Max Ravage, a Jewish immigrant who would later write a classic account of coming of age in turn-of-the century New York City, was politely peddling his candy for a penny a piece. A professional salesman watched in amusement and then pulled young Max aside. Raise your prices, he said, otherwise people will think your candy is no good. "Americans," he continued, "had no sense of value. They were so rich they didn't need any." And forget about being so polite, "Move along, elbow your way through the crowds.... Don't be timid. America likes the nervy ones. This is the land where modesty starves. And yell, never step yelling." Of course, it worked. Candy that Ravage had bought for well under a penny could be sold, he discovered, for a nickel a piece.[13] It was a new world, a modern world. Raskob intended to embrace that world.

By the time Johnny was working on the trains in the mid-1890s, he and his father had decided he would not go into the family cigar business. Neither Johnny nor his younger brother William ever learned how to roll a cigar, which is rather remarkable given that both their father and grandfather were skilled artisans. The boys were supposed to do better; and more pressingly, the prospects for the hand-rolled artisanal family cigar business were not good.

The cigar business had been good to the Raskob family for a long time. Jakob Raskob had begun making cigars just as the industry took off; in the early 1860s fewer than 5,000 men made cigars in the United States and per capita consumption of cigars had already nearly tripled since Jakob had first arrived in the United States. Most cigars were hand rolled by men who owned their own businesses and who employed just a few other men, often family members. There were no national brands or national distribution of cigars. Every cigar was handmade, and it took time to learn how to form the loose tobacco, roll it in the fragile outer leaf wrapper, and shape the cigar. Cigar makers had to master a multitude of styles, especially at the high end, where Cuban tobacco dominated. A cigar maker had to know how to make the corona, coquetta, perfecta, favorite, and many others. Cigars became more and more popular throughout the nineteenth century and per capita consumption soared. The five-cent cigar became the new industry's standard and competition became fierce.

By 1892 Johnny's father ran the family cigar business and employed a handful of cigar makers. Jakob Raskob, a widower for many years, still lived at 43 East Avenue but was listed in city records as a boarder not a cigar manufacturer. That Johnny's father had been able to take over the trade from his father demonstrated that the business was viable and that the Raskobs had succeeded where many other family cigar businesses had not. For example, Samuel Gompers, born the same year as Johnny's father, had also joined his father in the family cigar business. But the Gompers lived and worked in New York City and by the time young Gompers was a highly skilled cigar maker in the 1870s, he could make more money working for one of the big cigar manufacturers that were beginning to dominate the marketplace. Gompers went on to become a leader of the Cigar Makers' International Union of America and then the founder and president of the American Federation of Labor.

The cigar business was increasingly becoming a regional and national one and the Raskobs were still just a local concern, in competition with sixteen other cigar manufacturers just in Lockport. At the low end of the market—the canal boat crew end—cheap stogies made in mass using wooden shaping blocks and other less skilled production techniques were the popular choice. In the vast middle, five-cent cigars were increasingly made by cigar companies employing a thousand men (and by the early twentieth century, women). They could make a good cigar much cheaper than the small family-operated concerns. By the end of the century national brands, such as Antonio Y Cleopatra, King Edward, Garcia & Vega, and Swisher Sweets, were heavily advertised, promoted by professional boxers and celebrity actresses. Both John Raskobs, father and son, understood that the family cigar-making business was a dead end. Back in 1848, an agitated German political economist named Karl Marx had made note of the general phenomenon affecting the Raskobs' business prospects: "Constant revolutionizing of production, uninterrupted disturbance of all social conditions, everlasting uncertainty and agitation distinguish the bourgeois epoch from all earlier ones. All fixed, fast-frozen relations, with their train of ancient and venerable prejudices and opinions, are swept away, all new-formed ones become antiquated before they can ossify. All that is solid melts into air." John Jakob, namesake of two generations of cigar-making Raskobs who had made good lives in Lockport, was going to have to find his own direction.[14]

John had to choose that direction sooner than he had expected. His father died, unexpectedly, on June 4, 1898, at just forty-seven years old. The doctor at first thought he had typhoid, which explained the fever, nausea, and stomach pains, but the treatment for that disease failed and the father of four died at home seven weeks after he had become ill. The cause of death was liver failure. His son believed that his death was related to his years of making and smoking cigars. Whether he was right or not, John decided then and there that he would never smoke. Not long after his father's death he wrote a long letter to one of his closest friends: "Sometimes as I sit and watch an old man smoking and enjoying a pipe, I almost wish that I smoked too so that I could sit down and enjoy myself likewise at such times as I get the blues. Nevertheless I am afraid of it as I cannot banish the idea that smoking was partially the cause of my father's death in early life."[15]

John was not at his father's side when he died. The family had no phone and when his father suddenly took a terrible turn, he had run out to bring the doctor. When he returned, he saw his mother at the top of the stairs. He later wrote, "I shall never forget the agony on her face." He went up the steps. "She fell into my arms and said, 'Papa is dead.'" Twenty-eight years later, he wrote: "The impression on my mind could be no more clear than if it happened yesterday.... [N]ever in my whole life was my heart wrung as it was when I saw the anguish and suffering in my mother's face.... in that moment I passed from boyhood into manhood."[16]

In the manner of the day, John had not been that emotionally close to his father. Still, John and his father had shared a bond. Since he was a little boy, his father had talked to him about business. His father had shared with him some of the ins and outs of the family enterprise and had advised him as he looked for part-time work during his youth. John believed that his father had done right by him by letting him take on responsibilities at home and in the work world at an early age. His father, John said later in his life, had given him a strong sense of self-confidence.[17]

The funeral for John Raskob took place at St. Mary's Church. The Reverend Father Geysen, who knew the family well, spoke highly of "the manly qualities" that John Raskob had shown throughout his life. The large church was crowded with mourners and the *Lockport Daily Union* reported that the church was also filled with floral arrangements, including a commemorative pillow from Branch 31 of the Catholic Men's Benevolent Association and a harp from the *Saengerbund*, the German singing club to which Raskob had belonged since his bachelor days. John Raskob, the newspaper's short obituary stated, "was a man of qualities which endeared him to his family and a large circle of friends in business and social life."[18]

John's father's death set a pattern for Raskob that he kept for the rest of his life: when tragedy struck his family or friends he put his head down and he moved forward, fast. Those close to him never fully understood his emotional register.

John focused on his mother and his younger brother and sisters for whom he felt responsible, although the family was not destitute. John and Anna had diligently saved money and his father had a life insurance policy. All together Anna Raskob had about $3,000 and lived for free in the home her father-in-law had bought years earlier. If Anna took in a boarder or two—which she almost immediately did—and lived modestly, she and the younger children had enough to live on. But nineteen-year-old John decided he could not let his mother survive on that savings. He wrote one of his many friends: "I did not like to see her use this money when I was able to get out and work. I started out knowing I had to work and work hard which I did."[19] Up until his father's death, John had been having a lot of fun but he had not found his path in life, in large part because he had not been in any hurry to find it.

John had graduated from high school in 1897 and had then enrolled at Clarke Business School in nearby Buffalo. He left Clarke right after his father's death to go to work. He had done some coursework on bookkeeping, stenography, and other business skills, and he had been working part-time since he was a boy. He knew he was ready to do more and he accepted his self-appointed responsibilities eagerly.

John E. Pound, a leading lawyer in Lockport, immediately hired Raskob to fill in temporarily for one of his law clerks who was stricken with typhoid. Pound had known John's father and had watched John grow up. He wanted to help John make a start in life. It was Raskob's first real job. John Pound's younger brother and one-time junior partner, Cuthbert Pound, a graduate of Cornell University, was amused to discover that John, the low man at the firm without any legal training, "was the smartest boy" in the office, outperforming all the young law students who were apprenticing at Lockport's biggest and most prestigious law firm. Cuthbert, one of the few other young men from Lockport who would go on to big things, in his case a distinguished career as a New York state judge, also noted, with some ambivalence, that John had a restless "aggressiveness" about him.[20]

John, with a strong reference from Pound, then found work at a struggling manufacturing firm in Lockport, the Richmond Company. To secure the secretarial position, he had to supply his own typewriter, which he rented. It was not the best time to be looking for new work. The American economy was just recovering from the Panic of 1893, which had led to hundreds of bank failures and thousands of companies going under. In the mid-1890s nearly 20 percent of American wage earners were unemployed. While the economy was moving forward again in 1897 and would do so for almost the next ten years, many businesses were still on shaky financial ground and millions of people were still looking for stable employment. John thought he was lucky to find a decent job. Six weeks after starting at Richmond Manufacturing, his boss, Mr. Phinney, had still not paid him his promised wage of $5 a week. Raskob was out $2 for the typewriter rental.

John persevered and found a much more secure position at Lockport's biggest and most successful enterprise, Holly Pump and Machine Shops, which employed hundreds of skilled machinists and mechanics. Raskob was put to work as a stenographer. The firm hired him at $5 a week. He loved working full-time, though stenography was far from his favorite activity and he was earning a poor wage for a high school graduate with a year of business school behind him. Still, Raskob threw himself into the company's operations, seeking opportunity.

Holly Pump was a fascinating place. Back in 1864, old man Birdsall Holly, a self-taught engineer, had created a system for suppressing town fires that included a central water-pumping station, pipes, and fire hydrants. Holly then figured out how to manufacture all of the components, which another branch of his company installed for municipal customers all over the United States. Holly built on that success to launch and manufacture a central steam-heating system.

Holly Pump was a big, complicated, profitable business by the time John Raskob came aboard. Engineers dominated the firm, and it was a hierarchical, bureaucratized place.

John chafed against the lack of opportunity. He wanted to do more, and he very much wanted to be paid more. After several months, and near constant agitation on John's part, he received a 50 percent wage increase, $7.50 a week, the figure John had insisted upon, which was actually close to the era's median wage. His superiors then told him to be thankful for his good fortune and thereafter be patient; additional opportunities, they assured, would come his way.

Patience was never one of John's virtues. After almost another year had gone by, he asked for an additional raise. He wanted $10 a week. As John would tell the story, his superior was appalled at his "temerity" and told him to accept the salary "or get out."[21] John had hit a wall. Holly Pump was the best employer in Lockport, but his employer's assurance that additional opportunities would be offered to him had not panned out, at least not on Raskob's schedule. If he wanted more, he was going to have to leave his hometown.

Raskob was not alone in his frustration over the slow pace of promotion at Holly Pump. One of his supervisors, Sterling Bunnell, a few years his senior, had quit Holly after finding a better job at Johnson Steel in Lorain, Ohio. January 12, 1900, Raskob wrote Bunnell and told him he was looking for a new job: "The conditions here are perhaps better known to you than they are to me, but at any rate the Company is not living up to certain promises which were made at the time I entered their employ." Raskob asked Bunnell if he could use him as a reference and to please let him know "if you should hear of a position being vacant which you think I can fill."[22] Bunnell was happy to oblige and, better yet, told him of an opportunity.

Johnson Steel had a new president, Pierre du Pont, who had just turned thirty years old; du Pont was looking for a secretary. Raskob immediately wrote du Pont, applying for the job. Bunnell must have vouched for Raskob because within days Pierre du Pont personally wrote Raskob's other reference, the lawyer John Pound. He told Pound that he needed a stenographer and bookkeeper "trustworthy in every respect." Pound straightaway sent an effusive reply: "I have known Mr. John J. Raskob all his life time, personally, thoroughly, and well. . . . He is strictly honest, upright, and of excellent character and habits and is trustworthy in every respect. I commend him to you as a young man who I think would make an ideal stenographer and book-keeper in the capacity you seek."[23] Raskob's little network had come through for him. John Raskob's relationship with Pierre du Pont would be the single most important of his life.

That relationship, however, did not begin as expeditiously as John Raskob hoped. After Pierre du Pont checked out Raskob's references, he did not follow up on hiring Raskob. What Raskob did not know, at that point, was that du Pont was in the middle of liquidating the Johnson Steel Company. He had much on his mind besides hiring an assistant.

John had little else on his mind and fired off a series of letters. First, he outlined his thoughts about salary. Never one to think small thoughts, he decided to advance himself the $10 a week salary he had demanded at Holly Pump months earlier and, for reasons only Raskob will ever know, double that amount. Raskob calculated that $80 a month would be an appropriate beginning salary. It was an audacious bid. In 1900 that amount was a little more than twice the average wage in the United States and a great deal more than twenty-year-old stenographer-bookkeepers were paid. After a couple of weeks had passed with still no word from Mr. du Pont, Raskob asked politely but insistently: "What disposition you have made of the matter. Thanking you in advance for the courtesy of a reply, I remain, yours respectfully, John J. Raskob."[24] The letter was handwritten in an impeccably neat copperplate-like style.

Pierre took another week to answer. Addressing himself to "John Raskalb," du Pont wrote back with some amusement: "While I had not expected to pay the salary you mention at first, I would be willing to make such an arrangement provided I found in you the man desired." Pierre du Pont was, at that point, making $10,000 a year as president of Johnson Steel. "Disappointment in this regard," he continued, "might result in my making a change. But if you feel that your abilities warrant making a trial I would be pleased to hear from you as to when you could arrange to come to Lorrain."[25]

John was thrilled. He probably should have taken a little more time to reply as his high emotions and his lack of polish showed throughout the letter which was excessively long and also, uncharacteristically, revealed that John was anxious about the leap he was preparing to make. He wanted du Pont to know who he was: "[I] wish to say that my education is good and I have a good idea of business principles.... I have always liked book-keeping very much, since the time I first commenced to study it in school and I have not the slightest doubt as to my ability to satisfy you in this line." He promised that he was a great typist with a particular regard for working with a Remington. But he also wanted du Pont to know that he was not the world's ablest stenographer and that, actually, he did not like taking shorthand and that he really hoped that a heavy burden of this sort of work would not be "what you would require of me." That understood, he concluded, "I would not feel at all afraid of accepting your offer."[26]

Then nothing happened. Du Pont was buried in work sorting out the disassembling of Johnson Steel that had been bought only in part by a massive combine, Federal Steel, orchestrated by the inimitable J. P. Morgan in his first foray into industrial consolidation. Pierre had begun work at Johnson less than a year earlier, in March 1899. He had been brought, in large part, to sell off the company's nonsteel assets, which were surprisingly diverse. Primarily he was concerned with two subsidiary divisions: the Sheffield Land Company and the Lorain Street Railway.

Pierre du Pont, a young man, relatively inexperienced in the business world, soft spoken and shy, faced a daunting challenge but he believed he was capable of the tasks to which he was charged. Certainly, he was formally and genealogically prepared. An MIT graduate with a degree in engineering, he had always been an outstanding student. He was also the great-grandson of Éleuthère Irénée du Pont who had founded the DuPont Company explosives business in 1802. He had been named for his great-great-grandfather, Pierre Samuel du Pont de Nemours, a French nobleman and noted intellectual whose economic writings influenced Adam Smith. It was this Pierre S. du Pont who had begun the family's American adventure when he avoided a likely beheading by fleeing revolutionary France in 1799.

At the end of the nineteenth century, the du Ponts were a very rich, very refined family headquartered near the family business along the Brandywine Creek just outside of Wilmington. Pierre's father, Lammot, had more or less left the DuPont Company in 1880, frustrated with the family's conservative business practices and refusal to give him more responsibilities. Backed by the family, in 1880 he stated his own business, the Repauno Chemical Company, to manufacture dynamite. The firm was a great success. Then on March 29, 1884, one of his workers gave alarm; a 2,000 pound tank of nitroglycerine had begun to fume. Lammot tried to stem the explosion, but he was too late. He and four workers were caught in the blast and killed instantly. At an age even younger than Raskob, Pierre du Pont had lost his father. Soon thereafter he took on the responsibility of looking after his mother and his many siblings—who came to call him "daddy." Their circumstances, however, were more than a little different than that of the Raskobs; each of the seven minor children received an estate worth more than $70,000.

Pierre had joined the DuPont Company immediately after graduating from MIT. Joining the family firm seemed a natural progression, and he assumed that he would, in time, take a leadership position. But he was shocked by what he found upon his arrival at the company's Upper Powder Yard laboratory where he was to be a chemist working with explosive powder and exploring new avenues of research and product development. "[T]he laboratory, so called, was in deplorable condition," he wrote. "Equipment was almost nothing. A common kitchen range and one small spirit lamp were the only means of heating for chemical work. No gas or electrical facilities and a common kitchen sink and one ordinary ¾ inch tap the water supply."[27] Over the next few years, Pierre discovered that the state of the laboratory was too typical of how the venerable company operated. Management, operations, research, finance all seemed to Pierre to be run haphazardly, even primitively. The family members who controlled the company seemed indifferent or incapable of improving the company's methods of doing business. Nor was anyone in charge interested in Pierre's ideas about how to modernize the company. Pierre was not an arrogant or demanding man, just the opposite, but he concluded, correctly, that his talents were being wasted and the company was being poorly served by the family members who ran it.

So in early 1899, when Tom Johnson of the Johnson Steel Company asked Pierre to become his new president charged with overseeing the liquidation of the company, Pierre accepted. He did try one last time to make some progress at the family company. His cousin Alfred spoke for the rest of the family: "Nothing more was forthcoming."[28]

Pierre du Pont had inherited a $100,000 chunk of Johnson Company stock from his Uncle Alfred in 1893 (which paid an annual dividend of $10,000). Uncle Alfred had given Tom Johnson his start in business back in the late 1860s when he employed him at his Louisville horse trolley line. Johnson owed and liked Alfred, and he had made an effort to involve the old man's favorite and talented nephew in his business. So, Pierre had been involved with the company, in particular its finances, for several years before he became president. He had played a major role in raising the money needed to keep the company afloat until the Federal Steel buyout was arranged. Still, he had no experience in the businesses that he had been asked to tackle, which included turning a profit on the Sheffield Land Company by building commercial and residential properties on the 3,000 acres of land the company owned surrounding their factory and figuring out how to sell off the company's trolley line. Even as Pierre tried to make something profitable happen with the company's remaining assets as he worked out the company's liquidation, he still had to find the revenues to pay off the debt burden the company had taken on earlier. In the midst of it, he lost interest in hiring Raskob; he just had too many other things going on.

Pierre instead passed Raskob's name on to Arthur J. Moxham, the man du Pont had replaced as Johnson Company president. Moxham was a steel man, and he had left the company after the Morgan interests had bought up Johnson's steel business. An immensely capable and innovative manager, Moxham had quickly secured a favorable new position running the brand new Dominion Iron and Steel Company in Sydney, Nova Scotia.

Moxham was a part of the du Pont business network. Pierre's uncle, Alfred du Pont, had worked with Moxham in the late 1880s to finance the development of the Johnson Company after Moxham had figured out a way to roll a new kind of steel rail for the new trolley cars that Johnson had devised. It had been Moxham, in the first place, who thought of bringing in Pierre, a favorite of his

Uncle Alfred's, to take his place. It was a game of connections and now Pierre was connecting Raskob to Moxham, who desperately needed a capable secretary in the far reaches of Nova Scotia. In early March 1900, Moxham informed Raskob of the change in plans and offered him $80 a month, with promises of more to come if he performed as advertised.

For John it was a wonderful career opportunity, if not the exactly the opportunity upon which he had set his sights. Sydney was well over a 1,000 miles by rail from Lockport at the eastern edge of Cape Breton Island. By fastest train it took three days and tickets alone cost at least $34 each way. He would be very far, in all respects, from everyone he knew and loved, and visits home would have to be rare. John knew no one in Sydney. The town was unincorporated and surrounded by huge coal mines and little else. To a friend, John wrote that he was being asked to take a job "in a God-Forsaken country."[29] His mother made it very clear that she did not want him to go. John was about to celebrate his twenty-first birthday.

Young John Raskob took the job. He had decided that he was not going to let his small-town roots bog down his life. The decision, not surprisingly, felt monumental to John, and he wrote friends then and for years after about it. He knew he might well be lonesome and he knew, he told a close friend, that it would be hard on his family, "not knowing at what time of the year I would be able to get home again and see those I loved." But he felt that he really had to do it: "A fellow has to leave home sometime in life and the sooner he leaves it the better he is off, for it will learn him to be more self-reliant and independent and make him feel more like a man than a baby dependent upon its mother."[30]

Part of him wanted to offload the guilt he felt about leaving his mother and younger siblings and so he explained to one of his Lockport buddies: "It was a case of necessity with me, though, Roy. It was almost compulsion as it was not possible for me to support our family on what I was getting at the Holly Shops."[31] John was not being completely honest with himself. His mother did not want him to go and the family could have gone on just as they had been, living modestly but without privation. Financial need played a role but John wanted to go. He was ready to make his move into the wider world.

Excited and anxious, John still took care with the financial details. He matter-of-factly asked Pierre du Pont to work out an arrangement with Moxham to pay for his train ticket, including sleeping car arrangements, from Lockport to Sydney, Nova Scotia. He notified du Pont that, by his calculations, he would also need another fifteen dollars for food along the way, a generous sum. Somehow, without anyone to ask for advice, John knew to secure not just his ticket but first-class meal expenses. He just knew how things worked in the business world he had yet to actually inhabit. Du Pont readily complied with Raskob's request.

On Monday, March 19, 1900, John Raskob boarded the eastbound New York Central. He had a packet of the *Tip Top Weekly* ($2 for a one-year subscription) featuring the inspirational adventures of Frank Merriwell to keep him busy. All he knew about the other end of his journey was that he had a room at Mrs. Crawley's Sydney boarding house and that his new boss expected him at work no later than Friday the 23rd. John kissed his mother and said goodbye, forever, to Lockport and his old life.

2

Pierre du Pont and John J. Raskob

John Raskob arrived in Sydney in March 1900 to work as the personal secretary to Arthur J. Moxham, general manager of Dominion Iron and Steel. For a young man interested in business, especially finance and corporate management, his timing in joining a major industrial operation could not have been better. In the 1890s the United States—and Canada—had begun a financial and management revolution. For the next several years of his life, Raskob would place himself in the middle of that world in a business culture that could not have been more distant from the family cigar business that his grandfather and father had spent their lives sustaining.

In an age of fierce competition, dynamic technological changes, and rapidly expanding markets, industrial companies were merging in massive numbers. To avoid merciless price wars, or price competition, single-owner and family-run manufacturers, willingly or because they saw no other choice, were joining together in huge trusts or mega-mergers. The Morgan-backed Federal Steel deal that had bought up Johnson Steel, precursor to the much larger 1901 US Steel incorporation, was a major case in point. Industrial incorporation was the order of the day. To survive and grow big enough to take out competitors and take advantage of emerging national and international markets, promoters, brokers, industrialists, and investment bankers were inventing new forms of financing and recapitalizing to scale up corporate America. Credit and capital were in huge demand. Smaller producers, the inefficient, and many who clung to older marketplace rules were crushed by capitalist visionaries, as well as by predatory operators—with the difference between the two sometimes in the eye of the beholder. Lots of money was being made by company founders who were gleefully cashing out their equity, by bankers and brokers who were managing and marshalling the capital markets, and sometimes by promoters, investors, and the corporate innovators who understood how this new game could best be played.[1]

In the United States, railroads had already gone through this process, and a market for railroad bonds and securities based on Wall Street was well established.

State and national regulations, prompted by active political pressure from both customers and investors, placed railroads at the advent of the twentieth century at least somewhat under the thumb of public overseers and made them generally responsible in reporting valid financial data to the public. Industrial concerns operated in a different regulatory environment, in part, because before the 1890s no real market for industrial securities existed. No solid sources for rating industrial securities were published and information was hard to come by. Even in those states, such as Michigan, that had laws on the books that mandated "a true statement of the accounts" of manufacturing corporations, often no penalty was attached to failing to supply information nor was the nature of the "true statement" detailed.[2] It was caveat emptor all the way.

Most well-to-do people, let alone the middle class, steered clear of investing in industrial securities—there was just too much asymmetry, as economists say, between what a prospective investor knew and what company owners or investment promoters knew about earnings and assets and other pertinent factors. Still, all kinds of profitable opportunities existed for people who could figure out how to gauge a company's prospects and use the emerging capital markets and debt instruments to buy and sell companies in the chaotic, volatile, and expanding turn-of-the-century American economy.[3] For somebody like John Raskob, who had an outsized gift for numbers and taking risks, the early twentieth century was a very good time to be a young man.

Raskob had not gone to Sydney because he wanted to learn about corporate finance or how to run a major industrial plant. He had no five-year plan or vision of exactly what he wanted. People then rarely, if ever, thought that way. Nor did his new boss anticipate exposing him to high-order duties. Raskob had been hired for his shorthand and typing skills. Despite his attempts to explain to anyone who would listen that he had a gift for bookkeeping, he was not going to get a shot at developing those skills at Dominion. Still, Raskob's position as secretary to the general manager placed him in a position to watch a new major enterprise develop; Dominion, which was established to be the biggest steel producer in the British Empire, had been founded less than a year earlier and had yet to begin manufacturing when John got off the train in Sydney in March 1900.

Raskob's boss, Arthur Moxham, was an innovative manager, as well as a serious steel man. He was entrusted by the Dominion interests, who were coal men, to set up the plant and make it profitable by taking advantage of the adjacent coal mines that would supply coke for the blast furnaces. He was very well paid for his expertise, enough so that he could afford to have his thirty-room mansion, the "Moxham Castle," disassembled stone by stone in Lorain and rebuilt, complete with an indoor swimming pool, in Sydney in late 1898 when he took on the Dominion position. Moxham was one of the few men in North America who understood how to build a giant steel mill. He had a fierce eye for expenses and was meticulous in setting out "cost sheets" for every aspect of the plant as it was being constructed.

Much of what Moxham wanted done passed through Raskob's hands, and John did not just type up the masses of instructions and memos and correspondence by rote; he paid attention and made himself figure out what Moxham was doing. He gave himself a crash course in industrial management. He worked ten- and twelve-hour days processing the paperwork that Moxham's frenetic activities produced. As a result, Raskob had inside knowledge of Dominion Steel's plans and development, and everybody in town wanted to know what was happening. Raskob could have made himself a popular man—and probably some money, too—by talking outside of shop, but he kept his mouth shut, a fact his boss observed. Moxham was impressed.[4] Raskob plowed through whatever Moxham piled on him and he did not make mistakes, in part because he understood what he was typing. In a few weeks time Moxham made sure that Raskob understood his appreciation; he upped Raskob's pay from $80 to $100 a month. In about ten weeks' time, Raskob had more than tripled his wage.

At 21, John was for the first time in his life living apart from his mother. He cut loose, at least some. Sydney was a hard-drinking place, and Raskob, a social fellow, learned to consume whiskey and beer, sometimes in tumultuous combination. He had a few raucous nights. At least one evening involved loud public singing that featured the popular comic ballad, "Lucky Jim, How I Envy Him," the chorus of which, he was later informed, he had repeated a great many times. He met a Miss Ousely, who caught his eye with her "very pretty brown suit," and Miss Forbs, "tall graceful and sincere." He made a good friend, Stanley C. De Witt, who was another up-and-comer at Dominion. His circle was composed of Sydney's relatively few respectable middle-class young men and women. He was on his own and was intent on having fun, but he ran no personal risks and developed no bad habits. Raskob went to church. He spent a lot of nights at his boardinghouse reading the latest installments of the Frank Merriwell series and Nick Carter dime novels. He practiced coin tricks and other sleight-of-hand maneuvers with which he had become infatuated when he was a teenager. He was not lonely, but he missed Lockport and his family.[5]

In mid-July, Moxham took a vacation and he told Raskob to do the same. Despite the distance, John immediately set off for Lockport. His mother was thrilled to see him and in an emotional state asked him directly if he would consider finding a job closer to home. Raskob had no intention of returning to Lockport, knowing that there were no positions paying even close to what he had with Dominion Steel, but he promised his mother he would look into something in the area. When he returned to Sydney, he told Moxham about his predicament. His boss of just over four months was warmly supportive and promised

Raskob that he would help him find a job back in the United States closer to his family. John had made another ally.

With Moxham's permission secured, Raskob again tried Pierre du Pont, explaining his circumstances. Du Pont immediately wrote Moxham and asked him his opinion of Raskob. Moxham wrote a short but strong recommendation: "I can speak favorably in every way of Mr. John J. Raskob." He told du Pont that Raskob was prompt, attentive, "and I believe he is thoroughly reliable in the matter of holding his tongue which, as you know, is a very important one." Du Pont had also asked Moxham about Raskob's bookkeeping abilities but, ironically, Moxham could tell him nothing, "As I have had no occasion to test this."[6]

Du Pont was satisfied. He had an opening. While he had hired a woman as his secretary-stenographer, the position about which Raskob had first made inquiries, du Pont now wanted to hire a young man, someone with whom he could travel on business. Du Pont was starting a new enterprise, and he needed someone who could combine secretarial tasks with bookkeeping duties. He remembered that Raskob had claimed those skills. In late July, du Pont wrote Raskob offering him the job starting September 1 at $80 a month, the amount Raskob had asked for back in January. Du Pont explained that "at present I cannot pay more than this though chances seem quite favorable for increasing the salary of the right man when found." Raskob wrote back saying that he was now earning $100 a month but was willing to take $80 "and shall earnestly endeavor to merit an increase in a short time." Du Pont did not budge. With that bit of fencing, the deal was sealed and one of the more productive and unlikely business partnerships of the early twentieth century was about to commence.[7]

Raskob moved to Lorain, Ohio, in September 1900. Lorain was about 240 miles from Lockport, west of Cleveland, right on Lake Erie. It was an industrial town about the same size as Lockport but, at least in Raskob's untutored eyes, a more sophisticated, wealthier place. In making his way from Lockport to Sydney to Lorain, Raskob felt like he had made a fundamental break with his past and had also proven something to himself and to his family and old friends. In the somewhat patronizing tone he occasionally slipped into when writing his old circle, especially when giving career advice, something he did all the time after he left Holly Pump, he explained, "It has been my experience that a young man does a great deal better away from his native city than he possibly can hope to do in it, the chief reason for this being that most of his friends upon whom he depends for his assistance at home look upon him more or less as a child or baby and are not willing to entrust to him affairs of more or less magnitude with which he would necessarily meet were he among strangers."[8]

Du Pont, who was essentially a stranger, did almost immediately entrust affairs of magnitude to Raskob. Many years later du Pont was asked why, almost from the very first days Raskob came to work for him, he treated the relatively untested secretary with such confidence in his ability. Du Pont, somewhat mysteriously, said, "It was his extreme candor in everything."[9] Du Pont thought Raskob might have modeled his behavior after his erstwhile boss Arthur Moxham, who was famous in Pierre's business circle for his bold pronouncements and air of certainty (Du Pont also believed Moxham to be much better at presentation than delivery, a charge that some would eventually level at Raskob). Du Pont was, at any rate, immediately taken with Raskob and much later he emotionally recalled, "I never knew anyone other than John who saw eye to eye with me from the beginning."[10] Du Pont had hired Raskob as a secretary and clerk. Within weeks their relationship became something quite different.[11]

Raskob was from the start given bookkeeping duties and du Pont immediately perceived that his new assistant could read a column of figures like it was a musical score. He could add them up and hear all the parts of an enterprise play—and he could tell which notes were sour and which were sweet. Numbers made sense to Raskob and they stayed with him. He had told all of his employers that he was confident of his bookkeeping skills but until he began working for du Pont in the fall of 1900 he had never had a chance to display his talent.

Raskob meant something more by bookkeeping than just the simple recording of financial transactions. He meant that he understand how to use financial information to make sense of an industry and to assess its value. In 1900, accounting was in its infancy in the United States; in 1896 New York became the first state to recognize and license the profession of certified public accountant. While major British enterprises had begun to use chartered accountants earlier in the nineteenth century, often to codify their complex international business dealings, few American companies followed suit; as a result, almost all of the first professional accountants in the United States were English or Scottish, sent over by British capitalists to try to safeguard their investments in America's booming, relatively unregulated economy.[12] Although the American Association of Public Accountants had formed in 1886, Raskob's essentially unschooled talent was still relatively rare. Du Pont had much the same gift and his years at MIT had given him a strong mathematical and statistical background, as well. The two men found that they could speak the same language. For du Pont, not only did his discovery of Raskob's talents take some of the burden off his heavily weighted shoulders, it meant that he had found someone who understood who he was and what he was trying to accomplish.

They were still very different kinds of men. Raskob loved company. He devoted himself to making and keeping friends. He remained fully committed to spying out and meeting attractive woman. He loved athletics and spent much of his free time going to the YMCA and playing every sport he could find—he even personally laid out and paid for the first tennis court in Lorain. At the same time, he was a devout Catholic who attended Mass faithfully. As for temperament, John could be brash, outspoken, and angry when he felt he was being wronged or people were not on the up and up. Pierre was, in these ways, Raskob's opposite. He had long ago put aside his Protestant faith. He was very shy (his high school headmaster had nicknamed him "Graveyard" for his quiet nature). He was not interested in women. He was inept at sports and all outdoor pursuits and he did not mind admitting it: "Ball games had no attraction and I never could throw a ball or stone nor judge the direction and position of an object thrown towards me."[13] He had, instead, a highly developed aesthetic sensibility. His manner was gracious, even elegant. Raskob observed with interest and respect du Pont's refinement and even-temperedness. Over time, he learned from Pierre the ways of the well born and sophisticated, but these were not characteristics that ever that much interested him. Still, the two men became not just a well-fitted business team; they became dear friends almost from the first.

Everything was not always perfect, though sometimes even their disagreements paved the way for their long-term partnership. A few months after John began work, du Pont assigned Raskob to complete a financial deal. The details are hazy but almost surely had to do with finding investors for the Lorain Street Railway, a light rail system that had begun in 1885 as a horse-drawn trolley and then been bought by Tom Johnson in 1894. Johnson had immediately electrified the system, an expensive transformation that was going on all over the United States in the 1890s. He also expanded the rail system, creating an 11.5 mile network, in part to foster real estate development in the lands he had bought around the steel works he owned in South Lorain. One of du Pont's main tasks was to find ways to use the railway, somehow, to increase the Johnson company's cash position so as to better service the company's large debt.

Du Pont had rounded up three local investors for the railway who had agreed to provide a cash infusion in return for an equity position. Du Pont, who never enjoyed hustling for investors, was relieved that he had secured some new funding. Meanwhile, as he was in the thick of investigating several different business opportunities and needed to travel to Dallas, he asked Raskob to finalize the deal. The papers had all been executed and Raskob was to be assisted by a lawyer. John was just supposed to oversee the signing of the documents.

Without talking to du Pont, Raskob decided to do some due diligence on the deal by himself. As Raskob told the story years later, he quickly ran around Lorain talking to anybody who knew about the Lorain Street Railway. He was trying to ascertain the value of its assets, its current and projected revenues, and its various costs and charges. At the turn of the century, this kind of information was often not formally codified; accounting for depreciation and asset value, in particular, were all over the place. Raskob deduced, after comparing what he had in the way of financial paperwork with what his sources were telling him, that Pierre had seriously undervalued the railway. He also learned that other investors were interested and that a better price could be had. The night before the deal was to be done, Raskob got wind that du Pont's investors were at Lorain's best restaurant celebrating. They had never met Raskob so he slipped anonymously into the booth next to the men. They were "laughing and having a good time, with wine and everything, at this steal that they were going to make, and how it was worth three times what they were getting it for." Raskob had his final proof.

The next morning he found some wiggle room on the deal. The meeting to sign the papers had been set for 10:00 a.m. When the investors failed to show up on time, Raskob called the men and informed them that since they had chosen not to attend the scheduled document-signing, "You have defaulted. The deal is off." The men were furious. They saw no relationship between their casual approach to meeting with du Pont's underling and defaulting on a carefully negotiated business deal made with his boss who they knew was out of town. Raskob rubbed salt in the wound by informing them that not only had their tardiness cost them the deal but that he had already arranged a better offer.

The men called du Pont in Dallas and insisted that he fulfill their agreement. Raskob, knowing that du Pont would likely call him and insist that he consummate the deal, hid out. Over the weekend he nailed down a better price with a different group of investors for a serious sum of money that substantially exceeded what du Pont had negotiated. Raskob had put together his first deal. Still without consulting du Pont, Raskob used the authority du Pont had earlier given him and signed off on the new agreement.

Raskob knew that du Pont might not be completely pleased with his audacity. Still, he hoped the additional capital he had brought in would more than make up for the unexpected change in plans. John was both right and wrong. When he and du Pont finally talked, Pierre, in his quiet way, dressed him down. In the version of the story that remains, Pierre said: "John, I'm very disappointed. You think, being young, that … [the larger amount] you were able to get from somebody else because you felt the property was worth more and you put your ear to the ground and you found out a lot of things [makes everything good]. John, this was letting your boss down."

Pierre wanted John to understand that he had exceeded his authority and that he had made Pierre look foolish: "You wanted to do one of two things, John. You wanted to prove to me, your boss, that you knew more than I did, or that I had been hoodwinked. I know that you did it with the best of intentions. But John you are my employee.…You're just a new secretary." He told John that henceforth he must "close on the terms I give you." There was a caveat, however, "unless I give you instructions to negotiate." Then he gave John a huge bonus, which Raskob immediately used to buy his first extravagance, an American Runabout automobile built in nearby Cleveland.[14] Pierre understood that he had hired a secretary and found a business partner.

John was a happy man. He had found his path in life. Du Pont recognized his worth and was a generous employer; Raskob's salary more than doubled again between 1900 and the end of 1901. Twenty-two years old, he was making more than $2,000 a year in salary (per capita income in the United States, at that time, was less than $200).

Just a few months after arriving in Lorain, Raskob had moved his entire family from Lockport. In the residential area that Pierre was developing in South Lorain, he shared a comfortable home with his mother, paternal grandfather, and two sisters. John, showing the kind of cool-headed attitude he brought to all matters financial, even those relating to his own family, asked his grandfather, who was failing physically and mentally, to pay board of $3.50 a week. The amount was to come directly from the rent his grandfather received for the property at 43 East Avenue in Lockport. His grandfather was too confused mentally to arrange the details, so Raskob asked his old employer and family friend, the lawyer John Pound, to secure the manner legally. John pursued the boarding fee in large part because he was frustrated that his grandfather's will left his entire estate, including the house in which John's family had for so long resided, equally divided among his several children. John felt that the house, which he believed, in an emotionally charged overestimate, was worth $3,500, should have been left to his mother. As a result he wrote Pound asking that the $3.50 a week be sent directly to his mother, who was, after all, caring for his grandfather, and that in the event the total fee was not paid for whatever reason that "the balance remaining unpaid at the time of his death is to be paid our [sic] of his estate." That John wrote "our" instead of "out" seems like a classic psychological slip of the pen. John also stated that his grandfather wished to put the house on the market and wrote Pound that his grandfather believed that given "the likelihood of the Pan-American Exposition at Buffalo and the erection of the new Federal Building at Lockport increasing the value of his property," it was an excellent time to gain a high price for the property.[15] Given that his grandfather was not doing well mentally, the property analysis and decision to sell was almost certainly John's. Pound, following John's direction, did put the house up for sale but in 1900 the Lockport real estate market turned out to be soft and the house remained unsold for several years; while the property was often rented out during this time, collecting the monthly sum turned out to be an almost endlessly aggravating affair for John.

Even as John showed his hard-nosed approach to financial issues regarding his grandfather's situation, he also demonstrated a softer side when it came to helping those who cared about gaining a foothold in the economic world. When his younger brother, called Willow by the family, finished a business course in Buffalo, John asked Sterling Bunnell if he had a spot for his brother at the Johnson Company. Bunnell replied, "If your brother is anything like the first sample of the family, I shall only fear that Pierpont Morgan may be after him before he has been with us two weeks."[16] John had secured his family financially and had reunited them. Pierre, who after his father's death had charged himself with that same responsibility years earlier, looked on with approval.

For perfect happiness, John felt he lacked only a wife or at least a girlfriend, and he was dedicated to the search for a suitable candidate. At the same time, he was in no hurry to marry. To one of his many remaining friends in Lockport he wrote just after Valentine's Day 1901: "Note what you have to say about the young ladies. Fortunately, or otherwise, I have not been able to get one since coming here. None have attracted my attention so much in the least. I, too, am a firm believer in being worth something like ten thousand dollars before 'hitching up' as there is no such thing as living on love these cold days. However, I will not swear that my mind never changes."[17] The sum of $10,000 is really quite something, more than $250,000 in contemporary dollars, even if it is in large part a kind of subtle bragging to his old friend, demonstrating how far Raskob has come in such a short time.

In the constant stream of letters that John sent to his friends in Lockport, he kept them fully apprised of his flirtations and daily doings. In the first years of the twentieth century, Raskob sent or received several letters a week to his expansive circle of male friends. Indicative of his sense of self and his near-obsession with record keeping, he kept all of them, including carbons of his sent correspondence. Never again would Raskob have the time or the inclination to write so many letters detailing his everyday life. In those letters, John records his steady transformation from a provincial young man to a nationally oriented man-about-town.

By mid-1901, John was a well-known and popular young businessman in Lorain with a social life as full as he could make it. He threw himself into the social whirl of the community. He was still a cousin, if not a twin, to the small-town booster and culturally narrow type of man-on-the-make that Sinclair Lewis would lampoon so well two decades later in *Babbitt*. But he was not a social climber, and he kept a generous interest in all of his friends from Lockport, many of whom were from humble backgrounds and several of whom were having a hard time finding career opportunities of their own.

John's efforts on behalf of his Lockport crew were monumental if undoubtedly exasperating for some of them. In John's opinion Lockport was a dead end and the sooner his friends realized that fact the better off they would be. Lorain, he insisted, was the place to be. Iterations of his conclusion that only by leaving home can you become a man in your own eyes and the eyes of others was offered repeatedly. The fellows needed to follow John's lead, find some fortitude, break with their past, and embrace opportunity…in Lorain. John's advice was heart-felt and obviously came from his own experience but it was also self-interested. He missed his Lockport friends, and he had not found a similarly loyal and dedi-cated bunch in Lorain. He would never again find such a group of friends. His first friends, especially Will Bewley, Roy Flagler, Tom Spalding, Frank Dole, and Rob Allen, who knew and loved him before he became a man of wealth and influence, would haunt his memories all his life.

John constantly lobbied his friends to leave home and offered to find them jobs. He had leads everywhere, he told them. When one of his friends told him about his pitiful pay and terrible working conditions at his job with the New York Central on the "extra board" out of the Lockport train station, John learned everything he could about the pay scale and opportunity for train work out of Lorain and then instructed him, in detail, about how to make the move.

His friend Tom Spalding, a fellow Catholic, was training to be a doctor in Buffalo, and John threw himself into investigating medical opportunities in Lorain. He interrogated the company doctor at the steel company, sussed out opportunities at Lorain's Catholic Hospital ("Should think you would stand a good chance of securing work there; the Sisters run it but I do not know what order they are"), and then learned what he could about the Ohio State Medical Board certification process after Spalding expressed some concerns about it. At the turn of the century, many medical schools offered anything but a rigor-ous science-based education, and states had just begun to create standards for doctors, generally devised and enforced by the newly incorporated American Medical Association. Raskob found that Ohio had a relatively rigorous licensing process, which he thought Spalding would like, since "it will prevent all these quacks from coming into your territory." Spalding, matriculating at a not so rig-orous medical school, was not so sure. Lockport seemed like an easier place to set up shop.[18]

To another friend, whose skill level was holding him back and making it hard, even for John, to locate a suitable, nearby opportunity, he came up with another idea; John would loan him the money to go to a school that would "fit him for a commercial life." John had worked out the math and it should only cost between $150 and $200, since his friend could live with him while he went to school. To broach this delicate proposition John began with a long story about Abe Lincoln who was stuck in a dead end job as a wood cutter and rail splitter. Only when he borrowed money from a friend "to enable him to complete his schooling" was he able to get his start "in life and eventually become President of these grand and glorious United States of America." John meant to be funny, and he was, in order to spare his friend the awkwardness of taking the loan. John could not help, though, adding that "I will never miss a hundred or two."[19]

Despite John's investigative skill, creativity, and exuberant encouragements, none of his friends made the move to Lorain. Family, a sweetheart, community roots, fear of the unknown, something always held them back, even after many of them had entertained the idea and encouraged John to explore the possibilities. On occasion John was frustrated by their hesitancy and even chivied them for their lack of gumption. He also explained that if they were not really interested they should let him know because he was putting himself on the line for them, talking to employers and contacts about opportunities. Other times, he wondered about his friends' seriousness of purpose.

So, when his younger friend Frank Dole informed John in March 1901 that he was thinking he would skip Lorain and just go straight to New York City for his main chance because he heard the banks paid really well there, John gave him a lecture. It was true, he wrote, that men in New York could draw salaries of $5,000 to $10,000, but "it takes hard work and earnest endeavor to get ahead in a City like New York." And how, Raskob wrote, did Frank think he would land such a position in the first place? "In New York," he informed his Lockport friend, "well-to-do people pay banking institutions and the like to take their sons in their employ and learn them the business."[20] How Raskob knew this to be true is a mystery, but he felt no compunction about hectoring his naïve friend. John was losing his patience for the dreamy talk of youth, and he had a hard time understanding how and why people would refuse to take a good but well-calculated chance to advance their fortunes. He and his friends, even just a year after he had left Lockport, were becoming different people.

Despite that rapidly developing distance, and the occasional patronizing tone, John kept his affection for his old friends alive whatever their station in life. John, then and later, never became a snob or turned away from old friends and family because of their small-town ways or lack of success, nor did he ape his so-called betters. Having Pierre du Pont as his boss and friend probably helped; in Lorain, Pierre's sophistication and social place were unmatched, but he never played on his status. Du Pont was plain spoken, direct, and judged his associates on their performance not social standing. Raskob did not, however, look to Pierre for cultural guidance or direction. Their nine years age difference might have played a part though it is likely that Pierre's character, built on gentle refinement, mild manner, and aesthetic orientation, was just too far from John's own personality to serve as a model. On matters of personal style, Pierre probably felt unapproachable. Instead John and his circle of friends, a few of whom were also moving up the economic ladder, albeit much more slowly, and some of whom were having and would continue have difficulties finding their way, endlessly discussed popular culture, style, courtship, and the ways of the world. Much time was spent discussing the cut of a suit and whether a fabric that was all the rage in New York City would look elegant in Lorain, Ohio, and Lockport,

New York, or just odd. They were all trying to figure out how to be proper men in twentieth-century America. They were between two worlds, an older one in which a community judged a person by his character and a newer one in which society quickly appraised a man by his appearance. In most aspects, John took the lead but not always.

Some of the young men, as was typical of the times, avidly followed partisan politics. While a couple were vaguely interested in political office, for most politics was more an entertainment and partisanship a matter of personal identity. Policy preferences or ideology did not come up. To all the political talk, Raskob remained indifferent. The day before the first presidential election in which John was eligible to vote, one of his closest friends, Frank Dole, wrote him to complain that John did not seem to have a horse in the race: "Say, John, what are you, I mean what party do you belong and do you cast your vote in Ohio this election or have you not lived in the state long enough to vote?" Dole made his predilections clear: "Tuesday, November 6 is the day for the great funeral and I tell you we will put the Democrat party so far in the rear that they will not have the nerve to run another candidate in 1904. What do you think about it?"[21] John did not reply. He had, in fact, registered to vote and he, too, supported the Republican McKinley against Bryan. Bryan's populist "cross of gold," inflationary economics platform had no appeal to Raskob, who already thoroughly identified with the capitalist class.[22] But Raskob had yet to develop any real interest in partisan politics.

John was far more effusive about the goings on in the world of theater. He had begun following the theatrical world while still a teenager in Lockport but in Lorain, with money in his pocket and Cleveland, with its five major theaters, nearby, John was in heaven. His letters to his friends recorded his obsession: "I see that Olga Nethersole is about to leave for London.... How did you like James O'Neil in 'Monte Christo.' I was up to see 'Hamlet' which played at the Cleveland Oper[a] House last week. It was pretty good, but I did not care much for Shakespeare's plays as there is not enough fun in them. Saw 'Mistress Nell' last night."[23] Raskob was amazed by great actors' ability to play a parade of diverse parts. He had no such talent but he was and would remain entranced by those who could mold their personalities to meet the needs of the moment. John's undramatic character seemed fixed from early days, but he was attracted to people who could take to the stage—whether at a theater, a business conference room, or a political rally—and use their mutable histrionic skills to charm and channel other men to a desired goal.

If John was and would remain all his life a theatrical spectator, he developed a different and far more active interest in Lorain: card playing. The big game among his set in Lorain was Pedro, an early version of auction bridge. Given his ability with numbers, John not surprisingly turned out to be a gifted card player.

He almost always won. John regularly entered and soon began organizing Pedro tournaments, often paired with his sister Gertrude who also had excellent card skills. The competitions usually featured a prize for the overall winning player or pair of players. John won everything in sight, including a rocking chair, a gold watch, a tie, and "a finely bound volume of *In the Palace of the Kings*."[24] John's card playing and successful gambling had only just begun.

Besides attending the theater, playing Pedro, and forming a literary society, John still spent plenty of time at the YMCA where he was a regular on the basketball court and an exercise enthusiast. He bragged to his Lockport buddies that he was working out regularly and that "the Y.M.C.A. here is entirely different from the one at Lockport. All the best people in the place take a deep interest in it…. There are lots of pretty girls there, too."[25] While John was becoming a regular at the Y's businessmen's banquets, he also loved to run around the gym at full speed playing "It," as he called it, especially if girls were involved in the tagging. Even as John was fast becoming a sophisticated businessman, he was still a very young man very much invested in having fun.

While in Lorain he continued to maintain a semi-serious relationship with a "little lower-town girl" in Lockport, but he was constantly checking out the nice girls in town, enlisting his sister Gertrude in the cause. To a matchmaking friend, he explained his preferences in detail, pondering "what class of girls I like the better, light or dark." Both, he decided, though "I think I like a nice, young, pretty, dark girl, one that is as pretty as a gypsy. However, get me one that is not cranky, for I do not enjoy any girl's company if she can be obstinate or cranky in the least."[26] John was writing one of his closest friends, a peer, and that is how they wrote to each other about young women. His mother could have read any of his letters without a blush. Scholars have longed argued that turn-of-the-century American men regularly visited brothels and employed a sexually explicit vocabulary. Well, not John Raskob or any of his close friends.

Religiosity, at least on John's part, might have been a deciding factor. John remained a practicing, faithful Catholic. With his mother and siblings in tow, he maintained a strong commitment to the Church, attending Mass, keeping Lent, and observing the holidays. He was particularly close to Father T. F. McGuire of the Church of the Sacred Heart, who helped John, his siblings, and his mother, in particular, settle into their new lives in Lorain. Appreciative of all that Father McGuire had done, upon McGuire's retirement in 1903, John sent him a large donation, his first major philanthropic gift, which enabled McGuire to purchase a spectacular bejeweled chalice, valued at $375 (more than a year's rent in most big cities), for his personal use. Later, in return for John's charity, Father McGuire sent John and his brother William "blessed beads" to which the Reverend explained, "There is an indulgence of 500 days for each Hail Mary said on them."[27] Raskob never seems to have given a contrary thought to his religious faith despite the example of his skeptical boss. His faith gave him ballast and a sense of order, rare commodities in his quicksilver life.

In most social and cultural ways, Lorain was a gentle step away from Lockport for John. But in the business world, his break with his past was far more pronounced and rapid. A year after leaving Lockport, he reported to a friend, "Without appearing conceited and in all frankness and honesty, would say that the position I vacated in Sydney with Mr. Moxham has not yet been filled to his satisfaction; he has had different people there since I left, but none of them have remained." His ambition and self-confidence rang out in the next sentence, which only appears to be a non sequitur: "John D. Rockefeller has said that he would give any man that could manage his affairs a salary of one million dollars a year."[28] In 1901, du Pont was not Rockefeller and John's salary was far from a million, but Raskob knew he had already proved himself to men of high status in the business world.

Pierre du Pont had hired Raskob because he wanted an assistant to accompany him on his business travels in pursuit of the takeover of a city electric railway system. Du Pont, with help from Tom Johnson, had devised a plan to take advantage of the shifting fortunes of the electric railways that had sprung up all over the United States in just a few years time. Many of these new lines were run haphazardly, were undercapitalized, and were facing ruinous competition. Few people had a good idea of how to make them operate profitably and as a result these railways were a financial mess. In that chaos and confusion, du Pont saw an opportunity. He had, he hoped, devised a way to buy a troubled municipal trolley line and then use the railway's own revenues to pay off the purchase price, improve the line, gain a major equity interest in the business, and then sell the line at a substantial profit. He was confident that he could manage an electric railway system better than most of the men who owned them. He enlisted Raskob in the operation. With du Pont in the lead, the two men would leap into the fray. At the turn of the century, the American economy was booming and men who took smart risks could make fortunes.

Raskob knew little about the electric railway business other than what he was furiously figuring out from his work with du Pont on Lorain's own system. He did, however, know something about the craziness that too often surrounded municipalities' eager pursuit of an electric trolley system. When John was just fourteen, a group of Lockport investors, working closely with the town government, had formed the Lock City Electrical Company to bring to their community a new fangled electric trolley car system and, hopefully, a profitable business. They hired a supposedly seasoned construction manager, Charles K. Lawrence, to set up the railway that they had transported to Lockport on a freight train. Lawrence, a con man, bribed a yard crew to hook up the freight cars carrying the entire railway, including rails, trolley cars, switches, electrical components, and everything else that made up the Lock City line, to another train. He used the freight train to steal Lockport's new electric trolley line, intending to sell it to another small town out west. His bizarre caper failed. He was caught, tried, and sentenced to two years in prison for "stealing one street railway."[29] The street car business was not for the faint of heart.

Du Pont had traveled all over the country looking for a line to buy and by early 1901 he had zeroed in on Dallas. One of Johnson's contacts, the Cleveland industrialist George T. Bishop, had pointed du Pont at the Dallas trolley car lines. Bishop managed a syndicate that had bought a major interest in the neighboring Fort Worth electric railway in June 1900. Although just six years older than Pierre, he was an experienced investor; he believed a good deal of money could be made by linking the Dallas and Fort Worth trolley lines with an interurban railroad. He thought the well-connected and forward-thinking du Pont would be a perfect partner. After a series of talks with the Dallas street car owners, in March 1901 du Pont went to Dallas and spent several days there investigating. He deduced that he could buy the three major Dallas lines for a little over a million dollars.

Du Pont wrote his cousin and likely fellow investor, Coleman, that the system "is strictly 'bum'. . . . The road is operating very badly, cars are dirty and run with little system. The track is so rough that riding is very uncomfortable."[30] Perfect, in other words, for du Pont's plan. Properly operated, a consolidated system in Dallas could be made more profitable. It already generated enough revenues to pay off the interest on the bonds du Pont planned to sell to buy the line with a small bit left over to fix up the line. Better run, the line could provide a dividend for the new shareholders—meaning du Pont and his circle of investors. The real money would be made through the purchase strategy. Du Pont would front very little money. Most of the purchase price would come from selling bonds, which would be serviced through the line's own revenues. Without having risked much of his own capital, du Pont would own all or nearly all the share equity in the Dallas line. Once he had his new company operating more profitably he would sell the line. He stood to make a fair amount of money if everything worked as planned.[31]

Upon Pierre's return from Dallas, he worked closely with John on the deal. Preparing the documents they would use to buy the railways, as well the bond divestures and other financial agreements, they spent long hours together. Everybody pushed hard at the young team. Du Pont tried to get Brown Brothers interested in the bond issue. A major investment firm, they demanded brutal terms. Pierre was pretty sure that Brown Brothers was trying to take advantage of him; he wrote Bishop for advice. Bishop told him that the bankers at Brown Brothers were stalling; that they meant to take the line for themselves. Bishop was right. Du Pont wrote the bankers and asked them about the rumor. They were decent enough to provide a blunt, if not totally honest reply: "The opportunity to purchase these properties came to us quite unsought and really unexpected."[32] John and Pierre worked faster.

At the same time, Bishop took advantage of the information du Pont had shared with him to demand harder terms on a deal to consolidate their interests. Du Pont pushed back at him, insisting that he was taking a far greater risk and therefore had earned a far greater share in the revenue split of any deal they made. Bishop shrugged off du Pont's complaint and told the younger man that in order to make any money on the railway he had to get the Dallas city government or the Texas state legislature to contribute to their consolidated lines by paying for infrastructure improvements; in particular, the city would need to pay to pave or repave areas the interurban line would travel. Bishop was himself in Austin, lobbying away. The head of another, smaller Dallas trolley line, knowing du Pont's plans, told du Pont that he was going to compete with the new consolidated line by building a rival interurban railway; he was clearly looking for a payoff.

Du Pont and Raskob just kept working the numbers and trying to figure out who was square and who was not and what they needed to do to advance the deal. John studied the Dallas line's contracts with its suppliers, particularly the Standard Light and Power Company. John quickly mastered "now in use" electric charges versus future use costs and other technical language. He was getting a crash course in how contracts and related legal documents structured corporate deal making. He traveled with du Pont to Dallas and other cities where they were exploring opportunities to sell the Dallas electric railway bonds.[33]

For Raskob the work could be exhausting but mainly it was exhilarating. He was handling a lot of the financial paperwork and daydreaming about relocating to Dallas where, du Pont had told him, he would be in charge of the operation's financial end. He told his Lockport friends about his rise in the world and about his likely move to Dallas, at that point a fast-growing city of about 50,000 people. Dallas, he now informed them, was the place to be: "Dallas is a very beautiful City.... it is there where one knows in reality what a sweet balmy breeze is.... Roses bloom ten months in the year down there and it is possible to stroll without an overcoat in the evening away long after Christmas time."

In early May 1901, John bragged to his friend Frank Dole about his previous weekend: "We worked until two o'clock in the morning and all day the following day (which was Sunday) and until three o'clock Monday morning. That is when he bought the railroad."[34] Du Pont, thirty-one years old, and Raskob, just twenty-two, had clinched their first deal together. While they both were often anxious, it was a lot of fun.

Over the second half of 1901, Raskob and du Pont poured themselves into the Dallas venture. Du Pont had bought three Dallas lines for $225,000 in cash, money that he and members of his family put up. The rest of the $1,075,000 would be furnished through the sale of bonds. Du Pont also gave the old owners

$50,000 out of the $1,500,000 in common stock he had created for the Dallas railway. Since Pierre had not actually sold any of the bonds, yet, he provided the sellers with a personal note for $850,000, guaranteed by his holdings and those of cooperating family members—it was good to be a du Pont. Here was Pierre's first independent business deal and there was John at his right hand, the newly designated treasurer and director of the company. Raskob could not believe the rapid change in his life. From Dallas, he wrote his mother: "Among others, I met the Presidents and other officials of the different banks, many judges and prominent men of Dallas."[35] Raskob was a bona fide businessman.

Selling the bonds proved to be much harder than du Pont had believed. Before the deal had been consummated, he had written George Bishop blandly assuring him that "it would be comparatively easy to float our bonds."[36] It was not. Du Pont ran into roadblocks. From his years in Wilmington, Pierre had connections to well-to-do investors and brokers in Philadelphia. But Philadelphians had participated in the first wave of trolley lines in Dallas, which had turned out badly, and were not interested. In Boston, he discovered that the sort of investment houses that could have brokered his bonds were already awash in their own trolley line deals. New York bond brokers turned him flat down except for one serious player, Alven Beveridge, who agreed to sell the Dallas paper. The only customer he found demanded a steep discount on the bonds and other terms that would have provided the buyer interest payments of 15.5 percent in the first year. Du Pont agreed that such terms made the bonds a wonderful investment, but they were a terrible deal for him. He declined to sell. Luckily for Pierre, the Dallas sellers were willing to extend the term of his personal note while he pursued investors. In the worst case, du Pont and the note holders knew, Pierre could almost certainly sell the bonds to members of his own family.

Meanwhile, under du Pont's management, which included hiring a new operations director, and John's financial scrutiny, the Dallas line was operating more efficiently and effectively; revenues were up. To push productivity, Raskob and du Pont studied operational and technical factors: train speeds, scheduling stops, and electric motor capacities. The deal was not running perfectly according to plan, but it was working. Both John and Pierre were fast learning about the national financial market, deal making, negotiating, management operations, and restructuring a badly run business. It would take time but eventually du Pont's foray into the madcap city railway business turned out well; after making improvements, working through the interurban consolidation, and turning over management to one of his younger brothers, du Pont sold off the Dallas line for a substantial profit. In 1901, Pierre had loaned John $600 on generous terms to buy fifty shares in the railway; in a few years' time John netted several thousand dollars in the sale. But well before the Dallas endeavor played out, a much bigger and far more fateful adventure began.[37]

3

Raskob and the DuPont Company

Everything changed for Pierre du Pont and John Raskob on January 28, 1902. Eugene du Pont, head of the family company, formally known as E. I. du Pont de Nemours & Company, died that day after a brief battle with pneumonia. He had held 20 percent of the company's stock. His two brothers and a cousin owned another 60 percent. The remaining 20 percent was divided between two younger du Ponts, Pierre's older cousins, Charles and Alfred. Pierre owned no part of the tightly held company and, having exiled himself from the company four years earlier, he had no title or role in it. But in the immediate aftermath of Eugene du Pont's death, opportunity presented itself.

The surviving major shareholders in the company did not want to lead the company nor did they want to turn over leadership to the two younger shareholders. Charles was sickly and would die a year later. Alfred was seen by enough of his elders as so lacking in "good judgment and business ability" as to be incapable of leading the company forward. The major shareholders, after some to-ing and fro-ing, decided to sell the company, founded exactly a century earlier by Éleuthère Irénée du Pont, to their primary rival in the explosives business, Laflin & Rand.

Alfred du Pont, then a temperamental, hard-headed man of thirty-eight with extensive experience in powder manufacturing, if not necessarily proven expertise in the business, was insulted and infuriated. He had never been an easygoing man. He had been orphaned at twelve. When his Uncle Henry and other family members had tried to foster Alfred and his four siblings out to relatives, Alfred grabbed a shotgun and the others, armed as well, had refused to leave their family home, Swamp Hall. They raised themselves. After dropping out of MIT in 1884, where his greatest achievement had been befriending the boxing champion John L. Sullivan, Alfred had joined the family business as a powder man. Technically gifted, he had excelled, churning out some 20,000 pounds of powder a day for the American military during the 1898 Spanish-American War. He felt he had earned the right to take command of the company.[1]

At the decisive February 14 meeting of the small number of family stock-holders, Alfred came straight from his work at the powder yards still dressed in overalls with his hands and face streaked with gunpowder. He formally demanded the right to outbid Laflin & Rand, arguing "that the business was mine by all rights of heritage, that it was my birthright." Somewhat flabbergasted by Alfred's emotional call to arms and dubious as to Alfred's executive ability, the other shareholders agreed, if only in principle, that Alfred could try to buy the firm. Only Henry du Pont, among the other shareholders, actually offered Alfred encouragement, but it came with very specific advice: if he expected a positive outcome, Alfred had best bring his two highly talented cousins, Coleman and Pierre, into the deal.

Thomas Coleman du Pont, just over six years older than Pierre, had already been thinking about joining forces with his cousin Alfred in a takeover of the family company. Coleman, unlike cousin Alfred, was a popular figure in the family. Standing 6′ 3″ and weighing a muscular 210 pounds, he was charming, confident, and fierce. After a time at MIT, he had gone to work for his father's profitable mining business in Kentucky, the Central Coal and Iron Company. There he had proven his mettle by crushing a strike led by the Knights of Labor; he had made a deal with local politicians to use convicts as strikebreak-ers. Then, like Pierre, he had inherited stock in the Johnson Company and decided to run some of that company's extensive operations. In 1900, he had moved back to Wilmington, the DuPont Company headquarters, where he was in the middle of a variety of ventures, none of which were working out to his satisfaction. Coleman loved a challenge and was thrilled by the prospects of leading the family firm.[2]

When approached by Alfred, Coleman carefully alluded to his concerns about Alfred's business leadership skills; he would join with Alfred but only if he was placed in charge of the company and received the largest numbers of shares. Coleman, like Henry du Pont, also instructed Alfred that they must have Pierre, as well. Pierre understood corporate finance and they were going to need those skills if they hoped to buy out the other family members and then raise enough money to reorganize and modernize the company. Alfred agreed to the terms; these conditions when combined with Alfred's temperament would later lead to troubles.

Coleman called Pierre in mid-February to make his pitch. Almost half a cen-tury later Pierre remembered the conversation: "Would I do it? This was the most important far-reaching decision of my life; no position, salary, or interest in the business was offered but the three minute allowance of a telephone con-versation was quite long enough for me to receive the account of the proposition placed before me, and to make up my mind and give my reply in one word, *yes*."[3] Immediately, Pierre asked John to join him. They jumped on a train and arrived in Wilmington in the midst of a blizzard. With Coleman, they would figure out how to finance the takeover of the DuPont Company.

The takeover was a family affair and turned out to involve no sophisticated maneuvering. A streamlined version of the financial model Pierre and John had devised to buy the Dallas railway would be redeployed by the cousins to buy the company. Despite the emotional tenor with which Alfred had at first challenged his elders, Coleman and Pierre brought a practiced hand and a cordial manner to the buyout, quickly producing an amiable resolution that seemed fair to all parties. In the end, the three cousins expended the grand total of $700 each of their own money in purchasing the largest explosives company in the United States.

On February 28, 1902, the old shareholders graciously accepted thirty-year 4 percent notes priced at $12 million for their shares. The 4 percent annual interest on the $12 million approximated the annual prior years' earnings of the company. In addition, the old owners received almost 25 percent share of the new company's stock of 120,000 shares, giving them a stake in the company's future, hopefully enhanced, profits. Coleman, Alfred, and Pierre received the rest of the stock with Coleman gaining the lion's share at 43,200. Pierre and Alfred split the other 43,200 though Alfred, as an old owner, also picked up additional shares and 10 percent of the 4 percent note. If Coleman, Pierre, and Alfred increased the company's earnings everybody benefited and, if they did not, the cousins were holding shares that could support no dividends and had little value, since the interest-bearing notes had first take on almost all of the profits the company had, in recent times, been earning.

There was no transition. The day after the deal was signed former owner Frank du Pont walked into the company office where his cousin Pierre, in a sign of things to come, alone had come to work. Frank turned to Pierre, his junior by some twenty years, and told him the company was now in his good hands.[4]

Pierre du Pont was worried neither by the responsibility nor the necessity of increasing the company's revenues if he and his co-owners meant to prosper. Immediately after the deal was done, he and John began a monumental evaluation of the DuPont Company's assets. They quickly realized that the cousins had gotten a very good deal. Using the most conservative valuations, they listed the company's assets at just over $12 million but that included the bonus of around $1 million in cash.

To check their work, du Pont hired a certified public accountant to make an independent audit, indicative of their approach to modernizing the company. Every year accounting professionals were arriving in increasing numbers, produced by the rapid reorganization of industrial America and investors' and operators' need for standard and principled valuations. The accountant arrived at a figure of well over $14 million; he gave much higher values to the large amount of shares that the DuPont Company owned in other explosives companies. DuPont's shares and its role in those other companies would be the very next order of business to be studied and acted upon by Coleman and Pierre. Officially, Pierre was DuPont treasurer and as of March 2, 1902, John was listed as a clerk in the treasurer's office.

In practice, John served as the company's assistant treasurer, a title he would not be given for several more years. More importantly to Raskob, his salary was almost immediately increased by another 50 percent to around $3,000. He had made the leap from a weekly employee scraping by at $5 a week to a monthly man—high status at the time—earning an upper-middle-class income. But surrounded as he was by financial deal making of a magnitude he could have scarcely imagined even two years earlier, he understood that his fortune would not be made via a monthly salary check. He began thinking about how to make real money. Although still young and with little formal power, he was fast learning that the world was full of opportunity. Men who could take advantage of those opportunities, who were unafraid of risk, could grow rich. The world, Raskob was discovering, was malleable and a man could use his talent and his will to shape it. Under Pierre du Pont's tutelage, Raskob was learning how to think and to act like a member of the elite.

Pierre and John faced a massive undertaking as they began to investigate the DuPont Company holdings. When Pierre and John began their financial tally, the DuPont Company was an old-fashioned operation. As with so many other contemporary industries in the United States, DuPont's previous owner-managers had concentrated their energies on controlling the price and profitability of their products by reducing competition. In 1872, the leading manufacturers of explosives formed the Gunpowder Trading Association. It was a cartel and the DuPont Company played a leading role. Cartels were, then, completely legal in the United States. To assure compliance the big companies, including DuPont, bought shares in the other tightly held companies (these companies rarely traded their shares on public exchanges). The DuPont men, as shareholders, then executed their rights as investors to look at the books of the other members of the cartel to insure that they were adhering to agreed upon sale prices, market divisions, and other association measures. DuPont, then, was an independent company running its own explosives business under the terms set by the gunpowder cartel, and it also was a sizable minority shareholder in almost all of the other major and some minor companies similarly involved in the explosive powder and dynamite business. As members of a price-setting cartel, the explosives companies, including DuPont, spent much of their energy and capital policing one another and new entries in the field, rather than seeking competitive advantage through price or innovation.

By 1902, when the cousins took over DuPont, cartels were illegal in the United States thanks to the 1890 Sherman Antitrust Act. Still, the federal government had shown no interest in investigating, let alone prosecuting the cartel's practice of price-setting and market controls. Regardless, Coleman and Pierre believed that the cartel system was an inefficient way to run their business and that they could make a great deal more money if they consolidated the explosives industry under their own forward-thinking control. Centralized administration, economies of scale, rationalized productions, organized research, new product innovation, and modern corporate financial controls all would lead to a massive expansion of the business under increasingly profitable conditions. Pierre and Coleman were ready to throw over the business model that their forbearers had embraced for the previous thirty years.

Throughout the spring and summer of 1902, John and Pierre took full advantage of DuPont's status as a shareholder in the cartel's other big companies to tear into the financial records of their main rivals. They needed to figure out how much the other companies were worth so that they could buy them out at the right price. The goal was to create a much bigger and, thus, they believed, more profitable DuPont Company. Again and again, John and Pierre were surprised by the conservative valuation other explosive companies gave their assets, particularly the factories and mills where they made their products. In some cases, they discovered that the owners of the target companies valued their own shares on their private books for far less than they were valued in the open market (though since few, if any, of the shares of these companies were regularly traded, a market price was a very rough guide to current value). Still, if Pierre and John were right about the other companies' undervaluation, they could buy them relatively cheaply compared to their worth. Raskob and du Pont were analyzing these companies based not on the actual value of their assets or sunk costs but on the earnings the companies were capable of generating. They were by no means the first men to compute a corporation's worth in this manner—the (in)famous financier Jay Gould had done so decades earlier—but such share price valuations were not, as they would be, conventional wisdom either.

Raskob and du Pont had to figure out how to assess value, and it took a long time to understand how the companies figured out their own worth and then to decide if their methods made sense. Nobody was hiding or making up numbers. And most of the figures were fairly transparent. The core number for assessing a company's worth, then, was revenues and the revenue figures were not in dispute. The old cartel system had put a premium on the transparency of that number, since each member of the cartel had to know it in order to police one another and keep to their complicated price and market share agreements. Much less agreed upon were the values of a company's production facilities and the relationship of those values to the company's total worth. John and Pierre tended to see greater value in the other companies' plants and other production facilities than the owners did, since they believed that the targeted companies were not efficiently run nor was their profitability maximized.

Then, John and Pierre had to craft a plan by which their most important competitors could be taken over. All of these rivals were already partially owned by DuPont under the interlocking procedures that the cartel system had created. They targeted two companies above all, Laflin & Rand, the very company that the older generation had lined up to buy the DuPont Company, and Eastern Dynamite, a massive holding company that controlled much of the dynamite business. DuPont had no independent dynamite production, which was a problem; in the early twentieth century dynamite was a big, growing, and profitable business.

In both cases, Raskob and du Pont deduced that the old Dallas trolley line buyout model would work to finance the purchase price. Once again, they figured that they could use each operation's own revenues to support a bond issue that would satisfy the current owners' financial demands; the addition of stock in the new DuPont Company would give the old owners a necessary additional incentive to make the deal. The du Ponts would use their shares in DuPont to guarantee the bondholders' investment.

The plan had an element of risk to it. If the reorganized company failed to make enough money to meet the bond interest payments, the bondholders could demand a big hunk of the DuPont holdings. But John and Pierre were confident that the acquired companies were worth more than the current owners believed. Ergo, the DuPont Company would begin from a financially secure position that should generate sufficient revenues to meet the bond payout. In addition, John and Pierre had bypassed the capital markets. In these early deals, they paid no fees, no commissions, and no equity stake to any investment house or brokers. They had used no bankers. John and Pierre had analyzed and structured the deal themselves and financed it internally.

Pierre was in charge of the finances, but he worked closely with his cousin Coleman on the transactions and the grand strategy. The expertise and connections of other experienced family members were deployed in the long process of negotiation with the many target companies, as well. Alfred du Pont was happy to leave these sorts of operations to his cousins and he was rarely even consulted; he was occupied with the more straightforward if vital task of managing the DuPont's main powder works. John had no final say in any of the decisions, but Pierre trusted him not only to work through the finances but also to help structure the deals.

Almost always John was right in the middle of the deals and was often charged by Pierre with communicating with the key figures as they worked out the details. Sometimes John and Pierre traveled together to the site of a powder works they meant to buy and negotiated directly with their target. And sometimes the deal was negotiated from afar. To insure secrecy when doing a long-distance deal, a few of the men, including John and Pierre, devised an elaborate code that allowed them to communicate by telegram without risk of the wrong people knowing what they were up to. So, for example, a transaction involving a California company reads: "PARABELN, SNIFFED BALADRASTE. ECANGUAIS holders considerable OBMOVEOR here NERTARBERG at SITIASTEIG. HAKLEDER." Decoded, this message reads: Referring to your message of 2nd, 18,000 it is correct. Have been informed that holders [of] considerable Common Stock here intend to sell at 99. Await our letter of 2d.[5]

John was privy to everything going on. His own numbers told him that the companies the du Ponts were buying were worth more than their owners thought they were. And he believed, with all his heart, that in the du Ponts' hands, the assets of the acquired companies would contribute, relatively quickly, to a major increase in the value of DuPont. He was sure that DuPont was positioned to make a killing. In those days, there was no such thing as insider trading. John knew that he should if he could find a way to buy into the corporate merger as soon as possible.

Neither DuPont nor the target companies regularly traded their shares publicly. Still John understood that in the buyout period, if he had sufficient cash, through his direct connections to all the parties he could find a way to buy shares of the most undervalued of the companies that DuPont was acquiring. If he did, he was positive he would make real money. So, with the grand sum of his $500 in life savings at hand, Raskob met with Levi L. Rue, the president of the Philadelphia National Bank, to make a proposal.

Nearly a quarter century later, Raskob sent Rue a letter recounting what happened: "I undoubtedly had more 'nerve' than any young man should have. I approached you for a loan of twenty-five thousand dollars offering as collateral one hundred shares of Eastern Dynamite Company stock." This stock, of course, was what Raskob needed the $25,000 to buy. Raskob was twenty-three years old and still was not sure where to buy a good suit. Raskob continued, "It may be that you have forgotten or do not know the whole story"; Raskob assured him that it was a story worth remembering "even though it sounds like an Aladdin lamp fairy tale."

Raskob reminded Mr. Rue that he had made the following pitch: "The balance sheet of the company reflected the fact that an ultra-conservative management had amortized the plants of the company down to one dollar. A study of the condition of the company's property and business indicated that the stock was quite valuable." Raskob, of course, had been the driving force in that study. Raskob then proposed that based on his analysis Rue should lend him the money to buy one hundred shares of Eastern Dynamite, since the company was really worth much more than that share price indicated. Raskob must have also told banker Rue that the DuPont Company was buying out Eastern Dynamite and that the Dynamite shares would, thus, be soon swapped for DuPont stock and notes. That paper, Raskob knew, not only would increase in value over time but it was certain—he trusted—to generate more than enough dividends and other monies to pay off the loan. Raskob was asking the Philadelphia bank to do for him what Pierre and Coleman were asking the other explosives companies to do for them—it was Other People's Money financing in a smaller key. Raskob believed the deal was bulletproof and pitched it with conviction. Remarkably, Rue agreed. The Philadelphia National Bank lent John Raskob, an unknown twenty-three-year-old, the $25,000 using only the Eastern Dynamite stock as collateral.

When Raskob wrote Rue in 1925, the banker already knew that Raskob had long made good on the loan. And Rue certainly knew who John J. Raskob had become. What Rue might not have known, Raskob wrote him, was that the 100 shares Raskob had bought with the borrowed money had a market value in 1925 of $510,000 and had generated cash receipts, dividends, and other payouts worth $410,000. The $25,000 loan had produced for Raskob a grand total of $920,000 (corrected for inflation that is equivalent to well over $11 million!).[6]

Between 1902 and 1904, Pierre and John devised the financial plans that the DuPont Company used to become by far the biggest enterprise in the American explosives industry. Between 1902 and 1907, DuPont used those plans to purchase 108 rival firms.[7] In 1903, the DuPont Company was formally incorporated, ending its venerable status as a family partnership. At DuPont everything was changing. When the cousins took over, DuPont was, in the words of the company's official history, "an aging industrial Gulliver, pinioned along both banks of the Brandywine by innumerable small ties to the past."[8] As fast as they could, Pierre, Coleman, and the new men that they were bringing in to manage the company (such as John Raskob) were cutting those ties. They were inventing a new modern, international company, built on research, product development, streamlined administration, and pathbreaking financial and managerial innovations.

Raskob was a player in only a few critical aspects of this transformation. He was Pierre's junior partner in transforming the company's finances. Above all, during those first few years in Wilmington, he focused on appraising business values and in devising the financial means to buy out rivals and arrange expansion. He and Pierre went back and forth probing and debating the advantages of using preferred shares versus common shares in their buyout strategies; they talked to lawyers about the various forms of bond investitures; they modeled different offerings using alternative mixes of bonds and stock; they devised sinking funds and collateral pools. For many of the acquisitions, they made up more than one plan, never sure what their targets would demand or, more importantly, accept. Their goal was always to use as little cash as possible. As Pierre would say many years later, it was almost impossible to know where, in their thinking and devising, du Pont left off and Raskob began. With Coleman, they figured, too, how to entice the best of the old owner-managers to join the new DuPont Company, using stock offerings and guaranteed salaries.

Raskob was in the middle of a major industrial consolidation. Pierre and Coleman switched strategies over time as they moved from just buying out their main rivals, to consolidating the larger explosives industry into a holding company, and then incorporating their expansive holdings into one corporate structure. John had little to do with the administrative and managerial strategies that were needed to make the many parts of the new DuPont into one profitable whole. To help with that massive project, Coleman and Pierre brought in their old mentor—and John's first real boss—Arthur Moxham. Moxham, who had been running big companies for decades, convinced Pierre and Coleman to unite all the separate companies that they had been buying by creating a central administrative apparatus to control them. Under the command of the executive committee, the DuPont Company's top men could exercise strong strategic leadership and create massive economies of scale by consolidating purchasing, inventory control, financing, marketing, sales, and all other core functions. The executive committees could also winnow out less productive production facilities, maximize the use of the best facilities, and invest in new capacities.

Figuring out how to do so and most profitably invest and allocate capital internally and externally led Pierre and John to hire trained accountants and men gifted in statistical and financial analysis. These men, supervised by Pierre and John, created in the first decade of the new DuPont the centralized accounting system that made the entire company's operations financially transparent. Once this data was available, the executive committee could make rational investment decisions; as one report decreed, there could "be no expenditures for additions to the earning equipment if the same amount of money could be applied to some better purpose in another branch of the company's business."[9] To measure the utility of such capital investments, the men in the treasurer's office computed the return the investment promised to make. Railroad managers had long used a similar analysis to model their investments but few industries had done so prior to DuPont, in large part because so few industrial concerns had so many competing claims on capital in the way of separate plants, offices, and potential avenues of expenditure all consolidated under one corporate structure. Raskob and DuPont could not guarantee the return on investment (ROI) numbers they projected, but they did everything they could to make those projected returns on investment as data-driven as they possibly could. And they could most certainly use the ROI model to appraise the company's far flung operations. A financial and mathematical prodigy named F. Donaldson Brown, who became Raskob's right-hand man, helped conceive and operationalize the ROI system that would govern much of the company's capital investment strategy, measure ongoing operations, and maximize the company's earning power.

Even before du Pont, Raskob, and other key men figured out how to fully rationalize the company's accounting procedures and financial decision making, Moxham had insisted that the company break away from the gunpowder cartel. He argued that the old cartel system hid inefficient producers beneath the veil of set prices and a whole set of duplicitous, even larcenous practices. After participating for a short time with Coleman in the policing actions of the Gunpowder Trading Association, Moxham insisted that the company end its cooperation with the explosives trust and embrace the open air of competition, innovation, and market expansion. That cartels were illegal under the Sherman Act was another factor Moxham and the du Ponts registered even as they had yet to face any government pressure. Pierre agreed, as did Coleman.

On March 30, 1904, DuPont withdrew from the gunpowder cartel. At around that time, DuPont controlled 70 percent of the dynamite manufactured in the United States and between 60 percent and 80 percent of most of the other key explosives made in America.[10] By the end of 1905, DuPont had sales of $27.7 million and a total net income of $5.1 million.[11] Compared to the steel and oil industries, DuPont was still a relatively modest sized company in a mid-sized industry, almost exclusively focused on manufacturing explosives, but it was on its way to the big-time, well positioned for opportunity and growth.

To best assess what worked and what did not in the big new incorporated company, Pierre and John were standardizing accounting procedures and studying the constant flow of data those procedures produced so that they could compare the profitability and productivity of all aspects of the operation. It was nonstop work. Twenty-five years old in 1904, John Raskob was a central figure in the invention and implementation of modern financial controls of a major industrial corporation. Of course, Pierre du Pont, the man in charge, was himself just thirty-four.

John enjoyed letting his old friends know that he was doing well, but he wanted them to know, too, that the work was tough. Starting in 1903, he began waking up at 5 A.M. and getting to the office no later than 6:30. Work, he wrote his old friend Will Bewley, was unending and while he hated waking up in the dark—he had never been a morning person—he now had a chance to end the work day in time to have some fun. "However," he finished, "you can gamble your small change that I do not remain out late in the evenings."[12] To another old Lockport friend, he groaned about not having time to meet any young women: "It seems an age since I had the pleasure of kissing a pretty girl. Poor Edith [his younger sister] has to suffer the consequences for she has to give up to ten kisses each day (in fact I get fifteen to twenty each day) and on Sundays she has to give me twenty five.... Wish that I could be there with you out there for there must be many pretty and witty girls." He added, as he would so many times over the years, how much he missed Lockport and "those good old times." Though just twenty-four, he sagely concluded: "As the days go by, I wonder more and more if there is not a whole lot of truth in the old saying that childhood days are the happiest ones in a person's lifetime."[13]

Still, he was not complaining. He had moved his mother and his younger siblings to Wilmington where they all lived together in a comfortable rental house. He arranged office employment at the company for his talented brother William. Money had long since stopped being a problem for the Raskob family. Steadily, often with direct loans from Pierre, John invested in DuPont stock. He was fast becoming a man of means.

John was also an increasingly public figure. While Pierre continued to be a reserved if immensely respected figure in the company, John was an active presence at the company and in the community. Almost immediately after relocating to Wilmington in early 1902, John joined the company baseball team and was immodestly pleased to be named its captain. Despite the press of work, he made time to play. He spent long hours at his desk, but he found ways to stay fit; his generation of middle-class men was among the first to think about exercise as a requisite part of a healthy life. On the weekends, he could regularly be seen in Wilmington and the surrounding countryside pedaling his "wheel," often with a friend or female acquaintance in tow trying to keep up with him. In the first couple of years in Wilmington, Pierre regularly lent John his auto—the unreliable Roadster had been left behind in Lorain—and with friends and family Raskob enjoyed racing through the streets and roadways. The police got to know Raskob well, as he frequently exceeded the cautious speed limit of fifteen miles per hour. His friends kidded him about the large number of speeding tickets he collected and the payments he made for mowing down "chickens, roosters, and the like."[14] In the evenings, he was still a regular at the theater, though he grumbled that Wilmington needed a grander playhouse. Raskob continued, as well, to attend church regularly. He was a man of faith but church, as he admitted to his friends, was also a good place to meet pretty girls. While John still missed the carefree days of his youth in Lockport, he felt like he was on top of the world.

In late 1904, Pierre gave John a chance to explore more of the dynamic world he inhabited. First the two men took an emergency trip out to California. They had discovered, thanks to the accounting measures they had implemented, that the DuPont man in San Francisco had embezzled close to $50,000 (over $1 million in inflation-corrected dollars). From the train window, Raskob had his first views of the great American West. He was transfixed and vowed to return.

The business in California was unpleasant but ended satisfactorily. Confronted with DuPont's scrupulous accounts, the culprit confessed and, in exchange for keeping the matter private, he made good on his theft and resigned his position. Raskob could now brag to his friends that he had been east to Nova Scotia and west to California. Du Pont and Raskob had no time for sightseeing, but the long train trip further cemented their friendship.

A few weeks later, they were off again. The company was looking to expand internationally and Pierre and John crossed the Atlantic to explore a major deal with the French explosives holding company, *Société Centrale de Dynamite*. The international explosives market, dominated by European firms, was still operating under cartel agreements that had been signed in the late nineteenth century. The DuPont Company had been a partner to those agreements, but the giant French company had not agreed to the latest terms and was fighting DuPont for the growing Mexican explosives market. Pierre and Coleman hoped they could take a controlling interest in the French company and join forces instead of competing with it. Pierre expected to use the same financing tools he had been deploying to take over DuPont's American rivals. The *Société* negotiator, however, was an impressively savvy Austrian operator named Siegfried Singer. He had his own ideas on how to structure a deal and his own ideas of his company's value, which was higher than the value Pierre and John had given it. In the end, the cautious Pierre, backed up by DuPont's executive committee, decided no deal was the best deal for DuPont, a decision celebrated by most of the production men at home who did not think much of the French operations in Mexico, anyway.[15]

John was disappointed by the entire enterprise and honest enough with himself and his friends to admit it. He had been looking forward to the ocean voyage and to seeing something of the splendors of Europe. He discovered, on the rough Atlantic crossing, that he became seasick much too easily. Sounding like a very young man, he wrote his mother: "Water, water everywhere…both Mr. du Pont and I were sea-sick and in bed for thirty-six hours."[16] And then while they were in Paris, they worked nonstop. He had no fun, saw no sights, and then the deal fell apart. He wrote his old friend Frank Dole, "It was cloudy the whole time we were in Paris and we were so busy while there that we see very, very little, in fact, I do not feel like saying that I have ever been in Paris."[17]

Instead of just coming directly home, du Pont and Raskob, joined up with some other DuPont men and boarded a ship for a long voyage to Argentina. Accompanied by Elias Ahuja, the DuPont's South American agent, they were traveling to Buenos Aires and then overland to Chile to investigate not further horizontal expansion but vertical integration. The DuPont executive committee, at the urging of Arthur Moxham, was looking to sew up its own supply of raw resources. Moxham had already begun the process by starting a plant in Michigan to manufacture charcoal using DuPont-owned timber. Chile was the home of most of the world's export nitrates, the key ingredient in explosives. For many years, DuPont had used agents to purchase the huge amounts of nitrates DuPont depended on for explosives production. Pierre and John were going to investigate buying nitrate fields in Chile's vast and desolate, 450-mile-long nitrate belt.

When John and Pierre left France, they had been working side-by-side to remake DuPont for just over two years on a nearly nonstop basis. John occasionally complained about the long hours but mainly as a way to brag to his friends about his activities. He was young and had all his life been gifted with prodigious amounts of energy. He did not seem to know about being exhausted or in need of simple relaxation. Pierre did. Pierre, of course, carried a bigger burden. He had the firm's financial security largely on his back. Since he was a young teenager, looking after his younger brothers' and sisters' fortunes, as well as his mother's, he had been carrying a heavy emotional burden. On the long, slow ocean voyage to Buenos Aires, Pierre luxuriated in doing very little. He did talk some business with the men and made a point of sounding out Ahuja about his knowledge of South America and getting a feel for his business acumen. But mostly, he spent the trip lying around, listening to John and Elias Ahuja banter, and eating. By time the men disembarked, Pierre was in need of an entire new wardrobe from eating too much.

John, on the other hand, threw himself into shipboard activities. The sea, he reported, "was smooth and beautiful" and he had no problems on the crossing. The English ocean liner had every kind of game—which John played—and music and dancing every night. Formal dress was required at dinner and John took to the luxury. The ship made numerous stops, first in Spain, then Portugal, St. Vincent, Madeira, and then along the South American coast. John loved the adventure. He also, in his letter home, showed himself to be a typical white American of his times when it came to his understandings of race: "At St. Vincent and also at Madeira the minute the boat got in a lot of rowboats started out to it loaded with niggers who would dive into the water for money the passengers would throw to them. They were perfectly nude."[18] John was seeing the world and while he came at it from a conventional viewpoint he was thrilled by the novelty of it all.

Elias Ahuja contributed to John's fun. Although sixteen years older than John, he turned out to be a congenial character. Elias, Pierre, and John almost immediately became good friends; even as Pierre privately maintained some reservations about Ahuja's business skills. Not only was Ahuja bilingual (he had been born and raised in Spain but went to business school in Boston), making him a perfect guide in South America, he was also funny, charming, and companionable.

In Ahuja, John found a friend of an altogether different sort than the boys with whom he had grown up in Lockport. Unlike Pierre, Ahuja was a lot of fun. Like a favorite uncle, he teased John nonstop.

Ahuja was a worldly man, and he found John's Catholic faith, regular church attendance, and earnest respectability amusing. John took no umbrage though he defended the faith with energy, and both he and Pierre avoided whatever temptations the Southern Cone countries offered. Soon after the trip, Ahuja wrote John a long letter that began: "Notwithstanding my knowledge of your sporting habits, your extraordinary capacity for drinking, and constant visits to Clubs (always on the same errand), I never really discovered any really bad habit." Down the page, he then stated, "well, joking aside..." The most serious vice in which the three men seem to have indulged was eating large amounts of terrible, garlic-laden food served by garlic-breathed women with such sexy names as "Aunty." Ahuja did also write Raskob: "I have discovered a most touching love affair, a tale of unrequited love I fear" between a local woman and Pierre.[19] Given Pierre's lack of interest in women—he was then thirty-five and had never had a relationship with any woman—unrequited was surely the right word.

John's atypical disregard, even indifference to women during the long South American journey can be chalked up, at least in part, to a recent change in John's bachelor status. John confided in Ahuja during their trip that he had begun what might be a serious relationship with a young woman he had met at church in Wilmington in late 1904. On long walks in Valparaiso, the two businessmen discussed the young lady, to their mutual amusement, as a potential deal to be negotiated. The "option" became their phrase for describing John's potential paramour. Ahuja cheered John on and offered him advice on how to close the deal.[20]

The more pressing business of buying nitrate fields in Chile turned out to be another unsuccessful mission. None of the DuPont men felt that the business climate in Chile was stable enough to make a major investment; price inflation was rampant and despite official government policy welcoming foreign investment, land titles seemed uncertain even as the prices being sought by local owners of the fields seemed excessive. John was also floored by the Chileans' way of doing business. "The people down here," he wrote his mother, "are slow beyond imagination and it takes a long time to get them to do anything. Next few days will be holidays and it will be impossible to get any more work done in the way of advancing matters."[21] John, a man almost always in a hurry, took many long walks to burn off excess energy and his frustrations at the slow pace of Chilean life. In the end, instead of buying and mining their own nitrate fields, Ahuja set up a DuPont office in nearby Valparaiso and bought massive amounts of nitrates from the local companies, bypassing the previously used middlemen. Ahuja was also charged with keeping an eye on the possibilities of direct DuPont ownership, alerting the executive committee when conditions were right (which happened late in 1910).

On a very slow ship, John and Pierre made their way home, up the west coast of South America. They disembarked in Panama City where they stayed overnight in a memorably filthy hotel. Then they made an overland crossing of the isthmus of Panama—the canal would not be completed for several more years—and caught a ship home, returning to Wilmington May 1905. The two men did little but laze around on the way back and marvel at how long it took. Refreshed, Pierre immediately launched himself back into the business at hand. John did the same but his attention was fixed, as well, on closing the "option" he had discussed with Ahuja.

Helena Springer Green was a different sort of woman than John Raskob had been accustomed to meeting. She was not a "lower-town girl." While far from rich, she was genteel. She was an eighth-generation Catholic American. Her forbearer, Thomas Greene, had arrived on the aptly named ship the *Ark* with Governor Leonard Calvert in 1634 with a few dozen other English Catholics, seeking religious freedom in the newly chartered colony of Maryland. Greene became the second governor of Maryland. In the eighteenth century, the family was moderately well-to-do, owners of a large tract of land and slaves. They were of the plantation class—though not of the richest sort. In 1815 Benjamin Greene, Jr., in some financial dealing gone wrong, managed to lose most of that land. The Greenes' days as plantation owners were over. Helena Green's main line of descent stayed in Maryland. They were almost all farmers and they all piously followed their faith. While such tenacity of residency and religiosity had not by the late nineteenth century led to wealth, it did produce a sense of place and status. The Greens (the final "e" had been dropped somewhere along the line) were respectable people of proud lineage. Still, Helena's life had been difficult.

Helena was born November 30, 1884, and baptized soon thereafter at St. Francis Xavier's Church outside Warwick, Maryland. Her father was a farmer. Her mother died when she was three, and Helen and her two older sisters were taken away by their maternal grandmother, Elizabeth Corbaley. Helena's father remarried soon thereafter and had two sons, abandoning his daughters. Her maternal grandmother had already been widowed and had remarried another farmer named Samuel Corbaley with whom she had another set of children. There, at the Corbaley farm, Helena's grandmother gave her a new middle name, Springer, distancing her from her father's line and bringing her closer to her own; Springer was her mother's maiden name. Then Mr. Corbaley died. The little troupe of Greens and Corbaleys moved on to Grandmother Corbaley's son's farm. But in 1890 Grandma Corbaley died, too. Helena, still less than six years old, was taken in by her aunt Varina Corbaley who lived in Wilmington and made her living teaching music and directing the choir at the Cathedral of St. Peter. Varina was ultra-respectable but she was also a woman who had managed in the midst of the Victorian age to live on her own and make her own way, without husband or father. She was an unusual and unusually assertive woman.

Varina was a single woman when she took in Helena and she would never marry. Varina and Helena had inherited some small amount of money from Elizabeth Corbaley and that sum and Varina's modest income kept the two afloat. Varina was not thrifty. She and Helena lived as well as was possible, if not a little better than their income allowed. Varina summered with Helena at the fashionable Delaware Water Gap, staying at a charming hotel, the Mountain House. While they could not, as more well-to-do women did, spend the entire summer there, they stayed as long as they could; the Philadelphia newspaper, which actually listed who stayed where at the Delaware Water Gap on its society page, reported Varina and her charge as "late-arriving" guests. Helena had little money but was exposed to those who had it, and her aunt made sure that she had the polish to fit in. Everything about the spinster Varina indicated that she hoped that her young niece would find a gentleman of means to assure both of their futures.

Through St. Peter and her own circle, Varina had connections to the prestigious Catholic boarding school the Academy of the Sacred Heart directed by the Sisters of the Holy Cross in Lancaster, Pennsylvania. Sacred Heart had begun in the 1870s as a music school for young ladies and while it had expanded to include a full academic program it still specialized in music and art; it was a sort of finishing school for talented girls, Catholic as well as Protestant, who came from as far as Baltimore and Pittsburgh, as well as the relatively close by cities of Philadelphia and Wilmington. Musically trained by her aunt, Helena was a star performer. After graduating in 1902 with honors she continued her studies of music at the Leffson Hille Conservatory of Music in Philadelphia. No later than fall 1904, not yet twenty, she was living in Wilmington with her aunt, teaching piano and playing the organ on Sunday at the Church of St. Mary of the Immaculate Conception, a formidable red-brick affair built mid-century in the fashionable Byzantine Revival style. Helena's position had almost certainly been arranged by her aunt.

Helena Springer Green had seen her mother die, her father abandon her, and then her grandparents, after taking her in, also die in quick succession; all of this before she was six. Yet, somehow, she had weathered these early tragedies and emerged as a confident, independent woman. Perhaps her devout Catholic faith shielded her from the haunting sadness and then the economic and emotional travails of her years with her loving but eccentric Aunt Varina. It could not have hurt Helena's sense of self that at age twenty she was a well-educated, talented, slim beauty.[22]

A family story that fits well with the established record explains that John had made a habit of rotating his attendance at Wilmington's several Catholic churches in hopes of discovering engaging young women. St. Mary's, where Miss Green played, was an eastside parish and it was not the church closest to the Raskob family home on the west side of Wilmington. From his unfamiliar pew, John spotted Helena and was captivated. According to family lore, John quickly devised a plan to meet the church organist. He bribed the boy who operated the organ-bellows and took his place. Well-positioned, John then casually made his introduction.[23]

Their courtship was long and, for the times, adventurous. John escaped the Corbaley front porch and sitting room by using Pierre's auto to take Helena driving in the surrounding countryside, sometimes as far as Philadelphia. Some decorous picnicking seems to have occurred. John, his brother Willow, and a few other friends, most especially Helena, were part of an informal bowling club that met weekly in late 1904 and early 1905 by which time it was clear that John and Helena were an item. While John was away in Chile, he and Helena corresponded and in his letters to and from his brother during that same time, Helena was a subject of much discussion.[24]

When John returned from his long trip to Europe and South America in the spring of 1905, the courtship became more serious. John was five and half years older than Helena and was ready to marry. By mid-1905, his stock holdings and his rapidly increasing salary meant that he had easily passed the matrimonial bar he had set only a few years earlier; John was worth more than $10,000. John was a very good catch. In September 1905, John proposed and Helena accepted. A June wedding date was set. Family and friends were thrilled.

Elias Ahuja, who had coached John, gave him his blessing: "I congratulate you with all my heart and picture you now without that pining away look which used to come over you when I talked of the charming unclosed option." Elias also spoke for the majority of John's friends who had not yet met Helena: "I am certain I shall like Miss Green as she has shown good sense, say nothing of taste in accepting you; this being my 'true blue' opinion expect no 'chaucha' [Chilean slang for small coin] for expressing it."[25]

John's Lockport friends were less expressive in their congratulations. Several were themselves just married or about to marry, and they seemed to take the news in stride. Most seemed more interested in figuring out the wedding logistics, train schedules, housing arrangements, and wedding attire. Although John had been away for some five years and had, as they well knew, made an extraordinary success, they still took it for granted that they would be a part of the festivities as John had been a part of theirs.

For John, the most important vetting of his relationship came from Pierre. By this time the two men were extremely close. John had come to call Pierre

"Daddy," in the manner of Pierre's younger siblings. While their age difference was only nine years, John looked to Pierre as a father figure, as well as best friend, and advisor. For John, Pierre's blessing was sacrosanct and for Helena, she well knew, it was an imperative. Helena and Pierre had already met by the time of the fall 1905 engagement; at least once Pierre had accompanied—chaperoned—them on one of the countryside auto excursions. But in early February 1906, Pierre and his sister hosted a small formal dinner for John and Helena. In his invitation to Helena, Pierre wrote how pleased he was about their engagement and what a wonderful man John was. Helena, demonstrating her social skills and her confidence in her relationship with John, wrote Pierre a short charming letter in reply that indicated how well she understand what had been the most important relationship in her fiancé's life. "My dear Mr. du Pont," she wrote, the dinner invitation is "greatly appreciated" as were all the kind words about John: "It is so perfectly delightful for me to know how thoroughly Mr. Raskob is appreciated by his friends." She concluded with a carefully worded, almost Jamesian claim; she, too, expected to "be very good friends" with Mr. du Pont in the days and years ahead. Helena entered John's world, at least his burgeoning new social realm, as an equal.[26]

The wedding invitation was a simple but elegant one. It reflected Helena's family status and the couple's firm religious convictions: "Miss Varina J. Corbaley requests the honor of your presence at the marriage of her niece Helen Springer Green to Mr. John Jacob Raskob Monday morning June 18, 1906 9:30 at the Cathedral, Wilmington, Delaware."[27] John asked three of his old Lockport friends to serve as ushers. Considerate, as he always was, about his friends' economic situations, he wrote them in early June letting them know that they should not buy "a high silk hat," as he thought they were unnecessary and that "ties and gloves will be provided" so that they need not buy anything for the wedding service.[28] Pierre also served as an usher and John's brother was his best man. Two nights before the wedding, John hosted a dinner for the out-of-town guests at the Wilmington Country Club. Monseigneur John A. Lyons married the couple. Helena wore an elegant embroidered gown of chiffon and taffeta with a tulle veil and a wreath of lilies of the valley. As was typical of the times, the wedding at St. Peter's Cathedral was small with just a few friends present.

John had debated where to take his bride on their honeymoon. Ahuja had lobbied hard for a visit to Chile but Raskob saw the long voyage as impractical. He decided to take her to a place he knew well and loved, Niagara Falls.

They spent their first night as a married couple in New York City, staying at The Waldorf, the city's finest hotel. The next day the Raskobs saw the sights and John took his bride to the theater. He had secured seats at the Lyceum for the smash hit, "The Lion and the Mouse." It was an interesting choice for John; the drama was loosely based on the relationship between muckraker Ida B. Tarbell and John D. Rockefeller. John loved it. The couple took the "Day Line" up the Hudson to Albany; it was a leisurely and luxurious trip, with a band in the morning, followed by an orchestra. Then they took the New York Central, on a route John knew well, across the state, past Lockport to Niagara where his mother had spent part of her childhood. All this is known because John wrote a long, descriptive letter to Pierre.

The travelogue was really just a preface to what John wanted to express to Pierre. He wanted Pierre to know how happy he was, how much in love: "No one could ever be more dear, thoughtful and upright, honest and loving than Helena, and I only hope that her husband will prove worthy of her. My love for Helena seems to have grown as much during the last few days as it did in the weeks and weeks before." He vowed to never "betray" his bride's confidence in his love for her. "I wish, Daddy," he wrote Pierre, and given Pierre's long disinterest in women, it is an interesting wish, "that there was another girl somewhere in the world, as good and dear as Helena, for you." He concluded sweetly that he hoped that Pierre would not think him foolish for pouring out his heart, but "I know you won't for we have known each other too long and too well for either to misunderstand or think the other foolish." Adding that "Helena wishes to be remembered most kindly to you and would send some of her love were I not so selfish," he signed off.[29]

John was now twenty-seven years old. He was happily and successfully married and in no time at all he and Helena began to create a houseful of children. His ties with the extraordinarily gifted Pierre du Pont and his place in the meteoric DuPont Company were strong and secure. He was a man in the world, well positioned to let his talent and his zest for life take him to extraordinary places. The next decade would be a whirlwind.

4

Too Big?

During the first years of the twentieth century, before the Great War, Raskob was first and foremost Pierre's man. John lived in an economic, social, and political world formed by his roles in the DuPont Company and his allegiance to Pierre du Pont. He loved Pierre for giving him the opportunity to be in that world. His devotion left him largely but not completely uncritical of both the company and the man. But as the Progressive Era swirled around him and Americans struggled to make sense of the new industrial world that the DuPont Company was helping to build, Raskob began to consider his place in society. John would never lose faith in the DuPont Company, his friend and mentor Pierre du Pont, or the capitalist system. But in the years that preceded the advent of World War I, he would lose much of his innocence as he gained a fortune, a growing sense of autonomy, and a greater understanding of how American elites fought for power and influence.

Unlike John Raskob, most Americans were not sure what to make of the giant business corporations that were suddenly taking over much of the American economy. Nor were many Americans sure how to feel or what to do about the wealthy few who profited most from the rise of Big Business. Just before the turn-of-the-century a popular movement, based largely in the country's interior, had risen up to pull down the new corporate masters. Claiming to speak for America's rural millions, as well as the fragmented working class and small producers, too, the People's Party—the Populists—demanded that the great corporations be broken apart, their rich owners chastised, and the corrupt government officials that enabled their mutual rise be thrown out of office. The Party's platform read: "The fruits of the toil of millions are boldly stolen to build up colossal fortunes for a few, unprecedented in the history of mankind; and the possessors of those, in turn, despise the republic and endanger liberty. From the same prolific womb of governmental injustice we breed the two great classes—tramps and millionaires."[1] These Populists did not see themselves as class warriors seeking to overturn the capitalist system. They just wanted protection from predation and greed. They wanted their hard work to be rewarded; they wanted their dignity respected.[2]

The Populists' champion, William Jennings Bryan, joint nominee of the People's Party and the Democrats in 1896, had been beaten back then and again in 1900 by Republican William McKinley, the first candidate to run a modern, mass-mediated campaign. That campaign was made possible by massive, unprecedented donations from America's business elite. But McKinley became capitalism's first American martyr. He was assassinated in 1901, gunned down by an unemployed, self-proclaimed anarchist. His unlikely successor, the forty-two-year-old Theodore Roosevelt, took over the presidency and shocked McKinley's rich backers by excoriating some of their brethren. He insisted that the new corporate elite develop a higher moral standard. Cautiously and ambivalently, Roosevelt took up the case of trust-busting.

After Roosevelt left office in 1909, President Taft confounded his conservative business supporters by continuing Roosevelt's selective antitrust campaign and actually expanding it. The DuPont Company was one of the Taft Administration's many targets.

John Raskob watched the entry of his government into the affairs of his corporate and economic life with suspicion, frustration, and eventually a measured amount of anger. At DuPont he was not responsible for government relations; nobody was, though Coleman du Pont thought he had the federal intervention under control. But, as was Raskob's way, he interjected himself where and when he could. In the years preceding the Great War, the high times of Progressivism, Raskob began to understand how interconnected were the worlds of politics and Big Business.

The first attack on the DuPont Company came in early 1906. A former employee, Robert Waddell, had left the DuPont Company after twenty years of service to start the Buckeye Powder Company. Waddell had learned what he knew about the powder business working for DuPont, where he had risen up to the position of head of sales operations. He knew, too, that DuPont had long relied on combination and collusion to control prices and market entry in the industry. Although he also knew that the company had already left the gunpowder trust, he averred that DuPont used its immense, monopolistic power to deny him a fair market opportunity. The du Pont family, he stated, "daily, continually, and openly defy and break [antitrust and other] laws of states and the United States."[3] Specifically, he charged DuPont with a range of market-restraining infractions and with using undue influence to monopolize government explosives contracts. Waddell mixed his attack on the family and the company that bore its name without much distinction between the two, which was reasonable enough given the cousins' tight control and ownership of the enterprise.

Trusts and monopolies were under scrutiny in the early twentieth century as never before, and not just by radicals. Back in 1890, Congress had responded to widespread anger against new industrial combines by overwhelmingly passing the Sherman Anti-Trust Act. The Sherman Act outlawed any business practice that aimed to restrain or monopolize trade. But the Department of Justice, its hand partially stayed by the Supreme Court, had almost completely ignored the Act after its passage. The law had become, in the words of Theodore Roosevelt's secretary of war William Howard Taft, "almost a dead letter."[4] But the rise of such giant corporations as US Steel and the Standard Oil Company put a new spotlight on monopolistic practices.

Shining that light the brightest was a coterie of "muckraking" journalists. Henry Demarest Lloyd had led the way in 1881 when he pilloried Standard Oil for its competition-crushing tactics in the pages of the *Atlantic*. More than twenty years later, a more anxious public crowned Ida Tarbell the queen of these so-called "muckrakers" when she fleshed out the case against the Standard Oil Company and its fantastically wealthy leader John D. Rockefeller in the pages of *McClure's Magazine*. Her impressively researched charges were given even wider play with the publication in 1904 of her best-selling book, *The History of Standard Oil*.

President Roosevelt responded cautiously to the public fervor that the muckrakers had helped to stir. At the beginning of his presidency, he had argued that "combination and concentration should be, not prohibited, but supervised and within reasonable limits controlled."[5] Like so many other Americans, his feelings about the giant corporations that ruled key sectors of the American economy were mixed. He respected the wealth and general prosperity that the great corporations and their leaders produced. He wanted no harm done to "good" corporations, no matter their size or power. At the same time, he believed that something needed to be done to insure that the American economy served all its citizens and not just the most clever or devious capitalists.

Roosevelt was no populist but like many other Americans he hoped to develop some kind of moral capitalism. By 1905 he spoke out frequently on the subject: "Business success, whether for the individual or for the Nation, is a good thing only so far as it is accompanied by and develops a high standard of conduct—honor, integrity, civic courage. The kind of business prosperity that blunts the standard of honor, that puts an inordinate value on mere wealth, that makes a man ruthless and conscienceless in trade, and weak and cowardly in citizenship, is not a good thing at all, but a very bad thing for the Nation."[6] He insisted, "In order to insure a healthy social and industrial life, every big corporation should be held responsible by, and be accountable to, some sovereign strong enough to control its conduct."[7] Roosevelt struggled to find a regulatory solution to America's seemingly indomitable giant corporations. According to historian Richard Hofstadter, President Roosevelt's efforts were always a "hundred times more noise than accomplishment."[8]

Despite reservations, after the 1904 election Roosevelt did embrace trust-busting.[9] So did a majority in Congress, especially after another "muckraker," David Graham Phillips, published a nine-part series of incendiary magazine articles, beginning in February 1906, titled "The Treason of the Senate." Phillips exposed the corrupt relationship between a number of US senators, still appointed by state legislatures, and America's most powerful corporations.

When Waddell aired his accusations against the DuPont Company in early 1906, he did so at the invitation of the nervous, suddenly attentive members of the US Senate Appropriations Committee; this committee took on the matter because of DuPont's many government contracts with the military. Waddell's charges were amplified by America's leading newspapers, including the Hearst chain, which was among the first to mass market its wares through scandal and sensation. Even the *Chicago Tribune*, normally a great respecter of the prerogatives of businessmen, headlined Waddell's charges, "Nation in Grip of Powder Trust," and continued, "Robert S. Waddell of Peoria Files Charges Against the Du Pont Company—says Law is Violated—Unites States Declared to be Mulcted of $2,520,000 a Year in Illegal Profits."[10]

Raskob and the rest of DuPont's big men knew, in advance, that Waddell had gained a Senate hearing. They were not sure what if anything they should do about it. As the Appropriations Committee hearings progressed, John, at least, knew that Waddell's accusations were being read and discussed around the country. One of John's close friends from Lockport wrote him, warning that even in upstate New York the press was printing Waddell's attacks against DuPont.

Probably taking his cues from Pierre, John scoffed at the accusations and the likelihood of any adverse government actions. Writing his friend Tom Feeley, who had become the business manager of the Lockport newspaper for which John had delivered papers just fifteen years earlier, Raskob assured him, "The pieces you see in the papers lately about the so-called 'powder trust' are very much exaggerated and we believe there is no cause for worry."[11] John was genuinely not worried.

Working closely with Pierre, John kept digging away at DuPont's financial expansions, structuring deals and finding capital. Raskob had the title of assistant to the treasurer, but he was often working as financial point man on many of the company's deals. Pierre was doing his best to turn over as much of the day-to-day business of running the company's financial affairs as he could to John.

In 1906, Pierre had bought a large plot of land outside of Wilmington and was already beginning to turn his attention whenever time permitted to planning out the opulent gardens, greenhouses, and fountains he yearned to create. John loved the hurly-burly of deal making and financial scheming, but despite having one of the great business minds of his time, Pierre's heart lay elsewhere. To the degree that his strong sense of family and personal responsibility allowed, he was, though just in his mid-thirties, already looking for a gracious exit from his crushing business obligations so that he could pursue his horticultural desires. It would take many more years before he could commit himself fully to overseeing the garden and fountains of his boyhood dreams, but already in 1907 Pierre was looking to give John as much responsibility as he could profitably manage. In partial return, he was also always willing to support whatever business adventures and speculations Raskob cooked up. He did his best to make sure that the rest of the du Pont family and other important men within Pierre's grand orbit saw John as he did. That trust and influence would become a vital asset when Raskob sought to redirect the DuPont Company and steer its financial future.

Certainly Pierre's talented younger brothers Lammot and Irénée, both of whom shared Pierre's business talents and were being groomed for top leadership in the company, recognized Raskob's gifts. In 1906 Lammot invited John to join him in managing the Southern Trust Company, a small operation that financed book publishers and entrepreneurial authors who sold books to the general public on the installment plan. Generally they sold leather-bound editions of classic English and American writers' works or handsome oversized volumes of maps such as a collection of Civil War battles. Their intended customers were the newly minted middle class who were looking for highly visible signs of their respectability and sophistication in an increasingly mass society; these were the same people who were making upright piano makers, also sold on the installment plan, a mint during these years. Lammot and John supplied the capital and the bookkeeping, respectively, while leaving the hands-on management to others. The installment book business quickly proved to be an annoying enterprise filled with difficult-to-manage publishers and slow-paying customers. It took up more time than it was worth. Still Lammot and John kept at it for more than six years and it drew the two young men together. John made little money, but he did end up with a bookcase full of leather-bound editions of Emerson, Hawthorne, Longfellow, Lowell, Holmes, Whittier, and Chaucer, as well as a pictorial history of the Civil War, none of which John seemed to have read.[12]

Raskob had more success and fun going into business with Irénée, whose company he greatly enjoyed. For a while they used to meet up regularly on Thursday evenings with a couple of other young DuPont high-fliers and hold mock executive committee meetings, playing out various business scenarios and arguing with each other over corporate strategy. Occasionally they even believed that they came up with a good idea and they would pass it on to Pierre.[13] In spring 1907, just a few weeks after John's first child was born, Irénée and John, looking for a chance to try their hand at a little nonexplosives business, pooled together a bit of extra cash and bought a stationery company in downtown Wilmington. Raskob had already been involved with the business, McIntire and Company, for a short while as its treasurer, but he decided that the owners were much too lackadaisical for his tastes. So he and Irénée arranged to buy the business's store-front on Market Street. They renamed their store the Bee Hive.

John found managing the small-scale enterprise entertaining. He spent stolen hours fussing over the Bee Hive's affairs. He personally hired and fired employees, kept an eye on the stock, and maintained the company's books. He, with Irénée's approval, also decided to refocus the business, adding a substantial line of cigars, pipes, and tobacco. In a few years, John moved the Bee Hive to the Hotel Du Pont, where it became the town's leading cigar stand. The store was quite profitable but soon after setting up the little business John's time was much more profitably spent elsewhere. Nonetheless, for many years he maintained an active interest in his cigar stand. What would have been for many men a full-time job was for John a hobby. He never wrote about the decision to own and actively manage a cigar stand but his father's memory surrounds the unlikely enterprise. John's business decisions were not always fixed on the bottom line.[14]

During these years, John was constantly investigating investment and entre-preneurial opportunities, as he would be for the rest of his life. He invested in some local real estate ventures and, as an expensive lark, he bought into a pecan operation in Florida. The pecan farm turned out to be more scam than substantive business and it soon went bust, though not before John received hundreds of pounds of pecans that he enjoyed handing out to friends and family. These were by no means John's only investments and usually he was rigorous in his research, looking to make real money. He had begun investing in the stock market, picking up shares of US Steel and a few other big companies; most of his attention was fixed on buying DuPont shares whenever and wherever he could find them. He had also begun, in earnest, investing money for his wide contingent of friends and family. Sometimes he put in a good word with a banker in Buffalo or other upstate locales that allowed his friends to finance their stock purchases. More often, he lent money directly to his old Lockport buddies, or advanced them money, so that they could buy a few shares of DuPont or some other stock—some of these personal loans, it turned out, played out for decades and John kept meticulous records on them, paying close attention to interest owed, as well as remaining principal; he was not a man to forgive a loan, even to a penurious friend. Still, he was hardly looking to profit off of these loans; his intent, always, was to help his intimates make money. Many of his relatives and old friends became, if not rich, then quite comfortable because of Raskob's advice and willingness to loan them the money they needed to take advantage of it. He was also buying stock for his sisters and for his mother, enough so that they did become well-to-do in their own right.

The occasional DuPont share could be bought on the New York Curb—the less prestigious Wall Street market—as early as 1906 and regularly by 1910; and its preferred stock, as well as bonds, were sold, on the New York Stock Exchange in late 1909. DuPont was also listed on the San Francisco Stock Exchange. John was personally accumulating DuPont shares through a bonus program that he and Pierre had set up to reward leading executives in the firm. John could not have been more bullish about DuPont's prospects. He was willing to bet his fortune and that of his friends and family on the company's future.

At the end of 1908, John set his sights on a big block of Alfred du Pont's shares. Alfred had been bobbing in and out of the company, in part due to a somewhat scandalous marital realignment that had resulted in his resettlement in North Dakota for six months, a relatively divorce-friendly state, especially compared to Delaware. That divorce and Alfred's temperament kept Alfred's relationship to most of the family and to the company in a continual state of uncertainty. John saw opportunity in that state of affairs and began negotiating to buy 1,000 of Alfred's DuPont common shares. As yet, no large block of DuPont shares traded on any public exchange.

In early January 1909, Alfred du Pont responded formally and with some condescension to John's interest in his shares. He allowed that he was interested in selling what was for him a small slice of his stock ownership, but he asked for a price well over the amount that the shares had last sold. Since John needed to finance the purchase, using a loan for that purpose, Alfred admonished him to gain Pierre's approval and endorsement of the loan. Alfred added a few sentences suggesting that he was willing to "sacrifice" a few of his shares, since John had been such a loyal employee of the company.

Raskob was by early 1909 far from a neophyte in the financial world, a fact Alfred seemed either not to know or to recognize. It was true that Pierre continued to help John financially, loaning him money on friendly terms when John sought to make investments, but Raskob did not see himself, anymore, as an appendage to Pierre or as his mere assistant, as Alfred's letter implied. So John wrote back a blunt note that said as much about John's sense of his place in the business world as it did about his temperament. "I have your letter of even date," he wrote upon receipt of Alfred's terms, "and in reply would advise that I cannot accept your proposition, for three reasons." He then explained that, one, Alfred was pricing his shares too high and that, two, John had no intention of having Pierre sign for any note he and Alfred worked out. Finally, he stated, "I would rather treat this whole matter on a purely business basis than on a basis of sacrifice or concessions." Raskob ended his letter curtly, "I do not like to dicker back and forth in a transaction of this kind, as it appeals to me as not being good business."[15] John was not a young clerk; he was, evermore, a tough and confident negotiator. He knew that he understood a great deal more about complex financial transactions than did Alfred du Pont. Alfred du Pont, a self-characterized manly sort of man, actually appears to have approved of John's tough stance: he agreed to John's terms and he did so with grace.

In October 1910, John, undoubtedly in league with Pierre, attempted to buy a much bigger block of Alfred du Pont's holdings in the company. This time John approached Alfred with some care. Alfred had told him that he was uncertain of the company's future and that he felt unease at "having so many eggs in one basket." By this date, as John well knew, Alfred had become openly hostile toward the company leadership of his two cousins. Alfred only rarely attended the company's executive committee meetings and had even gone so far, as Pierre and John saw it, as to assist the Justice Department in their antitrust actions taken against DuPont.

So John knew that Alfred, who for so long had run the company's production facilities at the Brandywine mills, was himself a powder keg ready to explode. John followed up on Alfred's gambit, if that was what it was, by asking him if he meant that he would like to sell "a substantial amount of your holdings in E.I. du Pont Nemours and Co. stock. If you would consider such a step, I should like very much to have the opportunity to make a proposition." John then, at some length, made the case for a low price for the company's stock: "Personally, I am very optimistic as to the Company's future. There are, however, certain drawbacks in connection with the stock as an investment, principal among which is that no matter how valuable the stock may be, it is so closely held and the market for it is so limited that in case of forced sale, it is certain the holder would have to accept a substantial sacrifice." John then, somewhat slyly, worked to exercise Alfred's existing anxiety about just such a fire sale by outlining how and why such a fearsome event might soon unfold given "the pending Government litigation, the general hue and cry against corporations, the agitation of governmental control of large corporations, etc. etc., all of which however, may be considered as part of the natural troubles that must be expected in the lifetime of a young man," at least a young man such as John Raskob. A more mature and well-settled man, however, such as Alfred, might not wish to endure such "troubles," intimated young Mr. Raskob. John then offered to buy twelve to fifteen thousand shares of Alfred's DuPont holding at $210 per share, an unexpectedly high price. John would provide 10 percent in cash up front; the rest would be arranged through what might by that time be called typically Raskobian terms. Alfred did not bite.

Pierre's involvement in this negotiation remains unrecorded but there can be little doubt that John kept Pierre fully apprised and would not have gone forward without Pierre's approval and, in this case, likely suggestion. Soon after Raskob's failed attempt to weaken Alfred's holdings in the company, Pierre and Coleman, frustrated by their cousin's various maneuverings and on-again-off-again attitude toward the company, guaranteed his enmity. They forced Alfred out of the work he loved, managing powder production, and "promoted" him to do work he hated and had little to no likelihood of performing, analyzing reports and accounts as a vice president on the finance committee. Alfred became an absentee owner. John was nonplussed by the family wrangling but lined up without question on Pierre's side.[16]

Raskob did not see his DuPont investments as a gamble. As he honestly told Alfred, he felt very, very good about DuPont's position. While he was busy with a multitude of endeavors, his days were still spent overwhelmingly working closely with Pierre on DuPont's massive expansion and consolidation. John was the money man. A good test of his growing skills had come even as he had been in the midst of his purchasing of a hunk of Alfred's shareholdings.

In 1909, Raskob figured out a way to free up a substantial sum of DuPont money by rethinking how the company paid for the massive quantities of nitrate of soda that it imported from Chile. Raskob's solution, as well as the context in which he drew it up, speaks not just to John's financial savvy but also to the fraught and perilous economic realm in which he and the rest of America's big businessmen operated. In the early years of the twentieth century, Raskob and his kind were operating without much of a rule book, which allowed for a good deal of creativity in the midst of a great deal of social, political, and economic uncertainty and risk.

DuPont's problem was simple to describe if not to solve. DuPont needed massive quantities of nitrates mined in Chile every year to make its line of explosive products. Since DuPont had chosen not to buy its own mines in Chile, it needed to purchase said nitrates either directly from the Chilean mine owners or from nitrate brokers. Americans did operate as nitrate brokers and would accept payment in the United States in dollars for the product they imported, but they charged a hefty fee for their brokerage and import service; basically they marked up the price of the commodity. DuPont, wishing to be economical in its business practices given the massive size of the annual purchase, did not want to pay the mark-up. But to buy the nitrates directly in Chile at a better price, DuPont's agents, led by Elias Ahuja, had to find a form of payment acceptable to the Chilean producers. International businessmen and traders, obviously, had for centuries needed to find acceptable means for arranging such international economic exchanges. Carrying large packages of universally acceptable currency or gold was not the practical solution. Ergo, trusted financial institutions—banks, in the case at hand—were used to insure that payment drafts given by the buyer to the seller would be honored and duly credited in the currency desired by the seller.

For several years, DuPont had used Brown Brothers, the venerable Wall Street firm, as guarantor of their payment drafts. Brown Brothers notes were accepted in Chile because the American bank's paper was secured by Brown Brothers'

London connections. In Chile, like so much of the world then, London bankers rather than New York bankers stood behind international transactions; this fact is not surprising given that Great Britain still so dominated foreign direct investment, with the United States a very distant second. DuPont's problems came in the Panic of 1907 when a number of key New York banks became swept up in a Wall Street stock debacle, causing a major bank to fail, which produced a bank run, which resulted in a liquidity crisis in the United States; all of this caused a certain tarnishing of America's financial reputation. Brown Brothers responded to the Panic by tightening up on the credit it extended to America's business community. Specifically, it insisted that DuPont turn over more than $2 million in cash as collateral for the Brown Brother's guaranteed payment drafts the company used to buy nitrates in Chile.

Pierre and John absolutely did not want to tie up that much cash. From DuPont's perspective, they were being held up by Brown Brothers. They needed that money to continue the process of expansion and modernization upon which the company's long-term strategy depended. Quickly, they came up with a short-term fix that involved turning over more than a $1 million as collateral to a London bank that worked in tandem with a British nitrate operation, Gibbs & Company, in Chile. Pierre then charged John with finding a longer-term solution.

Raskob, who had been negotiating with banks with ever more confidence since the Dallas rail line days, got busy. He approached the National City Bank of New York, one of the biggest in the United States. In 1897 it had become the first American bank to open a foreign department. Raskob, his ear as always to the ground, knew that the bank was looking to expand aggressively its international presence and saw South America as a key market. With Pierre's backing, Raskob negotiated a deal with the New York bank that gave DuPont a $2 million line of credit that would be used to issue drafts that DuPont would be able to use to buy directly nitrates from Chilean mines. Those drafts, under an arrangement made by National City Bank, would then be sent to London banks where they would be credited to the accounts of the mining companies. Everybody could feel secure. Under the terms of the complex deal, DuPont would not actually have to meet payment for the drafts until ninety days after they were credited in London or, as Pierre cheerfully wrote DuPont's other key men, "about four months after they are issued. We are thus placed in a position to borrow continually $2,000,000, for which we pay at the rate of about 1 ½% annually." DuPont still had to deposit $500,000 in cash with National City Bank but that was a substantial savings over the alternatives. It was a very good deal for DuPont, freeing up a great deal of capital and even allowing DuPont's draft payments for the nitrates to float for up to 120 days, all at very little cost. Pierre insisted to the "President's Committee of Awards," which was DuPont's bonus committee, that John receive a special payment of 20 shares of common stock worth at least $2,400 "on account of the exceptional work that he has recently done in connection with arranging Chilean credits."[17] Overseeing the finances of an increasingly complex enterprise filled John's days—and sometimes nights—at the office.

Their work together brought Pierre and John ever closer together and further justified du Pont's confidence in Raskob's abilities. In March 1910, Pierre wrote John an intimate birthday letter: "It has been 10 years since you crossed my path," he wrote, "or rather since our paths came together.... 10 years may seem a lifetime for it does not seem to me that there ever could have been a time when I did not have you to look after me and my interests." Pierre was doing his best to relax and enjoy himself studying the great gardens of Europe, and he wanted Raskob to know that he could only do so because of his absolute faith in John's ability to look after the business of the treasurer's office while he was away: "Since leaving London I have 'gotten gay,' never think of business, don't read the paper, set my watch or know what date it is." At the same time, he assured Raskob that he was carefully reading John's letters detailing key events at DuPont while he was away and was fully appreciative of how John was handling the press of business: "I miss you a lot... [and] hope that you will have come to be proud of your achievement."[18] John, in turn, cherished Pierre's faith in him.

During these years of steady company growth and consolidation, the Justice Department continued to investigate the charges against the DuPont Company raised by Robert Waddell. For most of that time, John, following Pierre's lead, paid little attention to the government's case, even though the Department of Justice brought suit against the company on July 31, 1907, for violating the Sherman Antitrust Act. Coleman du Pont, who was still president of DuPont through this period (though his continuing health problems put him out of the picture for long periods of time, often leaving Pierre as acting president), charged himself with meeting the challenge. Coleman worked closely with his uncle, Henry du Pont, who happened to be one of Delaware's US senators.

Given the hullabaloo raised in 1906 by "The Treason of the Senate" articles and the common charge that the Senate was a corrupt millionaires' club, this strategy was ill-advised. Senator du Pont was pilloried, inaccurately, in newspapers across the United States as the real leader of the "Powder Trust." Some even unfairly charged that he became senator in 1906 only to protect his family company, which was untrue. He became a senator because he wanted to be a senator.[19] As he and other family members unapologetically saw it, protecting DuPont was just a natural outgrowth of his official duties given the company's major role in Delaware's economy. He did pursue that duty enthusiastically, pushing his congressional colleagues to accept various measures that aided the company's growth and profitability. Coleman, who had political ambitions of his own, was during this time a leading player in the Republican Party as well. He represented Delaware on the Republican National Committee and held the highly visible position of Chairman of the Committee on Speakers. He, too, was relentlessly attacked in the press, so much so that his fellow Republicans asked him to step down from his committee chairmanship. The Hearst empire, a chain of some thirty newspapers, found the du Ponts and their eponymous company a particularly ripe target, quite useful for stirring up public enthusiasm and thus newspaper consumption. William Randolph Hearst, while an ever increasingly wealthy media magnate, was a zealous Democratic Party supporter and had been one of the very few major newspaper owners to support William Jennings Bryan in his presidential bids. Hearst championed the antitrust movement and pushed his editors to attack giant companies with whatever evidence, however scanty or dubious, they could gather, a style of newspaper reporting dubbed "yellow journalism." In Hearst lingo the DuPont Company was the "traitor trust." DuPont, the Hearst papers headlined, "sold the Government bad powder" and had callously placed America's fighting men at grave risk during the past Spanish-American War and subsequent Philippines insurrection. That the charge was not true seemed to be immaterial.[20]

Coleman was furious over his public trashing and the Republican Party's failure to stand by him. He had Pierre's sympathy. Despite the hearings, the bad press, and the Justice Department suit, neither one of the cousins believed that the government would actually find the company guilty of anything. They believed that since they had broken with the Gunpowder Trust in 1904 they would be found innocent of restraint of trade by any court of law.

Only a few residual effects of the Trust were still in place by 1907 and DuPont had radically changed its methods of operations. The irony was painfully clear, at least to Pierre and Coleman; DuPont had been for decades the leading partner in a cartel but at the exact time when it was being publicly pilloried and investigated by the government it had almost completely moved away from cartelization to corporate consolidation. DuPont was just a very big, centrally managed corporation. That it controlled more than two-thirds of the explosives industry seemed irrelevant to the du Ponts as the company was not setting prices, not dictating market shares within the United States (there was still some international agreements along those lines but that was not the government's concern), and, above all, not "restraining trade," which was what the Sherman Antitrust Act aimed to stop. DuPont was just an ever better run company, increasingly dedicated to scientific research, safer operations, product innovation, and diversification. At least that is how the new generation of du Ponts, with good cause, looked at what they had done since taking over the company in 1902.

Raskob had no line responsibility for these kinds of government-driven legal problems. And Pierre was not seeking out his help or assistance in formulating a strategy to solve them. Pierre believed that Coleman, the charismatic, outgoing, and well-connected cousin, was perfectly suited to resolving this little contre-temps. It was just politics and it would blow over, Pierre wrote Coleman; the federal bench, long friendly to businessmen, would resolve matters satisfactorily. The du Ponts still believed that personal government connections and a sympa-thetic federal bench were all the political tools they needed to keep Washington out of their business.

John was not so sure. He had become well accustomed to operating in a busi-ness realm in which the rules were almost always unwritten and even bendable when they were knowable. But as he saw the antitrust investigation, the federal government was charging his company with a crime—with breaking a legally enforceable rule—but no one in the government was willing to tell DuPont exactly what it could and could not do to be in compliance with that law.

As far as John could tell, no DuPont man or any of the lawyers DuPont had hired had the knowledge to make good decisions as the suit was unfolding. John, because of his duties, was too aware that while DuPont was under investigation for breaching the antitrust law it was even still very much in the middle of buying even more powder and explosives companies, giving DuPont even more consol-idated control over the market to which it was charged with doing illegal things, even as no one could clearly explain to him what those illegal things were. John was a numbers guy. Politics was, in a worrisome way, not quantifiable.

Raskob's skills in other areas were not nearly as well developed as his financial skills though his interest in other parts of the nation's business had begun to percolate. He had very little to do with DuPont's labor relations, for example, though he had become well respected by the workers during the 1907 Panic when he had immediately responded to a cash shortage in Wilmington by creat-ing a scheme that provided all the hourly employees with DuPont-backed pay vouchers, in $1, $5, and $10 denominations, so they could pay their bills. In the abstract, however, John had begun to think about, as he put it, ways to "uplift or improve the relations existing between capital and labor."[21]

While still not politically active, he had become an avid reader. He subscribed to an increasing number of serious magazines and was on the lookout for books that addressed issues of political economy. From a distance he tried to make sense of the rise of the Socialist champion Eugene Debs and the formation of the International Workers of the World. Class conflict worried him; to his way of thinking it seemed counterproductive.

In December 1908, Raskob read an article by Andrew Carnegie in *The World's Work*, titled "How Labor will Absorb Capital," and exhibiting his usual pluck wrote directly to Carnegie, one of the wealthiest men in the world, with his own thoughts on the matter. "I have been studying for some time the problem as to how best interest laborers in the Companies by which they are employed," he informed Mr. Carnegie.[22] Raskob then offered Carnegie his plan "which seems to me should be productive of good results along the line." Written on New Year's Eve, Raskob's plan was impressively innovative, financially sophisticated, and quite detailed. It involved reserving 12.5 percent of a given company's earnings for shareholders and then using whatever additional profits remained to establish a bonus pool for all employees—not just high-ranking executives. Raskob then sketched out a complex means of distributing this bonus pool through a stock plan. The bottom line, Raskob explained to Carnegie, was that "there would be a double incentive for every man to do his best."[23] Carnegie responded immediately, praising his effort but, intriguingly, criticizing Raskob for reserving too much money for the investing class and not enough for workers: "The final form will not be reached until the capitalist and the workman are upon equal terms and share profits upon some agreed upon scale."[24] Raskob did not answer Carnegie's letter and made no attempt to implement his rough plan at DuPont. Raskob did not, however, stop thinking about the problem he had identified: how could workers and, for that matter, the middle class justly share in the rewards of a successful capitalist economy? John's social imagination was expanding with his wealth and social position.

Despite such turns toward broader concerns, John's actual responsibilities and interests were still limited at DuPont. He had no involvement at all with the business's operational side; unlike Alfred, he was no powder man and he showed no interest in becoming one. Nor did he understand the scientific and technical side of the business or the company's increasingly central research agenda the way Pierre did. John knew that there was plenty he did not know. He was content to leave many company issues to others. He was, however, intrigued by the company's tetchy political situation. John had always been, to be anachronistic, a networker, and politics seemed like the kind of networked operation he could understand and work well within. So, after watching Coleman and his people flounder and get publicly beat up in the process, John decided to become involved with the company's antitrust predicament.

Without consulting Pierre or the high-powered law firm that Coleman had hired to work on the antitrust suit, John devised an outlandish scheme. Raskob's basic idea was to get the attorney general of the United States, George Wickersham, on the record approving of the DuPont Company's consolidation of the powder industry. Once Wickersham's written approval had been gained, Raskob felt sure that the government lawsuit would disappear.

To get the attorney general's sign-off, Raskob would employ subterfuge. He would use his friend Tom Feeley, the business manager of Lockport's *The Daily Review*, as his front man in the operation. John was twenty-nine when he launched his first foray into the thickets of politics and public policy.

John instructed Tom to pass along a letter addressed to Wickersham that John had written. Feeley had to be sure to mail the letter in Lockport but only after copying it over onto his newspaper letterhead stationery and signing his name, not Raskob's. John warned that there could be no indication of any kind that the letter came from Raskob, the DuPont Company, or even the Wilmington area. The letter laid out a scenario: what if there was this company that never acted in restraint of trade but which, it so happened, already controlled more than 60 percent of an industry and which had plans to buy up more of its competitors so that it would then have 70 percent of the market of this industry? Would the Justice Department see this situation as having antitrust implications that could lead to charges being brought against the company and would that company then be found guilty of those charges in a court of law? "Please destroy this letter by burning after reading," John handwrote at the bottom of the page.

Tom did as John requested. Impressively, just a few days later Wickersham's chief clerk replied. Unfortunately, from John's perspective, the chief clerk wrote a curt note stating that the Justice Department could not give a legal opinion to a private individual. Tom passed along the news to John.

John was outraged. He dashed off an angry letter to Feely that Tom was again supposed to copy, sign, and send, this time addressed to President William Howard Taft. The president, John wrote, must instruct his attorney general to give him a proper answer: "It seems no more than fair that a citizen, desiring to undertake a project of the kind outlined in my letter, should have some definite means of knowing whether or not he is asking within the pale of the law." The content of this letter did not quite make sense coming from the business manager of a small town newspaper but neither Raskob nor Tom Feeley seemed to notice. Tom followed John's instructions and sent the letter to President Taft.

Again, somewhat shockingly, Tom Feeley quickly received a reply. This time it was much more polite and at pains to clarify the Justice Department's position. Clearly someone in Taft's office instructed someone in Wickersham's office to give the unknown newspaperman "T.T. Feeley" a more detailed response. While Wickersham's chief clerk gave a lengthy answer to the query it was not, from Raskob's perspective, satisfactory. Field explained that he could not answer the question. The Justice Department does not give its opinions, Field explained, to anyone but the president of the United States and the heads of the president's executive departments. The attorney general cannot give advice to "some private individual"; after all, he continued, it would be "embarrassing" if the attorney general told a person one thing and then the courts ruled differently. Field went on to explain that the attorney general does not and, of course, cannot control the courts and that it is a matter for the courts to rule on the legality of a given issue or situation or predicament as it relates to the laws of the United States.[25]

John's ill-conceived and remarkably naive scheme had failed. But John was intrigued; he really had not involved himself in the legal and political processes before. He was not at all chagrined or ruffled by his failure to make headway; he had learned something useful with the only cost being the time it had taken him to rough out his plan and write the two template letters that Tom Feeley had copied and sent to Washington. John had little formal education outside of business practices and sometimes he found the best way to learn about the world was simply to jump in with both feet. At the end of the odd affair, John passed along the entire correspondence to Pierre; unfortunately, no record of their conversation on the matter survives.

Coleman's complex if misguided strategy and John's amateur gamesmanship all led to the same basic result. In June 1911, the US Circuit Court for the District of Delaware found that Pierre, Coleman, and Alfred, as well as the DuPont Company itself and several other named executives, were guilty of the antitrust charges brought by Attorney General Wickersham of the Department of Justice. The Court ruled that the cartel system by which DuPont had for so long controlled the powder industry, though dissolved in 1904, led inexorably to DuPont's current position of monopolistic domination of the powder and dynamite industry. "The present form of combination is no less obnoxious to the law than was the combination under the trade association agreement," the Court stated.[26] The DuPont men should have seen it coming; earlier in the year Standard Oil had been found guilty by the Supreme Court of breaking the antitrust law. "The Great Octopus," as its detractors referred to Standard Oil, was to be broken apart in no more than six months' time into competitive companies. American Tobacco, another behemoth, had fared the same. So, too, ruled the court, must the DuPont Company be split up so that competition and unrestrained trade could be reintroduced to the powder and dynamite industry.

Pierre and Coleman were infuriated by the Court's ruling. Pierre summed up his feelings in a letter to an old friend: "The whole business makes one ashamed of his American citizenship and casts doubt on the sincerity of our Government officials and their friends."[27] Coleman remained, even after the ruling, in a state of angry, suspended disbelief. He wrote Pierre: "We are not a monopoly, cannot be a monopoly and are not in restraint of trade, nor can we be."[28] He blamed the lawyers for the adverse result. Pierre was, uncharacteristically, angry with Coleman. His cousin, in taking the lead in the legal battle, had claimed that he knew what he was doing. In fact, his attempt to use his many connections, including the business tycoon Charles P. Taft, the president's brother, had all backfired. President Taft, who was a man of integrity, had been incensed by Coleman's attempts to manipulate him, calling him "slippery as an eel and crooked as a ram's horn." The president later wrote his brother, whom Coleman had thought he could use to influence Taft, denouncing Coleman as a fool, like too many of the Big Business leaders with whom he had dealt: "That man T. Coleman du Pont is one such man. I have no use for him whatsoever. They do not see beyond their own noses. They think only of their own particular interest and don't take a broader view. They are in favor of special privilege in the sense of having themselves favored and everybody else prosecuted."[29] Taft brothers one, du Pont cousins zero.

It was not a good moment for the two talented du Ponts. As they saw it, their very success in creating a highly efficient, brilliantly financed, centrally administered, market-dominating corporation had been used against them. They were going to have to bust up what had taken so much work to create.

John commiserated with Pierre. He shared his boss's bitterness and took away from the antitrust campaign a skepticism bordering on cynicism about the role of politics and government in business. He was struck by the fact that a Republican Administration, supposedly the party of business, had done the backstabbing. Neither party, he concluded, could be trusted. But John was also less emotionally swept up in the affair. After all, it was not his family that was named as criminal by the US government. John was not directly implicated and he was fairly sure that he would not be personally or financially damaged by the Court's ruling.[30] More philosophically, John expected to take a few knocks as he went about his business, and he tried to accept with equanimity setbacks as part of the price success demanded. In the middle of the antitrust wrangling, he wrote his younger cousin Joe Moran, who had just lost his job: "Too bad.... But one can never foretell what the future has in store for them and after all life is a game in which we are likely to make many wrong and unsuccessful moves and, as in any other game, we must keep a stiff upper lip and fight to the end and feeling sure of winning sooner or later."[31] In the aftermath of the adverse court ruling, John followed his own advice.

DuPont's leaders faced what appeared to be no good options. They could appeal the decision to the Supreme Court, though recent rulings made that path seem unwise. In addition, the Justice Department let it be known that if the du Ponts chose to go that route, the Attorney General would ask the Circuit Court to place the company in receivership during the appeals process; this move could place the family's future control of the company in grave danger. Coleman tried to negotiate with Wickersham and did his best to involve President Taft directly in the settlement process. He failed on both counts.

At this point, Pierre du Pont and John Raskob took over and began banging around the numbers, trying to figure out how to break up just enough of the company's powder and dynamite business to satisfy the Court and the Justice Department. Pierre and John worked to create two independent companies that could successfully compete in the explosives business. They meant to do so, however, on financial terms beneficial to DuPont. Not surprisingly, given their expertise in corporate finance, they at least somewhat outwitted the government and the courts.

They acted in good faith in splitting off a substantial piece of DuPont's business and setting up the two rival firms, Atlas and Hercules. Both companies would be viable, profitable businesses. But in so doing they carefully preserved DuPont's capital position through artful negotiations with the government. Most important, in payment for disassembling DuPont assets, Pierre and John insisted that half the new companies' capital assets be kept in the form of bonds that would remain in the DuPont treasury. DuPont could use those bonds as collateral for their own financial operations. The other half of the new companies' capital would consist of common shares, which would be given to DuPont shareholders in exchange for DuPont shares. Pierre and John then used the new Atlas and Hercules bond issue to retire a sizable portion of DuPont's own long-standing bond indebtedness. Pierre was not happy about breaking off a piece of the company but he had done so, with John's assistance, in such a way as to strengthen the company's financial footing. As a bonus, the US military, in a campaign ably managed by the estranged Alfred, had insisted that DuPont be allowed to maintain its smokeless powder business, even if DuPont monopolized production; DuPont was a trusted and effective producer of the vital commodity and must be allowed to continue its long-standing relationship with the military, representatives of both the army and the navy testified. Mixing DuPont powder with other companies' products could, they argued, create standardization problems. Given the charges made by the Heart papers about the "traitor trust," the US military's stalwart defense of DuPont was sweet vindication.[32]

For Raskob, the antitrust fight was less an emotional blow than an intellectual lesson. Politics and business could not be separated. The government could not be wished away; it had to be managed. Watching Coleman du Pont bungle the fight taught Raskob that even a man he greatly admired and who seemed to operate in a world far above his own was only another operator with limited knowledge. Raskob was not shaken by the government's victory over his company, he was intrigued. Here was another complex, high-stakes game in which he might play. He was far from done with private enterprise but in the years ahead he would also enter the public sphere.

|| 5 ||

Raskob Makes a Rich Life in Wilmington

At the beginning of 1900, Raskob had been a provincial twenty-year-old with a dead-end job in small-town upstate New York. A dozen years later, he had a leading role in one of the nation's fastest growing industrial corporations. Raskob felt on top of the world, secure in the world he had built for himself in Wilmington. He was, he realized, a member of the elite. He could do more than manage DuPont's finances. And from childhood days, when Raskob saw an opportunity to do something, he took it.

Raskob was a member of a new cohort of professional men and women who began to apply their professional skills to the social realm. They were "progressives," which was for many of them not at all the same as being on the left of the political spectrum.[1] These lawyers, business executives, accountants, engineers, and educators disdained partisan politics and the corruption that pervaded most urban governments. They intended to make their communities run more economically and, when possible, more efficiently, too. Some of these new professionals were equally moved by a concern for social justice. Raskob was concerned about social justice. But in the 1910s he had only vague notions about how to bring it about. He had a much clearer sense for how to make his city, Wilmington, a better-run and higher-quality place to live, especially for the burgeoning business class. Raskob became a civic improver. It was his way into public life.

Raskob had only limited time to give to his civic projects. The DuPont Company remained his primary concern. When war broke out in Europe, the DuPont Company found itself in an enviable economic position. The Great Powers needed vast amounts of its explosive products. The war would change everything for the DuPont Corporation and, thus, John Raskob.

Throughout much of 1911 right through 1913, John and Pierre had to spend hundreds of hours figuring out the finances and financial implications of the antitrust breakup. Simultaneously, John was running the everyday work of the treasurer's office, which included all financial recordkeeping, monitoring, and managing the company's financial needs, and directly managing the company's financial relationships. In August 1911, Pierre had formally promoted Raskob to Assistant Treasurer but in everything but name John was the treasurer—a title he was finally given February 25, 1914. Raskob never complained about the near continuous paper blizzard he shoveled through every day; he gave every sign of relishing the challenge.

Raskob's only recorded criticism about his work during this period came at the very end of 1911 when he wrote a snappish letter to his old boss, Arthur Moxham, who had joined DuPont a few years earlier as a senior executive. Moxham had been charged with giving the company an organizational make-over. One of Moxham's major innovations was to institute a corporate commit-tee structure that he believed would integrate efforts and decision making across what was fast becoming a very large, geographically expansive, multifaceted organization. Raskob, accustomed to moving very fast on his own, or in partner-ship with Pierre, was peeved by the committee model.

Raskob's particular target was the accounting committee, which existed in part to standardize accounting practices across the company. Raskob approved of the standardization; he had been a leading force in pursuing it. And he admired the brainy men, many of whom worked for him in the treasurer's office, who were inventing new forms of corporate accounting at DuPont. He just hated the cumbersome decision-by-committee process. He argued that he, alone, could and should make the final decisions regarding the policy changes in accounting procedures. He had been doing so for years and saw no need for a collective decision-making process. The accounting committee should be dissolved or at least radically modified. What went for the accounting committee, he contin-ued, could probably be applied to all of Moxham's committees: "In our company it often times seems that there is too much quibbling over theory and over other things in which there is little more difference than there is between twiddle-de and twiddle-dum." Better, he wrote, that one person, such as himself, just makes decisions and then a committee could "disapprove of his decisions if they saw fit to do so, but the power of disapproving not to be exercised unless for some very clearly defined, practical reason." Raskob admitted that he pretty much believed in "one-man power...in order to facilitate work, secure quick decisions, and to fix responsibility absolutely."[2]

Raskob was not then and never became much interested in management theory. His boss, Pierre du Pont, ironically, was highly invested in managerial reorganization and had a brilliant administrative mind. Raskob's disdain for such administrative and managerial processes was a weakness in an executive charged with running a company as large as DuPont, which demanded organized communication and integrated decision making across complex, diverse units often separated by large geographic distances. John could get away with his "one-man power" style, in part because he had Pierre's complete trust and also because he was willing and able to take on a workload few other men could handle. He could work much faster, especially with numbers, than the other men; he relished the personal responsibility; and he loved to be very, very busy. Raskob's rush to decision and impatience with consultation, coordination, and cooperation, then and later, would cost him credibility in the corporate hierarchy.

Raskob seemed not to care about any displeasure that his one-man show generated among his colleagues. He just kept moving. In 1912 and 1913, he took on a whole new set of projects. While carrying on as treasurer and running the Bee Hive and restlessly investing in stocks and bonds for himself and an ever larger circle of friends and family and having a passel of children, John decided to be a real estate operator and civic improver. John made himself a central player in the building of Wilmington's biggest architectural masterpiece, the Hotel Du Pont and, to his great delight, the leading figure in the creation of the Playhouse, a state-of-the-art theater built directly behind the new hotel. The hotel and theater were constructed as part of the massive DuPont Building; the first stage, offices for the DuPont Company and the Wilmington Trust, had been finished in 1907. Pierre had been in charge of that effort. John, looking for something new to do, asked Pierre to hand off the next stages of construction to him, which Pierre gratefully did. John decided unilaterally to add the theater building to the site. His Wilmington circle cheered him on; most had long bemoaned their small city's lack of cultural amenities. The hotel and the theater were, as one of his new friends in Wilmington, observed, John's babies.[3]

Much of what Raskob did was what, by this time, John had long done. He worked out the financing of the projects. The hotel was relatively easy; the DuPont Company provided all the money. Raskob established the Du Pont Building Company, which was capitalized by the parent company at $3 million of which $1.5 million was in the form of capital stock and the other $1.5 million was in the form of a 5 percent bond. He developed the far less expensive playhouse himself. He issued a $120,000 bond, and he and Pierre put up a big chunk of the cash. Several other leading men in Wilmington invested as well. Raskob meticulously oversaw the project. He made his way through every bid and cost, checking out contractor's bills and overseeing payments. John brought in the project at the agreed upon financial specifications. But if taking care of such accounting details took up the bulk of the time John devoted to the project, it was not all he brought to the development. Raskob made sure that the Hotel Du Pont and the Playhouse were spectacular.

The hotel, opened in 1913, was an elegant creation. The lobby was lined with travertine stone and its ceiling was adorned with 14-carat gold leaf. On the top floor, Raskob established a private men's club aimed both at Wilmington's elites but also visiting businessmen, another cosmopolitan feature Wilmington had until then lacked.[4] For many years, the du Pont family, through its many branches and exogenous relations, had essentially served as social arbiters for Wilmington's elite. Raskob, the self-made man from Lockport, wanted a different kind of social arena for the area's elite businessmen and for the increasing number of important men who came to Wilmington on business matters. The new club was a bold statement, a declaration of sorts that Raskob, now thirty-four years old, was his own man, a social as well as a financial figure to be reckoned with. He became the first president of the City Club.

The Playhouse enterprise was, at least for a time, where John really enjoyed himself. First, he made sure that the theater was altogether first-rate. The building was set out as a 120-foot square with modern acoustical design and a stage flexible enough to be used for a variety of theatrical presentations. It seated 1,200 people. John personally worked out an arrangement with the New York-based William A. Brady, one of the nation's premier theatrical producers, to lease the Playhouse for five years at $11,000 a year. It was a sweetheart deal for Brady but Raskob, here at least, was not looking to make money for his group of investors. Raskob just wanted Brady to provide Wilmington with a "theater in which first-class shows could be played" and the bargain lease was Brady's incentive to do right by his patron by reducing the Playhouse's financial imperatives.

Brady was a bit of an odd choice, given Raskob's commitment to "first-class shows." William A. Brady was an ever on-the-hustle showman, a genuine "rags to riches" character, who had learned to use his fists growing up poor in the Bowery. He had first gained his fame in the entertainment business by managing the heavyweight boxer James J. Corbett in his successful 1892 bout against the aging pugilistic great John L. Sullivan. Brady went on to make Corbett a theatrical sensation in the smash hit, *Gentleman Jack*. By 1913, Brady still promoted boxing matches but was best known as one of the busiest theatrical producers in the country. He described his own career as having "had a good deal to do with the old-time tradition of piracy and plagiarism."[5] Brady was a charming rascal and Raskob, at least for a while, found him and his entire theatrical family irresistible. It was big news in the Raskob household when Brady's talented daughter Alice, who sang light opera professionally, spent the weekend as their guest. After all those years of following the theatrical greats and waiting excitedly to see a touring company appear in Lockport and then Lorain, John loved being a theatrical insider. Not only was he a backstage presence at the Playhouse but Brady supplied Raskob, at a price, with top-drawer tickets to a slew of Broadway shows. Brady helped introduce John to midtown Manhattan.

Their working relationship was not fated to last. Raskob was not a passive investor in the theater. He constantly second-guessed Brady's decisions and in a flurry of letters complained about Brady's poor choice of shows for the Playhouse. Several of the plays, Raskob believed, were too vulgar and downscale for the Wilmington theater crowd. Raskob also became increasingly incensed that Brady was putting on some shows without the full orchestra that Raskob deemed absolutely essential: "There is a howl of protest in Washington against the attempt of the management of the Playhouse to put on musical shows with no orchestra." He wrote Brady that after the orchestra-less first act of "Stop, Look and Listen," he "went out and raised the devil with Allenmann [Brady's house manager] about the matter, saying that he could not possibly hope to be successful in managing the Playhouse if he was going to bleed the people in Wilmington in this fashion, that they are not a lot of rubes and boobs but on the contrary know when things are right and wrong."[6] Raskob, then and later, was ever quick to take offense at anyone who he felt was patronizing him, treating him with any modicum of disrespect, or not living up to their end of a bargain.

Brady tried to explain to Raskob that he did not think that any of his good friends in Wilmington were rubes or boobs. He appealed to Raskob's business sense; to make the Playhouse a financial success he had to think about costs and he needed to produce a variety of shows, some more aimed at a popular audience than others. Ironically, given Raskob's economic perspicacity, he rejected Brady's expert advice. A little over three years into Brady's lease, Raskob fired the New York impresario and personally ate the loss on the remainder of the contract. Brady had many other balls in the air and he took the parting well. The two men stayed on good terms for decades after.

Not surprisingly, Raskob had no better luck with Brady's successors. By 1920, the Keith Circuit, managers of a very successful chain of vaudeville theaters, told Raskob, still a very hands-on owner, that the only way to make any money with a theater the size of the Playhouse was to reach out to a wider audience. Raskob would not have it. He wrote that he would not allow the Playhouse to be converted "into a vaudeville house" as it is meant to be a "theater in which first-class shows could be played."[7] John sometimes had a hard time conceding that others might know more than he did about the specific businesses to which they, and not he, had devoted their lives.

Well before Raskob's hands-on decision making at the Playhouse led to a managerial crisis, he was having far better luck reshaping the immediate neighborhood where the Hotel Du Pont and the Playhouse were sited. As part of his development scheme, Raskob worked closely with city and county officials to tear down the old County Court House building that stood across the street from the Hotel Du Pont. The county building was relatively small in scale, especially as compared to the city-block sized, twelve-story hotel. It represented a time when Wilmington was a more humble town and John, as well as any number of other Wilmington boosters, thought the old building looked terrible standing right across the street from the city's architectural showcase. City and county officials had long complained that the building, which housed city and county offices, a jail, and court rooms, was both outdated and much too small. Urban and rural interests had been warring for years over the cost and necessity of replacing the old government building in Delaware's biggest city.

Quietly, Raskob met with the leaders of the Wilmington Chamber of Commerce who were thrilled to have Raskob take over the project they had long wanted for their city. Then, he did the unexpected; he held meetings with the Grange and other farmers' groups and explained why the city and the county needed new facilities, the likely costs, and how most of the project would be financed by the city of Wilmington and its citizens. Raskob won their support and the state legislature approved a bond issue. Raskob worked out the details and in a few weeks time he had $1.5 million in capital. That was enough money, in John's hands, to knock down the County Court House and buy a site at a "decidedly reasonable" price close by—but not too close—to the Hotel Du Pont, on which to build a brand new city and county building. The old County Court House site, facing the Hotel Du Pont, became a lovely public square; it was a delightful setting and offered a first-rate view for the office workers and hotel residents in the elegant new DuPont building. All these steps were accomplished, as compared to the great majority of similar public enterprises in other cities, with amazing efficiency and economy.

Raskob's efforts were hailed publicly as a hallmark of the Progressive Era, good-government public works. The *Philadelphia Inquirer*, newspaper of record for a city whose own grandiose municipal building had taken thirty years to build at a cost of $24 million, cheered the effort: "Wilmington Enters New Era."[8] The *Inquirer* reported that many in Wilmington wanted Raskob to be the city's next mayor: "He made such an excellent record in pushing through the joint city and county building project that numerous people are [supporting him]. There is no doubt that he would make a strong candidate."[9] The Democratic Party, the paper concluded, was seriously considering him as their nominee. Raskob, resolutely affiliated with no political party and still stinging from the DuPont antitrust run-in with the federal government, showed no inclination to follow up on his public success with a mayoral run.

In 1914, Raskob was becoming a well-known figure in financial circles in the United States. The *Wall Street Journal* and the business press more generally followed his career and ran small stories on his official elevation to the position of treasurer in the DuPont Company. He was an increasingly rich man. While his exact financial position is difficult to ascertain given the convoluted structure of his debts and assets, his holdings in DuPont stock, even before the advent of World War I, alone made him a net millionaire (which would make him worth more than $20 million in the early twenty-first century). While not, as the saying goes, a "rags to riches" story, only a dozen years earlier Raskob had had essentially no personal assets.

In late 1914 and early 1915, John's outside activities, even including his domestic life, were mainly pushed aside as two spectacular, intertwining events forced Raskob's work days on behalf of the DuPont Company and Pierre du Pont, not always the exact same thing, to the absolute limit. In August 1914, war broke out in Europe and soon thereafter France, England, and Russia contracted with DuPont for massive amounts of explosives. To make good on those contracts would be a herculean task; the company would have to vastly increase its productive capacities and figure out how to do so in such way as to maintain the profitably of its explosive business, which was no sure thing. At almost the same time, Coleman du Pont expressed his desire to Pierre to vastly decrease, even end, his involvement in the family company. He was thinking that he might like to cash in his stock, all of it. Coleman was the largest single shareholder in the company.

For several years, Coleman had been distancing himself from the company that he, Alfred, and Pierre had bought in 1902. In part, the separation had been unavoidable; Coleman had been suffering from severe health problems for years, so much so that he had asked Pierre to be the acting president of the company starting in 1909. He had always been an adventurous, risk-loving businessman, easily bored by the day-in and day-out aspects of managing any operation. As his wild student days demonstrated, he also loved a good time. As he suffered from very painful physical ailments and underwent numerous medical procedures, he had increasingly moved his base of business operations to New York City.

In New York, Coleman invested heavily in real estate. He also explored the pleasures great wealth afforded him, including, according to rumor, privileged access to the city's demimonde (i.e., chorus girls and the like). In late 1912, he had set up shop at the penthouse of the brand new McAlpin Hotel, the largest hotel in the world and one of his major investments. In partnership with several very wealthy men, including Charles Taft, with whom he enjoyed strong working relations despite the antitrust debacle with President William Howard Taft, he was lining up several other huge real estate developments. Most spectacularly, he wanted to build a skyscraper in Manhattan's financial district: the proposed Equitable Building was to stand forty stories high and contain some 1,850,000 square feet, which would make it the largest building in the world. To pull off the deal, Coleman needed to draw heavily on his own capital much of which was locked up in DuPont stock.

Coleman first discussed selling his stock with Pierre in late 1914, after war had broken out in Europe but well before it was clear how profitable the conflagration would be for the company. In those first discussions Coleman had explained that he wanted to sell some 20,000 shares to the new generation of executives, most importantly younger family members such as Pierre's brother Irénée, who were taking over top leadership roles in DuPont's strategic executive committee. Coleman needed the money for the Equitable Building but he also believed that by selling shares he was assuring that the company would prosper under the control of a new generation of du Pont owner-managers.

Coleman, at least, had figured to sell those shares directly to the company which would, in turn, provide them as a bonus, by one means or another, to the new fellows. In his typically imperious fashion Coleman told Pierre to explain to Alfred what he had in mind. Pierre did so and the two cousins agreed that the matter should be brought before the finance committee. What happened next would become highly contested, with Alfred and his allies holding to one version of the truth and Pierre and his allies, including John Raskob, insisting on another. National headline-making litigation ensued.

All parties agree that Pierre du Pont, after having discussed informally the possible sale with Alfred, brought the matter of buying a large block of Coleman du Pont's shares before the finance committee on December 23, 1914, and that Alfred du Pont rejected the offer because he believed that Coleman wanted too high a price for his shares. Later, Alfred would insist that he only meant to reject the offer until Coleman could be induced to lower his price. Pierre took or took advantage of Alfred's rejection to mean that the company had passed on Coleman's offering and that he, himself, could freely negotiate with Coleman to buy him out. The minutes of the finance committee meeting, signed by Alfred and the other members, state only that the offer had been rejected. Pierre reported to Coleman, who was ailing once again, that the offer had been rejected but that he had hopes a successful agreement could be reached fairly quickly. Coleman was not happy; he needed to sell to raise the capital required to make his real estate deal. Without it, he was in trouble.

Over the next few weeks the possible sale was further complicated by rumors on Wall Street that a large block of DuPont shares was up for grabs. Pro-British interests contacted Pierre du Pont and warned that pro-German interests were angling to buy the DuPont shares and thus arrange to sell the company's explosives to Germany or at least to stop selling to the Allies. Pierre feared that such rumors, though they were unfounded, could have grave consequences: the company needed the British to provide advance payments for their explosive orders in order to finance the building of the new factories needed to produce the massive amount of explosives DuPont had agreed to supply. If the British used the rumors to halt or even delay their advance payments, DuPont would be unable to finance the new factories and might well default on the orders. It was a potential catastrophe. To an unknowable degree, this international complication contributed to Pierre's decision to act quickly and independently of the company in securing Coleman's shares and thus stabilizing the company's status and reputation.

Then, too, Pierre was not at all averse to cutting the troublesome Alfred out of the company's leadership and, instead, further solidifying his control over DuPont. Pierre also very much wanted to assure that his younger brothers and the other men he, above all, trusted to run the company were suitably rewarded. By purchasing Coleman's major interest in the company he could do so. Pierre du Pont and John got busy developing a financial scheme not to arrange the DuPont Company's purchase of Coleman's shares but to buy the block directly. Coleman gave greater impetus to their effort when he told Pierre that he had decided to sell not just 20,000 or so shares but his entire DuPont holdings. Buying out Coleman would take a lot of money, more than Pierre and his band of brothers (and Raskob) had. Pierre, Irénée, Lammot, brother-in-law R. R. M. (Ruly) Carpenter, and Raskob agreed that they would try to find the money.

In February 1915, Pierre and John huddled in the DuPont Hotel dining room at their regular table to map out their financial strategy. By 1915, they had played the buyout game many times, and they could almost read each other's minds as they flew through the options. They decided to form a separate entity, Du Pont Securities (later renamed Christiana Securities), through which they would buy out Coleman. The five men would pool their capital, with Pierre providing the vast majority of it, and then borrow a big piece of the additional money they would still need in New York. Raskob, who had been dealing directly with New York bankers for more than a decade, would handle the negotiations. Many years later, John Raskob recalled with great satisfaction what happened: "The plan involved borrowing some eight million dollars, and as this seemed to us quite a sizeable amount of money to be borrowed all on one class of collateral [mostly Pierre du Pont's company shares] by young men who were just establishing their reputations we were very pleasantly surprised when the bankers we approached consented without question to make the loan." He continued, "It was smooth sailing from then on and undoubtedly this plan of Pierre's was the most successful thing we ever undertook. Of course, we did bigger things later, but then the things were done by giants, compared to the youngsters that created the Christiana Securities Co."[10]

On the afternoon of February 18, 1915, Raskob took the train to New York City. The next morning he met privately with William Henry Porter, a relatively new partner at the Morgan Bank. Raskob had not previously worked directly with the House of Morgan and later admitted that he had been nervous. But the Morgan Bank, closely involved financially with British interests, as well as coordinating Allied purchases of munitions and other war material in the United States, was well aware of the implications of the deal for the DuPont Company's fortunes under Pierre du Pont's expert leadership, and therefore, for its ability to grow fast enough and efficiently enough to manufacture the explosives England and its allies needed to fight the Central Powers, led by Germany. The Morgan bankers, lenders to the British, had a powerful incentive to make a deal. Massive by Raskob's standards, and even Pierre's, but not the Morgan interests, the deal was roughed out in a few hours. Throughout the nearly effortless negotiations, Raskob was treated by Porter as a man of consequence. It was a far cry from the first time, when Raskob had negotiated with New York bankers on Pierre's behalf back in 1901 when he had come with hat in hand seeking to sell Dallas electrified railway bonds.

John floated out of the Morgan building and boarded an afternoon train to Philadelphia where Pierre had hurried up from Wilmington to meet him. John told Pierre that they had the money. The two old friends celebrated at the Bellevue Hotel and made their way back to Wilmington. The next morning, Raskob, Pierre, Lammot, and Irénée du Pont, and Ruly Carpenter gathered at Pierre's office at the DuPont Hotel. Morgan banker William Porter called and confirmed that at least $10.8 million in credit was theirs.

Pierre immediately wired Coleman with an offer to buy all of his common and preferred shares in the DuPont Company. He wrote Coleman that he would give him $8 million in cash and nearly $6 million in a seven-year bond. By wire and then phone they ironed out the details and before the afternoon was over Coleman had agreed to sell everything. The newly created Du Pont Securities Company formally purchased Coleman's shares and the Du Pont Securities Company was on the line for an $8.5 million dollar loan at 6 percent interest that was made by the Bankers Trust Company, which was controlled by the Morgan bank. To secure the loan, the Du Pont Securities Company had to pledge a massive number of DuPont shares and had to agree, as well, that in the event of a loan default that the individual participants in the Du Pont Securities Company personally agreed to pay back the loan; Pierre agreed to carry up to $4.25 million of that personal liability and John signed on for $340,000. Raskob was not at all worried about the risk he had assumed. He understood that it was very likely he was soon going to become a very, very rich man.

Raskob had negotiated in secret with the Morgan bank. Pierre and his brothers had not told Cousin Alfred anything about their plans. When Pierre had first wired Coleman with the offer he had closed his telegram with the words: "Important this be kept confidential for present."[11] The men behind the Du Pont Securities Company, most especially Pierre and John, knew that Alfred and his supporters were going to be upset, maybe even enraged by their decision to buy out Coleman without conferring with them.

Alfred du Pont had made a tactical error in not immediately accepting Coleman's initial offer to sell a large block of his shares to the company. At the least, he should have made sure that he participated in negotiating, on behalf of the company, for Coleman's shares. But he had not. It was not, to be generous, his style of management to take a hands-on approach to company financial matters. He had always given Pierre a free hand in managing all of the company's money matters. This had given Pierre the opportunity to do what Pierre believed to be in his own interests and what was in the best interests of the company, which he wanted to be led by the men, most especially his two younger brothers, he trusted.

Once Alfred figured out what Pierre had done, he maneuvered with his family allies to bring suit against Pierre and the other men who had used the Du Pont Securities Company to buy Coleman's shares. Alfred insisted that Pierre had no right to buy the stock on his own. The finance committee had voted to negotiate with Coleman for a better price; Pierre had never raised the possibility that he intended to buy the stock personally. Furthermore, Alfred's lawsuit charged, Pierre had used his position in the company to arrange the credit with Bankers Trust that he and his conspirators needed to buy out Coleman.

Not surprisingly, given the DuPont Company's central position supplying explosives to the Allied forces, the lawsuit, filed December 9, 1915, made newspaper headlines throughout 1916. In part, the family rift, with cousin pitted against cousin, and numerous other family members forced to choose sides, made for a dramatic, human interest story. Alfred's side was dominated by those du Ponts who had been almost completely shut out of the company's upper management, while Pierre had the allegiance of those who had risen to leadership since the cousins' takeover only a dozen years earlier.

As the value of the disputed company shares grew spectacularly as the DuPont Company's wartime earnings skyrocketed, the case fascinated the newspaper reading public, who were still shocked and amazed by the fabulous wealth the new American industrial giants were capable of creating. The *Philadelphia Evening Public Ledger* front-page headline trumpeted: "The Great Powder Romance: A True Story of Strong Men and Their Millions." The article accurately noted in its January 28, 1916, coverage of the suit that "putting the case mildly... [Pierre du Pont] profited more by war than any other individual in the country."[12] By the end of January 1916, the shares owned by the Du Pont Security Company had increased in value by almost $40 million, a fantastic sum at a time when Henry Ford had only just revolutionized the American workplace by doubling prevailing wage rates, giving his assembly line workers the grand total of $5 for a day's labor.

The lawsuit against Pierre du Pont also named John Raskob. Reporters noted that this Raskob had put up collateral of $340,000 in securing the Bankers Trust loan that had allowed Du Pont Security to purchase all of Coleman du Pont's stock. While Raskob had been named in the press before for his role in the DuPont Company and for his civic activities in Wilmington, for the first time, journalists became interested in how he had become a figure to be reckoned with in America's elite financial circles. The Philadelphia papers noted that it was Raskob, not Pierre du Pont, who had lined up the deal with the Morgan bank.

While Pierre dominated the newspaper coverage, Raskob, the papers reported, was a "startling figure in the 'get-rich-quick' group." Raskob, the *Philadelphia Public Ledger* reported in a biographical feature story, began his work life as a "conductor on a street car in Lorain Ohio and that he first came to the attention of Pierre S. du Pont when he returned change for a $5 bill given him a week before."[13] The story was utter nonsense and the article went on in a similar vein, offering likely proof that Raskob had chosen not to cooperate with journalists covering the story. Where the reporter did get his information remains a mystery, though the generally pro-Alfred du Pont slant of the *Ledger* suggests that it was probably someone in that camp. The article's erroneous information would figure in several other early stories on the rise of John J. Raskob, who quickly became in the stories that began to accumulate a proverbial "rags to riches" fellow. While the facts surrounding biography were not to be trusted in these first accounts, the newspapers' fascination with the great du Pont family legal battle over Coleman's shares and company's future put Raskob, for the first time, squarely in the public eye.

Raskob had relatively little to do with the long, complicated legal battle that began on June 28, 1916, though he was put on the witness stand several times to defend his own actions. Opposition counsel John G. Johnson, one of the nation's preeminent corporate lawyers, lambasted Raskob personally, arguing that Raskob, "a $12-a-week clerk who was advanced to treasurer" only because of his loyalty to Pierre, "knew that he could not have obtained any such loan [from the Morgan bank to buy out Coleman] if it had not been for his connections with the DuPont Company and the Morgan's knowledge of his knowledge of the vast profits that were in sight for the company."[14] Raskob stayed cool, did not bother to correct the various errors regarding his salary or his rise in the company, and explained dispassionately and technically how he arranged the loan. The trial went on for months and a decision was only reached April 12, 1917. In a surprise ruling, the trial judge declared that the DuPont Company shareholders must be given the right to vote as to whether or not the company should buy back at a fair price the shares purchased by the Du Pont Securities Company from Coleman du Pont. Pierre was outraged, especially since the judge went out of his way to accuse him of having acted in bad faith and having betrayed the shareholders of the DuPont Company. It was another bitter blow from the courts.

This time, however, all ended well for Pierre, John, and the rest of the men who had engineered the buyout. A majority of shareholders, still overwhelmingly members of the du Pont family, voted in favor of the Pierre-led buyout. It, of course, helped that Pierre and his men, including Raskob, owned a substantial, though not a majority of the outstanding voting shares. Coleman du Pont's shares were not counted in the vote, though it also helped Pierre's side, too, that Coleman did publicly and forcefully declare that he supported Pierre and not Alfred in the affair. That Pierre had made it clear that he would quit the company if the vote did not go his way no doubt also played a role in the outcome. Most important was the fact that under Pierre's leadership the company's value had grown spectacularly and shareholders had all done very, very well. A clear majority understood that they owed their fortune, not to Alfred and his men but to Pierre and his.

Raskob, as always, worked side-by-side with Pierre during the uncertainty created by the trial and the shareholders' vote. He helped draft key correspondence with the shareholders and assisted, as always, with both strategic and tactical decisions. Again, he remained remarkably calm throughout the affair and did his best to keep Pierre from boiling over. Even when the court ruled against them and declared that the DuPont Company shareholders would decide the outcome, John kept his cool. Immediately after the verdict, Raskob wrote his brother who was visiting relatives in Indiana: "I am not at all fearful of the result of this [shareholder] meeting which should end the case, although the meeting is bound to be more or less unpleasant on account of the many scurrilous remarks that I feel will be made by Alfred and his crowd.... Please give my love to all the folks and don't worry about this suit. It is disappointing to have a decision as it is, but I am not at all worried about the final outcome."[15] Raskob was not a man easily made anxious.

Throughout that difficult time, Raskob was far more fixed on financing the company's extraordinary expansion during World War I. That successful expansion allowed the powder company to supply much of the Allies' explosives needs. By the spring of 1917, the powder industry in the United States, still overwhelmingly dominated by DuPont, had increased annual capacity from less than 15,000,000 pounds before the war to upwards of 360,000,000 pounds.[16] Production boomed even higher when the United States joined the war in 1918. DuPont reaped unprecedented profits. The Great War made the DuPont Company an industrial juggernaut.

During the war years, as the various branches of the du Pont family continued to wrangle bitterly over control of the company, Raskob came to fully understand that he would never move further up in the DuPont Company hierarchy. The very top spots were reserved for du Ponts. Raskob had no problem with that line of succession; Pierre had long made it clear to John that his younger brothers Irénée and Lammot were being groomed to succeed him as company president. John, well aware by 1915 that his role was limited in the company, instead had begun looking outside of the company for new major opportunities. By 1915, Raskob had come to believe that an unstable, upstart auto company, the General Motors Corporation, offered the best opportunity.

Billy Durant

At the beginning of February 1914, Raskob asked one of his stockbrokers—he already had several—to tell him everything that he knew about two relatively new corporations, General Motors and the Texas Company (better known as Texaco). Both companies had been in the business news and were widely seen as high-flying, speculative stocks. The broker, Henry A. Rudkin, a well-connected, rising star on the New York Stock Exchange, played up to Raskob, praising his instinct and telling him that both stocks looked like winners. He admitted that he really did not know much about the Texas Company but said that he was confident, without giving any reasons whatsoever, that "the stock will do even better than it is now selling for . . . but I could not at this moment give you any well considered opinion. I will do what I can to find out something authoritatively."

Rudkin had a good deal more to say about General Motors. "I have just received a letter today from a friend of mine whose family is a large holder of General Motors stock," wrote Rudkin. The friend, who is in the "manufacturing end of the business in Flint," says that Buick—then GM's biggest seller—will sell 50 percent more cars in the fiscal year 1914 than it sold in 1913: "This is going to be the banner year for the Buick." Rudkin concluded, in a very soft sell, "As a matter of interest, I might add my personal friends and acquaintances in the Company own 25% of both issues of preferred and common stock."[1] Rudkin never said it outright, but it is a reasonable possibility that his friend with the inside information on Buick was the one and only Billy Durant, who had bought a controlling interest in Buick in 1904, created General Motors in 1908, lost control of the company to his bankers in 1910, and was at that moment assiduously scheming to regain control of GM. By 1914, the effortlessly charming Billy Durant knew just about every major stockbroker in New York City and most counted him as a good friend. Rudkin got a hold of GM's 1911, 1912, and 1913 annual reports and sent them straight away to Raskob.

Raskob studied the reports. That's what he did; he studied reports. What he saw sold him on the company. The numbers told him that General Motors' share price was relatively low because the company had yet to issue a dividend even though it had excellent earnings. This was a reasonable approach; GM was not paying dividends because the company's cautious managers were rapidly paying off debt and building a large cash-reserve. Raskob understood that once this highly profitable company was out of serious debt and began paying out large dividends, its stock would rise sharply, and he bought more than 500 shares of GM at a cost of just over $70 a share.[2]

Raskob, by this time assisting dozens of friends and family members with their forays into the stock market, urged others to do likewise. He wrote William Brady, the impresario Raskob had coaxed into running the Wilmington Playhouse: "In regard to General Motors, I think that this stock is easily worth double what it is selling at at [sic] the present time.... The Company is most excellently managed, has tremendous resources, and a very small capitalization indeed, and I do not hesitate in strongly advising you to buy this stock even at present market prices."[3] Brady bought a few shares. Other friends and family members followed suit. John made a strong pitch to Irénée du Pont, laying out all the reasons the motor industry was about to boom. Irénée later said that he really had not paid much attention to the auto industry and knew little about General Motors, but John was "such a bull on the future of the motor industry" and he "certainly had enough faith in him to take a fling."[4] Irénée bought 400 shares. Most of all, John insisted that Pierre take a piece of the action. He made the case repeatedly, but Pierre remained unconvinced. Finally, in April 1914, John walked into Pierre's office and, in front of Pierre's brother-in-law H. Rodney Sharp, poured out the reasons Pierre should invest in GM. Rod Sharp, many years later, recounted to Raskob what happened: "Pierre listened attentively to your enthusiasm, without showing much interest." When John ran out of steam, Pierre had looked at him warmly, as he had so many other times, and said, "John, you're crazy to be buying motor shares." Then du Pont bought 2,000 common shares of General Motors at $80 a share.[5] Pierre recalled years later: "I invested in the stock without knowing anything about the company." Du Pont bought because Raskob told him to: "It was purely a speculation on Raskob's recommendation.... He kept talking with me about it and finally I said I would make the investment to get rid of him!"[6] Satisfied that he had at last gotten Pierre on board, John took the train to Philadelphia and, once again, convinced his banker there to lend him money using as collateral the stock he meant to purchase with the loan. Raskob borrowed some $75,000 to buy another 1,000 shares of GM for himself.[7] That was just the beginning; Raskob and du Pont would buy many, many more shares of General Motors stock.

During the war years, DuPont business continued to take up almost all of Raskob's time, but his increasing investment in General Motors demanded more than just money. General Motors needed what Raskob and Pierre du Pont had or could command—financial expertise, corporate know-how, lots of loose cash, and good relations with New York bankers. Between 1915 and 1918, Raskob moved in stages from DuPont to GM and from Pierre's ablest lieutenant to his own man. As his investments in GM increased, and even as he convinced Pierre to invest more of his own money in GM, and then as he won over the DuPont Company Executive Committee to sink tens of millions of dollars into GM stock, Raskob remained almost completely under the spell of GM's founder, Billy Durant. At the same time, though, Raskob gradually came to understand that Billy, though a lovable, charming, spectacularly shrewd business visionary, had to go.

General Motors was the brainchild of William Crapo Durant, known to his legion of friends and admirers as Billy. Durant was a spectacular entrepreneur, a capitalist risk-taker of the first order, a man who could, in the near legendary words of his onetime employee Walter Chrysler, charm a bird out of a tree. He had been born at the end of 1861, making him a generation older than Raskob, and his upbringing could not have been more different than Raskob's. Durant's maternal grandfather had been a successful businessman, railroad president, and then the governor of Michigan; his uncle was a US congressman. The family was full of hard workers, men and women of integrity who had made good and served their communities honorably. At the same time, Billy's father, also a great charmer, proved himself to everyone's satisfaction to be a ne'er do well, a something-for-nothing stock-market plunger, and a drunk. Durant's father came and went during Billy's early years, finally disappearing before Billy turned ten. His mother returned to live with her well-to-do and ultra-respectable family in Flint, Michigan. Fatherless, young Billy Durant, in the words of his biographer, "was buried under waves of maternal cosseting...garbed like a little prince."[8] Durant saw it much the same way, telling a journalist, with tears in his eyes, that his mother "always thought I was a wonderful boy. And I have tried not to disappoint her."[9]

Billy Durant, child of a scandalous marriage and spoiled by his adoring mother, grew up to be man of uncanny confidence with little sense of limits. He was blessed with a talent—too much a talent, it turned out—for business risk and financial improvisation as great as any person alive in the early years of the twentieth century. A salesman of prodigious ability, by his late thirties he had mastered the world of business by creating the largest horse-drawn cart business in the United States and Canada, overseeing sixteen factories and a spectacularly successful sales operation. But in the very first years of the twentieth century, Durant left the horse-drawn cart behind. He had seen the future in the automobile before almost anyone else, and though without mechanical knowledge or aptitude he made himself one of the avatars of the brand new industry.

When John Raskob took interest in General Motors, less than six years after its incorporation, Durant had already taken the auto company on a spectacular roller coaster of a ride. Durant had joined the auto-mania of the early twentieth century by buying a major interest in the failing Buick Motor Company in late 1904. In ten months' time, he had increased the capitalization of the company from $75,000 to $1.5 million. Flint bankers and businessmen supplied almost all the money. They had been brought to the table and won over by the pictures Durant painted in the sky of a new industry aborning and booming in their hometown. Under Michigan's elastic securities laws, Billy and his lawyer took a few liberties in outlining their stock offerings. As Durant's lawyer explained, "Billy... just soared high, wide and handsome."[10] John Raskob had quit his small town to find his main chance; Billy Durant found another way: he reinvented his hometown, moving it smartly from one century, in which horses had supplied horsepower, into the next, where they did not, and the townspeople of Flint loved him for it.

By 1908 Buick was a success. With sales of some 8,500 autos, Durant's company was the new industry's leader. About 62,000 cars were sold in the United States that year, more than forty times as many as had been made in 1900. Durant's colleagues were in awe of his energy; he held meetings at 3 a.m. and some nights he skipped sleep altogether. Durant rolled by train across the country lining up investors, picking out factory sites, making deals. For a Detroit dinner held by his colleagues in the auto industry, a poem was penned in his honor:

> A special lightening cannon ball
> Brings William into town—
> Her steam gauge shows a sudden fall
> When William gets to town....
> Drones are converted to bees
> When William comes to town.
> Partners with work and worry mad
> With countenances sad
> Exclaim, 'My God, we'll be glad
> When William leaves the town.'[11]

Still, though turning around the fortunes of Buick was exhilarating, demanding work, it was only one piece of the puzzle, as Durant saw it. Durant knew what the du Ponts and so many other industrialists in that era knew: to make money and keep making money, a given industrial sector had to be scaled up and consolidated. There were too many auto companies competing, beating each other up over price, bidding up skilled labor costs, disseminating technical talent too widely, keeping unit costs too high, and defeating all attempts to reach a consensus on how to standardize parts and production and make sense of the dizzying array of technological possibilities and options. Durant meant to consolidate the auto industry and to scale it up. From a financial perspective bigger was better and much bigger was much better. Durant wanted to control his supply line of parts and accessories and wanted to incorporate a broad array of automobile brands under his control, as well.

Durant was not the only one thinking about the future of the auto industry. His friend and fellow auto entrepreneur Ben Briscoe was playing the same game, and he had contacts at J. P. Morgan Company. These bankers, in a rare gamble on the auto business, had arranged for Briscoe to get $250,000 in start-up capital. Briscoe, money in hand, believed that the Morgan interests could be convinced to finance a major automobile industry merger. He called Durant and asked him to take the lead by contacting some of the other big boys so that they could cook something up. Briscoe, with visions of US Steel dancing in his head, wanted to bring together a dozen or more of the 40 or so auto companies that were competing to sell cars to the American people and create one industry-defining, market-controlling corporation.

Durant, somewhat ironically given his later plans, thought a consolidation of so many separate companies was unworkable. But he did think a few of the biggest and best companies could be brought together to take advantage of economies of scale and so gain control over the marketplace. He contacted R. E. Olds, a relatively long-time leader in the industry and head of the booming Reo Company, and Henry Ford, who even before the roll-out of the Model T already had the second-best selling auto company in the United States. Durant, in his soft-spoken, irresistible way, asked them to meet with him and Briscoe. Durant had in mind a holding company that left individual companies mostly self-operating under a general set of guidelines set up by an executive committee. Or something like that; Durant was not much for the administrative details.

A week later the four car men rode to New York City and met with an influential Morgan lawyer, Henry L. Satterlee. He agreed to sort out the legal and financial arrangements for a major auto industry merger. It appeared that a big, industry-defining deal was on the horizon. But a few weeks later the mercurial Henry Ford became suspicious. Ford believed that the auto industry needed to lower prices on cars if it was to boom, and he had come to understand that the whole purpose of industrial consolidation was to hold prices steady or even increase them. When the others demurred on his concerns, he became sullen and finally said that he would sell out to the fellows for cash and then find something else to do. He wanted $3 million up front—no bonds, no promises, no securities, just cash money right there and then. This sort of outlay was not what the Morgan interests or Durant had in mind, and Ford, who may well have never really intended to sell, walked away. Satterlee was frustrated. The auto industry did not seem worth so much effort or, certainly, risked capital. He and the other Morgan men did not imagine the auto industry to be in the same league as steel or even the farm implement business, which they had also recently consolidated. Durant spoke about selling 500,000 cars a year but to the Morgan interests that sounded like a pipe dream. The auto industry in 1908 was relatively small-time, not even as large as the explosives industry. Satterlee told Durant that he felt like he was stuck on a "sinking ship." After what felt to Durant like endless negotiating, a barrage of nettlesome requirements, and personal insults, the Morgan people walked away from the deal.[12]

Durant, while suitably disgusted with the New York money men, took the setback in stride. He decided to steam ahead on his own power. In 1908, he created a new corporation, the General Motors Company, to contain his auto empire. He began to buy suppliers and a slew of smaller car companies. He could not reel in the well-known auto man R. E. Olds and his new car company, The Reo Motor Company, but he did buy Old's former company, Oldsmobile, which had fallen apart but which still had a well known, if misleading, nameplate. Durant paid a premium to get it. He took a stab at buying out Ford, offering him in late 1909 a total of some $9.5 million, most of it in stock, but the financing never quite came together and, again, it was not clear if Ford would have taken the deal anyway. Billy had more success with the great auto engineer Henry Leland, who made the best-quality production car in the United States, the Cadillac. Durant bought Cadillac, reluctantly paying mostly in cash, and kept old man Leland in charge. He bought the Oakland car company later known as Pontiac. Between 1908 and 1910, Durant found ways to buy out dozens of other auto and auto supply companies including Michigan Motor Castings, Reliance Motor Truck, Cartercar, Elmore, Bedford Motors, Champion Ignition, and Welch Motor Car. A few of these companies and their products were destined to become household names but many of them were destined only to be failures.

Durant was buying a new company, on average, every month. Unlike Pierre du Pont and John Raskob, who were doing much the same at almost the same time, Durant was not buying up companies with clear financial records and proven production methods in a long-standing industry. He was swooping in to buy up companies and talent and ideas in the great but greatly uncertain high-tech industry of his time. It was all a marvelous gamble. Durant explained his predicament, as he saw it, to one of his long-time cronies: "They say I shouldn't have bought Cartercar.... Well, how was anyone to know that Cartercar wasn't going to be the thing? It had the friction drive and no other car had it.... And then there's Elmore, with its two-cycle engine ... maybe two-cycles was going to be the thing for automobiles. I was for getting every car in sight, playing safe all along the line."[13]

Many sophisticated business leaders in the United States still believed that the automobile industry would fizzle. And even among those who had faith that a big market for personal autos existed, nobody really knew what would work

mechanically and what would not (though there were a few technically sophisticated automotive engineers and savvy auto men who could have provided some
well-informed opinions if Billy Durant had thought to ask them). But that was
not his way. Durant made little attempt, often none at all, to test his hunches and
hopes. When it came to making, marketing, and selling cars he believed—and
not without good reason—that he knew as much or more than any man alive.
When *Motor World* magazine the *Wired* of its day, asked Billy in 1910 if he had
not acquired "a lot of 'lame ducks,'" he replied that under his hand "the lame
could be made first to walk upright and then to gallop to the goal of prosperity."
Motor World, however, did have the last word: "Some of the General Motors
purchases, however, [have] proved very lame indeed."[14]

Durant had done his best to use as little of his own money as he could in
buying out large swathes of the auto industry. He spent upwards of $54 million,
some of it cash spun out of Buick's earnings but most of it borrowed or arranged
through extravagant stock offerings. Durant sold his vision of an auto nation to
friends new and old and at least some bankers and investors and car company
owners saw, or thought they saw, what he pitched them. He had told the Morgan
bankers in 1908 that soon, very soon, car sales would total more than 500,000 a
year; by 1909, he was telling reporters that there were ninety million Americans
and every one of them was "just aching to roll along the roads of this country in
automobiles."[15] They all would be his customers. It was an extraordinarily pre-
scient dream but in 1910 the whole complicated, highly leveraged fragile giant
that was General Motors hit the skids when car sales suddenly declined. Durant
and GM were on a collision course with financial reality.

Durant had no real forecasting tools. Mostly he just believed in his own hype,
which was in the long term a pretty good estimate of the American car market.
But given Durant's full-bore, nonstop approach to acquisitions, expansion, and
car production, short-term fluctuations in car sales meant big-time oscillations
in General Motors' revenue stream. In early 1910 GM was short of money to pay
its bills. Durant's cash cow, Buick, had been milked dry. Without a cash reserve,
GM was sinking in a sea of debt.

GM's money problems were exacerbated by GM's debt structure. Given the
big money men's resistance to his pitch, Durant had been forced to find some
of the cash he needed to finance his expansion and cover some of his operating
costs by exercising his charm directly on dozens of small-town bank presidents
scattered around the country, each of whom provided him with relatively small,
callable loans that totaled some $8 million. Alexander Hardy, one of Durant's
old friends who he had made a GM director (pliant directors were a Durant
specialty), claimed that at one point he, Durant, and A. H. Goss, a major GM
shareholder, met on a train after a particularly frustrating excursion in search of
bank loans. Later that night, the train stopped in Elkhart, Indiana, in a pouring

rainstorm. Staring out the window, Durant spotted an electric sign "far down the dark and dismal street…A BANK." Durant shook Goss: "Wake up, Goss," he said. "There's one we missed."[16] Paying off those existing loans on top of keeping GM's many other creditors at bay during the downturn was quickly becoming troublesome, despite Durant's maximal personal oversight of his relationship-based business practices.

Still, Durant firmly believed that once the auto market picked up, a time which he assured one and all was just around the corner, GM's legion of creditors would be mollified and General Motors would be fine. Unfortunately for Durant, his skittish network of small-town bankers was unwilling to wait. Just before the auto slump hit, a Texas banker had given an impassioned speech at a national meeting of bank presidents warning them that the auto business was on shaky ground and that they had best watch out for their loans to car dealers and manufacturers. The Texan's words reverberated in the bankers' wood paneled offices when the auto market slowed. In May 1910, the Main Street bankers began calling in their GM loans.

Durant needed millions of dollars to pay off the bankers and float his way around a floodtide of creditors. He reached out to Wall Street but was, again, rebuffed. Hauling Wilfred Leland, the highly capable son of the founder of Cadillac, with him, Durant rushed around the Midwest trying to talk Chicago bankers, St. Louis bankers, any bankers, into giving him more credit. By early September 1910, in the midst of the downturn, Durant was forced to sell off assets; his mighty General Motors had begun to implode. The First National Bank of Boston, on the hook for more than $7 million, tried to find new money for GM; the Boston bankers arranged a meeting between Durant and a group of major East Coast bankers in New York. Durant and his key men laid out their situation, emphasizing that in the 1909 fiscal year they had earned some $10 million on sales of nearly $30 million and that all they needed to push forward through the current market blip was a loan equal to one year's earnings. Wilfred Leland states in his account of those terrible days that after the meeting a few bankers asked him to meet with them privately. Without Durant in the room, Leland was able to interest them in bailing out General Motors.

The bankers who showed the most interest were from two major investment houses, Lee, Higginson and Company and J & W Seligman. James Jackson Storrow of Lee Hig, as it was known, took the lead. That Storrow saw an opportunity in GM after almost all other major bankers had turned it down was not surprising. Although on the surface Storrow seemed an archetypal Boston Brahmin banker—he was a Harvard man, and on the surface fit in well with the conservative investment house he had joined in 1900 after a decade as a successful corporate lawyer—he was an unusual man in many ways. To begin, Storrow's wife was an unconventional woman for her class and time. She and

Storrow had met in Switzerland on a mountain path high above Zermatt; hiking was a strange enough activity for any young American in the 1880s, but it was especially unusual for an eighteen-year-old girl. Helen Osborne Storrow was descended from a family famed in American history for championing abolitionism, women's suffrage, and any number of other Progressive causes. And James, surely in part through Helen's influence, became a bold Progressive in the late nineteenth century, championing the cause of America's immigrants. He and Helen would work for this and other causes for the rest of their lives. At a time when many men of his kind were openly hostile to the legions of Catholics and Jews pouring into the United States, he worked to assure them equal workplace opportunity. Thus, it is not surprising that Storrow agreed to team up for the GM bailout with the Jewish banker Albert Strauss of J & W Seligman, which had been known in the late nineteenth century as the investment house of the "American Rothschilds."[17] Such arrangements were still uncommon at the time; the Morgan bank, for example, did its very best never to work with Jewish bankers.

Thus, Storrow was an independent thinker. Progressive political leanings aside, he was also very much dedicated to changing his bank's business culture, which most insiders believed had become too conservative and hidebound. Storrow pushed his bank hard to make decisions based far less on long-standing personal relationships built on trust and character and much more on hard-nosed statistically-based risk analysis. While Storrow did not trust Billy Durant, he did trust enough of the numbers GM generated to believe that a multimillion dollar loan to the foundering auto company was a good bet and that an investment in the auto industry could pay big dividends in the years ahead.

Still, Storrow and his partners at J & W Seligman were well aware of the financial risks involved in propping up General Motors. GM, they believed, had been badly run by Durant, who, careless with company money and credit, had needlessly overexposed the company to financial risk. Storrow felt that Durant allowed the many companies he had bought to operate without sufficient coordination or control. The bankers were willing to bail out GM but only if they exacted steep concessions from GM's board of directors. They were merciless.

They began with the following terms: GM would pay off the entire loan of $15 million in five years at 6 percent per annum. To guarantee payment, GM would mortgage all its assets, which would be forfeited to the bankers if the five-year note was not met. The bankers also rejected the financial information GM—Durant, in essence—provided in its yearly statements; they would do their own appraisals, which not surprisingly turned out to be much lower than GM's. Lee Hig and Seligman insisted on a massive commission for making the loan, as well as a huge piece of GM's stock. Finally, Storrow held firm: the deal would not be made unless Durant stepped down from operational control of the company. In his unpublished memoir Durant wrote: "I was forced to accept [the brutal terms] to save my 'baby,' born and raised by me, the result of hectic years of night-and-day work, deligence [sic], and application."[18]

Durant was allowed to stay on as a company director, but under the terms of the deal the bankers, operating through a voting trust they controlled, were for the next five years in charge of General Motors. Storrow became GM's new president and worked tirelessly to modernize Billy Durant's ungainly but spectacular creation. Almost every Monday morning, week after week, Storrow boarded the Boston to Detroit train and spent the next several days figuring out how to make GM more productive and more profitable both by coordinating the multitude of companies and divisions Durant had brought together and by trying to find the right combination of incentives and controls that would make GM's many rival managers, whom Durant had given near complete autonomy, work together for the corporate good. Storrow was a banker, not an engineer or an experienced industrialist, but he did have good success in pushing GM forward. He kept at it for some two years before selecting the highly capable auto man Charles Nash to take over. Nash had worked for Durant but had never been a Durant man.

So in 1914, when Raskob began to take an interest in GM it was a very different company than the one Durant had pieced together between 1908 and 1910. In 1914, GM was on sound financial footing. Durant would never admit it, since he despised the bankers for the terms they had forced on him and for removing him from control of the company he had created, but those bankers had saved the company. Of course, Durant had been right, too. The auto market, after the sharp downturn in 1910, had rapidly picked up again and GM's revenue stream was strong. Despite the return of a robust demand for autos, the bankers had put a stop to Durant's acquisitions binge and had instead begun to prune GM's wild growth. They were cautious men, not much interested in innovation or expansion. Durant was appalled by their timidity and planned to regain control of GM at the end of the five-year term set up by the banks' financial bailout.

When John Raskob began to buy GM stock, bringing a reluctant Pierre du Pont in with him, he had no thoughts of also investing his time, talent, and energy into the actual management of the car company. But throughout 1914 and early 1915 he became ever more bullish on GM and on the auto industry more generally. He talked about the industry and about GM, in particular, with his assistant in the DuPont treasurer's office, Donaldson Brown. Brown, who was always much better with numbers than with words, later wrote that Raskob told him at the time that he had "great enthusiasm for the potential future and expansion for the automobile industry" and was surprised that the business was "not held in very high regard by the general banking and investing community."[19] Raskob was certain that the bankers and the investors were wrong, that the auto industry was on course for a spectacular rise. GM's stock, he insisted, was ridiculously undervalued.

By the end of the summer of 1915, even as the DuPont Company began to ramp up its production of explosive powders on its own way to spectacular growth, GM's stock did boom. By August, the share price passed 200, then, in early September, it passed 300. The boom was puzzling, in a way. Although its balance sheet was strong, GM still had not issued a dividend. Raskob watched with interest; it was clear that something was afoot. He figured that someone was gobbling up GM stock and was willing to pay a large premium for it. So despite the big potential profit, Raskob sold no stock and he urged others to hold on, as well.

Around the time GM stock passed the $300 mark in early September Pierre du Pont and Raskob attended a board meeting of the Chatham & Phenix Bank in New York City. The DuPont Company did considerable business with the bank and Raskob and du Pont had recently joined its board of directors. After the meeting ended, du Pont received a request from Louis G. Kaufman, president of the bank, to join the board of General Motors and attend the September 16 meeting in New York City at which the five-year trust agreement that Billy Durant had signed to bail out GM in 1910 would be resolved. Kaufman, who was working closely with Durant, assured du Pont that GM had successfully paid off its $15 million loan and that Durant controlled enough trust certificates to regain control of the company he had created. Pierre, still just a relatively small shareholder in GM, was intrigued. John's GM flier had produced an unexpected turn, and Raskob and du Pont decided to go together to New York and see what was what. It made for an entertaining change from the frenzy of activity at DuPont that had long been monopolizing their time. Both men also realized that the offer of a board directorship to Pierre signaled his growing power and reputation in the larger business world.

There was good reason for Pierre du Pont's new visibility. By this time, du Pont, Raskob, and the rest of their team had pulled off the acquisition of Coleman du Pont's stock. Raskob had taken the lead in working out the establishment of the Du Pont Securities Company and the shares in that new entity had been divvied out: Pierre retained the vast majority of the Du Pont Security shares; he owned 29,125 out of 75,000. His two younger brothers, Lammot and Irénée, controlled 10,953 each. John had 3,780 shares.[20] All of these men, even before the explosive growth in DuPont Company share value, had a lot of financial leverage but Pierre, most of all, was sitting on a fast-growing fortune. The financial community was well aware of his growing wealth.

When Raskob and du Pont arrived at the GM board meeting, they quickly learned that Kaufman had not been completely square with them about the day's planned business meetings. Durant was pulling out all the stops in an attempt to take back control of GM. He had regained his industrial moxie during his years in exile from GM by starting another auto company from scratch, Chevrolet. He had bet most of what he had on his newest "prize baby," working his financial magic from his new headquarters in New York City. While the company foundered at first, and car designer Louis Chevrolet was driven away by Durant's enthusiastic interventions, Chevrolet was by the end of 1914 a profitable juggernaut. With Chevrolet-generated cash and credit at his disposal, Durant had come back more confident than ever.

General Motors was clearly in play, but according to James Storrow, who had been running GM directly and indirectly since 1910, Durant still did not have the shares to take control of the company. No love was lost between Durant and Storrow or Storrow's hand-picked president of the company, Charles Nash. Durant summed up his feelings in a letter to one of his allies the very morning of the board meeting: "Nash is acting like a baby and Storrow is so disconcerted that he is willing to resort to blackmail to secure even decent representation."[21]

Kaufman brought Raskob and du Pont to a private meeting in New York held several hours before the scheduled official meeting. The men attending the private meeting, Durant and his allies and Storrow and his allies, were there to measure each other's strength and work out the shape of GM's new board of directors. At the official meeting, GM's current board members would nominate a new slate of GM directors whose service would begin at the moment the five-year trust agreement made between Durant and the banking interest expired. The nominated slate would then have to be approved by all of GM's shareholders in a vote that would be held soon thereafter. Whoever controlled the GM board controlled the company.

At the pre-meeting meeting, du Pont and Raskob were nonplussed to discover that they had been placed by Kaufman in the middle of a proxy fight in which neither side was confident that they could win a shareholder battle. For the two old friends there was a little frisson of excitement as they realized that they had stumbled into a corporate war in which their next move was uncertain and their role unclear to the other men in the room. Taking quick stock of the situation, John and Pierre were instantly aware that they could trust only one another. There was nothing new about that; since their Dallas railway days they had been trading glances in rooms filled with men whose interests were often at cross purposes with their own.

Durant, their nominal host, was his usual low-key charming self and indicated to the pair that he was only interested in assuring that GM emerged from the bank trust period in competent hands. John and Pierre believed that Durant was telling them that he was not interested in returning to an active management position with GM.[22] Whether that is exactly what Durant intended du Pont and Raskob to understand is unknown, but it is certainly not what Durant intended to do. Pierre and John would eventually learn that such misunderstandings, to use a gentle term for it, were a risk one took when working with Billy.

The meeting went on and on with neither side in clear command as they vied for control of the board. Du Pont and Raskob, at this point, owned or controlled only a few thousand shares and were in no position to play a major role in the battle royal, or so they thought. They were nominally allied with Durant, through their connection with Kaufman, and Kaufman and Durant wanted du Pont to be one of the board members on their slate which was nice but John and Pierre had no certain stake in the outcome of the fight and, at first, they did little more than watch events unfold.

After several fruitless hours of deadlock in which neither side convinced the other that they had the right to name a majority of board members, James Storrow offered a compromise. He agreed with Kaufman and Durant that Pierre du Pont, a responsible and respected business leader, should be named to the board. Then he suggested that the board be expanded to include 17 men in total. Durant's group would pick seven and Storrow and his group would select seven. Then he dropped his bomb: Mr. du Pont should be made chairman of the board and he must then be allowed to name three additional non-aligned members. Storrow did not know du Pont personally but he knew enough about him and how he ran the DuPont Company to offer him an extraordinary power over the future of General Motors.

A surprised Durant quickly agreed. He believed that du Pont was on his side. Du Pont, committed to no man in the room other than Raskob, signed on to the deal without any hesitation. He had gone to New York having already committed himself to serving on the board. Now he was in the amazing position of being asked to name three other men to the board. Given the stand-off between Durant and Storrow, du Pont knew that he was being offered the power to have a major voice—maybe the strongest voice—in determining GM's major policies.

Du Pont and Raskob conferred and in the frictionless manner in which they had reached so many other decisions they quickly decided to name to the board Lammot Belin, Pierre's capable and faithful cousin, who was already based in New York looking after business, and J. Amory Haskell, one of the grand old men of the DuPont Company who had Pierre's complete trust. Raskob, who had been following GM's affairs far more closely than had du Pont, took the third board membership.

Soon after, at a shareholders meeting, the new slate of directors was approved and Pierre du Pont was formally named chairman of the board of the General Motors Company. It was all quite unexpected. Right after the September 16 meeting, James Storrow wrote du Pont: "May I congratulate you and Mr. Raskob most sincerely upon the success of your day's work in New York? Certainly it was an irksome job for all concerned; but it seems to me pretty clear that the stockholders are much better off than would otherwise have been the case."[23] The battle over GM's future was far from over but its short-term path was set. Soon after the new board was elected, GM issued a massive $50 a share dividend. But GM's split leadership agreed on little else. Both Storrow and Durant were still fighting for control of the company. Pierre and his trusted team were the men in the powerful middle. Both Durant and Storrow courted the DuPont men, with Storrow concentrating his attention on Pierre and Durant working his wiles on John.

Storrow respected both men and he wanted either Pierre or John to take on the critically important position of chairman of GM's Finance Company. He made it clear that he would be happy to get either one of them for the position. Just as Storrow did not know du Pont, he did not know Raskob personally, either. Bankers such as Storrow recognized Raskob's talent; it was Storrow's business to know who Raskob was and what he had done for the DuPont Company. Storrow believed that a strong finance committee was necessary to keep GM running on the stable footing that he and his banking compatriots had placed it. More importantly, he knew that only a strong, un-charmable finance committee chairman could reign in Billy Durant if he managed to regain influence over GM in the uncertain days that lay ahead now that the trust agreement banning Durant from company management had come to an end.

Neither Raskob nor du Pont was willing to consider the Finance chairmanship offer seriously in late 1915. Because of their work with DuPont they knew exactly how much work such a position would demand, and they could not afford to make such a commitment. The timing was just wrong. First of all, members of the du Pont family were reaching a slow boil over the Coleman stock sale and Pierre was not sure what cousin Alfred had in mind. Second, and more important, the DuPont Company was expanding its productive capacities at a breakneck speed to meet the unprecedented munitions needs of the British and their allies. While DuPont counted on the money the British, the French, and the Russians advanced them to build new production plants, John was hard at work on finding the additional money the company needed to make good on its commitments. Some of that work was just reaching fruition when John and Pierre began their unplanned foray into GM's peculiar situation in the fall of 1915.

On October 1, 1915, the major restructuring of DuPont's finances that Raskob had been working on for several months, under Pierre's general direction, went into effect. It was a highly technical masterpiece that gave the company less debt and more ways to raise money. Most basically, Raskob reincorporated the company in Delaware—it had been previously incorporated in New Jersey—under a slightly different but therefore new official name, E. I. du Pont de Nemours and Company. Most importantly, under the new terms of incorporation DuPont would be able to increase the amount and kind of securities the company could issue. It was a complicated affair that involved buying up all of the old company's securities so that they could be issued in different form and type under the new corporation's name.

To put it simply, the new plan eliminated a good deal of the old company's long-term debt by trading in bonds for equities. To convince bondholders that this was a good and necessary trade for them, Raskob included numerous changes in securitizing the new company, including the creation of what he called "debenture stock," an idea he got while studying the ways in which British munitions companies raised money. This debenture stock, he argued, was a more secure and better income-producing instrument than the old preferred stock, while admittedly being not quite as certain an investment as bonds. Raskob made a complicated case for the advantages of his "debenture stock" that only the most sophisticated of investors would have followed. He did make it clear that by trading in certain of the old company's bonds for the new dividend-paying stock, investors would gain substantially more income immediately, which given DuPont's spectacular wartime growth was a most accurate claim for both the short and the long term. Raskob's main purpose in creating the new securities was to replace old bonded debt with stock. Reducing the debt on the company's balance sheet better positioned the company to access more credit at better terms to expand for war production. Raskob loved engineering these financial schemes. The financial reorganization was reported on the front page of the *Wall Street Journal* and Raskob's handiwork was impressively recounted.[24]

The plan was a success. Targeted bondholders overwhelmingly went for the deal. Immediately after the corporate reorganization was approved, Raskob worked out a massive loan with J. P. Morgan. During the war years, financing giant, new production facilities, making sure that costs were properly accounted for, working out payment policy, and setting prices appropriately—a loaded term, if ever there was one—would be as technically complicated and time-consuming a process as anything Raskob and the men associated with him had ever done before.[25]

Raskob was under a great deal of pressure during the early years of the war, but Pierre was under much more. Pierre du Pont not only was working alongside John, and sometimes directing him, on every major financial decision; he also had final say on every major decision undertaken by the company. With his family divided, Pierre understood that if he made a poor decision the company his family had controlled for over a century could be destroyed financially or politically or both. Then, too, if his company failed to make good on his promise to supply the Allied forces with explosives, the war would be lost. While few people in the United States would sympathize with the ever more spectacularly wealthy Pierre du Pont, the man was carrying on his shoulders a massive load.

Nonetheless, in the midst of all this pressure, du Pont had agreed to chair GM's board. Despite how it looks in retrospect, the timing of the request was actually good. While family troubles were brewing, they had not boiled over and du Pont could not know that they soon would. And while the war was only becoming more intense in late 1915, Pierre had good reason to be confident that his company was ready for the challenge. John Raskob, the GM enthusiast, really wanted him to take on that challenge. By this time, the two men never refused one another anything of importance. Then, too, Pierre was riding an unusual emotional high when the offer of the chairmanship had been broached. Pierre, the life-long bachelor who had never shown romantic interest in the fairer sex, was getting married.

Pierre du Pont married his first cousin Alice Belin on October 6, 1915. He was forty-five years old and she was forty-three. Alice had traveled with Pierre and two other couples, both married, in early 1913; from London they went to Paris where they took a car and drove 1,500 miles to Rome, touring twenty-two Italian villas and gardens as they wended their way across the country. Just weeks after that trip, Pierre's mother had died. Pierre, who had long served as "Daddy" to his brothers and sisters, was deeply affected by the loss of his mother at whose home he had often spent the night after particularly taxing work days. By all accounts he suffered emotionally after his mother's death and began to turn to Alice for comfort and support. Still neither she nor other members of the family expected their relationship to change so dramatically.

Pierre's lack of interest in women suggested to some that his sexual preference might have run in a different direction. That he had a very handsome, dark-eyed, working-class young man named Lewes A. Mason, officially his chauffeur, living in an intimate arrangement with him at Longwood beginning in 1913 after the death of his mother, a young man for whom he obviously and visibly cared a great deal, adds to the speculation, as does the fact that their living arrangement did not change, even after his marriage to Alice. Whether or not du Pont was what we today would call a homosexual or, perhaps, a bisexual is an open question. What is knowable is that his friends did not think of him in that way. John Raskob, who knew him as well as any of his friends and who had traveled with him around the world, never considered that Pierre was not heterosexual; he just thought he was shy around women. John was simply thrilled that after so many years his friend and benefactor had found a wife.[26]

John and Helena attended Pierre and Alice's wedding held in New York, since Pennsylvania, the home of Alice's family, forbade first cousins from marrying. Rodney Sharp, Pierre's brother-in-law, served as best man. To help Pierre after his mother's death, the Sharps had invited him over to dinner regularly; Alice had been invited, too, and she and Pierre had strengthened their bond at the Sharps' table. Indicative of the social gap that still existed between Pierre and

John, despite the power and importance of their fifteen-year-long relationship, Pierre had turned to family and not John in the troubled times that had followed the death of his mother. For Pierre, family always came first and John knew it and understood.

Immediately after his two-week honeymoon with Alice, highlighted by an auto tour of the fall foliage in Pennsylvania, Virginia, and West Virginia, Pierre and John decided to go to Detroit and Flint to see firsthand what they had gotten themselves involved with in regard to the General Motors Corporation. Pierre asked Alice to accompany him and so John asked Helena to do likewise. For John, it was one of the very few times he ever went on a business trip with Helena. They had a houseful of children to manage, even with a large and growing staff that included nurses, cooks, chauffeurs, and assorted others.

The trip was eye-opening. Du Pont and Raskob talked with many of the key men involved in operating GM. They met for the first time with Walter Chrysler, whom James Storrow had brought to GM in 1911. Chrysler was a force of nature, a self-made man from Kansas who had worked his way up from apprentice machinist at his hometown train yard to head of Buick Motors; he seemed to know everything about manufacturing cars. They talked with one of Durant's first bankers, Emory Clark of First and Old National Bank of Detroit, who was a GM director, trusted by both the bankers' faction and by Durant. GM President Charles Nash spent a long time with them, giving his perspective on Durant and the company's future. Du Pont and Raskob were impressed by the men they met, but they were not just interested in listening. They also did some talking. Based on what they had learned in New York from Storrow and Kaufman, they believed that GM had to restructure its system of financial controls and decision making. As far as they could tell, despite the measures taken by the banking trust in the post-Durant years, GM still had no sound system for evaluating how to invest capital internally and externally; the auto company had no way to assure that money went where it would generate the greatest return. The DuPont Company had such a system and they told everyone they met that GM needed a powerful finance committee to monitor costs, govern investments and acquisitions, and rationalize securities and credit strategy. Raskob found the auto business fascinating. He had been an early adopter of the new technology; at a personal level he got the appeal of owning an auto. As an investor, he believed that the industry's growth numbers promised a boundless future. He came back to Wilmington more enthusiastic than ever about GM.

In early 1916, Raskob asked his assistant treasurer Donaldson Brown to go to New York and talk with James Storrow about General Motors. Brown had been working for Raskob for just over three years and John had unlimited faith in Brown's financial acumen; it had been Brown who had worked out many of the key accounting practices and statistical procedures that the finance committee and key divisional managers used to measure performance and direct internal investment. Raskob was by this time a brilliant financial strategist, and he was not modest about his talent, but he understood that Brown had a more rigorous and trained understanding of corporate accounting and financial measurement. Brown had become his sounding board.

A tall, slim, socially awkward man, Brown was a genuine prodigy; he had graduated from Virginia Tech with a degree in electrical engineering when he was just 17 and mathematical analyses seemed to come to him effortlessly. Raskob had great respect for Brown's gifts and sending Brown to New York served two purposes. First, Raskob wanted to apply Brown's talent to GM's financial situation; introducing him to Storrow was a step in that direction. Second, Raskob wanted to demonstrate to Brown, who had just turned thirty years old, that he believed in him. He wanted him to know that he thought him capable of doing a great deal more for the company than work out measurement formulas and standard accounting principles. Raskob had never had a protégé and Brown was probably the closest John would ever get to taking a younger man under his wing. Raskob and Donaldson Brown never developed the kind of personal relationship John had with Pierre but the very fact that Raskob was looking out for his own brilliant young assistant demonstrated the change that was coming in John's life.

John was at a crossroads. He had always been comfortable serving as the loyal, youthful assistant to Pierre du Pont but by spring 1916 he was thirty-seven years old. While he was still fairly fit, his black hair had thinned considerably and he had noticeably thickened around the waist. He was a husband and already the father of eight children. He was no longer the young man in the room. In Wilmington, he had stepped up and taken on leadership roles in the city and among the business community. Wall Street bankers knew and respected him and New York stockbrokers vied for his business. He was a multimillionaire and well onto his way to becoming an extraordinarily rich man. But in Wilmington and New York he was still known, above all, as Pierre du Pont's man. And Raskob knew it. His love, and that is not too strong a word for it, for Pierre made that hierarchical relationship anything but problematic for John. Still, Raskob was not content to stay at any level for too long.

When Don Brown came back from his meeting with Storrow, he and Raskob had a long talk about General Motor's prospects. Brown told him everything Storrow had said. Not surprisingly, Storrow had spent almost their entire time together badmouthing Durant. Billy will always be, said Storrow (according to Brown), "the promoter type with a complete lack of grasp over the requirements of financial control." If Durant regains control of GM, "financial difficulties would inevitably ensue." Durant has too many "shortcomings."[27]

Raskob heard Brown out, but told the younger man that Storrow was only half-right. He told Brown that Storrow missed the big picture. "Mr. Durant," he said, "had extraordinary ability as an operating man and possessed great vision as to the potential possibilities of the automobile industry." Storrow and the other bankers, John argued, "lacked a vision and remained highly skeptical of the growth potentialities" of the automobile business. John readily acknowledged that "Durant had serious shortcomings on the score of the financial side of the business," but he insisted that "weakness in that quarter could be overcome by suitable organizational procedures."[28] By spring 1916, Raskob had become a Durant man. The bankers were too risk-adverse. Raskob, like Durant, believed that the automobile business was going to become the next big thing in America, and General Motors, if it was led by the visionary, risk-taking Billy Durant, "The Dream Maker," as his biographer called him, could and would make millions upon millions selling into that market demand. Raskob wanted a piece of that dream.

7

Family Man

Raskob's increasing involvement in General Motors would change his personal, as well as his business life. GM's corporate and financial headquarters was in midtown Manhattan while its main operational and manufacturing center was in Detroit and Flint. Durant and the other key men at GM had to bounce back and forth between New York and Michigan. The DuPont Company, too, had facilities scattered around the country and Raskob traveled regularly for business, especially to New York, but for more than fifteen years he spent almost all his time in the Wilmington corporate headquarters. It was in Wilmington that he and Helena had made a life together. Neither Raskob foresaw it but the war years were the last years that John and Helena would live together, day-in and day-out, in harmonious intimacy. In the 1910s, in his family life, John seemed to have found a counterweight to his need for constant motion and change and new challenges. That balance would soon shift.

By the mid-1910s, Raskob's investments were fast moving him from the realm of the rich to the inner circle of the truly wealthy. He was not and would never be in Pierre du Pont's class. Du Pont, even before the war's end, had become a member of America's fabled few. But Raskob's leveraged purchases of both DuPont and then, to a lesser degree, GM stock had made him a capitalist of the first order, no longer beholden to salary or bonuses or even the largess and support of Pierre. Raskob had become his own man. Raskob's private life reflected his changed circumstances; even as he continued to invest aggressively, he began to spend real money. While Raskob's whirlwind ride would soon change the intimate register of that private life, the years right before the United States entered the Great War were among his most happy and triumphant. Raskob's war years were in some respects reflective of the two cultural realms that were colliding in the United States: an older, almost Victorian order of family and faith and an emergent era of personal expression and materialist celebration. Raskob lived happily, without any apparent sense of contradiction, in both.

During the Great War, Raskob had become the head of a large and growing family. In 1900 his mother had been his emotional lodestar. In his thirties, Raskob maintained that close and loving relationship with his mother, as well as his siblings, all of whom he had relocated to Wilmington. Increasingly, his wife and children had become the center of his emotional life.

Marriage, in those days, completely agreed with Raskob. A couple of years after he and Helena had wed, he wrote to his friend Rob Moore: "I have quite come to the conclusion that a happily married man is the most contented person in the world."[1] In the eyes of his old friends, to whom he still looked for the measure of his success, Raskob's marriage had put an exclamation point on his rapid rise. Helena charmed John's old Lockport crowd, as well as the far more sophisticated circle in Wilmington. She, like John, moved effortlessly across social realms.

At the end of March 1907, John and Helena had had their first child whom they named, at Helena's insistence, after John. For those who were counting, "Junior" was born nine months and 12 days after their first night of marriage. John was thrilled to be a father and spread the news to everyone he knew: "Both he [the baby] and Helena are getting along very nicely, and we are all very happy. I can see no resemblance to either of us in the baby, however, he does look almost exactly like a picture of me taken when four months old. He is a very good baby."[2]

Raskob's family life increased at a nearly unbeatable rate. Helena gave birth to a little Raskob almost every year. After Junior's birth in March 1907 came William Frederick II (named after John's brother) in June 1908, then Helena Mary in June 1909, Elizabeth Ann in June 1910, Robert Pierre in October 1911, Inez Yvonne in October 1912, Margaret Lucy in February 1914, Josephine Juniata in July 1915, Nina Barbara in October 1916, Catherine Lorena in April 1918, Patsy Virginia in November 1919, Mary Louise in August 1921, and Benjamin Green in December 1922. The Raskobs clearly followed the Church's teachings on marriage and procreation.

Helena gave every indication that she welcomed her almost constant state of pregnancy. Physically fit and well cared for by her doctors, she moved through her pregnancies and near-annual child birth in excellent health. She was a loving and attentive mother, generously assisted by a bevy of nurses, maids, and cooks, while gardeners and groundskeepers kept their relatively small estate groomed and green. John and Helena each had a chauffeur and several autos at their disposal. By 1914, John was being driven back and forth to his offices in the DuPont building (though he still loved to drive himself around at excessive speeds in a growing collection of roadsters) in an elegant six-cylinder Stevens-Duyrea automobile, which he had customized to include four doors, electric lights, and a self-starter. The auto was big enough—though not for long—for the entire family to ride to church, where they appeared every Sunday. The Raskobs cut quite a figure in the community. The couple was far from overburdened by their large family. The household, while a complex mechanism with many moving parts, was in excellent working order, its daily affairs supervised by Helena and its finances carefully, even obsessively, watched over by John.

John made it clear to one and all that he loved his many children. After number seven entered the family, he wrote his old friend Frank Reynolds, with an air of amazement: "I have a very strong natural liking for children."[3] Friends and family regularly received letters recounting the children's progress and their various illnesses. After "Junior" suffered a bout of pneumonia, John wrote Elias Ahuja, "We had two doctors and a nurse, all of whom were pretty badly scared. Naturally Mrs. Raskob and I were very much worried. In fact it was about the worst experience I have ever had." [4] John also regularly sent his good friends family photos. Ahuja, after receiving a group portrait, wrote in typical style: "It is quite fortunate they have a very remote look of their father as they are quite pretty. That is rough on you, but still it cannot be helped."[5]

John was an emotionally involved father but the day-to-day management of the children was entirely Helena's responsibility. John did take on two aspects of the children's lives. He provided the young children with a modest weekly allowance on the condition that each child kept scrupulous account of his or her money. John went over each child's account every Sunday morning and lectured them if he felt, as he often did, that they had been profligate in their spending. John D. Rockefeller, the Standard Oil octopus, had done the same with his progeny and John might have learned of the Great Industrialist's practice through Rockefeller's well-oiled publicity machine but almost certainly the like-minded John had simply devised the practice on his own. Second, John took a hands-on approach, with an enthusiasm that surprised some of his friends, to the disciplining of the children. In accord with the custom of the time, he used corporal punishment, at least with the boys, personally delivering a "whipping" when he felt the occasion demanded.

In 1915 and 1916, whippings aside, the Raskobs' home was a happy one. John and Helena had also created a rich and satisfying social life in Wilmington. While John's relationship with Pierre remained fundamental, the Raskobs' evenings and weekends were rarely spent with Pierre, nor did they regularly attend the many du Pont family functions that dominated the area's social calendar. The Raskobs helped lead an alternative social whirl that became increasingly gilded in wealth as John's involvement in both DuPont and GM produced buckets of cash. One of their more memorably spectacular and expensive events proved to be a bit of an embarrassment as it produced a good deal of publicity at a time when Pierre, at least, was trying to keep the powder company's wartime good fortunes under wraps.

At the end of 1915, John and Wilmington's leading stockbroker Frank Lackey decided to celebrate the spectacular financial success of the year with their social set. Mr. and Mrs. Raskob and Mr. and Mrs. Lackey invited nineteen couples to join them for a long weekend in New York City. The couples had all met and become friends at a regular weekly dance lesson held at "Miss McClafferty's studio in Pythian Castle." The invitation read: "Leave your pocketbook at home." Lackey and Raskob, afloat in DuPont wartime dividends, would be paying for everything. The two men hired special Pullman coaches for the trip and rented out an entire floor at the Astor Hotel. With the assistance of their friend and fellow dance school compatriot Ernest Tate, who managed the Hotel Du Pont, they arranged cabaret suppers, dinner dances, hotel luncheons, and excursions up the Hudson. Traveling in a large and glittery group they were highly visible and New York's highly competitive press corps took note.

The headline in one of the New York newspapers reporting on the extravaganza read: "'On with the Dance' Cry of Wilmington Party Here to Burn up Money." The New York press, in a tone that combined awe with a bit of mockery, noted, "As spenders they are expected to establish a new mark, even for the high altitude of the Powder City." To its New York readers, the *Evening-Telegram* explained: "The party is made up of those who have acquired almost fabulous wealth within the last six months from the rise in Du Pont common and General Motors. Several million dollars have been cleaned up in Wilmington and men rated as possessors of millions are as common here as loungers on a park bench in Madison Square—almost."[6] Similar sensational stories appeared in *The New York World* and the *New York Sun*. Philadelphia papers picked up the story as well.

John was shocked at the newspaper coverage his all-expenses paid excursion produced. He pulled out all stops in trying to suppress the story, which he feared reflected dangerously on the DuPont Company and its war profits. Thanks to connections Raskob had made through business with the Western Union Telegraph Company, he found some satisfaction. The general manager of Western Union's Eastern Division, A. G. Saylor, wrote Raskob a long and detailed message: "As quickly as Mr. Casey [Raskob's connection] got in touch with me Friday night, we communicated with the various newspapers and press associations through the influential members of the organization with good success.... The City Press Association which covers all the Afternoon and Evening editions agreed to kill any stories that might be put up to them by their reporters from that time and the Associated Press and the United Press agreed to put out nothing further over the wires from New York." Saylor, a jaded New Yorker, did his best to explain and apologize for the media frenzy to Raskob: "You, of course, realize that the New York City papers always pick up anything which may be of local interest where prominent people are concerned and they play it up for all and everything it is worth. There is not any malice in what they do."[7] Raskob, rather remarkably, took the efforts of Saylor as his due and the press censorship as a matter of course. The press coverage was unwelcome but the weekend, otherwise, went off without a hitch. John enjoyed every minute of it. It was good to be rich.

Wealth and careful oversight, as the business of the unwanted publicity demonstrated, could not, however, completely wall the Raskob family off from problems. John maintained a near constant state of war with Helena's one-time guardian, Aunt Varina Corbaley. Right after the Raskobs married, John had bailed Miss Corbaley out of legal troubles involving her misuse of the small trust fund that had been left in her hands after the death of her mother (Helena's grandmother). By 1915, John completely supported Corbaley, who constantly ran up bills that she expected John to pay which, usually after much complaining on John's part and sometimes coaxing on Helena's part, he always did. Raskob hated her indifference to staying within her reasonable allowance and her casual disregard for John's constant harangues that she keep a strict accounting of her expenses: "I wish there was something I could say to you that would bring you to a full realization of the value of money and the importance of keeping account. Please read this letter over and then read it again and again until you thoroughly understand the statement."[8] For John keeping accounts was as much an aesthetic and moral issue as it was a purely financial one. He hated the mess Miss Corbaley made of her accounts almost as much as he was frustrated by her apparent lack of gratitude for his benefaction.

In 1916, after one of John's reprimands, Corbaley wrote to Raskob from her Annapolis home, paid for by the Raskobs. She told him that he must be mistaken, that she thought that she had, more or less, kept to the fairly humble $60 a month that Raskob had allotted her for expenses. Raskob, his patience long gone, told her that, no, he had not made an accounting mistake, she had not stayed even close to within her budget, she had run up expenses of $2,081.54 in the first eleven months of the year. Exasperated, Raskob insisted that she stop writing Helena, a soft touch, to ask for more money. On that score Raskob had no more success than he did in keeping her within her budgeted allowance. Raskob, whose day job was keeping the DuPont Company's books, still found time and still had the unquenchable need for financial order to track the expenses of his wife's maiden aunt down to the last penny. Miss Corbaley lived a long life; she and Raskob squabbled over her allowance (which was substantial by the early 1920s) and her finances until the very end.

More seriously, health problems, both minor and major, also afflicted the constantly expanding family and the Raskobs' circle of friends. Not surprisingly, viruses of one kind or another occasionally swept through the household; in 1911, for example, Helena and three of the children all had measles at the same time. Not long after the measles, John, who was rarely ill, caught and ignored an upper-respiratory ailment; he came down with pneumonia, which took some four weeks to clear up. Most troubling, daughter Yvonne, born in late 1912, was plagued from infancy with severe allergies, a growing list that would include eggs, pork fat, silk, velvet, and horse-hair mattresses. Her diet and surroundings had to be carefully supervised. Yvonne also suffered from eczema and, more danger-ously, asthma, which the family and Yvonne called "the puff." Her lungs were weak. Sweet-natured and rarely heard to complain about her troubles, she was almost never well. Everyone rallied around her and her older brothers and sisters kept a close and loving eye on her. Yvonne was exempt from her father's some-times heavy-handed discipline, and he and Helena showered her with gifts and small comforts. From an early age, her father called her "Mrs. Goshwhatapile," because she so often was the recipient of so many presents, which she responded to with transparent delight. The Raskobs had medical specialists of all kinds attending to Yvonne but treatment remained palliative and Yvonne remained always in fragile health.[9]

John's friends, too, suffered in those pre-antibiotic days when infections too often could turn deadly and when even relatively simple surgical procedures went terminally wrong. Although he and most of his old friends were then still only in their thirties, death came into their circle more often than later genera-tions could have imagined. Then and later, John suffered the loss of the men and women with whom he had grown up in Lockport deeply, as if a piece of the always cherished innocence of his youth died with them. In 1914, for example, Agnes Reynolds died unexpectedly and inexplicably. She was married to John's boyhood friend Frank Reynolds and the three of them had grown up together. John had nursed a crush on Agnes as a teenager and was rocked by her loss in a way he had not been even when his own father had died. "Words cannot express my sympathy for you," he wrote Frank, "in this great and terrible affliction, and why our good Lord should ordain that the life of one so sweet and beautiful as Agnes…should be taken from us is thoroughly beyond comprehension of an ordinary mortal." In his long letter of condolence John reminisced of their times together at dances where Agnes was so popular and at visits with her when he and Frank and the other boys just wanted "to listen to her talk and to be near her as she was always so sweet, gentle, and cheerful with everyone." John ended by calling on their mutual faith, urging Frank to think "of the very high place she occupies in heaven, and feeling that her watching over you and your dear children and eventually meeting her there is too tender for words."[10] John stayed close to Frank for years to come, saw him on his not infrequent visits to Lockport, and, several times, John had Frank and his motherless children visit the Raskob estate.

Although tragedy, illness, and worries did enter the Raskobs' intimate life, in general, the household was happy, safe, and secure. As of 1916, the rest of

the Raskobs' children had escaped serious scrapes and illnesses. The older children dutifully attended local Catholic schools and, while keeping the children
attentive and respectful during Sunday Mass demanded more effort than John,
at any rate, often felt was reasonable, the children's religious indoctrination was
steady and without any cause for concern. John was still working daily in nearby
Wilmington, a short commute, and he was a presence in his children's lives. He
took interest in their schooling and activities. His hours at the treasurer's office
could be long and while he traveled fairly regularly to New York City on financial
matters, he was not pushed and pulled around the country on business as he
would be soon enough.

Given their seemingly fixed position in Wilmington, the Raskobs decided
in 1915 to celebrate their good fortune by building a spectacular home for
themselves. Already in 1910, the Raskobs had moved out of their large home
on Wilmington's west side to a far lovelier country estate, "Archmere," which
included grounds of 23 acres just outside the city in Claymont, overlooking the
Delaware River. The Raskobs paid $27,000 for the estate.[11]

In 1913 John and Helena decided that Archmere had become too small for
their ever-growing family and too humble for their tastes. In the summer, after
talking over the matter with Helena, John had consulted with a locally prominent architect to renovate and expand their elegant old home, going so far as
to have a rendering drawn. But the Raskobs could not quite put their finger
on what kind of home best expressed their evolving desires and chose not to
move forward. Raskob did continue to buy neighboring lots so that in 1915 the
Raskob estate covered around 70 acres in Claymont, at the very northern tip of
Delaware.

By that fall, just a year after the advent of the Great War, Raskob's wealth had
grown dramatically, and he and Helena decided to build a new home on the
exact same site as their old house to take advantage of the spectacular view of
the Delaware River through, as the estate's name suggests, an arch formed by
two rows of stately old trees. They would plan the new house together. Money
would not be an object. At least that was their original thought. Helena Raskob
wrote: "It was our opinion that no site was so beautiful as the one on which the
old house stood. Accordingly, we decided to build our new edifice as nearly as
possible on this old location." The new Archmere, she continued, would be "the
home of our dreams."[12]

The "dream" they meant to make real appeared to the Raskobs on one of
their frequent trips to Florida in the winter of 1915, in a romantic moment on
a "beautiful, balmy day." In Helena's words: "As every plan of life springs from
a tiny thought or desire, so also came the suggestion for the plan of the new
'Archmere.'"[13]

The Raskobs found their inspiration for their new home in a Spanish Renaissance Revival-styled hotel, the spectacular Ponce de Leon in St. Augustine. They were not the only ones inspired by the hotel. Back from England for a brief spell, Henry James visited Florida on a grand American tour and wrote in 1907: "The Ponce de Leon, for that matter comes as near producing, all by itself, the illusion of romance as a highly modern, a most cleverly-constructed and smoothly-administered great modern caravansary can come … and is, in all sorts of ways and in the highest sense of the word, the most 'amusing' of hotels."[14] Not exactly the Raskobs' sentiments but instructive of the cultural divide between the impossibly refined mind of Mr. James and the more sentimental feelings of the Raskobs. The Raskobs found not the illusion of romance but the real thing at Florida real estate developer Henry Flagler's amazing "caravansary."

The Raskobs, like many of their wealthy friends, wintered in Palm Beach. They had started vacationing there in 1912. Until then, John had kept to more familiar ground, returning regularly with Helena to the Lockport area where they often spent a few romantic days at nearby Niagara Falls. Florida had become a getaway for the East Coast elite only in the late 1880s when Henry Flagler of Standard Oil fame began his developments.[15] Palm Beach, by the second decade of the twentieth century, was the most spectacular of the Flagler-led resort developments but the Ponce de Leon Hotel in St. Augustine had been his first foray in transforming the east and southeast coast of Florida from a muggy, sandy wasteland into a premier tourist destination for the well-heeled. In 1915, the Raskobs were on their way to the Breakers in Palm Beach when they stopped at the marvelous Ponce de Leon.

The hotel was a massive 640-room edifice that helped stamp a "Spanish" architectural style on Florida's burgeoning real estate development. But what the Raskobs found most captivating was the Mediterranean-styled inner courtyard of the complex. Helen lavishly described the court "with its brilliant flowers and palms, its golden sunshine and cool shadows by day; its trickling waters, silver moonlight and mystical shadows by night, with the sky above ever its canopy, we knew we loved the Patio."[16] Little more than a decade earlier, Helena had vacationed, if only briefly and very occasionally, at the Delaware Gap with her nearly impecunious Aunt Varina, breathing in the cultural airs of her economic betters. Now she was the confident wife of a rich man and she was just delighted by the magic of the "Spanish" courtyard that had been created by Henry Flagler's team of talented designers and architects. She wanted to have such a court of her own and she and John had the funds to make it so.

When the Raskobs came home they talked about their dream home and Helena began to sketch out what they wanted, most especially a great open inner courtyard. By fall 1915 the Raskobs had selected a thirty-eight-year-old architect, James Alexander Harper who with his engineer partner James McClure had worked on Raskob's theater building and had done some drawings for Pierre du Pont's planned greenhouse at Longwood. Harper had worked for several years with the leading American architectural firm of McKim, Mead and White and then taken a year to travel in Europe. In Italy, he spent months studying and sketching the great Renaissance palazzi and villas. It was soon after his return that he had worked, with New York engineer Clay McClure, on the theater building in Wilmington.[17] Two years later, in the fall of 1915, Raskob contacted him and asked him to propose a design for a new Archmere.

The Raskobs had definite ideas about what they wanted. Harper should make use of his expertise to design their home in the manner of a Renaissance villa. The Raskobs, too, by this time had toured Italy and had greatly admired the elegant facades of the grand homes they had seen. Helena also instructed Harper that a music room was a necessity and a library, too. Many, many bedrooms were needed. Most important was that the house should be designed around an open-air inner courtyard like the one they had discovered at the Ponce de Leon. They knew that Delaware, with its cold winters, was not balmy Florida but somehow they had come up with a solution to that impediment. They learned that in 1910 the Pan-American Union Building in Washington, DC, had been built with an open-air inner court protected during inclement weather by a retractable skylight. The Raskobs instructed Harper to come up with something similar.

Harper took the Raskobs rough ideas and offered them what he knew best, a home in the style of a fifteenth-century Florentine villa built around an elegant cortile—albeit one with a retractable glass skylight. The home, Harper estimated, would cost $374,200. His fee would be an additional 10 percent. He proposed a new, architecturally compatible "garage," as well, which would include work spaces, laundry facilities, bays for several autos, and quarters for the chauffeurs; that would be another $56,200. Harper did not include a fee for this building in his proposal; possibly he assumed that Raskob would understand that the architect's normal fee of 10 percent would apply. This assumption did not sit well down the road with Raskob. The Raskobs' dream house, Mr. Harper detailed, would cost approximately $467,800, or well over $9 million in today's dollars.[18] At the time a ten-room, fashionable apartment in New York City sold for around $9,000 and a large upper-middle class home in Wilmington cost no more than $6,000. In 1917 Billy Durant bought a thirty-seven-room, white stone villa with exquisite gardens, ponds, and fountains from the estate of Regina and Jacob Rothschild, outside of New York City, for $115,000.[19]

Raskob fiddled around with his holdings to finance the project, creating a separate holding company, a limited liability corporation aptly named Archmere, to which he transferred a majority of the stock he had held personally in the Du Pont Security Company. Once the new estate was completed, Archmere Inc. would be used to hire all employees, make all contracts, and pay all expenses associated with the Raskobs' home. Archmere Inc. would be the first of several specialized corporations that Raskob would create over the years to handle the costs or investments associated with his various ventures, either to manage various tax liabilities or to leverage credit and avoid personal liability. Such multiple holdings or legal entities, all of them established within the rules of whatever government authority existed, would frustrate government taxing authorities for years to come; they would also create fantastically complicated paperwork, which never bothered Raskob, master of arcane financial record keeping, in the least. Raskob's Archmere files alone would eventually contain some 10,500 carefully organized documents including every bill he paid, every invoice he received, and every piece of correspondence regarding the property he sent or received.[20] Raskob kept such documents for good fiscal reasons but it was more than that; Raskob liked having his life documented, he liked the sense of order his personal records created; he liked to see the evidence of the complexity and increasing expansiveness of his life.

With the deal done, Harper and McClure moved to Wilmington to work full-time on the new Archmere estate. It would take them and the skilled artisans they hired two years to raze the old home and build the Raskobs a Florentine masterpiece in Claymont. The Raskobs, rather casually, bought the mansion adjacent to their own estate and moved in there while their new home was built.

Helena spoke often with her architect and was immensely pleased by his dedication and his artistic taste. John, by all accounts, was pleased by the house though his letters to friends mention the project rarely. He did chide Harper about costs, including his own fee. Raskob was particularly annoyed by a suite of elegant and very expensive furniture that Harper had selected, reminding Harper that the Raskobs' home was filled with children who should not be made to feel that they were living in a cold and comfortless castle filled with regal objects that allowed them no room to play. Raskob probably wondered, too, if his children would not make short work of such pricey finery. The furniture stayed, suggesting that someone with the power to overrule Mr. Raskob weighed in. When it came to their homes and to the children, Helena always had the last word.

In the courtyard, with its massive retractable skylight, Charles Keck, a prominent New York based sculptor with whom the Raskobs grew close, created a marble fountain whose base featured images of the Raskobs' children at play; he carved bas-reliefs of the children, as well, on the marble roundels on the lunettes around the courtyard. Tutored by Harper, Helena quickly became expert in the architectural terminology that described her dream home. Everywhere the best wood paneling was used; a Welté-Mignon organ was installed in the music room, its walls hung with carmine velvet, and in the library, with its Persian book bindings, a large portrait of Helena hung over the room's stately fireplace. The second floor was filled with bedrooms for the children and also a host of named guestrooms: "Ye Olde Fashioned Roome," "The English, or Tulip Room," "The Fringe, or Green Room," "The Italian Room," and the "Filet, or Gray Room." Helena loved it all.

The Raskob estate was a statement. Some of the du Ponts had equally magnificent homes; some were even bigger and grander but none were modeled after an Italian Renaissance palazzo. Pierre's house was of a far simpler sort. He, too, just before the Raskobs began their project, had doubled the size of his home, a stately farmhouse he had bought in 1906, but it was still an unostentatious structure with functionality its base theme. Of course, Pierre had bought his home for the grounds, which included a rare and astonishing growth of old trees. Pierre would spend the rest of his life building Longwood, as he named his estate, into one of the great garden and fountain sites in the world. Unusual for a man of his time and place, du Pont planned that his gardens would be open to the public and that grand annual fetes would showcase his works to friends, family, neighbors, and the general citizenry. His dream was nothing like that of the Raskobs. Helena and John had imitated no one in creating their Archmere and they had not allowed any sort of modesty to impinge on their vision. They had built a home fit for an Italian Renaissance prince and princess at a Medici-like cost.

While Helena managed the household, became pregnant again, gave birth again, and walked across the grounds from the Raskobs' temporary home to watch and offer her thoughts to Harper and McClure on Archmere's rise, John was even busier than usual taking care of business. Raskob was rich and celebrated in his adopted hometown of Wilmington. But he was far from satisfied with his accomplishments. GM beckoned.

The General Motors Deal

The Great War produced massive flows of money in and out of the DuPont Company and Raskob gave order to the sums. He worked closely with the banks to maximize DuPont's financial leverage and he oversaw the financial committee as it wrestled with costs and prices and rates of return on investment. Raskob, working closely with Pierre, worked out stock dividend policy and bonuses for the company's leading executives. These issues were touchy as the press and the American government scrutinized DuPont's profits and the spectacular wealth those revenues produced for the du Pont family, company managers, and shareholders.

Public oversight of the DuPont Company grew exponentially as the American government began in late 1916 to build up the US military's war preparedness; when Congress formally declared war in April 1917; and then in late 1917 when the American government realized that the US military role in Europe would be substantial. From 1916 on, DuPont was under the microscope as public figures realized that the DuPont Company, which in 1902 had been a relatively small industrial concern, at least as compared to giants like US Steel and Standard Oil, was minting money as it sold tens of millions of tons of its explosive wares to the various belligerents. In 1916 alone, DuPont profited by some $82 million and returned $62 million of those dollars just to its common stock shareholders in the way of dividend (corrected for inflation that is about $1.6 billion and $1.2 billion, respectively).[1]

The federal government, to the cheers of the public and to the amazement of the DuPont Company's leaders, singled out the powder company industry for a special wartime tax. The tax bite was unpleasant and seemed to Raskob and du Pont to be nothing more than an unwarranted penalty for corporate success. Pierre responded to President Wilson's election-year championing of the tax surcharge by lobbing a massive donation of $92,500 to Wilson's Republican opponent, Charles Evan Hughes.[2] Despite the government levy, all of DuPont's major shareholders received returns that no one, not even Pierre and John, could have imagined when they worked out the 1902 leveraged buyout that began the company's great transformation from traditional family firm operating within the confines of a price-setting cartel to a modern corporation dedicated to maximizing return on investment in a cutthroat global marketplace. John raked in huge dividend payments on his significant DuPont holdings and picked up large bonuses of additional company shares on top of his not insignificant salary. He was richer than he ever dreamed possible.

DuPont's war profits and large dividend payments put massive sums of money into the Du Pont Securities Company, as well, and Raskob looked after that money. By late 1915 he was already investing some of it outside the company. On January 7, 1916, Raskob wrote all the members of the relatively new holding company asking them to approve a measure that would allow him, Pierre, or Irénée, individually or in partnership, to invest the Securities Company capital whenever opportunities presented themselves. Raskob worked out how to apportion such investments among the participants. A Cuban sugar cane deal had precipitated Raskob's interest in working out the company's investment policy but soon after getting the members' approval, Raskob urged the men involved in the Du Pont Securities Company to invest as individuals in one of Billy Durant's auto schemes.

Raskob had been keeping in close touch with Durant. Billy was hell-bent on taking back control of GM from the bankers. He was in the midst of pulling off a high-wire act that would give him a clear majority of GM's stock. In typical Durant fashion, he announced the successful completion of his takeover bid before he had actually launched it, so sure was he of its success. What Durant did was to increase the capitalization of Chevrolet, his new booming company, by many tens of millions of dollars by selling stock to the public, even as he retained a large majority of the shares through a syndicate he controlled. Then Durant announced that he would exchange five shares of Chevrolet stock for any one share of GM stock. On paper, at least, this exchange guaranteed a GM shareholder a sizable profit. Durant also told the business press that the DuPont interests were solidly behind his effort to take over GM through this stock exchange offer. This was news to both Pierre du Pont and to Raskob, though by this time John was firmly in Durant's corner and neither man publicly repudiated Durant's unsupported claim. Pierre insisted that Raskob and the rest of the du Pont men stay neutral in Durant's takeover attempt, and John did comply with his boss's request, though reluctantly.

By early 1916, John believed in Durant and he believed that the auto business represented an incredible opportunity for the DuPont Company, as well. Raskob, beginning in mid-1915, had urged Pierre and the DuPont finance committee to retain, as Don Brown tells the story in his noncaptivating way, "a substantial proportion of the extraordinary earnings which had then accrued or were in prospect as a result of the successful completion of large allied war orders."[3]

Raskob believed, and Pierre was in complete accord, that the company's war-time earnings gave them an incredible opportunity and an imperative need to diversify outside of their traditional powder business. Retained earnings would give them the ready capital to pursue these new opportunities, which they would need to find; otherwise when the war ended and the company's massive capacity to manufacture explosive powder was no longer needed, DuPont would be the unhappy owners of too many powder manufacturing facilities, useless laboratories, and assorted empty buildings; the company would also need to fire many redundant employees, including high-performing executives. Pierre and his younger brothers had already begun to focus these diversification efforts on related manufacturing businesses such as the production of chemicals and new materials. These ventures would soon enough involve tens of millions of dollars and turn DuPont into a very different, very successful diversified corporation better known for its innovative products than its explosive powders. But Raskob had no real role to play in this sort of product diversification, which called for scientific and technical training, as well as a feel for the marketing of chemical compounds and abstruse substances about which he understand little and cared less. Raskob kept his eye on Durant and General Motors.

Not only did Raskob believe that GM was primed to make serious money in a rapidly expanding industry but he also believed that DuPont could make GM a much better run and more profitable company. DuPont had what GM most needed: talented managers who understood how to run a big company through financial controls. Perhaps given his relative indifference to the actual and, for that matter, projected businesses in which DuPont made its money, it is not surprising that Raskob saw financial management, even more than, say, product development, as the key to industrial corporate success. He told his assistant, Don Brown, that "all essential matters of operating and procedure were dependent, in the final analysis, upon financial considerations and attention to problems of coordinated control should be centered in the financial department."[4] DuPont had more men of proven financial capabilities than it could possibly use in its postwar business, but GM had too few such men. By 1916, Raskob believed that DuPont should take a big interest in GM both as a way to invest those "retained earnings" and as a way to use its overflowing talent pool.

In April 1916, Durant actually accomplished what he had announced he had done months earlier: he had taken back his "baby." The Chevrolet for GM five-for-one stock swap had worked. Durant controlled the company. Storrow and the other members of the anti-Durant banking group immediately resigned from the board of directors; Durant undoubtedly would have thrown them out. GM President Nash resigned, as did several other executives who had been loyal to the bankers' ancient regime. Pierre tendered his resignation, as well, figuring that Durant would likely create a board composed of loyalists, but Durant surprised du Pont by asking him to stay on as chairman and stating that he hoped the other DuPont men would continue as well. Durant understood that the DuPont men brought him legitimacy in high financial circles that would be impossible to gain otherwise. Since Durant controlled a strong majority on GM's new board, he believed he had nothing to fear from the DuPont men serving on his board of directors.

With his board in place, and the title of president of GM once again his, Durant wasted no time getting back on track. He started buying companies. Among his first actions was to buy up a string of auto parts and accessory manufactures to make good on the vertical expansion he had been forced to curtail back in 1910. To buy the targeted companies, Durant created yet another semi-independent holding company, the United Motors Corporation, which he created with 1.2 million shares at no par value. He kept a majority of the shares for himself.

Raskob could only smile as he watched a master at work. He chipped in, working with Durant to bring members of the Du Pont Securities Company, as well as some other favored members of the du Pont family, into the United Motors underwriting syndicate. Raskob arranged for his group to subscribe for 80,000 shares, of which he took 9,000 for himself. He convinced Pierre to take 15,000.[5]

Durant used some of the 1.2 million shares in the new holding company that he had retained, in a bit of creative financing, to buy, among other companies, the Hyatt Ball Bearing Company, which was owned, in large part, and managed in total by a perilously thin, sharply dressed forty-one-year-old named Alfred Pritchard Sloan. The ball bearing company was a strong addition to GM. Durant's decision to woo Sloan and convince him to become the head of his new parts and accessory company, legally independent of GM but in fact completely intertwined with it, was an even better move.

Like everyone else who met Billy, Sloan was, at first, completely taken by the man who acted, Sloan later wrote, "in the manner of a gentleman striving to be harmonious with the world."[6] Sloan was a far less harmonious man. He brimmed with nervous energy and could not keep his knees from jiggling during meetings. Sloan's ball bearing company was based in New Jersey and when he became head of United Motors, he worked out of Durant's cramped New York City offices where he watched with near disbelief Durant's instinctual decision-making processes. Sloan was a patient and attentive listener: in fact, his intensity of expression while others talked often unnerved people, many of whom did not realize that Sloan was evermore hard of hearing and had to stare intently if he meant to follow what they were saying. But listening to Durant issue orders and wheel and deal on the set of telephones he had lined up on his office desk did not align Sloan with Durant. Sloan's brain worked much faster than most men's, including Billy Durant's, and it would take him only a short time to be driven nearly mad by his impetuous and impulsive new boss. Sloan was an MIT-trained engineer who always knew to the last decimal point the numbers needed to make a rational business decision. Soon after Sloan took up his duties, Raskob met him in New York at Durant's GM offices. The two men, both at home with numbers though opposite in so many other ways, hit it off and as each man's importance to GM grew, they looked to one another for information, advice, and support.[7]

Raskob, throughout 1916 and early 1917, became convinced that General Motors, as well as Chevrolet, represented an extraordinary investment opportunity. He kept buying GM and Chevrolet stock, including a massive, leveraged purchase of 5,000 shares of GM in May 1916 alone. As was becoming his practice, at that same time, he also bought 375 shares in Helena's name. He counseled his siblings to buy GM and Chevrolet stock, loaning his sisters the money to do so. He urged his wide circle of friends, who counted on him for investment advice and assistance, to buy into Durant's enterprises, as well. Pierre du Pont was, by this time, a major investor; by the end of 1916 he owned about 14,150 shares. On paper, at least, he had netted over $800,000 (well over $15 million when corrected for inflation) on the investment Raskob had convinced him to make. Despite Raskob's public and genuine enthusiasm for GM, he still did not entirely trust Durant.

Again and again, Raskob insisted that GM needed to adopt a DuPont-like system of financial control. But Durant did not move in that direction in the months that followed his successful coup. In the late summer of 1916, du Pont wrote Durant, probably at Raskob's urging, asking him why he had not moved forward on instituting financial controls: "It is my understanding that you wish to talk to me on the subject. As I have not heard from you I fear that through misunderstanding I have failed to communicate with you as to a convenient date of meeting."[8] Although few men would read it so, du Pont was fuming. Regardless, he could afford little time for GM affairs; he trusted Raskob to look after their interest in GM and to keep Mr. Durant on the right side of fiscal responsibility.

Just a few weeks after du Pont's letter of concern, Durant decided to make official what his actions had almost already accomplished. He decided to reorganize the GM board of directors. The new board, Durant declared, would have just five members, a small executive committee, and no finance committee at all. In effect, Durant would be free to act as he thought best, allowing the company to move forward nimbly whenever opportunities presented themselves. It would be, as Raskob had once described his own desire for executive power at DuPont, "one-man rule."

The plan took Raskob by surprise and he was not happy. Raskob believed in Durant but he also believed that Durant's entrepreneurial genius needed to be reined in by someone who understood corporate finance. With Pierre's full support, Raskob pushed back hard, speaking directly to Durant and lobbying the existing board. Durant always did his best to avoid direct conflict, especially if it involved public exposure that might hurt share prices. He backed off his bid for more absolute and formal control over GM. Still, Raskob was worried.

Durant was almost completely ignoring the GM finance committee, even depriving it of basic financial information, which rendered it nearly impotent. And he was using his multiple controlling interests in the legally independent GM, Chevrolet, and United Motors corporations to move money across the companies wherever he or the managers he trusted wanted it to go. From a simple accounting standpoint, Durant's casual and personal placement of investment capital, reckoning of company earnings, and approach to company assets was a dangerous muddle that skirted and probably crossed legal requirements. Raskob hated the mess; it was Aunt Varina magnified a million-fold. He was sure that Durant was creating unnecessary tax liabilities and increased costs by not integrating the three holding companies into one efficient unit that could direct revenues rationally, avoid duplicate and excessive inventories, and create a coherent strategy for financing expansion, paying off debt, and dispersing dividends to shareholders. He also understood that Durant wanted to keep things as they were so he could assure his power to act as he wished without interference. Raskob also understood that Durant controlled everything.

Nonetheless, he continued to believe in Durant. The United Motors venture was a stroke of genius and throughout 1916 GM and Chevrolet were minting money and providing large dividends. GM's share price floated around the $200 mark. As Raskob had always said, Durant was amazing, even if he made almost everyone around him crazy. That year Durant declared a personal income of $3,419,835, an incredible sum for the time.[9] Raskob continued to invest in the Durant auto empire and kept counseling friends and family to do likewise. While Raskob's personal fortune was far more tied to his holdings in the DuPont Company, he had committed his circle to Durant's auto companies. And, of course, he had deeply involved Pierre in GM, as well. Faith in Durant aside, Raskob kept pushing for financial reform, in general, and he kept making the case for the integration of GM, Chevrolet, and United Motors, specifically.

Durant kept putting Raskob off. It was frustrating and, worse, it was awkward given Raskob's assurances to everyone that GM was a sure thing. GM and Chevrolet were making money and paying strong dividends but Raskob was anxious. On top of the crush of his DuPont duties, Raskob felt the pressure. In February 1917, with temperatures in Wilmington hitting record lows of eight degrees, John and Helena escaped to Palm Beach, where they stayed at another grand Henry Flagler resort, the Royal Poinciana Hotel. Pierre and Alice took off at the same time, traveling to Santa Barbara. John wrote Pierre: "Hope your trip, Daddy, is doing you as much good as mine is doing me."[10]

While Pierre spent his time relaxing, John recreated with a vengeance: "Breakfast at eight, tennis with Mr. Button at nine, swimming at twelve, lunch at one, read and listen to music from two to four, then bicycling till six, dinner at seven, then walk, talk, dance, read or any old thing 'till eleven. Lots of exercise and we are all burned with the sun." John went fishing, as well, but as always got seasick: "must have been funny to see me fish for a while, then hand my pole to someone while heaving ho, then fish again, and so on."[11] Raskob also reported to Pierre that the hotel had hydroplane rides and he was thinking of going up—he had flown the previous summer for the first time while in Atlantic City. He casually mentioned to Pierre that he was planning to start an aviation corps back in Delaware to train military pilots for when the United States entered the Great War.

John came home revved up and ready to take on Durant. On March 6, 1917, he wrote Durant and asked him to convene a meeting of the finance committee at GM's New York offices. Raskob told Durant that the time had come; they had to discuss "getting everything onto one company including Chevrolet and also the United Motors companies. This would make a magnificent company with a splendid organization and would result, I am sure, in elimination of a great deal of waste and a savings of large amount of money."[12] Billy Durant's biographer observed: "*Magnificent* and *splendid* were words that appealed to [Durant], though he was usually the one to use them on others. Raskob had an odd way of turning him from a salesman into a prospect."[13]

Raskob, being Raskob, did not just suggest the merger casually. He prepared for the meeting by spending hours working out exactly how GM could use a stock offering to raise the capital to work out a stock swap that would bring the three Durant auto companies together under the GM corporate umbrella. Raskob tried to meet Durant in New York before the scheduled meeting but Durant, not particularly thrilled by Raskob's insistent attempts to manage him, characteristically kept putting Raskob off. As a result, Durant had little warning of exactly what Raskob had devised.

With Pierre at his side, Raskob made the case to Durant at the GM finance committee meeting that Durant had finally consented to hold. Durant was not happy but he allowed that Raskob made a good argument. Pushed into a corner by Raskob's detailed work, Durant agreed to have an outside accounting firm drill down into GM and Chevrolet in order to see if the numbers worked out the way Raskob said they did. If so, the deal should move forward, said Durant in his open-ended way.[14]

America's declaration of war on Germany June 4, 1917, interrupted Raskob's GM-Chevrolet merger plans. The American economy, most especially the stock market, was roiled by the uncertainties of war mobilization. The DuPont Company remained immune, of course. The war declaration only added to DuPont's future profits though in the short-term—and the longer-term, as well—it would bring ever greater scrutiny to America's biggest producer, by far, of explosive powder.

Even before the declaration of war, DuPont had begun to increase the amount of powder it sold to the American military; war preparedness had been escalating for more than a year and had grown in intensity after the Germans began a campaign of unrestrained submarine warfare on American shipping. DuPont would have serious problems with the American Congress and the Executive branch negotiating cost structures, prices, and production schedules; the company's bottom line, however, would only grow fatter. But for nonmilitary manufacturers America's official declaration of war created great uncertainty. No one knew how war production and the wartime economy would affect American industry, employment, and the consumer marketplace. GM, which at that point had only just begun to secure military contracts as the American government began to ramp up war production, had no sure claim on potentially scarce wartime resources. It was hit hard by the war jitters. Durant watched his corporate babies wobble; their stock prices plunged amidst market uncertainties.

Raskob took note of the decline but as America entered the war, he shifted his gaze away from Durant and the auto business toward the war itself. Although he had never before shown much in the way of patriotic enthusiasm, he was swept up by the American war effort. Since the Great War had begun, Pierre had insisted that everyone at the top levels of DuPont keep out of the public debates that had been swirling around American intervention on the side of the Allies. Du Pont understood that the company was an easy target and was already fending off multiple charges of war profiteering. Even in his private letters, Raskob had stayed neutral and whatever feelings he had about American intervention, at least through the first few months of 1917, he kept to himself. But once American intervention became inevitable, Raskob become involved in the American effort on behalf of the Allied cause. At thirty-eight, Raskob was well over the draft registration age of thirty and never considered joining the military. He had, he thought, a better way to serve his country.

After roping in the almost always agreeable Pierre du Pont and the enthusiastic Irénée, Raskob began the aviation school that he had mentioned in his letter to Pierre just a few months earlier. They set up operations in Claymont, not far from John's estate. The three men funded the purchase of several airplanes, including four "flying boats" or seaplanes, and hired experienced aviators to run the operation. The idea was to provide free training for "young men who are willing to enter the aviation corps."[15] As a somewhat natural extension of his early interest in the automobile, Raskob was an aviation enthusiast and believed that airplanes would play a major role in the war, as well as in modern life more generally. Raskob bragged to an old Lockport friend that he was going to take lessons at his school, too, and expected to be flying around the country in just a few weeks. John's nemesis, motion sickness, got in the way of that particular notion but the flying school was up and running by the time the United States entered the war. None of the three men made public mention of their role in establishing the aviation school.

Raskob took a far more public role in urging his corporate peers to contribute to the Red Cross. Busy parceling out DuPont's tens of millions in wartime earnings, he had come up with the idea of paying out a special 1 percent dividend with all proceeds directed to the American Red Cross to help the organization with its war work. Raskob took his idea to Washington for a special meeting of the Red Cross War Council, which had already received major support from J. P. Morgan and John D. Rockefeller. High-ranking executives from US Steel, AT&T, and other major corporations attended and enthusiastically supported the plan. A week after Congress declared war, DuPont followed through and presented the Red Cross with $600,000 (about $10 million in contemporary dollars).[16] Several other major corporations did the same including General Motors; Pierre du Pont personally asked Billy Durant to do so. The 1 percent dividend effort was well publicized and while Raskob acted from the heart he was also well aware that the DuPont Company, pilloried by Secretary of War Newton Baker and other high-ranking figures in the Wilson Administration for the wartime bonanza it was reaping, could use all the positive publicity it could generate.[17]

Proof that Raskob was not just after good public relations came two weeks later, when without fanfare, Raskob quietly donated $5,000 of his own money to the Red Cross. He also signed on as chairman of the executive committee and vice president of the newly formed Delaware State Council of Defense, which prodded both business and labor to work together to maximize war production. Raskob continued to support war relief work throughout the next year. In late May 1918, Raskob arranged for an unpublicized $750,000 charitable gift from the Du Pont Securities Company. He told the Du Pont Securities board that given the immense war profits they all were accumulating it simply was the right thing to do. With the board's approval he divvied out the money to the American Red Cross, the YMCA, the Knights of Columbus, and the Jewish Relief Fund. Such an ecumenical gift was an incredible rarity at the time, demonstrative of Raskob's growing cosmopolitanism.

Restless as always, Raskob was becoming ever more interested in the world outside of the treasurer's office. By this time, Raskob was president of the Wilmington City Club. And his experiences dickering with the Grange, civic associations, and various business groups on the new court house and county building had exposed him to the organized interest group politics that were becoming commonplace in the United States. More directly, Raskob's increasing interest in and capacity for public leadership was an outgrowth of his ongoing work with the Wilmington Chamber of Commerce and the US Chamber of Congress.

The US Chamber had been founded in 1912, and Raskob had joined the Wilmington Chamber of Commerce in late 1913. The national Chamber had begun at the express invitation of President Taft, who wanted businessmen to provide a Washington-based counterweight to the power of organized labor. Quickly enough, the Chamber became by design a potent lobbying force, pushing back against Progressive Era economic regulation, public spending, and tax policy at both the local and the national level. Raskob fully approved of that mission; the passage of the 16th Amendment in 1913, giving the federal government the power to levy individual income taxes, was particularly galling to him.[18]

Raskob had joined his local branch of the Chamber with no great agenda in mind. He had not been a leader in organizing the group. But Raskob was always looking to make new connections and the Chamber showed promise in that direction. Most of the prominent businessmen in Wilmington were joining up. Almost immediately, he found the Chamber more interesting than he had expected.

The national Chamber published regular, nonpartisan reports on state and national legislation that affected business and businessmen. Raskob somehow found the time to read and digest the reports. He liked what he saw. Partisan politics had never interested him, but economic policy, he decided, was intriguing and after the DuPont antitrust mess and the federal government's ongoing attempts to restrict DuPont's wartime earnings, he understood the relevance of the Chamber's work.

Raskob had always been a reader, but his interests had run more toward novels than anything else. The Chamber reports pointed him toward books on political economy and public policy. Raskob, who had never attended college or systemically studied government policy or economics, for that matter, was intrigued. He avidly followed the role that the US Chamber was playing in Washington as an effective lobbyist on behalf of business interests, in general. He was particularly enthusiastic about the Chamber's antitax efforts, since he had almost immediately come to hate the federal income tax, which at that point, unfairly he believed, only applied to America's wealthiest citizens (nor was he happy about the subsequent wartime surtax on high-income Americans). By 1914, Raskob had become active in the Chamber. Through the Chamber he met, for the first time, a number of other major businessmen around the country. Raskob's work with the Chamber of Commerce movement was pushing him into a wider circle. It laid the groundwork for his nationally celebrated effort to provide the Red Cross with corporate donations at the advent of America's entry into the Great War.

Raskob's Red Cross campaign was characteristic of his public and, for that matter, corporate work. He worked almost completely behind the scenes, talking on the telephone with other business leaders as he set the project in motion.

He made no speeches and he made no attempt to talk to reporters about the work. Raskob was not a good public speaker and he demonstrated no interest in becoming one. But he knew how to talk to other businessmen and could lay out schemes, whether they were financial ones or philanthropic ones, in ways that made sense to them. While he always made sure the numbers worked out with an exactitude that proved his seriousness of purpose, he was ever an enthusiast about whatever plan he had set in motion. He convinced his peers to partici-pate in the Red Cross fundraiser not only because he had figured out a clever way to raise money but also because he threw himself into selling it. He was no Billy Durant but Raskob, as Pierre du Pont had long known, was not just a numbers guy, but a man who could sell ideas with an enthusiasm that was often contagious.

Raskob needed all his talents to sell what would become his biggest or at least most expensive idea ever: the DuPont Company's direct investment of tens of millions of dollars into General Motors. Raskob had been thinking about how to involve the DuPont Company in General Motors' affairs for some time. He had been eyeing the growing pile of retained earnings that DuPont was fast accumu-lating and sketching out how those dollars might be usefully invested in Billy Durant's empire. Those speculations came to a head in the summer of 1917.

GM's stock price had begun to fall in June and kept dropping. Investors pre-dicted a major slowdown in car production as steel, in particular, was rationed and directed to war production. Given GM's debt structure, and its financial his-tory, a slowdown in car production and thus sales could well have been disas-trous; experienced stock pickers had not forgotten Durant's misadventures in 1910. By September GM's share price had dropped more than 50 percent from its high of just a few months earlier. This fall in share prices was dangerous for Durant, who had used GM's earlier high valuations to leverage his United Motors deal and other stock market forays. In typical Durant style, he responded to the drop in share prices by attempting to buy even more shares of his companies.

Durant had an emotional response to naysayers who doubted the ever upward direction of his "babies." He particularly hated short sellers of his companies, those market bears who bet on dropping share prices. Ignoring the general war nerves of stock market investors during the latter half of 1917, Durant had decided that GM, in particular, was being set upon by manipulative short sellers. He later wrote: "This drive was without rhyme or reason. It is not because of any inherent weakness in the financial position of the Company or the Company's business outlook."[19] Ergo, he decided to punish the short sellers of his beloved GM by forming a syndicate to buy up GM stock and thus drive up its price. Durant enlisted Raskob in his syndicate.

The reasons for Raskob's allegiance to Durant's scheme remain murky. Certainly, he did not want to see GM prices decline; he had bet his own money, as well as the money of a good many of the people about whom he most cared, on GM. But a short-term decline in GM share price, as wartime stock market investors worked through the uncertainties of the day, should not have been a major concern for Raskob. It is, however, likely that Raskob had bought some of his recent GM purchases using the stock itself as collateral as he had been doing ever since his earliest investments in the DuPont explosives companies' mergers. He certainly had not paid cash outright for his huge 1916 GM stock purchase. Raskob, busy paying for the glorious new Archmere, would be in an awkward financial position if his bankers or brokers were forced to call in his GM position in the event the share price fell too far. Bottom line: Raskob became an active partner in the Durant syndicate that fought to push up the price of GM shares.[20]

In the very short term, the syndicate succeeded in pulling up GM's share price. As soon as Durant stopped buying, however, the stock started falling again, suggesting that the decline was not caused by a small cabal of short sellers but was a response to more general market uncertainties. Unfortunately, the continuing slide put Durant in a dangerous position. To help fund the stock syndicate, he had borrowed heavily against his own GM shares to raise the capital needed to buy additional ones. He had also bought on margin additional shares on his own account. Unlike 1910 when GM as a whole was in financial trouble, this time it was Durant who was facing, as was said at the time, grave financial embarrassment. Raskob believed that if Durant's personal exposure blew up, it could create a general run on GM stock as investors began to doubt the financial stability and integrity of the company itself. Raskob was well aware that, if the company tanked, his own investments, as well as that of his intimate circle, would be flattened.

Raskob had several ideas on how to escape the mess. First, he and Durant tried to get the GM board to bail Durant out by having the corporation lend a substantial sum of money to him so he would not be forced to sell out his stock position. Even Pierre balked at this slippery plan and the board squirmed out of this proposal. As a compromise, the board did give Durant a $1 million salary, payable immediately, a fantastically high executive salary in those days; previously Durant had taken almost nothing for running GM, making his money instead through stock sale and dividend payments. But a million dollars was just a drop in the bucket; much more money would be needed to bail out Durant...and others who had bet against a major drop in the value of GM's share price. Raskob had kept Pierre abreast of everything that was going on with General Motors and Durant but now he needed Pierre's help.

In mid-November 1917, Pierre du Pont, John Raskob, and Billy Durant sketched out a deal whereby Pierre and a small group that would have likely included Irénée, Lammot, Raskob, and a few others would create a new holding company that would then buy $12.5 million worth of GM and Chevrolet shares, much of it directly from Durant. That was enough investment capital, everyone figured, to stabilize the share prices. Pierre, as head of the new holding company and undoubtedly the major provider of the capital by a big margin, would have roughly the same control over GM as Billy Durant. Under such a scheme, the men agreed, Pierre du Pont would control the auto companies' finances while Billy would retain operational control. Durant acceded to the plan though he had no actual intention of turning over GM's finances to du Pont or anyone else.

The problem was that, even for Pierre, coming up quickly with that many millions of dollars would have been a stretch. Pierre would have had to borrow large sums against his DuPont holdings. It was not a simple solution but the men certainly could have made it work. After all, the same men with far less personal resources had pulled off a similar gambit only a few years earlier when they had bought out Coleman du Pont's stake in the DuPont Company. This time, though, the plan did not go forward. Instead Pierre and John, with Durant's excited support, decided to do exactly the opposite of what they had done when they had bought out Coleman. This time the DuPont Company would be asked to make the deal and assume the risk.

Raskob had been thinking about this option for some two years. He and Don Brown had talked about investing DuPont's retained earnings in GM ever since Brown had come back from his 1915 meeting in New York City with the banker James Storrow. So while there was a degree of self-interest in Raskob's bid to use DuPont Company capital to shore up GM's stock price—Raskob and his family had a lot riding on their personal GM investments—he had been preaching GM's virtues for years and he had been advocating for a large-scale DuPont investment. Raskob absolutely believed that buying into GM at the moment when its stock price was historically low, when it was, Raskob absolutely believed, undervalued was the right move for the Company. DuPont, he knew, had an incredible opportunity to realize a very high return on its investment, a return no other opportunity presented. And there were, as Raskob had also been preaching for some time, other distinct advantages for DuPont in taking a strong interest in GM.

On December 19, 1917, with Durant in New York but completely clued in to the plan, John Raskob finalized his written proposal for the consideration of the leaders of the DuPont Company. Pierre was completely on board and ready to throw his weight behind the plan but this was John's deal. Raskob wanted DuPont to invest $25 million in General Motors. It would be one of the biggest investments one corporation had ever made in another.

Raskob had, as always, nailed down the numbers and worked out a spectacularly clever financial strategy. To gain approval, he needed to march the plan through the DuPont administrative gauntlet. With Pierre and Irénée already committed, a schedule was set up for fast track approval. First, the finance committee would meet on the morning of December 20th, a Friday. The finance committee was comprised of John, Pierre, Irénée, and Henry du Pont. Only Henry needed to be brought on board. Immediately thereafter the finance committee would discuss the plan with the executive committee. Here, with men representing other corporate interests, a real debate was likely to ensue. Nonetheless, Pierre and John had scheduled a full board meeting for the very next morning, a Saturday. For the meetings, John had prepared a detailed report that provided the relevant financials, the structure of the deal, and the rationale. It was a tour de force and Raskob presented it confidently, with the full force of his enthusiasm. He was thirty-eight years old.

"During the past two years, our Company has been doing big things," he told his DuPont colleagues. "After the war it seems to me it will be absolutely impossible for us to drop back to being a little company again and to prevent that we must look for opportunities, know them when we see them and act with courage." The men listening to Raskob knew the underlying facts; in 1914 DuPont had employed around 5,300 people, by 1918, 85,000 worked for DuPont; assets had quadrupled; and profits were 700 percent higher than they had been right before the Great War had broken out.[21] But Raskob was speaking about more than facts when he asked the men to refuse to go back to "being a little company" and, instead, to "act with courage." Raskob was speaking from his own convictions. He was speaking from his own life experience. Corporate men do not often get the chance to take big chances; Raskob was offering his colleagues a free market adventure. "If our fundamentals are sound," he continued, "as they certainly seem to be in this case, the control of the General Motors will be a task worthy of the best there is in us and will I feel afford many opportunities to keep our important men occupied with big things after the war."[22]

Raskob carefully worked through the financial data. He reminded the men that even after investing $35 million internally in new product development and plant expansion and even after retaining $5 million for working capital, they still had $50 million in retained earnings. "It is imperative," he argued, "that this amount be employed, otherwise the earnings of our Company after the war will be insufficient to support our dividend policy and the matter of properly employing this money in a way that will result in proper return to our Company is one of most serious consequences."[23]

Durant's auto business, Raskob argued, was the exact best place to invest a substantial sum of that money. Shading nothing, he reported: "The growth of the motor business, particularly the General Motors Company, has been phenomenal as indicated by its net earnings and by the fact that the gross receipts of the General Motors-Chevrolet Motor Companes [sic] for the coming year will amount to between $350,000,000 and $400,000,000. The General Motors

Company today occupies a unique position in the automobile industry and in the opinion of the writer with proper management will show results in the future second to none in any American industry." Raskob's emphasis on the phrase "with proper management" and his explanation of what he meant by it was the only spot in his report where he allowed himself a degree of optimism not fully substantiated by the proven record: "Mr. Durant... is very desirous of having an organization as perfect as possible to handle this wonderful business." Durant, he continued, because of his experiences working with Pierre du Pont and the other DuPont Company men who had served on GM and Chevrolet boards of directors, has expressed a "desire on his part to have us more substantially interested with him, thus enabling us to assist him, particularly in an executive and financial way, in the direction of this huge business."[24] Raskob undoubtedly believed what he was saying and Durant had surely given him reason to think what he was saying was true. But by this time Raskob should have known Durant well enough to understand that Billy, once DuPont had invested the money, would give up his "one-man power" only grudgingly and would fight the DuPont attempts to rein him in every step of the way.

Raskob ended with a patriotic flurry. He told his colleagues that the auto industry was "the most promising industry in the United States" and that the United States "holds greater possibilities for development in the immediate future than any country in the world." DuPont would reap a fortune by investing its wartime profits in what Raskob was sure was going to be peacetime America's brightest industrial sector. Raskob was on the money; Jazz Age prosperity was around the corner and the automobile business would play the biggest single role in the economic boom that was coming.

Not everyone at DuPont bought into Raskob's prophecy or found his GM investment proposal compelling. The debate went on for two exhausting, intense days. The men successfully pushing DuPont into new product lines raised the strongest reservations. Raskob, they warned, was taking the company in the wrong direction. They wanted to know why the company should not instead continue to buy into areas in which they already had technical and operational expertise. The Company had already bought key manufacturers of heavy chemicals, enamels, lacquers, pyroxylin plastic, dyes, varnishes, and rubber-coated fabrics.[25] Chemicals, not cars, were DuPont's future, they argued. Others expressed doubts about the wisdom of expending so much money at a time when the Company might need that money to dramatically expand its powder works to meet its US government military contracts. These were serious and quite reasonable objections.

Raskob countered sharply and Pierre had his back. First, Raskob promoted synergy: "Our interest in General Motors will undoubtedly secure for us the entire Fabrikoid, Pyralin, pain and varnish business of these companies, which is a substantial factor."[26] Ignoring any possible antitrust difficulties with the federal government or the possibility of hard-nosed decision making by GM's operation men, Raskob had a point; if DuPont had a controlling interest in GM, the car company would be an almost sure buyer of some of DuPont's new products. Pierre followed up, making a related but different point. While DuPont worked through its diversification plans, GM would be more than a good market for its new products, it would supply the Company with big cash dividends during a period when the new product divisions might well need capital subsidies, even if only in the short to mid-term. This clever argument appeased most of the men involved in the diversification effort. Pierre also followed up on Raskob's argument that after the war was over DuPont might not have a place for some of its most talented managers. He believed that GM needed what DuPont had in abundance, financially astute executives who understood how to keep a multi-divisional, geographically dispersed company profitable. Once Pierre weighed in, vocally and firmly, serious debate ended. For nearly sixteen years, Pierre had been driving the Company forward; he had everyone's trust, faith, and confidence. He knew that and he knew that his open support of Raskob's big plan was all that was necessary to make it happen. So did John Raskob. The board approved and John got to work implementing the decision.[27]

After Christmas and the New Year, Raskob worked out the financial strategy that he had reported to his DuPont colleagues. He established and financed a new holding company, eventually called the Du Pont American Industries, to buy over $25 million in GM and Chevrolet stock. The DuPont Company owned the holding company. Only about $3 million in shares was bought directly and indirectly from Durant, allowing him to keep a huge interest in his companies. The rest was bought on the open market, which had the deliberate effect of stabilizing the market price well above $90, taking all the pressure off of Durant and his leveraged shareholding position. DuPont owned 23.83 percent of the soon to be unified GM-Chevrolet stock.

Once Raskob had worked out the deal, he asked Pierre to make the news public in a big way. John arranged for Pierre to announce the completed deal on February 21, 1918, at the Metropolitan Club in New York City. At a festive dinner attended by several of the biggest bankers in New York City and Philadelphia, Pierre du Pont, shy and uncomfortable as always in the limelight, outlined the DuPont Company's major investment in General Motors. DuPont would bring its proven record of financial expertise to the General Motors Corporation. A more powerful GM finance committee was to be formed, ruled by DuPont Company officials and headed by John J. Raskob. Durant followed du Pont at the lectern and in his trademark, low-key style outlined General Motors' accomplishments to date and all the great things the DuPont-GM relationship promised. The press had been invited and cheered on the new arrangement.

The business world took notice not just of the DuPont-GM arrangement but of the role John Raskob had played in it.

John had pulled off the biggest deal of his life. Pierre now looked to him to safeguard their $25 million investment in General Motors. Pierre hoped he could step away from corporate life. At DuPont he was, in stages, turning executive power over to his trusted and talented younger brother Irénée. While he intended to stay on as chairman of the board at GM and at DuPont, Pierre was looking forward to spending more of his days at Longwood building greenhouses, designing gardens, and devising fountains and waterworks of all kinds. It seemed like there was to be a passing of the guard. John still had much to do at DuPont, but his focus would now be on managing the finances of General Motors. He expected to be working not for Pierre but alongside the irrepressible Billy Durant. John Raskob was moving up, his sights set on General Motors' corporate offices in New York City and its main operations in Flint and Detroit. His time at home with his wife and children at Archmere would become rare. His personal life, as well as his public profile, would never again be the same. Little would turn out as it appeared it would in the early months of 1918, but John Raskob, nonetheless, was soon to become a famous man in Jazz Age America.

9

Man of Influence

By the end of the Great War, Raskob's holdings in General Motors and DuPont were worth millions. The DuPont-GM deal he had engineered had made him a celebrated star in the business world. Raskob was, increasingly, a man of influence. He had, for the first time, the corporate power to reach beyond the financial deal making that had made his name. Between 1918 and 1920, Raskob would change how the auto industry did business. Raskob would make history, giving shape to the consumer culture that was transforming American life in the first decades of the twentieth century. The short time between the end of World War I and the advent of the Jazz Age were for John dangerous, exhilarating, defining years.

John had always been smart, at least in certain ways. His talent with numbers seemed to be innate. His maternal grandfather had been a bookkeeper and his cigar-making father and grandfather had both been at home with numbers. His sister Gertrude had trained to be a bookkeeper, too, and though she had worked only briefly before her marriage her talent showed though in her sharp card playing. Younger brother William had followed his brother to DuPont, where John made sure he had a good position, but William's own high-level accounting skills had made him a trusted senior executive in the treasurer's office. The Raskobs had a gift for numbers. But John was more than mathematically nimble. He had ambition and fierce drive, and he thrived on risks and challenges. And as Pierre du Pont had noticed almost immediately on meeting Raskob, John fortified his talent with an extraordinary confidence that grew with his every success. After the GM deal went public at the end of 1917, men of influence and power took notice of Raskob's role and word of his talent and character spread; people wanted him in on their action. Raskob, his mind whirling, stepped lively, jumping at the opportunity to do more and more.

John had not been unrecognized before the deal was done; Pierre and his younger brothers had long treated him as an equal, Wilmington's civic elite counted on him, and Wall Street bankers knew him as a man to be reckoned with. But after the GM deal people saw him as a powerful player in the nation's life, as one of those men in the United States who could make things happen on the biggest stages.

John got a sense for his new status soon after the GM-DuPont deal had been struck. As part of the agreement that Raskob had engineered with Durant, Raskob took over the seemingly buffed-up GM finance committee. The appointment had been made public with some fanfare, as was Raskob's next big announcement. In March 1918, Raskob made clear to his peers in the business world that he was serious about his new responsibilities at GM. He resigned his hard-earned, long-in-the-making position as treasurer of the DuPont Company. Raskob was far from done with DuPont; the day he resigned his executive post he was named a company vice president and he retained his board membership. But Raskob sharply curtailed his day-to-day responsibilities at DuPont so that he could focus on GM, and he made sure that his colleagues in the banking and corporate world understood his new commitment.

Soon after his public change in corporate allegiance, Raskob took the train to New York to meet with Billy Durant and Sam McLaughlin, who ran an independent auto company that manufactured GM brand autos in Canada in collaboration with the General Motors Company. With GM's latest financial imbroglio settled thanks to the DuPont investment, Billy was hyped on the idea of buying up the McLaughlin Motor Car Company, which had been under contract to make Buicks in Canada since 1909 and Chevrolets beginning in 1915. John traveled with Pierre to New York for the meeting but as would be true for the next couple of years, at GM Pierre took a back seat to John.

McLaughlin was one of Canada's leading manufacturers. The company had been founded in 1867 as a carriage maker by Robert McLaughlin, Sam's father, and had grown rapidly until it was the largest carriage maker in the British Empire. Sam McLaughlin, born in 1872, got bit hard in the early twentieth century by the auto bug. McLaughlin, like so many others who had scrambled to enter the auto business, had had a miserable time manufacturing an automobile from scratch. His cars just did not run right. McLaughlin knew Durant from the carriage business and asked for his help. They worked out an arrangement whereby the McLaughlin Motor Works imported GM-built auto engines and other key components and then assembled vehicles in Canada for the Canadian auto market using car bodies his company designed and built. The Buicks manufactured in Canada took advantage of McLaughlin's well-earned reputation as a quality carriage producer and were sold under the nameplate of McLaughlin-Buick. Their Buicks were quite stylish cars, proof of which was visited upon GM's executives shortly before the buy-out meeting in mid-1918.

At the request of GM's ever attentive vice president for parts and accessories Alfred Sloan, McLaughlin shipped a McLaughlin-Buick to GM's New York

City office so that some of the GM executives could get a sense for what the Canadian manufacturer brought to the table. The delivery man, unable to locate a loading dock, parked the Canadian-made Buick on the street right in front of GM's headquarters. Indicative of the excitement that surrounded automobiles in 1918, a crowd of usually jaded New Yorkers flocked to study the novel-looking, well-appointed Buick. Several floors above, Sloan, who missed little, got wind of the uproar and yelled at one of his subordinates: "Get that thing out of here and quick. It's gathering crowds and no more like one of our Buicks than a St. Bernard is like a dachshund."[1] McLaughlin was a gifted car man and a brilliant character all around.[2] Durant very much wanted to work out a deal to bring not just McLaughlin Motors but also Sam McLaughlin into the GM-fold.

Durant was no slouch at engineering such simultaneous company buy-outs and executive buyins. He had done it many times, though he had often enough ended up driving away the men he had brought aboard, such as Louis Chevrolet and Henry Leland. McLaughlin had known Billy for years, well enough to respect his gifts but also to worry about his untamed exuberance. In New York for the meeting, McLaughlin saw that Durant was now carrying some useful ballast. Maybe Billy was no longer flying so close to the sun. He had never met John Raskob but he knew his name and he knew what he did. McLaughlin was in New York because he wanted to sell out to GM, but he wanted to do so with some certainty of GM's future stability. He needed to sell because his lease arrangement to manufacture Buicks and Chevrolets in Canada was always at risk; GM could end the arrangement at any time if a more economical opportunity came along, leaving McLaughlin with nothing but the capacity to make auto bodies nobody wanted. But McLaughlin also knew that GM had regularly faced financial debacles. Raskob's presence at the table gave him hope that GM would, thereafter, be on a more steady financial footing. By mid-1918, John Raskob was a known quantity. McLaughlin trusted Raskob and he made the deal, selling his company and also becoming a member of GM's executive team.

Raskob meant to do a good deal more at General Motors than simply transfer his reputation for financial deal making and money management skills from one company to another. He had a big idea that he believed could change how cars were sold in the United States and so help bring about Billy Durant's vision of mass auto ownership in the United States. Raskob wanted to bring the kind of financial leverage he had exercised on behalf of the DuPont Company and his own investments to middle-class American consumers. Raskob wanted GM to finance its own sales. GM could make cars far more affordable not by wringing out every excess production cost or narrowing its own profit margins but by bringing installment buying to the car business.

Overwhelmingly, in 1918 new cars were sold on a cash basis. And new autos were expensive. Henry Ford was doing everything he could to make his Model T affordable but even with Ford's relentless efforts to reduce the cost of his assembly-line produced, stripped down Model T, his cars demanded a level of savings relatively few American families could afford. A well paid white-collar worker would have to come up with savings equal to about three months of his salary to buy the Model T, the cheapest new car on the market. A typical working man would be lucky if half a year's salary would put him in the driver's seat of a Ford Model T. Few could do so. And GM cars cost more than Ford's. Even GM's lowest priced car, the Chevrolet, could not compete on price. Most of GM's cars, especially Buicks and Cadillacs, cost a lot more. Too few people could save enough money to buy new cars, especially a GM auto, to create the millions of sales that Billy Durant and John Raskob envisioned.

Raskob saw the obvious answer: "other people's money." Car sales should become a credit business. Raskob also believed that GM could use the same financial arm to provide its auto dealers with credit so that the dealers could expand and stabilize their inventory. More cars on the dealers' lots and in their showrooms, even during slow buying seasons, meant more sales and more cash flow for GM. In early 1918 Raskob proposed to the GM board that a committee be formed "to study the whole subject of the installment selling of automobiles."[3]

Raskob believed that his bid to put GM into the auto installment business had to be rolled out carefully and convincingly. In part, he had to get his fellow executives on board but more importantly he had to convince Wall Street bankers that the new business was credible. Raskob had to assure his cautious friends at Morgan, in particular, to support GM in the credit market when it pursued the large sums it would need to establish its own credit arm. After the 1917 troubles, few big-time bankers were excited about providing Billy Durant with a big cash infusion that would be used on what appeared to be an untested proposition.

Raskob did not see the auto installment selling business as inherently risky. Installment buying had been around for a long time in the United States. In the mid-nineteenth century, the farm machine business could not have boomed without some form of consumer credit and an installment buying plan. Cyrus McCormick understood that American farmers, most of whom were happy to earn $300 a year, almost all of it at harvest time, would never be able to buy his $100 to $160 mechanical reapers unless he came up with a payment schedule they could afford. Once they did, his business took off—even though a sizable number of farmers defaulted on their installment contracts. McCormick quickly discovered that people would pay a good deal more for his products if they could pay for them over time; to shore up his own capital position he offered big price cuts to cash purchasers but about two-thirds of his customers preferred or more likely could only afford to buy on time. Done with at least some care, installment sales were highly profitable.[4]

If McCormick proved that relatively small producers would embrace debt in order to finance improved productivity and income, Edward Clark and I. M. Singer of the Singer Manufacturing Company figured out how to use installment buying to sell the first widely adopted household appliance. By the late nineteenth century, Singer was by far the market leader, offering its sewing machines with a simple and effective sales pitch: "dollar down, dollar a week."[5] By the early twentieth century, installment buying was taking off in the United States. Department stores sold clothes and furniture on the installment plan; piano makers rapidly expanded their businesses with a variety of payment schedules; and, as Raskob knew well, middle-class homes featured elegant sets of leather-bound volumes paid off in monthly installments.

This credit boom and installment buying were made possible by the steadily improving wages Americans were earning. By 1920, Americans had the highest wage scale in the world and the average American worker had double the purchasing power of his counterpart in 1860. American workers and their families were becoming consumers. In 1918, when Raskob asked GM to investigate the installment selling of automobiles, he knew that American wage earners still had limited savings—indeed most Americans had no or almost no savings at all—but most did have an ever-increasing amount of disposable income. Millions of Americans could afford a car if they did not have to come up with a large up-front payment for it but could instead pay off most of the price over time. The math backed up Raskob's insight.

Raskob, of course, had direct experience in the installment sales business. In 1906, he and Lammot du Pont had gotten in on the ground floor of the installment book buying business when they invested in the Southern Trust Company. The Southern Trust Company provided working capital for book publishers who sold their wares to the reading public on the installment plan. Based on that business Raskob knew that financing consumer purchases could be risky; people reneged on their obligations and even with the law on their side, sellers often had a hard time recovering their property or what was left of it. Installment sales carried risks but the rewards, Raskob believed, could be well worth it.

Raskob also knew that other businessmen, including some in the auto industry, had begun to make their own forays into auto financing. In 1912, a few Chicago auto dealers had begun to offer to finance new car purchases, advertising "easy payments." A handful of West Coast dealers did the same. But these dealer-supplied credit plans were severely limited by the dealers' own credit problems; they were constantly scrounging for cash to pay off the manufacturers so that they could put enough makes and models in their showrooms and lots to offer car buyers an enticing array of choices. Dealers just did not have a rich enough cash flow to support their own finance schemes. But a sharp-eyed, San Francisco based entrepreneur named L. F. Weaver noticed the demand and in 1913 he started the first auto finance company. Weaver extended credit both to consumers and to dealerships. He was a good businessman, but his operations were local, and relatively speaking, small-time. Two years later, on November 1, 1915, a much bigger operation started up in Toledo, Ohio. The Guaranty Securities Company teamed up with the Willys-Overland Company to finance the popular Overland auto, which competed directly with Chevrolet. Guaranty's owners realized that the auto finance business was a potential bonanza and in 1916 they split off from Willys-Overland and moved to New York where they began an aggressive campaign to raise capital.[6] Raskob, keyed into the capital markets, must have gotten wind of their plans. By the end of 1917 they were making a serious go of it. Guaranty was financing both individual car buyers and car dealers. All told, including their huge involvement in financing dealers' stock, Guaranty held notes on more than 50,000 cars. Guaranty's loans were short term; they had to be paid off in eight monthly installments.[7]

Intriguingly, GM's increasingly ubiquitous executive Alfred P. Sloan was a director of the Guaranty outfit. Before Sloan had sold his ball bearing company to Durant and joined him in managing the GM empire in the spring of 1916, Sloan had made roller bearings for the Willys-Overland and was on good terms with company president and founder John N. Willys. When Guaranty was just getting off the ground in late 1915, Willys had recommended Sloan to the Toledo businessmen that began the operation. Despite his close involvement with Guaranty, Sloan did not promote installment buying at GM. Sloan had an extraordinary business mind and saw profitable opportunities quicker than almost anyone else. But in this case he did not make the connection between what Guaranty was just beginning to do and what General Motors might do in a much bigger and better way. Years later, in a rare moment of candor, he admitted that he perhaps should have made such a connection and promoted the idea, but in 1916 and 1917 he was fixed on the management problems before him, running GM's loosely organized parts and accessory division and trying to understand his boss's sometimes impulsive decision-making process. He was not yet thinking much at all about how to sell cars and work with GM's growing network of auto dealers. He would be soon, though, just in time for him to team up with Raskob.[8]

Raskob did see the opportunity that Guaranty and a few other smaller outfits had begun to exploit. What he did not know was that executives at Ford, the industry leader, had seen the same opening but had passed on it. In 1916, around the same time that Sloan became Durant's much junior partner, Henry Ford's son, Edsel, had hired a consultant to look into Guaranty's business and explore its implications for his father's company. The consultant, an economist named

Edward Rumely, concluded: "The automobile industry will pass from a cash basis to a time basis."[9] In his carefully argued report he made a strong case. Edsel Ford believed him and tried to convince his father that they needed to establish some kind of credit arm.

Henry Ford, as usual, rejected his son's advice. In this case, he dismissed Edsel based on what he considered moral grounds. Ford hated bankers. The major reason Ford became an infamous anti-Semite was because he believed that Jews controlled the banking and loan-making industry that he despised. Ford also hated debtors. He did not want to become the former nor create a new class of the latter. While Ford was not one to quote Shakespeare, he believed in the maxim given voice by *Hamlet's* Polonius, "Neither a borrower nor a lender be." Ford concentrated on making his Model T as inexpensive as he could so that people who avoided frivolous purchases could buy one. A cheap, reliable, easily-repaired, unadorned vehicle, he believed, was the answer to the American people's transportation needs. Ford believed in thrift not credit. The stubborn carmaker had a different vision of what a mass consumer capitalist marketplace could and should look like. It was not the vision that would prevail.

Raskob was no lone genius who dreamed up the auto finance business out of whole cloth. He patched his idea together from existing bits and pieces, some of them, such as the Guaranty Securities model, fairly well-formed pieces. But Raskob, unlike Henry Ford or even the excessively perspicacious Alfred Sloan, not only knew about the installment sales business and the forays others were making specifically into auto installment sales but he also believed in it and had the status and will to make it happen at General Motors and on Wall Street. He drove his auto company into this new, still uncertain, still relatively untested business with complete faith. Raskob just knew the business would be a gold mine. His confidence was well placed.

Raskob worked with a team of men to study installment buying and figure out how to make it work best for General Motors. They worked the numbers and studied how other finance companies, especially Guaranty Securities, structured the business and safeguarded their loans. Guaranty kept the ownership paper on the cars they financed and insured them both against loss and default. The insurance was mandatory and both individual consumers and auto dealers had to buy the policy from them, up front. The insurance added a chunk to the buyers' cost and profits to Guaranty's business. Still, the insurance backstop against defaults was a tricky and risky business. At a time when no national credit rating agency existed, one of the biggest questions was how to determine who was eligible for credit and how much to charge people for the privilege of receiving it. Along the same lines, Raskob and the rest of the men had to figure out what to do about buyers who defaulted on their loans. Guaranty, a public corporation by this time, did report on their defaults and in all of 1917, at least, it was spectacularly low. They claimed that they had made over 50,000 loans and had been forced to repossess only 45 cars.[10]

Raskob found an early supporter of his financing scheme in Alfred Sloan. When Raskob first pitched the installment sales idea, Sloan knew that Guaranty Securities had been making good money financing auto sales almost from the start. There was no good reason for GM not to do the same. And Sloan, already by this time, liked and trusted Raskob.

Sloan reacted to the increasing presence and influence of Raskob, as well as Pierre du Pont, the same way the Canadian manufacturer Sam McLaughlin had. He was thrilled to have somebody on board who might be able to restrain Durant and possibly redirect the company into new profitable areas. Sloan was throwing himself into his GM work, but he was a nervous executive. By virtue of his 1916 buyout deal with Durant, more than half his wealth was tied up in Durant's various stock schemes. By 1918, Sloan was not at all sure that he had made a good decision.

Sloan commiserated regularly with Walter Chrysler, who made millions for Durant running Buick but who often found himself cooling his heels outside Durant's office for hours at a time while Billy used his row of desk-top telephones to play the stock markets or to reach out to the hundreds of men who thought of him as a trusted friend and investment advisor. Chrysler, whose own deal with Durant in June 1916 to run Buick included a hefty amount of GM stock, had watched Durant nearly go under in November 1917. He later wrote: "His door was standing open, which was extraordinary in itself; Billy was standing there, staring at the wall as if in a daze. He seemed completely unaware of me and just stood there staring blankly, as rigid as if he had been turned to ice."[11] It was a not a confidence-building picture of his boss.

Sloan, like Chrysler, welcomed the DuPont intervention into GM's nerve-wracking affairs. He wasted no time reaching out to Raskob. By late February 1918, the two men were good friends. With their wives they took a two-week trip together to Raskob's new haunt, Palm Beach. The occasion was social, but for both Sloan and Raskob the trip was also supposed to cement their business alliance at General Motors. Both men were, relatively speaking, outsiders at GM. Long-time Durant loyalists made life complicated, or worse, for the talented by-the-numbers businessmen that Billy had been bringing into GM to keep the ever-expanding combine running profitably. Billy was not always so hot on the new men himself. In 1918, General Motors was factionalized and Durant often used the lack of trust between the men who had been with him for years and the men whom he had brought into the company in 1916 and 1917, often only because he had no other choice, to his own purposes.

As a result of the divisions within General Motors in 1918, Raskob had no idea how much backing his planned installment sales and credit arm plan would have. He knew that he had the support of the chairman of the board, but Pierre was, at this point, a hands-off, distant presence at GM. Sloan's enthusiastic and well-informed support was, then, much appreciated and valued. Working with fellow DuPont-turned-GM man, Armory Haskell, as well as other financial men he brought to GM, Raskob oversaw a careful analysis of the installment business.

Raskob and his team engineered one major change from the Guaranty model. Rather than have GM keep the title, or in some other manner be financially responsible for cars purchased through the installment plan, Raskob's team decided that GM dealers would have to endorse every consumer loan on the cars they sold. In other words, GM's auto dealers, not GM's credit arm, would be on the hook if an installment buyer stopped paying off his auto loan. Such an arrangement was called "recourse liability" in the credit business. That such an arrangement was sure to create tensions between GM and its dealers was not something Raskob worried about. Nor did he worry, at that point, about how GM would make sure that its dealers did not seek out other credit providers who might offer them less risky, "non-recourse" deals, even if such loans would mean higher interest charges for consumers. Quickly enough, these points of contention would sharpen. Raskob probably anticipated such problems—little about credit markets escaped him—but he chose not to discuss such eventualities in launching the plan. He wanted to move the idea forward, not raise barriers; others could work out the details.[12]

The General Motors Acceptance Corporation launched January 24, 1919, with strong support from the DuPont imports to GM but with just over $2 million in capital, a relatively paltry sum given the number of GM's sales. Despite its humble launch, the new business was novel enough to warrant a top-of-the-fold story on the Sunday business section of the *New York Times*.[13] Exercising caution, Raskob and his team spun this first newspaper story on GMAC so as to assuage Wall Street concerns. Neither GM's share price nor its creditworthiness were affected. The article stated only that GMAC would "assist dealers in automobiles and trucks in financing their products."[14] No mention was made of the seemingly more noteworthy—and risky—business of lending directly to consumers.

Raskob kept his fundamental role in GMAC out of the news though all of GM's top men knew that it was his baby. Amory Haskell was made president, and a former vice president of the Guaranty auto financing companies was brought on to manage operations. Raskob decided only to be named to the GMAC board. He did his best not to take a hands-on approach to GMAC, leaving day-to-day management to others, but he championed GMAC in GM's ceaseless internal wars, fighting to ensure that his creation received the capital and people it needed to grow and prosper. GMAC opened its first office in New York City with fifteen employees and by March was providing credit to dealers and individual consumers with branch offices in San Francisco, Chicago, Toronto, and Detroit. Despite the January 1919 news story that GMAC would lend money only to GM dealers, in its very first year a good deal more than half of GMAC's credit was issued to consumers.[15] According to an auto salesmen involved that first year in installment selling: "We gave everyone and anyone credit, feeling that we could always repossess the car if worst came to worst."[16]

Raskob made the rounds ensuring that GMAC's managers knew they had a champion. At the car dealerships, the salesmen were thrilled. One of the first to hear about the innovation remembered: "We were utterly amazed at the daring of the corporation to extend credit to both its dealers and its customers on the sale of such an expensive article as an automobile."[17]

At the end of 1919, Haskell and Raskob hosted a party in New York for all of GMAC's managers, many of whom were younger men fresh out of military service and hungry for success. Raskob, uncharacteristically, gave an emotional, impromptu, and highly charged speech. He told the men that they were at the forefront of a major change in American life and that within a year GM was going to need to increase GMAC's capital position tenfold to meet demand. Credit, he said, was the lifeblood of the new American economy.

On GMAC's 30th anniversary, Alfred Sloan, who had attended that first big GMAC meeting, celebrated Raskob's galvanizing speech. He reminded GMAC's employees that in 1919 few Americans, let alone industrial leaders, anticipated a time when "consumer durable goods" would be seen as a major part of the American economy, let alone be considered "a necessity of the American way of living." He continued: "Such thinking was advanced only by the most imaginative. It was decried by those who considered themselves more realistic." Many, and here Sloan got in a dig at Henry Ford, said that consumer credit "constituted a danger of the first magnitude calculated not only to undermine the business prosperity, but the morale of the American people as well." Echoing Raskob, Sloan concluded, "Yet, everyone had the ambition and perhaps, from the American point of view, the right to own such things."[18]

In April 1920, just a little over a year after GMAC had launched, Raskob and his team released a massive study, based on survey data, of their consumer loan business through September 1919. The survey findings were publicized, as was the intent, by major newspapers around the country. The survey was directly aimed at showing bankers that GMAC's consumer customers were creditworthy and that the new business was, therefore, sound and creditworthy, too. The publicity surrounding the survey was also, more subtly, directed at potential borrowers, letting them know that going into debt to buy a car put a person in the company not of life's losers but of society's more successful citizens.

The lead in the *Washington Post* read: "Of more than passing interest to bankers and others are figures recently compiled by the General Motors Acceptance

Corporation as to the financial responsibility and resources of purchasers of automobiles on the deferred payment plan."[19] The report highlighted that a sizable number of GMAC's customers were bankers, lawyers, dentists, and other professionals. Farmers, businessmen, and many others representing a broad swath of the middle class availed themselves, too, of GMAC's services. The subtitle of the *Post* piece read: "Average Purchaser has Monthly Income of $275 and owns $6000 Real Estate."[20] Economically secure, middle- and upper-middle-class Americans, GM could demonstrate, had embraced the auto installment buying plan.

Exceeding even Raskob's early expectations, by the end of 1920 GMAC loaned out more eighty million dollars in the United States, with $46,693,170 going to individual consumers. By April 1922, GMAC had financed 146,937 sales to consumers.[21] GMAC was from the very beginning a massive success and, as it grew, John Raskob emerged as the well-publicized and celebrated champion of consumer credit. The men who took on the management of GMAC were not faint in their praise for their founder: "GMAC was conceived, as we say, in the practical imagination of John J. Raskob. There may have been other people who had some such idea in mind, but whatever such claims might be, it was Mr. Raskob who beat them to the goal, and no one could take that distinction from him."[22]

Throughout 1918 and 1919, most people within Raskob's business orbit believed that John was marching from success to success. He certainly appeared to be maintaining a fierce and undivided focus on the GMAC launch and on untangling GM's financial knots. Only a few people knew that his family, like so many other families around the world, was being decimated by the great influenza epidemic of 1918 and 1919. Most people did not know because John showed little, if any, sign of being affected by the tragedies that surrounded him.

Little remembered today, the "Spanish flu" pandemic killed some thirty million people around the world. Some 650,000 people in the United States died from the virus. The flu first struck in March 1918, disappeared, and then returned in a far more deadly strain in August. By November millions around the world were dead. All over the United States people were infected, an estimated 25 percent of the population. The deadliest wave of infection in the United States struck in late October and lasted through November. The pandemic did not stop killing Americans until the spring of 1919.

When the virus was at its most rampant, the Raskob's infant daughter Catherine Lorena became ill. So did Helena. In nearby Wilmington, at almost the exact same time, John's brother-in-law, William Dole, who was married to his sister Edith, was infected. Will, who had long worked as one of John's assistants in the DuPont treasury office, was the first to die. Just days after Will's death,

Edith gave birth to a daughter. A week later, the newborn baby died of the flu. The very next day, Catherine Lorena died. Helena survived. John and the other children were uninfected.

John reacted to the deaths in his family much as he had when his father had died. He pushed on. He went to work. He carried on almost as if he were untouched.

On November 21, 1918, he wrote one of his closest Lockport friends, Bob Moore, with the news. But first he replied to the letter that Bob had written him a few days earlier celebrating the end of the Great War. Bob already knew about Will Dole's death but had heard nothing about the other deaths in the Raskob family. Moore had concluded his handwritten note to John by expressing his condolences over Will's death: "We hope that the smiling face of his little one will cheer the mother and lighten the burden."[23]

The first sentence of Raskob's reply reads: "I was glad to receive your letter of the 18th and I too say 'Hurrah.' It is certainly good to have the war over and particularly to have won such a complete victory." Then Raskob joked that Bob, being such a "rock ribbed Republican," was probably disappointed that the war was won "under a Democratic administration." Only after a few more sentences of good-humored badinage did Raskob write: "Helena has quite recovered from the 'Flu,' but is still a little weak. We lost our baby, Catherine Lorena, six months old. She died a week ago today. She had been sick for some time, but was so far recovered that we had really ceased to worry about her, however, such is life and I am sure that we are very thankful that we have nine others left." Then he told Bob his other news: "It certainly is too bad about Edith's loss. She had a baby born a week after Will's death but the baby died a week ago yesterday. She is very very brave however and is getting along splendidly." Only the double "very" communicates that John feels something about what had happened to his family.

Then John wrote another paragraph asking after Bob and his farm. As was his practice when writing his Lockport friends, he offered his usual somewhat patronizing if well intentioned observations about the life course Bob had chosen by default: "I often wonder whether it would not be well to give up the farming business and go into some other business, but, of course, it is hard to tell for I know nothing of farming, except, that it has always seemed to require a tremendous lot of very hard work with not very good results." This last paragraph of the letter is written as if the one before it carried no emotional weight or news of grave significance.[24]

One possible explanation for Raskob's stoic response to the death of his infant daughter, newborn niece, and brother-in-law appears in the oft-repeated sentiments John wrote in reply to the condolences he received from his friends over his daughter's death. To his old supervisor Sterling Bunnell, he wrote, "Crosses of this kind, I believe, make one appreciate how much real love there is in the world as it takes expression in the very pleasant messages received."[25] On December 7, a little over three weeks after his niece and daughter had died, he wrote a reply to the message of condolence sent by his Lockport friend Tom Spalding, who was a doctor. Again Raskob began in good humor: "I was glad to receive your letter of the 3rd and to know that you are still alive and kicking. The physicians all over this country certainly have had a hard time of it during the past two months and I am glad to know you survived so well." Then John replied directly to his old friend's emotional expression of sorrow over John's loss: "It is indeed hard to lose a child, but when I stop to think of Edith's trouble it seems as though I have no good cause for complaint." He assured Spalding: "We all are well down here now and things look much brighter. It is a grand relief to have the war over and people seem to have relaxed a very great deal indeed."[26]

As John's pointed reference to the end of the war indicates, he was very aware that his personal tragedy was occurring at a time when millions of families were also mourning their dead, whether killed in battle or by the pandemic. In reply to Walter Chrysler's condolences, he said as much: "I appreciate very much indeed your kind thought of me as expressed in your letter of the 18th. It is indeed hard to lose one's child, but when we look about and see the suffering of others it really makes us ashamed to complain too much."[27] Raskob was also responding to the loss of his daughter and niece just a few years after a time when nearly one in ten infants in the United States did not live to celebrate their first birthday. Still, Raskob's resolve and ability to place baby Catherine's death in contexts that made his loss less emotionally powerful and immediate was characteristic.

At the same time, John was not unmoved by what was happening to his family, friends, and community. He immediately began to look after them in the ways he was best able. In action, Raskob felt most himself.

John instantly took charge of Edith's financial situation and was able to explain to her that economically she was going to be fine. John had long before begun to manage her finances and he reported to her that she had assets of $497,689.38, most of it in Chevrolet stock that John had arranged for her. He would continue to manage her resources and he assured her that she would have a very comfortable income. She need never worry about her economic situation.

John also reached out, without delay, to the family of his old Lockport friend Rob Allen, another of the pandemic's victims. Rob was one of Raskob's oldest friends, but they had seen little of each other for several years. Rob was among the last to sicken and die from the flu epidemic, catching a deadly form of the mutating virus in late January 1919. He had been in touch with John just a few months earlier, asking for financial help, as he had done several times in the past. John had tried to lure Rob to Lorrain way back in 1901 and had offered him advice and financial aid to leave Lockport, Rob had stayed and married his hometown sweetheart. Although he had eventually resettled in

Ohio, he had scraped by financially ever since. At his death, his family was in rough economic shape.

John, unasked, stepped in and within days of Rob's death had set up a trust to support Margaret Allen and her children. He placed 100 shares of his GM holdings in the trust, which generated, in 1919, $1,200 in dividends, which was only about $200 less than the average annual family expenditure in the United States. Over the years John kept all stock splits and other accruals in the trust so that it would generate additional income. In 1922, when GM paid no dividends, John provided the Allens with their accustomed and needed income out of his own pocket. He wrote Margaret soon after: "I often think of Robert and wonder why the Lord in all his wisdom finds it necessary or desirable to take such splendid men from among us. Were he alive he would have so much to be proud of in your accomplishments and in what all his children have made of themselves under your splendid direction."[28]

In typical Raskob fashion, John kept watch over the Allens' little trust for years, tweaking it or reinvesting when he thought it was necessary to keep up their income. When Margaret Allen's youngest child turned 21 in 1937, John terminated the trust, advising Margaret of his decision well in advance and informing her and her three children that they now should be in a position to look after themselves. A few years earlier, Rob Allen, Jr., right after graduating from Ohio State University with additional support from Raskob, wrote John: "I cannot refrain from thinking about how wonderful the friendship must have been that existed between you and my father. A friendship that even death could not part! Today the children of Robert Allen live in respect and admiration for John Raskob, whose humanness has proved the existence of God in this great world of ours."[29] Allen had been John's friend but not by any means his closest or dearest, and the two men had seen little of each other for years. John always took extraordinary pleasure in aiding his old Lockport friends and he showed them an emotional side that few other human relationships touched.

John did, of course, have one great friend who was not from Lockport: Pierre du Pont. John remained exceptionally close to Pierre during these years. Still, despite that closeness, Pierre seems not to have consoled John or Helena in the days and weeks after Catherine's death, nor did John reach out to Pierre. The friendship that John and Pierre had built over the last eighteen years seemed to have had no room for the kind of tragedy both men were enduring in the season of the great flu pandemic.

Pierre's household, too, had been visited by the deadly virus. At almost the exact same time that John's daughter had died, Pierre's special friend, Lewes A. Mason, fell to the flu at just twenty-two years old. He had been with Pierre for some five years. Like Catherine Raskob, Lewes had seemed to be recovering from the virus, but this was one of the cruelest aspects of the 1918 flu strain.

A flu victim typically first suffered from a high fever reaching 104 degrees, body aches, sore throat, and severe headache, as well as vomiting and diarrhea. Then the fever dropped and the patient felt much better. But then, often but not always, the patient relapsed as the virus mutated; the fever returned with a vengeance. For many, that is when the disease turned deadly, causing massive pulmonary hemorrhages. Pierre had employed doctors from the nearby Chester County Hospital to watch over Lewes at the Longwood residence. But there really was nothing doctors could do about the progression of the illness except try to make the patient more comfortable.

Pierre suffered but with Alice at his side he, too, acted characteristically. To show his appreciation for the kind yet ineffective efforts of the doctors of Chester County Hospital, Pierre du Pont gave a donation of $1,000,000, a monumental gift in those days, to the hospital in Lewes A. Mason's memory.[30] It is possible that Pierre and John talked by telephone during these hard times, but no correspondence, at least, exists between them about the people they loved, in their own ways, who died during the great pandemic.

The speed with which John and, it seems, Helena moved on after the deaths in their family was somewhat remarkable. About a month after Catherine's death, John's Lockport friend Will Bewley wrote a kind-hearted Christmas note in which he mentioned, in an awkward but well intended aside, that he and his wife Lena were, as John knew, childless and how much he wished he could have had children. John replied, "It is indeed too bad that you do not have children of your own for they do so much to making life happier and are worthwhile; perhaps I had better loan you some. You and Lena can talk to Helena about this when you come down [for a visit in January]."[31]

By mid-December, John was already busy making plans for a blowout New Year's party at the Ritz-Carlton in New York City with GM General Counsel Standish Backus, Alfred Sloan, Walter Chrysler, and their wives. Sloan, who was an unlikely social director but who was also the only native New Yorker, was put in charge: "Our table will be in the main dining room as after careful inquiry I understand that this is really the best place. Mrs. Sloan and I will be there at 11 o'clock and ready to receive whenever you arrive." Sloan also arranged to loan the Raskobs his own car and driver, since "it is almost impossible to get a taxicab accommodation New Year's Eve." John was thrilled and, as was characteristic, responded in high good humor, telling Sloan that he and Helena were going to stay at the Biltmore and see the hit show "Sometimes" at the Casino Theatre on 39th Street before making their way to the Ritz "where you will have the pleasure of laughing at two country boobs (Mrs. Raskob and me) enjoying their first New Year's eve in New York."[32] The night cemented friendships that became an important part of John's life for the next several years. Walter Chrysler summed up the happy occasion, writing John a couple of days later, "I laughed so much

New Year's Eve in New York I was entirely laughed out."[33] Within a few short weeks, Raskob had put his family deaths behind him.

At the advent of 1919, John was chairman of the General Motors finance committee and a vice president of both DuPont and GM. He was not lacking for corporate work. At the same time, he continued to become much more involved in public policy issues and civic activism in Delaware. He spent a considerable amount of time hectoring Pierre, whose company duties had lessened considerably with the promotion of his brother Irénée to the DuPont presidency in early 1919, to do the same. John had already begun his latest public service push in early 1917 when he launched a major campaign to lobby the Delaware legislature to fund a State Highway Department. He knew first-hand, as an auto enthusiast, how bad the roads were in Delaware, and as an industrialist he knew, too, that bad roads cost the state's business community money and opportunities. Raskob gathered together fifteen business leaders in Delaware to give the campaign broader legitimacy, but he put up all the money, $5,000, needed to move forward. Most of the money was spent on lawyers and other experts Raskob hired to write a report and a model bill, which his group then presented to key legislators. As was usual, John then talked Pierre into giving a sizable contribution to the cause.[34] By mid-1918, as vice president and workhorse of the Delaware State Council of Defense, Raskob was in full stride, remedying a number of deficiencies he had identified in Delaware.

Raskob had taken his work at the State Council as seriously as he did most all of his duties. Analyzing Delaware's war-readiness capacities, he had discovered that compared to most states in the region, Delaware was in poor shape; its infrastructure and its educational capacities, in particular, were terrible and put Delaware at a severe economic disadvantage for the postwar world. On the education front, Delaware teachers were paid abysmally, which perhaps accounted for the fact that less than half of the elementary school teachers had even finished high school. Black teachers in Delaware's Jim Crow schools, which were racially segregated by state law, fared far worse. They worked in ramshackle buildings, many of which operated on a budget of less than a dollar a day, affording the great majority of black students, despite their teacher's best efforts, little opportunity to learn much of anything. Schools were poorly run, the school curriculum in most districts was backwards looking, and too many school districts in the rural parts of the state seemed to take an almost perverse pride in ill-preparing young people for the modern world they must soon join. John was appalled and insisted that something had to be done.

Knowing full well that his new commitment to General Motors was going to take him out of Delaware for extended periods of time and was not going to leave him the time to throw himself at the state's problem, John began another one of his pressure campaigns to convince Pierre to step into the breach. John had a specific plan in mind. He wanted Pierre to lead, personally and financially, a big, public civic organization that would study and fund major changes in Delaware's educational system. As usual, when faced with one of John's enthusiastic entreaties that lined up with his own general viewpoint, Pierre acceded. By this time, he had already given large philanthropic donations to a variety of public causes in Delaware and his sense of civic duty was more than well developed. John was pushing against an open door; his major contribution was to point Pierre in a specific direction, give organizational shape to the general principle of educational reform, and urge Pierre to provide committed leadership, as well as money to the cause of civic improvement.

In July 1918, Raskob got Pierre to co-host a meeting with him at the Du Pont Building. They invited eighty of Delaware's most influential citizens to join them and come up with a plan to do something, at last, about the state's failures. By this time, Raskob had been putting together groups of like-minded, civic-oriented men for several years; the previous year, for example, he had led a charge to improve the Delaware State Hospital and for that effort he had gained the support of many of the same men who he was calling on to reform the state's schools.

John led the meeting and explained that his organization, the State Council of Defense, was soon to end its work but that there remained "many conditions in Delaware susceptible to great improvements." Raskob looked at the men that he and Pierre had gathered together and asked directly that they, "intelligent and representative citizenship of the state...take charge of the ways and means of permanently bettering conditions" in Delaware.[35] Du Pont told the men that he had no specific plans but that he thought he should ask some well regarded individuals in the fields of education what suggestions they might have for the Delaware schools. He was hoping that everyone in attendance would publicly support the effort to put Delaware on a better footing. Shy Pierre, everyone understood, would supply the funds to commission the investigation and, at least initially, pay for the necessary reforms. He just wanted them on board, which was a wish easily granted.

Immediately thereafter, having secured the support of the state's political and economic elite, du Pont moved forward. With typical grace and without fanfare he set up a trust fund with $1,500,000 for the new Service Citizens of Delaware, more than enough to supply the organization with a sure and steady income. John was thrilled.

Several years later than most places in the United States, the state of Delaware had joined the Progressive movement. Du Pont directed that the Service Citizens of Delaware focus on public education. Not surprisingly, given Raskob's and du Pont's economic position, Delaware's Progressive reforms would take a more elite-driven and economically conservative form than many others. The Service Citizens of Delaware did not, then, address some of the issues that drove Progressives in other parts of the country, such as workers' conditions or rights, the need for state government regulation of industry, or efforts to regulate or improve housing conditions for the less fortunate. Nor did the organization or its main funder confront the Delaware school system's legally mandated racial segregation.

On the race issue, however, Pierre du Pont did make sure that massive sums of money, most of it his own, went to completely revamping educational opportunities for Delaware's black students. He personally provided the funds to build brand new school buildings throughout the state for black students, including the state's first black high school. Overall, du Pont donated more than $6 million to Delaware's public schools, building numerous new school buildings and pushing hard to restructure the state's entire school system. Pierre did more than donate funds; he took an active and public role working with state politicians and even accepted official state duties to further the cause. For du Pont, the effort, which lasted through much of the decade, was transformative at both a personal and a political level.

Both Raskob and du Pont embraced a very particular vision of social and political reform: efficient, rational, and practical reforms were best engineered by well-trained experts and the best sort of reform was that which improved opportunities for individuals willing to take advantage of them. Raskob, in particular, had begun to think hard about how he could and should use his wealth to help others to help themselves. He also was beginning to think about the role government should and should not play in aiding Americans in their efforts to gain good and productive lives.

After pushing du Pont into the fray, Raskob backed out of any leadership role in the newly formed Service Citizens organization, though he continued to advise du Pont on his philanthropic efforts. While Pierre threw himself into the work in Delaware, John chose to operate on a more national stage. Through both his civic and DuPont Company work during the war, he had come to know a number of the big men coordinating the government's industrial relations and contracting, as well as his new peers in Big Business, and those connections were producing interesting opportunities in the postwar era. Somewhat surprisingly, given his relative lack of interest in labor issues and working conditions at DuPont, in 1919 John became involved in the great debates over the "labor question" that broke out in the midst of a national tidal wave of labor unrest.

In 1919 some 3,600 strikes erupted in the United States involving more than four million workers. One of the first and biggest of these strikes hit Seattle in late January when 35,000 shipyard workers walked off their jobs. A couple of weeks later, some 75,000 workers joined a General Strike, championed by organized labor groups including the militant Industrial Workers of the World. Seattle was nearly paralyzed for five days. In April coal miners struck. Then in August nearly the entire Boston Police Department walked out after wage negotiations fell apart. The Great Steel Strike began in September; some 365,000 workers shut down steel production in the United States.

Workers had been fighting for the right to form unions and to earn a bigger share of the revenues that their labor contributed to their employers' coffers well before 1919. A wave of strikes had broken out in 1917, too, just as the United States began to mobilize for war. While the United States fought in the Great War, almost all workers had taken what they had been given in an act of national patriotism, assured, in part, by threats from the federal government made against any workers involved in work stoppages. After Armistice Day in November 1918 those same workers began to ask and then demand that their productivity and sacrifice be rewarded. To make their muscle felt they organized. In the uncertain economic times that followed the reconversion to peacetime production, most employers were loath to give their workers anything in the way of raises or to allow them to organize labor unions. Jack Morgan, head of the Morgan Bank after the death of his father in 1913, cheered on the hard line taken by US Steel President Elbert Gary. In a telegram that represented the opinion of most of America's capitalist elite, he wrote: "Heartiest congratulations on your stand for the open shop.... I believe American principles of liberty deeply involved and must win if we all stand firm."[36] Following the success of the Bolshevik Revolution in Russia, a good many middle-class Americans, too, saw the labor unrest of 1919 not as a democratic fight for economic equity but as the first stage of a "Red" uprising.

Such fears were not completely irrational. On June 2, 1919, in the midst of the strikes and walk-offs, seven bombs went off in seven cities, targeting individual members of America's political and economic elite. While the bombers managed to kill only one person, a night watchman at the home of New York Judge Charles Nott, and to blow up only the front of the home of US Attorney General A. Mitchell Palmer, the attacks were chilling. They were made even more so by a scattering of pink flyers left at each bomb site that read: "There will have to be bloodshed, we will kill because it is necessary.... We will do anything and everything to suppres [sic] the capitalist class."[37] The rich, at any rate, had cause to be anxious. The wave of strikes, labor unrest, and scattered acts of violence quickly produced a reaction: the United States had its first "Red Scare."

Raskob did not partake in the overreaction. Nor did he cheer on the antiradical raids launched by Attorney General Palmer, who declared the day after the his home was bombed, that he would rid the country of its "anarchist element," a promise he did his best to keep.[38] On December 20, 1919, federal authorities forcibly loaded 249 foreign-born radicals, including Emma Goldman, onto a recently converted battleship and sent them off to the newly christened Soviet Union. For the American government, it was an unprecedented act of forced, politically dictated mass repatriation.

Raskob made no comment public or private about the government's attack on radicals. He was, however, intrigued and worried about the labor unrest that was roiling the nation. He knew that many of his friends in the business world, especially those directly affected by events, were quite exercised about the unfolding events.

DuPont and General Motors were not directly affected by the wave of strikes. Both companies had relatively good relations with their hourly workers, in part, because both highly profitable companies paid well above the industrial standard in the United States, and DuPont executives, in particular, had pushed hard to make work at their factories much safer than it had once been. Still, Raskob understood that the future was uncertain; the "labor question" needed to be answered. Everybody was talking about it, and John knew that he could do more than talk idly about it; he could do something about it.

John had been vaguely interested in labor issues for a few years. Recall the letter he had sent years earlier to Andrew Carnegie in which he had pondered how to link worker productivity to business earnings so as to reward hard-working and loyal hourly wage earners. John had, ever since, inserted himself periodically into DuPont Company deliberations over worker compensation and benefits, too. Just before Christmas 1914, John had jumped into a major company debate about starting a pension program for employees. In typical Raskob fashion he started off his contribution on the subject by admitting "my thorough lack of knowledge on this subject." Then, in equally typical fashion, he gave a tough-minded analysis of the issue. He asked if the pension programs would be "adopted because of the practical necessity of caring for dependent old employees, or are they designed to be of distinct benefit to the corporation in the way of securing better men and holding those men to the corporation." In other words, he concluded, were company pensions a kind of compensation that good employees preferred to, say, slightly higher pay or were pensions a sort of "necessary evil" made necessary by many workers' inability, for whatever reason, to care for themselves in their old age? Raskob said that he would much rather pay men more in the here and now and let them set up their own form of savings for future needs; anything else, he felt, smacked of "paternalism." But Raskob also stated that whatever his feelings, the company should find out the facts—would good workers prefer a pension benefit to secure future needs or would they prefer slightly higher pay rates so they could decide for themselves how to save for old age? Raskob preferred that workers be bold enough to take care of themselves but in December 1914, at least, he was willing to let the workers' preference decide company policy. He was attempting to be open-minded and was actually interested in what DuPont workers had to say on the matter.[39]

So, in 1919, when the labor question was foremost in the minds of many Americans, Raskob chose to become more involved when opportunities presented themselves. He entered the conversation with certain vague principles about individual initiative, self-discipline, and personal responsibility fairly well fixed in his mind but with an unsettling and uncharacteristic sense that he had limited practical experience to draw on. He had no good answers to workers' demands that they be given a greater share of the wealth industry produced, safer working conditions, and job security. To one of his new friends at General Motors, Charles S. Mott, who had been a Progressive mayor of Flint with a powerful interest in the great social and political issues of the day, including what both men called the "labor question," John wrote, "My mind is very much confused on this issue but if I can crystallize my views in a few words I shall be glad to write you further."[40] But Raskob had no pithy answers or solutions, at least then, and he knew it.

John took what opportunities he could to explore and become involved in the labor question. At first, he did so in exact line with his earliest and long-standing interest in availing working-class and middle-class Americans with the kind of economic opportunities that their economic betters enjoyed. John collaborated with his new colleagues at General Motors to establish an employee's savings and investment plan. Set up in late spring 1919, the GM plan was, for the time, a generous way for hourly workers to gain a significant nest egg. As might be expected from any finance scheme with which Raskob was involved, the plan was somewhat complicated but also a good one. Basically, all GM workers could set aside up to 10 percent of their income, up to $300 a year, in a GM savings fund that paid 6 percent interest. The company would match that savings dollar for dollar by buying shares of GM stock that would be set in an individual investment account, which would, of course, also help to boost the price of GM shares. The plan involved a penalty for early withdrawal—individuals lost the entire GM stock investment portion of the plan if they took out money before each "class" of investment matured at five years—but it also allowed workers to use the money they saved to buy a house at any time without penalty. If workers kept paying in to their individual retirement funds they could end up with a tidy sum, unless, of course, the GM stock portion of their fund took a hard hit in a down market, which through most of the 1920s no one expected.

Judging by participation rates, workers liked the plan. John bragged to his old mentor A. J. Moxham that almost every worker was putting at least some money in the GM savings account and was therefore becoming a company shareholder, even if only a very modest one. The GM plan, Raskob believed, gave the workers a stake in the profitability of the company and during the prosperous 1920s it seemed to provide some level of harmony between the workers and their bosses. Raskob was and would remain proud of what he had done and while the savings and investment plan would become less generous over time it was a success. It paid out more than $100 million to employees in stock and interest payments in addition to the $142 million that employees saved; about 18,000 employees used the plan to save money to buy a home. The GM savings and investment plan was dissolved in 1935 when the Social Security Act went into effect.[41] As Raskob saw it, the plan best rewarded, as it should, those who had the discipline, tenacity, and willingness to help themselves.

Raskob's efforts at rethinking the relationship between labor and ownership at GM, as well as his prominent volunteer work with the Delaware Defense Council and his continuing involvement with the US Chamber of Commerce, brought him to the attention of a small group of corporate leaders who were similarly struggling with the "labor question" in the United States. Two of these corporate leaders, Owen Young of General Electric and Alfred C. Bedford of Standard Oil, as well as Charles Schwab of US Steel, wanted to get together a few top men from industry to think out loud and share ideas about how to manage their respective workforces. Very quietly, even secretly, with absolutely no publicity, they meant to create a group that would discuss frankly how to bring labor peace to their companies; the corporate leaders would meet once a year, and each company would select a labor specialist who would meet with his colleagues once a month to share tactics and strategy. The secret group would be called the Special Conference Committee (SCC).

Among industrialists and financiers, these men were, relatively speaking, liberals. They all were looking for ways to bring a peaceful resolution to labor unrest and to find a way to reconcile labor's interests with those of capital. Unlike some of their corporate peers, they abhorred violence and not just when it came from angry workers. They opposed, as well, company violence and coercion.

Standard Oil's special and leading role in the SCC came directly from the damning role John D. Rockefeller, Jr., believed one of his family's companies had played in the events surrounding the 1914 Ludlow Massacre when nineteen people, including eleven children, had been killed by Colorado National Guardsmen who had been ordered to end a strike organized by the United Mine Workers. Many of the striking miners were employed by the Rockefeller-owned Colorado Fuel and Iron Company. In the immediate aftermath of the massacre, a running gun battle broke out between workers and private mine guards and members of the state militia. Over the next several months, dozens more people were killed. The violence only stopped when President Wilson sent in federal troops to end the deadliest labor conflict in American history.

After the horror, a guilt-stricken Rockefeller asked Canada's Mackenzie King to help him solve the desperate state of American labor relations. King had gained fame in Canada as the country's first minister of labor and had won over both workers and capitalists with his successful plans to improve working conditions and tame labor unrest in Canada's booming industrial sector. Guided by King, Rockefeller began to support financially a new field of study, industrial relations, and to advocate for company labor unions. At its core, the new field of industrial relations promoted nongovernmental, private efforts to improve workers' wages, benefits, and conditions, and to allow workers to voice their own concerns and even demands through unions that were controlled and sponsored by the company that employed them. From the perspective of labor union organizers such as John L. Lewis, who ran the United Mine Workers, this sort of voluntary improvement of workers' terms of employment and the whole notion of company-sponsored unionism was laughable. Lewis and other militant unionists had no trust in their capitalist adversaries and were sure that at the first sign of any economic troubles, workers would be the first to feel the pain and would see their so-called company unions disappear along with their nice benefits and then their jobs, too.

Industrial relations counselors, as they came to be called, obviously saw it differently. And the SCC, begun in 1919, was the offspring of this effort. Historians would later call the Rockefeller-inspired movement welfare capitalism. John Raskob, who never saw the interests of workers and their bosses as inherently antagonistic but hoped that workers through stock ownership and other-related options could be convinced that increased productivity and corporate profits could improve their financial position, too, was intrigued and inspired by the welfare capitalist ideas. As soon as he heard about the SCC operations in 1919, he became a strong supporter. General Motors and DuPont joined US Steel, GE, AT&T, Standard Oil, and a very few other giant corporations as members. While most of the other big men at GM, at least, were highly suspicious of the committee's highly idealistic hopes about labor-management cooperation and the utility of a company union, Raskob tried to encourage the leaders of both GM and DuPont to participate regularly and to learn from the SCC's good works.

The SCC meetings and deliberations were very hush-hush. The whole point of the enterprise appeared, at least, to be highly collusive. Here, after all, were many of the biggest industrial corporations in the United States meeting to share cooperatively specific, practical methods to control labor unrest and quell workers' demands in their respective enterprises. Whether the participating companies were actually breaking any laws by sharing information about their labor practices and plans in their secret meetings is not clear, but the participants worried enough about it to keep record keeping to a minimum. As a result Raskob's exact role in this organization from 1919 through the early 1920s, the period when he participated and closely followed its progress, is more than a bit mysterious. For example, in a letter to DuPont Vice President Lammot du Pont, when he appears to be trying to interest him in the SCC's works, he writes, "There are one or two things in connection with their work that I do not want to put in writing but I should be glad to tell you about them."[42]

If Raskob's exact involvement with the shadowy SCC remains murky, his other major foray into the great labor issues of the day is not. In late 1919, Raskob accepted an invitation to be one of the five men representing the Chamber of Commerce at a well-publicized conference called by President Wilson to hash out a comprehensive response to the spectacular battles between labor and capital that were so roiling the nation.

Raskob was tickled by the invitation. He had been an enthusiastic participant in Chamber events and had strongly supported its efforts to roll back wartime tax rates, but he had not been an officer of the organization. His invitation, he knew, revealed his fast-growing reputation among those who counted in the world of business. President Wilson's strong supporter and key advisor Bernard Baruch, the financier and investor who had run the War Industries Board (the government agency that had coordinated all American war production and managed labor issues during World War I) likely was the man behind his appointment. Baruch, one of the great stock market investors of the day, knew John both from his Wall Street plays and from his leadership role at DuPont and GM.

At the National Industrial Conference meetings in Washington, John sat around a huge table, day after day for two weeks, hashing out the labor question with a who's who of American society. Representing the more moderate faction of organized labor was Samuel Gompers, the aging leader of the American Federation of Labor and one-time cigar maker. John L. Lewis, of the United Mine Workers, was there as well, standing up for the more militant labor faction. The most radical worker organizations, such as the International Workers of the World (IWW) had no seat at the table. But John D. Rockefeller, Bernard Baruch, Elbert Gary, and other leading capitalists were in attendance, as was the president of the US Chamber of Commerce, the head of the National Industrial Conference Board, and other luminaries including Robert S. Brookings and Harvard President Charles Eliot.

In the *New York Times'* extensive opening coverage of the conference, Raskob was described as such: "He has been much interested in improving the relations between employers and employees in the companies in which he is interested. He himself, less than twenty years ago began at the bottom of the ladder as a stenographer in the employ of P. S. du Pont."[43] John, perhaps because of his well-publicized rise from lowly worker to leading executive and almost surely because he had no record of any strongly worded prior public statements on the issues at hand, was immediately elected to be the conference secretary, in charge of the meetings. Raskob's brimming confidence was quickly apparent to all. Despite being one of the younger men in the room and certainly one with less direct experience in labor relations than almost any of the others, he took a leading role.

The labor men at the conference had one specific goal in mind: they wanted the conference to strongly support the rights of workers to join national unions— not company unions. Those national unions would then act as collective bargaining units for all their members. John L. Lewis, seen as the most radical of the labor men at the conference, wanted much more. He specifically wanted to see mines in the United States nationalized and miners guaranteed 30-hour work weeks at far higher pay than they currently received. On the other end of the spectrum was US Steel chairman and chief executive officer Elbert Henry Gary, who was in the midst of battling a long-standing steel strike. He insisted that the entire purpose of the conference should be to fight "for a principle fundamental to American institutions." "The issue raised here," he said, "should be the 'embracing the open shop.'"[44] Gary wanted the conference to reject collective bargaining of any kind.

Raskob came to the meeting with no sure answers. He probably approved of the remarks made by the always optimistic Secretary of the Interior Franklin Lane who assured the public at the conference's opening with these anodyne words: "Men say that this problem of labor and capital is unsolvable. You cannot say that to me.... We will draft here a declaration of dependence, not of independence."[45] As John observed the rancorous debates, he moved quickly to the side of his corporate colleagues, including Elbert Gary. Raskob had no sympathy for John L. Lewis's talk of nationalizing the mines or of mandating collective bargaining units run by national labor unions. If the only choice was between mandatory closed shops and open shops, he had no doubts as to which side of the debate he belonged. Using his role as conference secretary, John became a key player in pushing aside the labor men's most militant demands. The relatively liberal *New York Tribune* headline read "Employers win Delay on Collective Bargaining" and reported that labor leaders were furious at the conference failure and that Raskob took advantage of his role as secretary to play out the clock on the long meeting: "John J. Raskob talked the meeting across the adjournment time to the point where the session ended under the rules."[46]

Many had hoped that the conference would bring an end to America's industrial class warfare. But it was not to be. Just three days before the conference opened, President Woodrow Wilson had suffered a paralyzing stroke. No one outside the president's most intimate circle knew just how serious the attack had been. All that people knew for sure was that the president, who had long talked of bringing lasting peace to America's new industrial state, was absent from the great conference that he had called to solve the labor question.

Wilson did try. The onslaught of his illness made it impossible for him to appear or to speak directly to the factions. But on the conference's twelfth fruitless day, Wilson steeled himself and dictated a short note upon which he scrawled his signature. Secretary of Labor Lane brought the president's message to the conference and read it aloud: Could the delegates truly find no resolution to their differences? Could they offer the president nothing that he could announce to the American people? Did the delegates mean for him "to confess that there is no method to be found for carrying on industry except in the spirit and with the method of war?"[47] The delegates were moved by Wilson's plea, but their positions changed not at all.

Raskob was frustrated by the conference's failure to forge a consensus and blamed that failure on the labor men in attendance. He left the national conference a more conservative man than he had entered it, at least when it came to the "labor question." He was surer than ever that capitalists best understood how to maximize return on investment and create productive enterprises; workers' best chance at better living conditions depended on their willingness to yoke themselves to those enterprises that employed them. Raskob's effort to secure a savings plan for workers at GM was a step in that direction.

Shortly after the conference came to its close, Raskob read a short book by a California politician and writer named George Wilder Cartwright titled *Mutual Interests of Capital and Labor* that was making the rounds of the Chamber of Commerce circuit. Cartwright spelled out what Raskob had long believed. Cartwright argued that employers had to pay their workers a good wage both to keep them productive and also to assure that working people had sufficient disposable incomes to buy the items modern industry mass produced such as automobiles. Cartwright argued that a "scientific" basis could determine a fair wage and that it was employers' duty to calculate that wage and pay it. In turn, employees should work hard, be loyal, and consume the good things the capitalist economy generated. If employers failed to pay a "scientific" fair wage, then employees had the absolute right to quit and find better jobs. Raskob bought 500 copies of the book directly from the publisher and sent one or more copies to most every businessman he knew.[48] Raskob's thinking about the labor question pretty much came to a close. His fascination with America's political economy, however, grew more intense, especially as he realized that he was increasingly well positioned to do more than just study it from afar.

Even as John was joining policy circles in Washington and pondering the big social issue of his day, he was very much still focused on bringing financial rigor to General Motors, which under Durant's unsteady but magic hands remained both unruly and very profitable. War's end had brought social turmoil to the United States; it also brought economic uncertainty, chaos, and contraction to the American economy. In 1920 that downturn pushed General Motors to the brink—and Billy Durant over it. Raskob had a corporate crisis on his hands, a crisis that was in part of his own making. Pierre du Pont and Wall Street looked to him to make it right.

10

Crisis Manager

John was entranced by the sheer magnitude of GM's operations and scope. He was, moreover, having a hard time figuring out how to rein in the enterprise. The closer he got to Billy Durant the more he saw why Durant saw so many possibilities for expanding the business, even at astronomical cost.

Part of the challenge was that GM had an embarrassment of talent competing for capital to invest in an array of possible directions. For example, in the summer of 1919, GM's resident genius inventor, Charles Kettering, began a sustained campaign to convince Raskob to provide him with large sums of money to put GM into the aviation business. Durant had already turned Kettering down. Refusing to take no for an answer, "Boss Kett" focused his enthusiasm on Raskob, figuring that he had his hand on the money spigot at GM.

Kettering had come to GM in 1916 when Billy Durant had bought Kettering's Dayton Engineering Laboratory Company to secure Kettering's automotive genius; he was responsible for the electric self-starter and numerous other clever and profitable gadgets. Now, Kettering argued, he should be allowed to turn his attention to aviation. Raskob did not know what to do.[1]

Raskob was being asked to make all sorts of decisions about which he, and almost everyone else, knew relatively little. How do you figure return on investments in emerging markets on untested or even uninvented technologies? Durant had been trying to tell Raskob and those who had been second-guessing his decisions for years that it was not easy. As Raskob threw himself into GM's sprawling business, he was pulled in multiple directions at once. It was great fun, just the kind of high-energy situation he loved. He watched Durant operate and saw genius as Billy gamboled from autos to refrigerators to tractors to stock market operations that boggled the mind.

Raskob was too entranced. He was far from the first man to have his critical faculties derailed by Billy Durant. Caught up in the sprawl and possibility of GM's multiple endeavors, he was not efficiently or effectively figuring out how to bring financial order to the chaotic House of Durant. Instead, he helped Durant find more and more capital to invest in GM's growing empire. He was, in many ways, replicating the relationship he had with Pierre during the first years of the twentieth century when the two men had bought dozens of explosive companies to increase the DuPont Company's capacities. Only this time, Raskob was working with a man who was more a madcap, if also brilliant plunger than a careful, numbers-driven industry analyst dedicated to carefully managed risk and long-term growth. Raskob, at least sometimes, seemed to forget that in his partnership with Durant he was supposed to be the prudent skeptic not the ever-clever financial innovator who could always find more capital to grow.[2]

Still, Raskob knew he had to get a handle, at least, on GM's finances, which he tried to do throughout 1919 and into 1920. He brought over several high-powered, immensely capable numbers guys from DuPont to figure out what was going on. John Pratt, one of the first and best of the DuPont men to dig into the mess, gave a blunt appraisal:

> No one knew just how much money had been appropriated, and there was no control of how much money was being spent....When one of them [division heads] had a project, why he would get the vote of his fellow members; if they would vote for his project, he would vote for theirs. It was sort of a horse trading. In addition to that, if they didn't get enough money, Mr. Durant, when visiting the plant, would tell them to go on and spend what money they needed without any record of it being made.[3]

Raskob quickly took heed of the lack of record keeping and pounced on it. He sent two men over from his old DuPont office to create company-wide uniform accounting procedures.[4] Procedures were good, but they did little to rein in the widening gyre of Durant's flight of acquisition and expansion.

The DuPont men found that regulating and rationalizing GM's operations was slow-going. Durant had no interest in implementing their recommendations; he allowed his men to stall. Durant was at least as wary of the control and the inflexibility the new rules would create as his loyalists were. Indicative of Durant's charms, even as John Pratt reported to Raskob that Durant was putting up roadblocks and was not likely to adhere to or support the new accounting rules, he was falling under Billy's spell. Durant had responded to Pratt's investigations and concerns by asking him for advice. What did Pratt think about the future of aluminum? Should GM start its own glassworks? How about the battery business? A few months after the two men met, Billy asked Pratt to come work for him. Pratt, despite all his reservations, did.[5] Raskob was glad to have Pratt on the inside, hoping that the hard-nosed executive could figure out which of Durant's enthusiasms were most likely to actually make money and which, critically, would not.

In early 1920, Raskob thought GM was on the right track. His accounting men had begun to make sense of GM's record keeping, a necessary, if not sufficient, step in the right direction. What the numbers showed was that GM was making its big investors bags of money. Raskob had calculated that 1919 was going to be a very good year for GM but even he was surprised by the year-end figures. GM had sales of over half a billion dollars. He and Durant had the pleasant task of sorting out what to do with the $60 million in earnings the company had made that year.

Raskob calculated that since Billy Durant had taken back the company in 1916 GM's capital assets had grown nearly eightfold. He wrote Durant with the figures and offered him a bouquet of praise: "This is indeed a fine tribute to your foresight."[6] GM seemed to have become the corporate bonanza that Billy Durant had predicted only a decade earlier when the fledgling automobile industry had been dismissed by Wall Street and championed by only a relatively few men who had the know-how, tenacity, and guts to risk everything on a dodgy new technology and an untestable consumer marketplace.

Unfortunately, all was not as it seemed at the end of 1919. As Billy Durant's biographer points out, GM was immodestly profitable in 1919 and Raskob and Durant had good reason to celebrate, but the company also faced a great deal of risk. Most of all, GM had become a very expensive operation with a fixed investment of some $153 million, an inventory of massive proportions, and a payroll that clocked in at over 85,000 employees.[7] Just to keep the company running demanded a constant torrent of revenue, most of which had to come from more and more sales of cars and trucks sold at a high-rate of profit. To keep GM growing depended on the frequent and massive new equity offerings that Raskob and Durant gleefully engineered. A big chunk of that new money came from the DuPont Company, which sunk many more millions into GM.

Billy Durant had no intention of keeping GM simply running as it was. He wanted GM to be bigger and then bigger again. He had lots of expensive ideas. Rather than act as brake on Durant's ambitions, Raskob had his foot on the accelerator as well. Raskob, in particular, pushed forward on building a massive, very expensive new headquarters in Detroit that would house the centralized financial and administrative offices he insisted GM needed. Together, Durant and Raskob continued to raise new capital to make more acquisitions, build more production capacity, and make new investments to enlarge operations.

Given GM's rate of growth, investing more money in the company's expansion seemed to make perfect sense to both men, though they sometimes differed on how to expand and grow rich faster. Durant, for example, was no fan of Raskob's $10 million investment in GM's new administrative office building. But rather than fight each other they both—with Durant far in the lead—kept spending money. It was all a risky proposition given the uncertainties of

America's postwar economic situation. Despite all the money flowing into GM's coffers in 1919 and early 1920, the company was not in as strong a financial position as it would soon need to be; its cash surpluses were low and its ability to continually raise capital through the markets, even with all of Raskob's skills, was running up against increasing skepticism from the business community. Raskob, who had never made a big mistake in his life, especially not a financial one, was about to reap a financial whirlwind that was, in part, of his own making.

John had been working in corporate finance for twenty years. Under Pierre du Pont's tutelage, as a lad of twenty he had done deals with veteran industrialists. He had quickly learned how to pitch bankers and earn their trust. Certainly Pierre du Pont, chairman of the board of GM, trusted him and so did the other DuPont men who had seen their investments in GM produce spectacular returns. Even Billy Durant, ever the lone wolf, had come to trust John. Raskob was charged by the du Ponts with watching over Durant and Durant knew it. But nobody was charged with watching over Raskob as he became swept up in the grand adventure of the auto business. Pierre, the one man who could surely have pushed Raskob to exercise more caution, was not interested in spending his time second-guessing his most trusted friend and advisor.

In 1920, events conspired to bring Billy Durant to his knees and GM to the brink of bankruptcy. Raskob, who had never had to manage a big economic downturn, especially one he failed to see coming, contributed to that mess. He was also the man who then took out the broom, swept up that mess, and put Billy in the rubbish bin.

In 1919 and then into 1920, Billy Durant, with Raskob's full support, spent more and more money, around $79 million, betting on GM's future. Some of the investments, such as the $26.7 million spent buying a controlling interest in the Fisher Body Company, were horrifically expensive but brilliant long-term moves. Others were a colossal waste of money. Regardless of their strategic value, the acquisitions and internal investments stressed to the near-breaking point GM's financial position. Durant's loyalists had convinced themselves and then Durant that a postwar economic boom was going to fuel skyrocketing demand for cars and trucks; if they had the inventory, they said, they could double their sales. Even as Durant was listening to his inner circle and his own ever optimistic inner voice, even while he was buying and expanding and gambling on hunches, he was also becoming ever more disconnected from GM's best men, who were far more prudent about GM's short-term prospects.

Walter Chrysler, the operations czar who, among other tasks, ran Buick, tried to slow Billy down. But Billy would not listen to him and Chrysler was fast running out of patience. Part of it was personal; Chrysler just could not take the stomach-wrenching aggravation Billy's way of doing business produced. Chrysler had enough of Billy's last-minute summary demands that he appear before Durant in New York or Detroit and then be kept waiting for hours. Once Chrysler went to New York, cooled his heels for four days, and never even saw Durant. The waste of his time infuriated Chrysler, but it was, he believed, just one symptom of Durant's reckless way with people, money, and the company. What finally drove Chrysler over the edge was the 1919-20 buying spree. Chrysler called Durant on it publicly and loudly, at a GM board meeting: "What am I roaring about? I'm roaring as a stockholder, if you really want to know. Everything I have in the world is tied up in this company. I don't want to lose it."[8] A few months later Chrysler called it quits. Billy Durant, gracious as always, agreed to buy Chrysler's $10 million in GM in stock, even as he had to borrow money to make the purchase.

Alfred Sloan, GM vice president and key corporate problem-solver, saw the same risks. Shocked into action by Chrysler's blunt assessment and angry resignation, he tried to get Durant to at least tighten up the company's management and capital allocation procedures. Durant, with his usual charm, thanked Sloan for his carefully prepared report and then ignored everything. Sloan quietly informed Durant that he needed some time off and made plans to take an extended auto tour through Europe. Before he left, he contacted an investment banking house in Boston and let them know that he was open to a change in his line of work.[9]

Raskob was far more sanguine about the company's prospects. He still believed that Durant needed more financial discipline but, more importantly, he thought that Durant was right to be optimistic about GM's earning prospects and right to invest lots more money in the company's growth. He had run the numbers and predicted big profits in 1920 right through 1922. He even played out the calculations through 1928 and argued that GM's worth would increase threefold by then. He used those figures in January 1920 to assuage the concerns of some of GM's lenders, including his friend Seward Prosser at Bankers Trust, who had begun to worry about GM's finances in the face of postwar inflation and economic instability. A confident Raskob, in what Prosser described as a "long heart to heart talk," convinced the astute banker that GM was on sound footing and well positioned to take advantage of America's growing auto-mania.[10] Raskob had signed on to the Durant vision: GM had to expand to increase capacity so that they could fully exploit a booming consumer economy. Rather than rein in spending, Raskob worked hard to raise money to fuel the fires of expansion.[11]

In early 1920, Raskob and Durant ran into unexpected trouble. They had come up with a typically elaborate scheme to raise some $60 million by engineering a stock split, revaluing a chunk of GM common stock shares and offering the public a taste of the new equities. But the public had no appetite for GM's newest offering, especially as the country entered an economic downturn, engineered in part by the relatively new Federal Reserve Bank's deliberate anti-inflation policies. Durant usually had no problem luring his expansive circle of large and small investors into buying a piece of his latest action, but they claimed to be tapped out, at least when it came to purchasing more GM stock. In February, a surprisingly anxious Durant got a hold of Raskob at the Everglades Club in Palm Beach and told him that the stock offering was not going well; they needed to find some deep pockets.[12] In response, the DuPont Company, as well as Pierre du Pont, bought up some of the shares but more, much more investment capital needed to be found. Raskob went fishing for a big investor and came up with the British-based branch of the explosives giant, the Nobel Company, still flush with wartime profits. The British investors agreed to buy up nearly $30 million of the new GM stock, though in the next few months as GM's financial position softened, this seemingly done deal unwound to some extent, forcing Raskob to do a fair amount of scrambling. Still, it appeared to be a grand catch.[13]

Even with the British investment, Raskob needed much more money so, fatefully, he turned to his friends at the Morgan bank. In mid-April he arranged a lunch meeting, and accompanied by Pierre, asked the bankers to use their influence to sell GM equities to their various clients and affiliates. The bankers agreed, as well, to buy a substantial amount of the offering on their own account. But the deal came with stiff terms. The bankers would charge extraordinarily high commissions in their handling of the GM stock. They also insisted on having their own seats on GM's board and demanded, as well, that other well-known bankers and trusted industrialists be added to the board. Given the urgency of the situation, Raskob quickly agreed and assured the men that he could gain Durant's acquiescence and that he would personally convince each of the non-Morgan men to accept the board memberships, which he later did. Finally, the men at Morgan bluntly told Raskob that they did not trust Billy Durant. While they respected Raskob's position at GM, they told him that his influence on Durant and on GM's operation was insufficient; they wanted Pierre du Pont to play a larger role at GM. Pierre assured the men that he would step up to any challenge at GM that needed his services. Raskob did not inform Durant of this aspect of his conversations with the Morgan bankers.[14]

Raskob believed that the storm had been weathered and that GM's finances were once again on course. He celebrated by meeting that same evening at the Metropolitan Club with some of his new friends in the elite world of business. He, Pierre, Percy Rockefeller, GM executive Alfred A. Swayne, the industrialist Samuel Pryor, and others discussed reducing the burdens imposed by the relatively new federal tax law. Raskob, increasingly active in public affairs, thought they should act as soon as possible "as we may be able to secure a much better consideration before the Republican National Convention than we can later on."[15] Raskob also expressed his enthusiasm for Massachusetts governor Calvin

Coolidge, who had gained the national stage in 1919 by firing the entire Boston police force for participating in an illegal strike. Coolidge had taken advantage of his fame by publishing *Have Faith in Massachusetts*, a public relations effort aimed at securing the governor the second position on the 1920 Republican presidential ticket. Raskob had read Coolidge's work of self-promotion and sent out copies to dozens of his business friends, commending Coolidge's dedication to "the splendid ideals which governed our forefathers in framing the Constitution of the United States," by which Raskob meant that Coolidge was an ardent supporter of property rights.[16]

Durant was in a far less happy mood. The turn to the Morgan bank, as he saw it, had brought a predator into his peaceable kingdom. Ever since the Morgan interests had dismissed his first attempts to finance GM, he had mistrusted and even feared the lions of Wall Street. The bankers' coup of 1910 that had taken GM from Durant still haunted him. But he understood that GM needed the money and he trusted Raskob, so he acceded to Raskob's turn to the Morgan interests and accepted the Morgan men's hard terms. There was no way around it, the bankers were back. Durant did not need Raskob to tell him that the Morgan interests meant him no good but Durant, ever confident, thought he could use them without being used up, in return. Durant showed no fear as he made his rounds in New York City, demonstrating to his multitude of friends, whether at the opera or the brokerage houses, that all was well.

But Durant knew that, again, his place at the General Motors Company was at grave risk. He knew that the bankers would, if they could, depose him. Sadly, he would give them everything they needed to crush him. Billy Durant, a noble prince of commerce, was brought low by his own foolish desires. In the end, he was a silver-tongued pitchman who believed too much in his own patter. Who that makes John Raskob is an open question. Perhaps he is Horatio, the loyal friend who aimed only to serve Durant, his prince, as he had once served Pierre du Pont, his "daddy," before him. But if the theater-loving Raskob wanted to see himself as some version of the honorable Horatio, that is not how Billy Durant saw Raskob in his final moments on the corporate stage. Durant hated the bankers, but he blamed Raskob, too, for his fall. In letters to friends and allies, Durant termed Raskob his betrayer. In Durant's last days at General Motors, Raskob did choose to repudiate Billy though what choice he had is also a question with no easy answer.

Durant and Raskob were both wrong to spend so much money expanding GM's holdings and capacities in late 1919 and during the first six months of 1920. That summer the postwar economy took a hard turn. The world agricultural market, after years of war-induced shortages and the resulting high prices, was suddenly glutted. Commodity prices in the United States collapsed. More than two and a half million returning American soldiers flooded the labor market, while industries struggled to reconvert to peacetime production. Unemployment sky-rocketed, demand slackened, and prices fell across the board. Despite the crushing deflationary pressures, the Federal Reserve raised interest rates to guard against the invisible specter of inflation and the Harding Administration stuck to rock-ribbed conservative principles and ran a budget surplus to restore confidence in the economic system. The short-term results were a deep contraction. Economists have argued ever since over how to weight the various causes and consequences of the downturn.

All Durant, Raskob, and the rest of GM's leaders knew at the time was that in July 1920 the auto market began an out of control skid. While anxious people waited to see which way the economy would go, they had to keep buying food and paying for their housing; they did not have to buy new cars. In November 1920, GM sold only 12,700 automobiles; sales were off 75 percent from June. To meet its operational targets and capitalization requirements, GM needed to sell an average of 70,000 vehicles a month. By late 1920, everything stopped moving. John Pratt, ever practical, made his rounds and counted $210 million in unsold vehicles and parts. GM lacked the capital flow to service its debt and meet its obligations to its legions of creditors. GM's share price, which had already fallen to under $40 a share in spring 1920, began a long slide. Under Durant's hand, assisted by Raskob, GM was falling apart, again.

Billy Durant refused to believe it. He bet everything and more that the economic contraction, the decline in car sales, and the capital flow problems were nothing more than a hiccup. He began to buy up every share of GM he could, certain that the sell-off of GM stock would make him millions when the auto market recovered, a recovery he predicted was only weeks away. He bought up friends' stock or asked them to refrain from selling into the bear market, guaranteeing them against any loss. He used his many brokers to soak up big and small blocks of shares, buying on the thinnest of margins. Durant leveraged all he had, doubling down on his "Baby" one last time. But as car sales failed to recover in the late fall of 1920 and GM debt service began to wobble, the price of GM stock kept falling.

As GM's share price continued to plummet, Durant and Raskob worked with other GM executives, the DuPont Company, and the Morgan bankers to put together a syndicate to buy shares in the open market in an attempt to stabilize the price and restore the faith of both the public and GM's many creditors in the company. Morgan banker and GM board member Edward Stettinius ran the operation, a chore he took on with no enthusiasm and certainly with no interest in supporting GM's largest individual stockholder, Billy Durant. Stettinius and the other men at Morgan suspected that Durant was, as ever, running some kind of speculation and that they were being asked to bail him out. They grumbled amongst themselves: "Yes, Durant thanks us humble now for saving his life but within a week he will be cursing us for something else."[17] Durant personally contributed one million dollars to the stock syndicate while Du Pont and Raskob chose not to put in any of their own money. They did agree not to dump any of their shares or DuPont Company shares into the falling market. None of the men were, then, aware that Durant's offering was but a small percentage of the money that he was secretly throwing into the stock market in his efforts to gobble up massive amounts of GM's common shares. Despite these efforts, in the late fall of 1920, GM shares kept losing value. Each and every single point drop in GM's share price cost Billy Durant roughly $2 million, money he did not have.[18]

Stettinius, when taking over the syndicate, indicated that he would try to prop up GM's share price at around $20. He quickly concluded that too much air still remained in GM's stock valuation and so, rather than buy up shares, he began to reduce what shares the syndicate had already purchased or controlled, avoiding further loses. This public disinvestment by members of the GM board did not go unnoticed on the New York Stock Exchange. GM's share price dropped to $12.

Durant, for once, lost his cool and accused the House of Morgan of a willful act of sabotage. Stettinius scoffed at Durant's charges and threw back a charge of his own: Durant was operating in all manner of ways to profit off the GM debacle. He pointed out that Durant was in the midst of launching a kind of bucket shop operation aimed at the smallest of stock investors in which GM shares controlled or owned by Durant were to be sold at a profit to an uninformed public. To one of his Morgan colleagues, Stettinius later expressed his contempt for Durant: "It is of course perfectly obvious that Durant has lied continuously and persistently to all of us here and to all of his associates."[19]

In October, Pierre du Pont, too, registered alarm at Durant's brand new stock-peddling operation, dubbed the Durant Corporation, when he learned that Durant was directly marketing GM shares at above-board prices to Delaware's school teachers. He was appalled, in part, because he felt that Durant was implying in his advertisements that Pierre du Pont, hero to the Delaware school system, was connected to the special offer. He wrote Durant and asked him to please stop; Delaware teachers simply did not earn enough money to risk what little savings they had on GM stock at a time when the market looked so dire. At almost the same time, however, Pierre, acting on a request made by Durant that was brought to Pierre by John, agreed to a short-term, secured loan of over 1.3 million GM shares held by the DuPont Company to Durant for unspecified use. Even as du Pont was losing faith in Billy Durant, he was not yet willing to cut himself free from whatever Durant had gotten himself into, surely because John Raskob was advising him to hold on just a little longer.[20]

Durant denied to everyone that he was involved in any unseemly activities. To the degree that he was involved in market operations he was so, he explained to a sympathetic reporter from *Motor* magazine, only to protect GM stockholders

1. Raskob early portrait. In 1900 Raskob went to work for Pierre du Pont, launching his meteoric business career. This photo is taken soon after Pierre du Pont and Raskob arrived in Wilmington to restructure the DuPont Company. Used with permission of the Hagley Library and Museum.

2. Raskob family. John Raskob's sisters and father in front of their house. While journalists often stated that Raskob went from "rags to riches," in fact he came from a middle-class home in Lockport, New York. After his father died unexpectedly in 1898, John vowed to support his widowed mother and younger siblings. Used with permission of the Raskob Foundation for Catholic Activities.

3. Raskob on ship in 1905. In 1905 Raskob traveled with Pierre du Pont and other DuPont executives to Paris and then to Chile. On the long voyage to Chile, where the men hoped to buy nitrate fields, Raskob made a lifelong friend, the rakish Elias Ahuja (pictured with Raskob). Used with permission of the Hagley Library and Museum.

4. Helena Raskob. An oil portrait of Helena Raskob at the piano. Mrs. Raskob was stylish and socially gracious; she also was a highly competent and energetic manager of the family and the Raskobs' properties. Within the family she was always called "Skipper" in recognition of the tight ship she ran. Used with permission of the Hagley Library and Museum.

"Archmere"

The sky is the limit to our wishes for you and yours during 1929

The Raskobs

5. The Raskobs' Archmere Estate. In 1916, the Raskobs announced their new economic position by building Archmere. This photo shows off Archmere on the front of the Raskobs' 1929 New Year's card. Used with permission of the Hagley Library and Museum.

6. GM leadership in 1922. The men of GM gathered in Michigan in 1922 after weathering the financial meltdown that had resulted in William Durant's departure and the elevation of Pierre du Pont to the GM presidency. A beaming Raskob stands next to du Pont in the front row. The large man in the center of the front row is the can-do executive John Pratt and to his left is the future leader of General Motors, Alfred P. Sloan. Used with permission of the Hagley Library and Museum.

7. Raskob at the helm. In the 1920s, Raskob owned several yachts and sailboats. Proud of his great wealth, Raskob enjoyed dressing the part. Private collection.

8. Raskob family. "Skipper" and the twelve Raskob children; this photo was taken in 1928 shortly before John Raskob announced his role in the Al Smith presidential campaign. Raskob used this image as a bookplate in his private library. Used with permission of the Brooklyn Historical Society.

9. Smith and Raskob. Besides managing Al Smith's 1928 presidential campaign, Raskob counted Smith as one of his closest friends. Used with permission of the Hagley Library and Museum.

RUM AND ROMANISM
Must Not Be Permitted to Crucify Tom Heflin on the Papal Cross For Being Loyal to God, Home and Country

THE FELLOWSHIP FORUM,
339 Pennsylvania Avenue, Washington, D. C.

Dear Mr. Vance: I want to help RUSH another BIG HEFLIN SPECIAL EDITION into Alabama on October 25th, and help smash Rum and Romanism before it is too late. Enclosed you will find $.................................to cover cost of sending copies of The Fellowship Forum, with its truth revealing stories of the great fight for civic righteousness, directly to the voters of Alabama. I look upon it as both a privilege and a duty to help in this good work. My earnest prayers for victory go with my contribution. A Heflin landslide will mark a tidal wave for better government.

$25.00 Will Send 1000 Copies	Name ....
10.00 Will Send 400 Copies	Street or R.F.D...
5.00 Will Send 200 Copies	City ....
1.00 Will Send 25 Copies	State ....

Help Banish Rome, Raskob, Smith, Tammany Hall from American Politics.
MAKE ALABAMA THE TURNING POINT. GIVE DECENCY THE RIGHT OF WAY.

10. Heflin Campaign literature. Raskob was surprised at the virulence of anti-Catholic feelings in the 1928 presidential election. Alabama Senator Tom Heflin was at the front ranks of the anti-"Papists." Used with permission of the Hagley Library and Museum.

11. Al Smith, John Raskob, and Michael Meehan. After the failed 1928 campaign, Smith and Raskob joined forces to develop the Empire State Building. Here the two men are joined by their mutual friend, stock market manipulator extraordinaire, Michael Meehan, whose "pump and dump" maneuvers would be pilloried by congressional investigators after the Crash. Used with permission of the Hagley Museum and Library.

12. Pioneer Point. In the late 1920s, the Raskob family developed a spectacular 1,600-acre estate and working farm, Pioneer Point, near Centreville, Maryland. It was primarily run by Helena Raskob. Used with permission of the Raskob family.

PLATFORM AND ORGANIZATION

of the

American
Liberty League

Platform

1. To preserve American institutions which safeguard, to citizens in all walks of life, the right to liberty and the pursuit of happiness. Therefore to uphold American principles which oppose the tendency shown in many countries to restrict freedom of speech, freedom of the press, religious liberty, the right to peaceable assembly and the right to petition the government; and to combat the growth of bureaucracy, the spread of monopoly, the socialization of industry and the regimentation of American life.

2. To maintain the right of an equal opportunity for all to work, earn, save and acquire property in order that every man may enjoy the fruit of his own ability and labor, and thus have, in his declining years, the peace of mind that comes from a sense of security for himself and for his wife and children who may survive him.

3. To uphold the principle that the levying of taxes, the appropriation of public funds and the designation of the purposes for which they are to be expended are exclusively the functions of the Congress and should not be exercised by administrative officials.

13. Liberty League platform. In 1934, Raskob organized the American Liberty League, a "nonpartisan" group of economic conservatives, substantially funded by DuPont and GM executives, who hoped to derail the New Deal's liberal policy agenda and defeat Franklin Roosevelt's bid for re-election in 1936. On his way to a smashing victory, Roosevelt blasted the Liberty League, telling voters: "I welcome their hatred." Used with permission of the Hagley Library and Museum.

14. Raskob on Elephant. In 1935, Raskob tired of politics and went on an around the world tour. Here, he sits atop an elephant somewhere in south Asia. Used with permission of the Raskob family.

15. New York City View. The south view from the eightieth floor of the Empire State Building where John Raskob had a suite of offices. Throughout much of the 1930s, Raskob had far too much of the building to himself. Used with permission of the Hagley Library and Museum.

16. John Raskob, photographer. In the late 1930s and 1940s, Raskob roamed the West to buy land, operate mines, and seek out good times. At Bryce Canyon, in Utah, he volunteered to take a picture of this group of young women. Photo in author's collection.

17. Raskob in Palm Springs. Beginning in the 1930s, Raskob wintered alone in Palm Springs. He pursued good times but also bought a large tract of land. Used with permission of the Palm Springs Historical Society.

18. Raskob and grandchildren. Raskob, around 1943, at Pioneer Point surrounded by a few of his grandchildren. In his last years Raskob delighted in the company of his grandchildren; he played right alongside them on the estate's expansive waterfront. Used with permission of the Raskob Foundation for Catholic Activities.

19. John Raskob and Pierre du Pont, 1950. Raskob and Pierre du Pont were intimate friends, business partners, and political allies for fifty years. Used with permission of the Hagley Museum and Library.

20. Raskob portrait. John Raskob shortly before he died October 15, 1950, at the age of 71. Used with permission of the Hagley Museum and Library.

from "ruthless attacks on the part of manipulators." Durant somehow convinced the reporter, one of the media's savviest auto analysts, that "he has never speculated in the stock market for personal profit."[21] Durant had convinced himself that his market interventions, including his notion of selling millions of dollars worth of GM shares to small investors, was a selfless effort aimed only at shoring up GM's share price and that in short order those small investors would reap a profit. Raskob watched Durant's trapeze act with growing consternation. Like many a man before him, he suddenly found it harder and harder to reach Durant by phone, to schedule an appointment to see him, or to meet with him even when he had made an appointment.

Already by early October, Raskob was aware that Durant was not his usual self. Durant insisted that people were conspiring to ruin him by dumping GM stock and that the Morgan men were in the middle of it. Instead of buying GM shares to prop up the market, he accused them of selling off huge blocks of stock. Durant, Raskob believed, thought that he and Pierre were part of the Morgan cabal. Raskob wrote Durant—an indicator of how much difficulty he was having in arranging a face-to-face meeting—and assured him that he and Pierre were not selling any of their GM holdings, nor were the Morgan men, at that moment, selling GM, though he admitted that Morgan was not buying any shares, either. Morgan partners George Whitney and Dwight Morrow told Raskob that GM "stock was acting well in the market…and under the circumstance…[the] full buying power [of the syndicate] ought to be held in reserve." Raskob assured Durant that he had told the bankers that he "he felt some little support could be given" to GM's share price but that the bankers, so far, were unmoved.[22] Immediately thereafter, Raskob spoke with Pierre about the Morgan position. Du Pont agreed with Morrow and Whitney, instructing Raskob that the bankers' approach was "the only proper and indeed the only feasible way."[23] Raskob understood. Pierre, while still willing to offer Durant private financial assistance and public statements of confidence, was fast growing weary of him. It was time to back away.

In late October, Raskob wrote an angry note to Durant, who uncharacteristically was holed up in his beachside mansion in Deal, New Jersey. Raskob had worked through GM's latest numbers and was in near-shock over the amount of red ink he had found: Chevrolet and the Canadian division were each losing $400,000 a month; Oakland, Olds, and Samson Tractor were each losing $200,000 a month, the components and parts group was down $500,000 a month; other divisions were hemorrhaging money as well. Raskob was working at a feverish pace lining up short-term loans to cover the losses and pay off GM's creditors. What was Durant doing, why was he not focused on the crisis? "Everything," Raskob underlined, "must be done to reduce" the losses.[24] Prior to the financial debacle, Raskob's letters to Durant had always contained a note of jocularity and intimacy. Now Raskob wrote Durant in the cold and distant style he used with people who could not keep their accounts straight and their debts paid.

Durant did not write back. His attempt to hold back market forces by throwing everything he had in support of GM's share price had failed catastrophically. The stockbrokers with whom he carried massive margin accounts, as well as several banks from which he had borrowed substantial sums, were demanding payment. In mid-November he needed at least $1 million in cash to hold back his flood of creditors, but he had no money with which to make good on his personal debts. His entire holdings of GM stock, which he had used as collateral, were now at risk of liquidation. That liquidation could break not just GM's share price but the corporation, too. The fall of GM, were it to happen, would ripple throughout the economy; it could launch a panic that might put the entire American economy into a tailspin.

The end came in a rush. While Durant had somehow managed to keep his financial debacle secret, in part by misleading, if not outright lying, to Raskob, the men at Morgan had sources enough to suspect that Durant was in some kind of trouble. They asked Raskob and du Pont if they knew of Durant's "personal affairs, particularly as to his possible stock market operations."[25] Raskob and Durant demurred but agreed to set up a meeting with Durant so that the Morgan men could ask their questions directly. On November 10, Durant attempted to assure his financial partners that everything was fine. In reply to a direct question from Dwight Morrow, he insisted that he knew of no "weak" accounts in regard to any GM holdings. Du Pont, Raskob, and the Morgan bankers did not directly challenge Durant's claim, but the Morgan bankers insisted that Durant allow them to review his stock records and scheduled a meeting to go over the books of the Durant Corporation, the stock-peddling outfit Durant had just set up.

The very next morning, before the Morgan bankers had a chance to take their accounting, Durant phoned Raskob and du Pont and asked them if they might meet for lunch. They had no idea why Durant needed to see them, but they knew it could not be good. At lunch Durant dropped his bombshell. According to du Pont's record of the meeting, made soon after, Durant stated "that he had been informed that the 'bankers' had demanded his resignation as President of the General Motors Company, to which demand he was ready to accede, as he was determined to 'play the game,' for the reasons that the company as well as he personally, 'was in the hands of the bankers' and must act accordingly." Neither du Pont nor Raskob had any idea about what Durant was talking. Both insisted that Durant was in error and that GM was in no immediate risk from any bankers. They had heard nothing from the House of Morgan and, as Durant knew, Raskob had successfully arranged enough short-term credit to weather the downturn in auto sales. Durant refused to clarify his meaning but opaquely suggested that "he was worried about his personal accounts" and then left. Du Pont and Raskob tried to figure out what was happening.

Raskob was pretty sure that he understood; Durant had misled them all and had speculated wildly on GM stock. The next morning, he tracked down Durant and asked him bluntly how much he owed: was it "six or twenty-six million dollars?" Durant managed to shock Raskob by telling him that he was not sure, "he would have to look up the matter."[26] Raskob and du Pont gave Durant the weekend and Monday, too, to add up the calamity. On Tuesday, they waited for hours outside Durant's office. According to du Pont's laconic description: "Mr. Durant was very busy that day, seeing people, rushing to the telephone, and in and out of the room...it was not until four o'clock that afternoon that Mr. Durant began to give us figures indicating his situation." He knew for sure that he owed nineteen brokerage houses over $12 million, which needed to be paid immediately. Durant estimated that overall he owed about $20 million (or over $215 million in current dollars). But he admitted that it might be more. Raskob and du Pont were mortified. They were also "loath to believe the accounts in any way accurate."[27] They were right to be suspicious; Durant actually owed a good deal more. Meanwhile the Morgan bankers were demanding that Durant come clean to them. Durant told Pierre and John that he would rather not explain his predicament to the cold-hearted bankers, implying that the three of them might instead work something out. With Pierre now taking the lead, Raskob and du Pont made it clear that no side deals or arrangements were going to be made.

Immediately thereafter, du Pont and Raskob met with several of the Morgan bankers and began to compare their assessments of Durant's debacle. Stettinius, who had been at the center of perilous financial storms several times before, suggested to Raskob and du Pont that they must quickly and completely clean up Durant's mess so as to prevent not only GM's failure but a broader financial panic.[28] Working quickly, they agreed to borrow immediately $20 million from several banks to buy up Durant's debt.

Du Pont and Raskob returned to Wilmington to share the unpleasantness with their colleagues at the DuPont Company. On Friday, November 19, 1920, at 4 o'clock the DuPont finance committee held an emergency meeting. President Irénée du Pont and the other men urged Pierre and John to do what they must; the DuPont Company would stand behind GM.[29] Over the weekend Raskob, du Pont, and the Morgan bankers scrambled to set the deal in motion, which eventually included not just the $20 million dollar loan, but massive stock swaps, collateral arrangements, and the divvying up of Billy Durant's GM holdings. Raskob personally took charge, working out the massively complicated details.[30] Durant, fighting all the way, held on to sizable holdings, about 40 percent of what he had once had, though he had to agree to a valuation of his GM stock—the shares that he would have to give up to make good on his debts—at a bargain price of

$9.50. Durant would later claim that he had been forced to give up some $90 million in stock, if it had been fairly valued, to get out from under the debts he had incurred. At the same time, Durant also knew that he had not been totally frank with the men from DuPont and Morgan; he still had a number of outstanding debts, as well as promises he had made to his wide circle of friends to guarantee their GM losses, all of which would have to be made good out of the stock that remained in his hands. Worst of all, from Billy Durant's perspective, was an ironclad agreement at the heart of the bailout: Durant had to resign immediately from all duties at the General Motors Company. The good men at DuPont and at the Morgan bank had thrown him out of the company he had built.

Durant, not surprisingly, felt betrayed by these terms. In the months that followed his forced resignation, he badmouthed Raskob wherever he could, blaming him for GM's perilous financial situation. Somewhat oddly, he seized upon Raskob's insistence that GM build a new office building as the fount of all the company's troubles. He wrote Alfred Sloan, Sam McLaughlin, and many others reminding them that he had not been responsible for the new building and its attendant costs.[31] It was an odd performance, since the new GM building was not by any means the cause of Durant's downfall or a significant part of GM's financial difficulties in 1920.

Raskob was furious with Durant for trying to offload his problems onto him, which was not in Durant's best interest, since it was Raskob, and Raskob alone, who was charged with sorting out Durant's final financial settlement with GM. After the dust had somewhat settled, Durant wrote Raskob and demanded that GM pay him a final year's salary of $1.5 million and then provide him with substantial compensation for all the expenses he had incurred since taking over the company in 1916. Many of GM's major shareholders, Durant assured Raskob, believed this to be only fair and were angry with Raskob for not treating him more appropriately. Raskob was no longer amused by Billy's methods. What shareholders, he wrote in response, believed that such a package was appropriate? Would Mr. Durant please list their names? He then accused Durant of misrepresenting facts and figures, most obviously of claiming that GM owed Durant a specific sum of $250,000 when in truth that sum represented a loan Durant had made to himself from GM's treasury. As for a final settlement, Raskob was ice cold: "There was no agreement that I recall between us although you and I did have quite clear understandings as to the condition of the various items of accounts between us." Raskob felt that a lump sum payment of $25,000 would be more than generous. Durant ended up getting a good deal more but not what he thought he deserved.[32]

Between November 1920 and April 1921, Raskob was immersed in GM's financial affairs. He was not alone. In late November, John, who remained head of GM's finance committee, arranged for Donaldson Brown, his one-time protégé, to become GM's vice president for finance. With Brown in the lead, the two men took control of GM's inventory accounting procedures. Brown then began a sustained, monumental, and breathtakingly successful campaign to rethink and then institutionalize a new financial control, planning, and forecasting system for the entire GM company.

Brown worked with Raskob but both men had a new boss at General Motors. Pierre had come out of retirement to become GM's new president. Most involved believed that only Pierre du Pont could reassure Wall Street that GM was going to be all right and so provide the credit the company needed to resolve the crisis. Stettinius, the Morgan point man, was insistent. He wrote to a Morgan partner: "Pierre du Pont . . . is certainly the one man in sight who is able to assume immediate direction of the Company's affairs and whip the organization into shape."[33] Alfred Sloan, who was a most interested party in the transition, wrote: "I did not have to think twice to decide who I thought should be the new president." Du Pont, he continued, "was the one individual in General Motors who had the prestige and respect that could give confidence to the organization, to the public, and to the banks, and whose presence could arrest the demoralization that was taking place. The only other man in the corporation who might have been considered for president was John J. Raskob." Pierre was probably the only man actually considering John for the presidency but as he remembered many years later, "He was my choice but I cannot say I pushed it at all."[34] It was not to be. The banking community, on the line for many tens of millions, wanted du Pont, and both Raskob and du Pont understood.

Sloan, for one, was pleased that Raskob was not chosen. Sloan admired Raskob, calling him "brilliant and imaginative . . . a man of big ideas." But Sloan believed that Raskob was too "aggressive" and that his "impatient intelligence" was not what GM needed coming off of the Durant debacle.[35] He was right.

John did not want the job. Nor was he humbled by the mess that he had helped to create. As John helped to lift GM out of the troubles of 1920, he had complete faith that GM was soon going to be making lots and lots of money again and that he, Pierre, the DuPont Company, and GM's remaining executives were just going to be a whole lot richer as a result. He had total confidence that he was going to make that happen. And he was right.

Jazz Age Hero

Raskob had managed the GM crisis with calm, even unnerving competence. He never publicly revealed any self-doubt about his own role in GM's troubles. Nothing in his personal correspondence suggests he ever had any private doubts, either. Nor did he ever express any regrets about removing Billy Durant from the company he had founded. Emotionally, Raskob was well made for the hard business of business. Moreover, Raskob liked crises; he was at his best when problems needed to be solved quickly and he knew it.

Poor Durant had been right about one thing: the auto market was only suffering from a brief downswing. Perhaps if Raskob, du Pont, and the men at Morgan had worked harder to safeguard—manipulate—GM's share price in the late fall of 1920 or had provided Durant with a sufficiently large personal bridge loan, Durant could have survived his reckless stock market play and emerged from the crisis a slightly chastened, much wealthier head of General Motors. But Billy had burned up whatever good faith and trust he had earned with Raskob and du Pont and no Wall Street banker had ever wished Durant well. In the aftermath of his forced retirement, Durant threw himself back into the auto business and plunged into the deep end of the Great Bull Market of the 1920s but Durant was running out of comebacks. He would end his days penurious, kept afloat only by the charity of Raskob, Sloan, and a few others who never forgave him but never forgot him, either. A new era was beginning at GM and it was going to be, as Raskob predicted in early 1920, one of the most profitable runs in American business history.

GM's rapid recovery under new and much improved management made Raskob look and feel better than ever. At the end of 1920, he summed up the GM bailout to his old friend Elias Ahuja, who had some fifteen years earlier in Chile coached the young and relatively inexperienced Raskob on how to close "the option" with Helena: "We purchased Mr. Durant's holdings in the General Motors Corporation, which involved raising about twenty-seven million dollars ($27,000,000). This is quite an accomplishment and it was practically done in twenty-four hours and in one of the worst money markets we have ever experienced. We persuaded Pierre to take the presidency and I look to see things improve very fast indeed."[1] The expected improvements arrived almost exactly on the schedule Raskob predicted.

In the early 1920s Raskob was zooming back and forth from his home base in Wilmington to GM's corporate headquarters in New York City to GM's operational center in Detroit. During the week, when he was not in Michigan or any of the dozens of other places where GM had business, he could usually be found in his large sunny office on the southeast corner of the 24th floor of the GM Building at Broadway and 57th Street. At the end of 1921 he wrote DuPont Company president Irénée du Pont: "While it is not pleasant for one of such large family to be away so much of the time, the General Motors work is so extremely interesting that one feels a high degree of compensation for the sacrifice made."[2]

Durant's efforts to blame Raskob for GM's problems had failed. Instead, Wall Street, the business press, and the nation's leading businessmen praised Raskob for his financial legerdemain. His ability to raise money and refinance GM's short-term debt and then engineer the Morgan-DuPont rescue of the Durant holdings during the recessionary dark days of 1920 was seen as heroic. In particular, Raskob cemented his strong relations with the bankers at the House of Morgan. In the clutch, Morgan had worked closely with Raskob to assure GM's survival, remove Durant, and protect the DuPont Company. Raskob and the men at Morgan would team up throughout the decade. John made that bond clear in mid-1922 when DuPont's new treasurer, Walter Carpenter, argued that the DuPont Company needed to expand its banking network, seeking the best terms and arrangements. Raskob firmly disagreed, "I, personally, feel very strongly that all our financial arrangements, no matter how small, should be conducted through J. P. Morgan & Company and we should recognize them as our financial agent."[3] Raskob believed in relationship banking and his close involvement with the Morgan bankers was fundamental to his personal and professional life during the 1920s.

In just over twenty years, John's life had gone from local to regional to national and international. Everywhere doors opened. As the scope of his life widened, John dined at the White House, met regularly with New York's corporate chieftains, and both invested and gambled with some of America's wealthiest men. Yet he remained committed, as well, to the men with whom he had grown up decades earlier in Lockport. Raskob made sure that he kept up with their latest professional and family news. He helped them financially when they needed it—and many did. He gave them career advice, offered up his business connections, kept up a steady stream of stock tips, and even paid college tuition for several of his old friends' sons. His boyhood friends and his memories of Lockport seemed to give him the sense of psychological continuity he needed to square off against the extraordinary risks and ever-changing demands that character-ized his adult life. In appreciation of a gift of two old photos dated 1894 and 1895, Raskob wrote to one of his many friends who never left Lockport: "Those were happy days indeed and I seldom acquire more pleasure from anything that I do from recalling and thinking over old times."[4] Raskob normally kept whatever sentimental feelings he had in close check except when it came to his childhood and youth, the time, in other words, before his father died and he became, in his own eyes, a man with heavy responsibilities.

John remained devoted, as well, to his mother and to his sisters and brother. As late as 1922 he still referred to his younger sibling as the "kids," even though his brother "Willow" was by this time a successful, wealthy DuPont executive in his own right. He provided for his mother and widowed sister Edith, care-fully managing the considerable financial assets he had put in their names and he also made sure that his favorite sister "Gertie" and her family prospered, as well. His mother, who had moved close to John's family in Wilmington, traveled frequently back to Lockport and to Indiana to visit her extended family and old friends, and John often arranged the details of her travels himself. While she was away he wrote her regularly, keeping her up to date on his family's health, the weather, the general state of his affairs, and little tidbits of everyday life. In February 1922, Raskob sent his mother and Edith on a luxurious trip through Europe, calling on his extensive network of friends and colleagues in England, France, and elsewhere to look after them. His letters to his "gang," as he addressed Edith and his mother, during their extended travel were sweet and intimate: "I am glad you are going to have some extra time in Paris as you will enjoy this very much indeed. I presume you will be in Paris on my birthday and if I were there I would help you drink some of that white and red wine.... All join in sending love and hoping that you are most thoroughly enjoying your trip, I am, Your affectionate son."[5] He was and meant to be a good son and a good brother.

John continued to travel home to Archmere as often as he could, usually on weekends, to be with Helena and the children. By the mid-1920s, the oldest children went to Catholic boarding schools, but they too usually were home on the weekends and the whole crew knew that when their father arrived he would join them in play. When the pogo stick craze hit America, John brought at least one of the "toddle sticks" back from the Gimble Brothers Department Store and bounced around Archmere like a madman, taking turns—a long turn, in his case—with the children. Two days after Christmas, he wrote a friend: "I (the largest of the kids) of course, had to learn [to pogo] with the result that I really am quite expert already. Last night, much to the amusement of mother and some old folks, as well as the kids, I danced on it to the music of the gramophone quite successfully."[6] John still very much relished his household full of kids and was an enthusiastic host, as well, for his children's friends and his friends' children. "The household," he wrote in 1921 to Walter Johnson, one of his new GM friends, "is a bevy of excitement." John encouraged Johnson to "park" his children there at any time: "with eleven children a couple more can hardly be noticed."[7]

John offered weekend fun and regular discipline, but it was Skipper (as everyone called Helena in homage to the ship-shape fashion in which she ran the household) who provided most of the day-to-day affection and love. John and Helena had their last child in 1922. During the 1920s their marriage was changing; although Helena sometimes joined John in New York City for a weekend holiday away from the children, each was becoming more independent as their lives became less intertwined.

John was in the world. Through his new circle, he was discovering the New York demimonde. He watched his wealthy friends run wild; he became close to men who could not have been more different from Pierre. Prohibition, which went into effect January 16, 1920, made a night out on the town a different, more louche kind of experience, even for the rich. John, like all his friends, stockpiled liquor. In New York, Atlantic City, Palm Beach, and numerous places in between, he gambled. In 1922, John wrote one of his wealthy friends, giving him the low down on how to have fun in Palm Beach: "Bradley's is a famous gambling place there and to come within the law they conduct it in the form of a club, known as the Beach Club. It is here that the millionaire, multi-millionaires, and would-be-millionaires congregate every afternoon and evening for tea, dinner, and gambling and you will perhaps see a greater number and value in jewels here than any other place in the world, even including court functions."[8] John suggested that his friend use his name to gain entry to the club; he also reported that the real action at the tables did not begin until after midnight and generally ran until 3 or 4 A.M. Raskob was also a Broadway regular. He hosted opening night festivities, sometimes with Helena and sometimes without. He was also seen in the company of showgirls. John had always liked to have fun. Now he had the money to do what he wanted.

Even as Raskob strained the boundaries of propriety, he became more dedicated to his Church. He was richer than he had ever imagined he would become and began to share more of that wealth with his diocese and with the Vatican. In the last half of the 1920s, as John's corporate duties became less onerous, he committed much more of his resources and his talent to his Church and found new satisfaction in spiritual reward.

Raskob turned 40 in 1919. That was, then, to be a man of already advanced years; life expectancy in the United States in 1920 was less than 55. But John certainly did not feel old. In his forties, John took on ever more, trying out new arenas and seeking out new experiences. He expended his abundant energies across the spectrum of elite life in America.

In Big Business, the world in which he still spent most of his waking hours, everybody knew Raskob. He was closely identified with General Motors, but he kept his hand in at DuPont and he played the stock market with the big men. The papers and magazines covered his business moves, as well as his speculations and declarations. In 1925, *Time* magazine, in one of the dozens of articles in the 1920s that discussed Raskob's doings, paid typical homage to what its writers called "Mr. Raskob's foresight." *Time* reported that the DuPont Company, in large part due to its investment in General Motors, had just declared a 40 percent common stock dividend worth some $38 million. "Behind the declaration of this $38,000,000 'melon,'" continued *Time* in it is inimitable prose, "lies a story."[9] That story was John J. Raskob and his one-man campaign to invest DuPont's wartime capital surplus in the automobile business. While many sang Raskob's praises for his money-making gifts, his well-publicized suggestion that all Americans deserved an opportunity to prosper through stock ownership earned him even more acclaim.

John Raskob, the half-Irish, half-German Catholic boy from Lockport, had become one of America's best known businessmen, a high flier who was in tight with Wall Street; his offhand comments moved the stock markets; the mass media celebrated his rise to riches. In this decade that marked the zenith of his career, Raskob tried to keep up with everything: politics, public policy, new technologies, and new industries. He kept GM financially strong, helped invent the modern auto consumer marketplace, made the company's top managers millionaires, and made tens of millions for himself. Raskob was a New York heavyweight in America's business-obsessed, stock-market worshipping Jazz Age. Once again Raskob was reinventing himself and his timing was spectacular.

"John J. Raskob of Wilmington, Delaware, is to-day the organizing genius of this country," reported Samuel Crowther in the October 1920 issue of *The World's Work*.[10] The timing of this bold claim was a bit odd given the considerable troubles that were at that moment plaguing General Motors but Crowther, one of the nation's leading business writers, was looking to situate Raskob in a broader context than GM's fourth quarter problems. *The World's Work* was among the preeminent business-oriented magazines in the United States and it did not try to cover breaking news. For its readership of sophisticated professionals, investors, and corporate managers, the monthly magazine sorted out international financial and political developments and explored the changing face and place of business in American society.[11] The article, "John J. Raskob and the World's Largest Business," aimed to alert readers to the astonishing role this financial genius had played in bringing together two of the world's most enterprising operations: the DuPont Company and General Motors.

Crowther was himself a sharp operator and not a disinterested observer of American business. He profiled Raskob for a couple of reasons. First, he had an interest in getting in close with the nation's leading businessmen and he was good at gaining their trust, an ability that he used to secure lucrative writing assignments. After Crowther wrote his generous piece on Raskob, he and John developed a lasting and mutually advantageous relationship. While keeping on the right side of GM's leadership, Crowther was also buzzing around the notoriously difficult and already quite famous Henry Ford. Within a few months of publishing his profile of Raskob, Crowther had worked out a deal to "co-author" Ford's autobiography, which was published in 1922 and quickly became a runaway best-seller. Second, Crowther was no muckraker, a journalistic type that was fast disappearing from the business-friendly media of the 1920s. He was a Big Business true believer. Raskob was the anchor for a big, attention-grabbing piece on the future of American business and the rise of a new investor-friendly corporate economy.

Raskob, he explained to his readers, "is not the successor of Harriman, or of Morgan, or of Hill, or of George Perkins, or of any of those dead giants who consolidated and built along their own particular lines. He is in the way of being the founder of a new dynasty. He has effected the greatest combination of interests—potentially and actually—the world has ever seen—a combination greater than the Steel Corporation, greater than the loosely connected series of interests which are known in a general way as the Standard Oil Group." Crowther continued, "This new combination manufactures and sells many hundreds of different sorts of finished products in practically every part of the world and under dozens of corporate names.... In almost any part of the world you can make your living by working for these interests or you can buy from them the motive machinery with which to construct, or to travel, or you go to them to deck out yourself or your house, or, your fancy changing, you may call on them for whatever is necessary to blow up your friends or whatever you have constructed." Crowther understood Raskob's business world rather well. It was a realm in which the particularities of product or even industry mattered little; the hard-played game was profitable investment of capital. While Crowther snuck in a bit of a low blow with his fillip about DuPont's willingness, if "your fancy" changes, to sell you "whatever is necessary to blow up your friends," he did have a point. Raskob took no offense. Both men believed that whatever ghosts of amorality haunted the system in the hunt for profitable investment, the more significant fact was that jobs were created, incomes improved, and prosperity spread.[12]

The real focus of the article and the reason that Crowther focused on Raskob and not Pierre du Pont or Billy Durant or any of the other big men associated with the "greatest combination of interests...the world has ever seen" became clear only in the last page of the long profile. Tellingly, it had nothing to do with Raskob's small-town, "immigrant" boy background or rise from $5 a week stenographer to industrial giant. The exaggerated "rags-to-riches" approach that had been a staple of press coverage of Raskob just a few years earlier had lost its hold on the public's imagination—or at least on the imaginations of the generally well-off readers of *The World's Work*.

Raskob, Crowther explained, is "a man with an extraordinarily keen business sense, a vivid but not at all a fantastic imagination, and power of translating imagination into figures and then convincing others that the dream can be made to come true." Crowther was impressed by Raskob's vision of what the new capitalist society that he and his colleagues were building could and should mean not for the elite few but for the many.

Raskob's vision, Crowther argued, pointed the way out of the labor troubles of the past few years. He let Raskob make the case in his own words: "The largest problem that I see in modern industry is to obtain capable managers and workers," Raskob states, but "unless a manager or worker has an interest—a financial interest—in what he does, he will hardly develop his capability. He is not content to see all the money he makes going to someone else." Thus, Raskob argued that all big corporate employers should offer all their employees stock options: "We calculate that any man working for twenty or thirty years will thus have a fund on which he can retire and live not merely comfortably but very well indeed."[13] This sort of plan was, of course, exactly what Raskob was implementing at both DuPont and GM and not just for top managers. Raskob wanted everyone to be a capitalist committed to the profitability of the business that employed him.

This financial stake, Raskob continued, was necessary but not sufficient to win an employee's loyalty and greatest effort: "Together with money he must have complete responsibility in his own sphere. He must be more than a cog.... All ideas cannot come from the top."[14] Raskob offered a far less well developed model for assuring every worker that he was "more than a cog." He only insisted that all well-run businesses had to avoid rigid centralization of authority and that top executives had to find ways to give their employees' opportunities to develop the ideas that would keep their company competitive and profitable.

Crowther praised Raskob's vision. While noting that Raskob's investment strategy linking together DuPont and GM had produced a massive industrial combination that might raise a previous generation's concerns about trusts and monopolies, he assured his mostly well-to-do readers: "These are not the old ideas of combination: they are new. The principal thought is not combination but work. It is an enlarging—not a shutting off—of opportunity through something that might be described as a kind of socialization of money in the hands of individuals."[15]

Crowther's lengthy profile was picked up the next month by the popular digest magazine *Current Opinion*. An abridged, rewritten, and retitled version appeared as "A New Captain of Industry: A Rising Luminary of Industry and His Vast Orbit."[16] The long sections on the du Pont cousins, Billy Durant, and the rise of both the DuPont Company and General Motors were gone. The piece was squarely focused on Raskob. It began with a vaguely nativist nod to the "Alger" boy notion: "The name Raskob does not seem to suggest romance. Yet John J. Raskob, of Wilmington, Delaware, who, a few years ago, was a stenographer in the du Pont employ, is today recognized as one of the organizing geniuses of this country and is by way of being the most important asset of the largest corporation in the world." Amid the generous praise that followed, which also included a typical tip-off to Raskob's stature—"the Napoleon of industry"—the article honed in on Raskob's vision of a class-conflict-free society made whole and prosperous by a new corporate order in which "every man in the organization [is given] a chance to buy stock and then adding out of the profits of the companies to the stock that he buys."[17] Raskob, the piece suggested to a larger audience, offered Americans an alternative to the bitter labor wars of the past few years while also assuaging the concerns many middle-class Americans had about the threat giant corporations presented to their dreams of workplace autonomy built on individual productive labor. John Raskob had become an apostle of a new kind of American prosperity.

Raskob was not by any means the only person promoting the widespread ownership of corporate stocks and bonds. Already by the turn of the century a few leading economists had made similar arguments, concluding that the wealth-producing characteristics of the capitalist system needed to be—and easily could be—made to benefit far more people. John Bates Clark, one of the most articulate of these advocates, described a company stock-ownership plan in which "the men who work will have a proprietary interest in the tools of labor and share in what the tools produce. The socialist is not the only man who can have a beatific vision."[18] Even before Raskob had helped to develop an employee stock plan at the DuPont Company and then at GM, the industrialist and Morgan banker George Perkins had led the charge to implement employee stock plans in 1903 at US Steel and McCormick, on whose boards he served.

Despite such growing enthusiasm for stock ownership, most advocates still urged caution. Perkins, following the lead set by John Bates Clark, believed that if working- and middle-class people were to invest more broadly in corporate stocks, the government needed to lend a hand by providing sufficient regulation to the securities business to keep the unscrupulous seller from cheating the unsophisticated buyer. Many supported some sort of government oversight, including the administrations of all three of the Progressive Era presidencies. Roosevelt, Taft, and Wilson all worked to craft some form of federal regulation of the securities business, in general, and the workings of the leading equities market, the New York Stock Exchange, in particular. All failed to impose any real federal regulation.

Despite the headline-making charges produced by congressional investigators of the equities business, who demonstrated a range of corrupt practices, well-connected and politically influential members of the banking community and the corporate world, as well as key members of the New York Stock Exchange, made too strong a case—an argument well-backed up by their financial relationships with key members of Congress—that federal regulation would damage the nation's credit markets and the well-honed workings of the market system. Self-regulation and investors' own scrutiny, they successfully argued, were sufficient checks. While most states created some form of corporate reporting regulation during the first two decades of the twentieth century, the securities markets still operated, in the final analysis, on the principle of caveat emptor. As a result, many economists and financial experts still worried that most people lacked the tools, information, and necessary safeguards needed to invest in the stock markets as the Jazz Age began. Stock market investment, they argued, remained a risky business.[19]

Few working people at the advent of the 1920s were dreaming of investing their savings in stocks and bonds or hoping that their employers would offer them a stock investment plan. Most industrial workers, as the great strikes of the immediate postwar years demonstrated, thought their best hopes for economic security lay in collective bargaining. But in the aftermath of the postwar red scare, the crushing of the steel strike, and the failure of the Wilson Administration to find some middle ground between workers and their bosses, many people across class lines were seeking some alternative solution.

As Crowther recognized, Raskob thought he had an answer—though given the obvious risks associated with stock market investing, especially for the ill-informed general public, Raskob did not yet champion universal participation in the equities markets. He did believe, quite firmly, that employee stock-ownership plans offered employees a way to build a stable economic future. Raskob was proud of the plan he had set up at GM for hourly workers and was pleased by the attention the press gave it at the end of 1920.

Raskob had, at least in part, instigated the press coverage of his exploits and ideas through a rare bit of authorship. Somehow, in the midst of GM's troubles, he had found the time to write a long, sometimes awkwardly phrased article on Big Business and the labor question. He had been batting the issues around, talking about them with his colleagues, since the 1919 Washington, DC conference. In October 1920, the nation's most prestigious journal of business management, *System*, published his essay. It was his first publication and, unlike later articles published under his name, he seems to have written this one by himself.

Raskob began his article with a long justification of "Bigness" in American industry. In a look backward at the antimonopoly, antitrust movement of the first two decades of the twentieth century, he made a strong case that Big Business was good for America. At the same time, he was careful to explain that he was not advocating for monopolization. Today, the only people who approve of industrial monopoly, he wrote, are the socialists: "The socialists say that industry should be monopolized by the state and is then right."[20] Raskob argued that state monopolies were no better than capitalist monopolies. Monopoly, no matter the sponsor, he wrote, "leads to restricted trade at high prices," which produces a limited marketplace that provides no incentive for innovation or increased productivity. But a very large corporation in a competitive marketplace, he explained, can centralize a number of its functions, create competition within its own organization by applying tough financial controls and thereby lower costs and prices and so create an ever larger market for its products. Innovation, he insisted, not stability, pushes forward economic development. Competition, Raskob argued, both internally and externally, produces the prod that makes people and companies work better for their customers.

Raskob then veered off in an unexpected direction. "I should carry this thought of competition," he wrote, "into the labor side of industry." In a long aside, he sketched out a novel idea. Rather than organize labor into "closed shop" collective bargaining units and thereby create an inefficient, anticompetitive labor monopoly in a given industry, why not create competing labor organizations "so that I, as a manufacturer, might be able to ask bids on having a thing done—that is, I could say to the American Federation of Labor and to the new organization, 'Which service should I buy?' Then these organizations would submit their bids on a business basis." Such labor competition would, Raskob argued, "raise real wages . . . because so many men refuse to do a day's work for a day's pay" but in a competitive bargaining model they would have a collective incentive to perform their work productively and so maximize their ability to gain profitable work contracts.[21] Any shop floor manager or production manager in the early 1920s could have explained to Raskob the disruptive impracticality of his idea of competitive, organized mass-labor forces in mass-production facilities but as a future model for flexible, team-based contracting Raskob was onto something. Of course, Raskob understood the practical limits to his thought experiment, as well. He mostly intended to pull the tail of the labor union organizers with whom he had been negotiating in late 1919 at President Wilson's invitation.

More relevant to Raskob's actual work was the detailed case he made for employee stock-ownership plans. At the top end of the new corporate economy, he had lived through the transition from owner-managers to manager-owners and he was personally aware that "today in the big corporation we no longer have the strict relation of employer and employee." He explained: "Not many years ago . . . big concerns were owned on the family basis and no matter how high an 'outsider' rose, he remained a salaried man. . . . But in this day of corporate ownership, it is the exception rather than the rule not to find the leading executives with a fairly strong stock interest. That establishes their identity with the company, they hold the dual position of representative of capital and servants of capital. They hold a position that every man working for the corporation can and should attain. And when all do we shall be rid of the idea of working for the soulless corporation." Raskob detailed his plan for stock ownership using a variety of hypotheticals that demonstrated how stock-ownership plans would lift employees "out of the usual blind alley of work and we need not bother about pension funds or other charitable undertakings." Raskob concluded, "No man ever got rich just by saving his wages—he gets rich by making use of the money he has saved."[22] Raskob was not the only person pitching a mass-investment society in the first year of the 1920s, but he was the only one who could back it up with his own rise from $5 a week stenographer to multimillionaire deal-maker extraordinaire, and the publicity that followed Raskob from 1920 onward likely convinced an increasing number of Americans to put their money into the stock market.

Raskob's forays into the public sphere were still very much limited by his full-time obligations. GM needed a lot of attention after Durant was officially shown the door on December 1, 1920. Working under Pierre's calm and calming leadership, Raskob, John Pratt, Donaldson Brown, Armory Haskell, and Alfred Sloan began a massive corporate reform effort. Raskob had a vital role in the reorganization, not the least because Pierre still had total trust in him. Raskob's position was strengthened by his physical proximity to Pierre, which now included the long train trips they took every other week, often accompanied by other top GM men, back and forth to GM's operational center in Detroit and around to other GM facilities. There they spent three or four packed days meeting with various high-ranking executives. Du Pont and Raskob talked together about everything and both men delighted in their renewed working relationship. But much of the actual work that had to be done to repair General Motors and prepare it for the expected upsurge in consumer demand called for skills John did not have. Alfred Sloan quickly became Pierre's and GM's most indispensable man.

Sloan, like Pierre du Pont, had graduated from MIT, earning his degree in the hot new field of electrical engineering. Like Raskob and du Pont, Sloan had spectacularly good quantitative skills. Sloan also had a brilliant administrative mind, a seemingly innate talent that he had assiduously developed during the seventeen years he had run his own business, the Hyatt Roller Bearing Company and then after Durant bought Hyatt during his five often frustrating years as a divisional vice president at GM. In 1920, he turned forty-five years old.

Sloan demonstrated his potential utility to du Pont even before Durant's demise. In September 1920, when the corporate chaos had pushed Sloan nearly to the brink, he had sent GM's chairman of the board a document blandly titled

"Organization Study." The short but detailed document explained how GM's slovenly corporate structure could be effectively remade. Sloan had previously presented the plan to Durant, who graciously thanked Sloan for his thoughts and promptly discarded it. If Durant did actually look at Sloan's analysis, it must have appeared to him as equal parts gibberish and complaint. Du Pont loved it.

Sloan had created a management model somewhat similar to the structure that Pierre and his men had instituted early on at DuPont. Sloan maintained the centrality of GM's two existing overarching executive committees: the executive committee and the finance committee. But Sloan had gone much further in plotting out a highly rationalized decentralized corporate scheme that in his words "will definitely place the line of authority throughout [GM's] extensive operations as well as to co-ordinate each branch of service, at the same time destroying none of the effectiveness with which its work has heretofore been conducted." Building on GM's strong divisional strengths—the fiefdoms that Billy Durant had allowed to run with great autonomy except when he felt otherwise—Sloan's plan continued to give GM's division heads a great deal of responsibility and authority in running their operations. But Sloan made them answerable to the two master committees that looked after overarching corporate strategy and profitability. There would be strict accounting: division heads would be rewarded when they performed and punished, even fired, when they did not.

The Durant-built, jerry-rigged conglomeration was to be restructured into neat, coherent and measurable boxes. Every box on Sloan's organization chart was connected to another, creating corporate hierarchy but also divisional freedom and producing a delicate balancing act. Pierre studied Sloan's creation, tweaked it slightly, and with total delight pronounced it good, very, very good. Beginning on January 3, 1921, GM's executives began to implement the grand plan. It would take until 1924 to realize fully Sloan's vision. A great deal of housekeeping was necessary, including the retiring of a few of the old Durant loyalists who had been running key GM divisions. Sloan, named vice president of operations, was in the middle of much of this reorganizing. Raskob, the reluctant administrator who never relished committee work, was not, even though he, too, was appointed in mid-January 1921 to the reorganized executive committee. In 1921 alone, the executive committee, chaired by du Pont but managed by Sloan, met an extraordinary 101 times. Basic policies aimed at bringing strategic coherence to GM were created and plans for implementation were detailed.[23]

In April 1921, Sloan also took on the chairmanship of a special committee to analyze GM's product policy. Working closely with Charles Mott, the former mayor of Flint, veteran industrialist, and long-time GM man who ran the car and truck division, Sloan came up with a breakthrough strategy that he presented two months later to Pierre du Pont and the other members of the executive

committee. Rather than compete directly with the market-leading Ford by producing an innovative, economical car, Sloan believed GM should turn their current happenstance assemblage of various automobile lines—Chevrolet, Buick,
Oldsmobile, Cadillac, Oakland, Sheridan, and Scripps-Booth—into a coherent
strategy, creating what he later called a "car for every purse and purpose." While
Ford believed that the great majority of people simply needed a mechanically
sound automobile that would get them efficiently from one place to another
at the lowest possible price, Sloan saw other possibilities. Automobiles could
represent consumer's style and economic status. They could be fashionable,
with model changes every year. Massive marketing and advertising campaigns,
Sloan insisted, were well worth the cost to make sure consumers—a word Sloan
adopted well before most other manufacturing executives—knew about GM's
broad array of enticing products.[24]

Sloan was quickly proving himself to du Pont and the rest of GM's leadership,
Raskob included, as a corporate genius of the first order. Officially, Sloan was
vice president of operations but he had his hand in almost everything. With du
Pont's support he was laying down administrative principles that magnified and
consolidated his authority. His base of power was the executive committee and
in the early 1920s that committee was the site of most of GM's most important
and adventurous decision making.

Sloan's control of the executive committee limited Raskob's power at GM. To
a large extent, Raskob had ceded this control to Sloan or at least had not fought
for it. Going back to his days at DuPont, Raskob had never been much interested in operational control or in the kind of time-consuming committee work
that GM's new and complex decentralized organizational structure demanded
from its top executives. Raskob was still important; he was the vice president
of finance and, simultaneously, the head of the finance committee. At DuPont,
the finance committee was in the thick of much of the action and it was far from
unimportant at GM. Officially, it was equal in importance to the executive committee insomuch as it was charged both with overseeing the financial controls
that governed strategic decision making and with working out GM's debt financing, as well as resource allocation. But almost all of these duties and responsibilities were not what Raskob did best or most enjoyed. He had become ever more
adept and well-known for his skills at financing expansion and development. In
the early 1920s, GM did not need to find more money to expand and develop;
it needed to reorganize, prioritize, rationalize, strategize, and cut loose some of
Durant's more feckless acquisitions.

In December 1920, Raskob's first major decision in the post-Durant era was
to move his old assistant, Donaldson Brown, from DuPont to GM. While Brown
never got the kind of accolades at GM that Sloan did, or the public recognition, the work he did in the next few years was of central importance to GM's

long-term success. Using many of the same measures he had invented at DuPont, Brown set up the forecasting and measurement tools that allowed GM to figure out how best to distribute internal investments, plan production, discover low or negative returns on capital, and pinpoint and reward success. Brown brought financial visibility to GM's many precincts. Raskob was, nominally, Brown's boss and he oversaw the development and implementation of these policies, but it was Brown who was the essential man.

Raskob was hardly idle at GM. In the immediate aftermath of Durant's departure, Raskob took charge of refinancing GM's massive debt. In particular, he partnered with the Morgan bank to rework the DuPont Company's financing of the Durant debacle cleanup. He also oversaw the last steps of the takeover of all Chevrolet equities by GM, an arrangement that Durant had never quite finalized. Even as Raskob structured these complex financial maneuvers, in the first four months of 1921 he also served as du Pont's eyes and ears on the inventory assessment and reorganization committee. Raskob and John Pratt, as well as a team of able executives, working nonstop, figured out exactly what the company had, where everything had been stored or dumped, what had to be liquidated or discounted, and what the company would need once orders picked up. It was a perfect job for Raskob and his order-seeking intelligence. The committee worked out that GM had a total write-off of $84.9 million. It was a big gulp, but du Pont did not hesitate to make the numbers public, demonstrating GM's new financial rigor and transparency.

Together Raskob and Pratt oversaw the invention of a new cross-divisional system that integrated purchases with production needs while accounting for finished products. GM had become a very big operation and under Durant too often economies of scale and coordinated activities had been lost in the uncharted thickets of the company's many dispersed and uncommunicative plants, divisions, and facilities. Raskob and Pratt were trying to bring order to that chaos. Here, too, Brown stepped in to help organize the data and produce the formulas that allowed other executives to make use of the system. On April 21, Raskob was able to announce to the executive committee that they had created an integrated management system that should prevent future inventory pileups, even in the event of a demand shock like the one they had just suffered.[25]

Raskob had plenty else to do at GM but once again he understood that he was not going to run the show—even by mid-1921, Alfred Sloan's star was clearly ascendant—and that his role at GM would not demand all of his time. With Don Brown overseeing the complex internal financial issues and questions, Raskob was by late 1922 released from much of the everyday business of GM's financial offices, a situation made certain when Brown was named GM treasurer in 1921. Absolutely, and somewhat remarkably, none of this bothered Raskob. He was behind Brown's promotion and he applauded Sloan's rise. Raskob liked doing things, lots of things, and he certainly liked accumulating wealth but he really did not care about company politics or titles. He did not want to do what Sloan did and he took pride in Brown's smashing success. To his credit, Raskob was the kind of man who cheered on and was cheered by his associates' successes.

By this time the day-to-day oversight of corporate financial data did not intrigue and excite Raskob the way it had even five years earlier at DuPont, though keeping his own meticulous personal financial records still very much appealed to his sense of good order and disciplined responsibility. Raskob also recognized that Sloan was much better than he was at managing and administering, and he was happy to see his friend rise to the challenges his new opportunities at GM afforded him. Raskob was fine with how things were turning out at GM and was suitably pleased when the company began making money again that year. By early 1922, just as Raskob had predicted, GM once gain began turning a big profit.

The GM roller coaster ride from summer 1920 to spring 1922 had, in fact, left Raskob feeling elated, not just because the company had emerged from crisis stronger than ever. During that time, he and Pierre had worked in perfect tandem, just like in the old days. While Sloan, Brown, Mott, Pratt and several other top GM executives were doing much of the corporate reorganizing and strategic implementing, Pierre had looked to Raskob, as he had for so many years while they were together at DuPont, for constant support and advice. Du Pont had great respect for Sloan and he quickly surmised which of the GM men could be counted on but always it was Raskob upon whom du Pont placed his trust and with whom he shared his concerns.

Pierre had not wanted to come out of retirement. He loved his gardens, his fountains, and the good works he could quietly perform in Delaware. But Raskob had convinced him that GM needed his competence and Wall Street needed his presence at GM's helm. While du Pont took on the leadership of GM, above all, to safeguard his family's and his company's massive investment in General Motors, he had also done it because John had asked and because John had promised that he would do everything in his power to assist him.

From the moment du Pont took up GM's presidency, Raskob was, as promised and as Pierre desired, at his side. Pierre had stepped down from the DuPont presidency May 1919 and even before that Raskob had moved out of Pierre's immediate orbit to take up of his duties at GM. Years had gone by since the two old friends had shared the kind of day-to-day activity and sense of linked fortune that had structured both of their lives for so long, almost from the first time they had met in 1900. Both men had missed that partnership and that intimacy.

Raskob felt for Pierre du Pont more than he ever felt for anyone else, including his wife and children. The two men understood each other. They had shared an extraordinary adventure together. When they met, Pierre was a well-born fellow with an excellent position and strong prospects. And John, though very young and with no decided advantages, had already proven himself to be a gifted and aggressive business talent. But they had both, in their own different ways, been young men struggling to find their way in life. Raskob, certainly, but du Pont, too, had no lock on the future. They had no sure sense that they would each become, in two decades' time, nationally renowned and extraordinarily wealthy corporate giants. Together, they had.

John understood that without Pierre he would never have risen so far. John never saw himself as Pierre's equal. Raskob had a remarkably unqualified faith in his own ability, but he understood that Pierre du Pont had changed everything for him. He believed that he owed Pierre everything.

In May 1922, John took a few days off from family and work to nurse a bad cold. Alone at the Hotel Monticello in Atlantic City, Raskob wrote du Pont an extraordinary letter. He wanted Pierre to know how indebted he felt to him and how much, indeed, he loved him. First of all, John wanted Pierre to know just how exhilarating it was to be working again with him: "I am, and have been, walking on air for the past year and a half, and the best part of it all is that you continue to keep me there, the ties of friendship and bonds of love seeming to grow tighter all the time." In an outpouring of emotion, unlike anything John expresses in any of the thousands of letters he wrote to others, he told Pierre: "You have put it within my power to really enjoy some of the pleasures of life, and the best part of it all is the affection and love you feel toward me. It has been brought home to me often in the past eighteen months that money counts very little in this life of ours, what we really need is happiness and believe me, you have been the source of happiness and joy to an extent that I never expect to be able to repay." He continued: "You have made my work a real pleasure, my life a happiness, and have implanted yourself in my soul as a real ideal, one whom any-body would be proud to emulate.... Truly, you are just wonderful, Daddy, and I love you more than I can ever explain."[26] With GM's financial problems largely solved, working alongside Pierre again, and with his personal fortune booming, John felt himself a very lucky man.

In spring 1923, Raskob began work on what would turn out to be his last major contribution to the success of General Motors. At du Pont's urging and in accord with everything he himself had been preaching for the last several years, Raskob set out to create a stock-option plan for General Motors' top executives. The plan would assure that GM's managers would become loyal owners with every incentive to maximize GM's earnings. Working closely with Don Brown and in constant consultation with Pierre, Raskob threw himself into the task. The Management Securities Company, as GM's executive stock-option plan would be called, was the last big corporate financial maneuver John and Pierre would work on together. The idea was simple: set up a stock bonus plan for GM's top executives that would reward them for their achievements and also bind them to GM. Financing this plan would be anything but easy.

In late spring 1923, Raskob and Don Brown decided that they had to escape from GM's headquarters in New York to work out the plan. No matter what they did, so long as they were in New York they would never be left alone long enough to focus on the task at hand. Raskob had been planning a summer family trip to Lake Placid in the Adirondacks and he proposed that he and Brown take a suite of rooms at the Lake Placid Club and stay there until they figured out how to structure and find the money to finance and maintain the stock-option plan. Brown agreed and the two men, without staff support, took the train up to the splendid isolation of Lake Placid. Surrounded by documents, they began working the numbers. Their goal was to devise a scheme that simultaneously maintained the DuPont Company's controlling interest in GM, as well as the bond payments GM owed DuPont, while finding sufficient GM shares that could be given to deserving GM executives at little or no direct costs to the men. Holed up for days, the two corporate finance masterminds began trying out a variety of scenarios.

They devised a plan that defies simple description. Basically, they began moving GM equity assets from an already existing DuPont holding company that Raskob had previously created to hold some of the GM stock bought during the Durant debacle to a newly devised GM holding Company—the Managers Securities Company. They worked out medium-term notes to finance that move, as well as to purchase additional shares of GM stock from the DuPont Company's massive holdings. To reduce tax exposure and financing costs, some of these movements of shares involved complex debt swaps and trading of assets. At the same time, Raskob and Brown decided, GM would use a portion, at first 6 percent, of its earnings, to contribute stock to the GM holding company. Finally, Pierre du Pont, himself, would sell a big bloc of GM stock into the new Managers Security Company in exchange for some cash and a large bond issue that would be financed through a portion of the dividends earned through the holding company's GM shares. As always, the deal involved a great amount of leveraging of assets through debt-financing.

Once sufficient GM equities had been accumulated, this holding company, the Managers Securities Company, would distribute stock to selected GM executives, via instructions from the General Motors Company, for a modest initial payment. Then these deserving executives would use subsequent GM dividend distributions to pay off the price of the stock over time. So long as GM made money and distributed sufficiently large dividend payments the executives would make money. If GM earned a good deal of money and if share prices went up as well, these men could make a great deal of money. If GM could not distribute share dividends and if the price of GM stock collapsed, the men could make nothing, would be on the hook for installment payments on the shares they had already agreed to buy, and could even lose money—that is, unless GM's leadership chose to bail out their leading executives during hard times by paying off the stock option costs directly, a scenario made quite possible by the fact that executives participating in the Managers Securities Company were GM's leadership.

In late June, Pierre du Pont and Alfred Sloan weighed in on the plan. Both men were enthusiastic and impressed. Perhaps not surprisingly, the two men only differed over the plan's implementation. Du Pont wanted to spread the benefits of the plan widely so as to include some 150 top executives. Sloan, who would in all likelihood receive a lion's share of the stock, made the case for a smaller pool of recipients. Sloan won the argument. For the next several months interested parties at DuPont, including President Irénée du Pont, debated the details of the planned program. They intended to make sure that the DuPont Company was not losing in the transactions or risking its interest or profit in its GM holdings.[27]

These debates continued episodically through the summer and fall and John was on call at both General Motors and at DuPont to explain, defend, and, generally, champion both the overall strategy and specific method of implementation. Early on, Irénée du Pont and DuPont treasurer Walter Carpenter suggested that perhaps Raskob and Brown had over-thought the idea and that GM's executive committee might just instead simply hand out individual stock bonuses, as was done at DuPont, to deserving executives. They saw no need for a semiautonomous holding company controlled by a large, select group of GM executives who were charged with collectively managing the holding company's large GM shareholdings, a portion of which would then be annually distributed to members based on performance as judged by a special committee chaired by GM's president. Even saying it was a mouthful. The whole thing, Irénée du Pont and Carpenter argued, seemed needlessly complicated.

Raskob, supported by Pierre du Pont, explained that putting the holding company under the group ownership of the leading GM executives was the beauty of the plan. Even as an element of competition would still exist between the men over whose performance warranted what amount of shares, the group nature of the enterprise would serve to create a sense of linked purpose among the men. Top executives, many of whom would be running separate divisions within GM, would see each other not as competitors for either corporate resources or for a limited bonus pool but as allies seeking to create profit for the whole company since a part of that profit—roughly 6 percent—would be used to enlarge the group's stock holding, which could then be handed out according to individual performance. To coin a phrase, it was one for all and all for one. Or as Alfred Sloan put it in conversation with Brown and Raskob, the plan aimed "at registering effectively in the minds of the members of the exclusive club that what was good for General Motors was good for them."[28]

By October, under pressure from Irénée du Pont and Walter Carpenter, Raskob had revised the plan to slightly decrease DuPont's exposure and costs and to slightly increase General Motors' contribution to the Managers Securities Company. Raskob had not been overly wedded to any particular detail of the plan and was amenable to most any suggestion that seemed reasonable and that moved the process along. He did his best to stay away from the squabbles that broke out between GM's Don Brown, the former DuPont treasurer, and Walter Carpenter, the new DuPont treasurer, as they fenced over tax liability issues and other, sometimes highly technical and even arcane matters.[29] Raskob strongly believed in the principle of manager-ownership and focused his energies on selling the overarching idea at both corporations.

When it came to corporate finance, Raskob was usually a detail-oriented man who played the role of both strategist and technician. But that September he found himself in the somewhat unfamiliar position of corporate hand-holder, just trying to get everyone to sign off on the creation of the GM executive stock-ownership plan. Right before the plan was to be finalized, Alfred Sloan, of all people, got the jitters: "I firmly believe that any plan that puts any man in business for himself is a constructive one, but due to the magnitude of this thing and the number of men we are taking in, I think we ought to be more than certain that the work-out is going to be entirely satisfactory."[30]

With Pierre du Pont's constant support, Raskob just kept assuring everyone involved that the plan was good and necessary. By November 1923 the Managers Securities Company was a done deal. As GM's profits soared and as its share price exploded in the 1920s, so too did the resources of the Managers Securities Company, easily allowing the enterprise to pay down its originating debt and parcel out huge rewards to participating executives. Alfred Sloan took charge of the committee that oversaw the plan's implementation, deciding who was in and who was out. Raskob was one of the seven men who served on the Board of Directors. He was also the secretary-treasurer of the Managers Securities Company. The business press would celebrate Raskob for his role in creating what came to be called the Millionaires Club, which created immense wealth for the dozens of men who had earned the right to be its beneficiaries. John Raskob, of course, was one of those men. In 1927 alone he would receive bonus shares of Class A stock worth $612,660 (or about $7.6 million when corrected for inflation).[31]

Pierre du Pont, confident that General Motors had been put right again, had stepped down as its chief executive officer in May 1923. As had been long planned, Alfred Sloan had replaced him. Raskob wrote du Pont right after Sloan's formal elevation praising the result: "We have done a splendid job in electing

Alfred president of General Motors Corporation because we have promoted a good man, a man who demonstrated his fitness and ability for the position and PRINCIPALLY BECAUSE WE HAVE PROMOTED A GENERAL MOTORS MAN, and I feel that the reaction throughout the entire organization has been splendid."[32] Raskob had long believed that the DuPont Company had to be cautious in placing too many of its people in high-ranking positions at GM, lest GM's own executives feel crowded out. Nonetheless, John remained as vice president of finance and head of the finance committee. Du Pont stayed on as chairman of the board and he remained invested and involved in GM's affairs but his biweekly train trips to Detroit with John stopped. Pierre was stepping away from both companies. He began to spend more and more of his time at his Longwood estate, looking after Delaware's schools, overseeing his gardens, and planning elaborate music and water shows on his grounds. While his adventures with John were far from over and new mutual concerns would excite them to collective action, their lives would never again be so intertwined.

Raskob did not drop any of his GM commitments but already by late July 1923 he was able to step back from the long, grinding days he had spent working out the Managers Securities plan. After turning in his draft of the stock-option scheme, he spent several pleasurable weeks at the members-only Lake Placid Club. His children swam and learned to sail, a recreation that would soon become a Raskob family favorite. John joined the children in their waters sports, cannon-balling into the lake, playing tennis, taking long energetic walks, and generally keeping himself as busy in the outdoors as he normally did indoors at work. At the end of the summer, he and Skipper left the children under the care of their staff and John's brother, William, and took off for a grand European tour. Raskob was ready to turn his attention in new directions.

12

Catholic Interests

The summer of 1923, Raskob began plumbing his feelings in a way he had never done before, including an uncharacteristic inquiry into his religious beliefs. Now in his mid-forties, he began to read much more widely in a deliberate attempt to expand his intellectual horizons. He spent hundreds of dollars a year at New York City bookstores at a time when a new book cost between $1 and $2.

As a general intellectual backstop, he bought two complete sets of the twenty-volume, deluxe edition of the *Pocket University*, published by Doubleday, which was an expansive collection of short or shortened works of fiction and nonfiction, including excerpts from essential plays and novels, speeches, and essays—as judged by the reigning cultural arbiters of the early 1920s. John had one set delivered to his New York apartment and the other to Archmere. He then methodically followed the directions laid out in the *Pocket University* introductory essay. The *Pocket University*, readers were informed, was intended to be studied section-by-section, in order, over the course of a year. Raskob worked his way through Milton, Shakespeare, Browning, Tennyson, and many dozens more, including a large number of American authors published by Doubleday Press, many of whom have long since dropped off the literary canon.

The publisher Nelson Doubleday got wind of Raskob's dedication and asked Raskob if he might craft a few sentences explaining why he liked the *Pocket University*. John obliged, noting that the collection was "very helpful and most interesting. The course of reading prescribed is one which can easily be followed as it is not arduous and with a little persistent attention in the beginning the following of the course soon becomes a habit, and habits once established are, of course, easy to follow."[1] Doubleday was delighted with Raskob's businessman-like approach, which so perfectly represented a style of mind that was rippling across the American cultural landscape. He asked Raskob if he could use his endorsement to advertise the *Pocket University* and John readily agreed. Raskob, celebrated as the one-time stenographer who had without benefit of a university education become one of the nation's "organizing geniuses," was in 1924 a celebrity endorser of Doubleday's sensible guide to great works of literature.

By the mid-1920s, Raskob was seeking out ways to slip free of the narrow business-minded world that had long been his domain. Especially at the end of the summer of 1923 and well into 1924, when the press of his corporate responsibilities at both DuPont and GM had lightened, Raskob's reading took him far afield from the kind of Chamber of Commerce recommended economic and political tracts that had previously interested him. Raskob could not be easily pigeon-holed. His bookstore receipts, which he carefully recorded, suggest that he read a great many works of serious fiction, including the erotic novel *Venus in Furs*, and openly shelved the multi-volume memoirs of Casanova in his New York City apartment.[2] He also read *The Varieties of Religious Experience; A Study in Human Nature* (1902) by the Harvard philosopher and psychologist William James and *The Meaning of God in Human Experience: A Philosophic Study of Religion* (1912) by William Ernest Hocking, one of James's students who joined the Harvard faculty after World War I as the Alford Professor of Natural Religion, Moral Philosophy, and Civil Polity. Raskob also read Harvey O'Higgins's much more accessible work on psychoanalysis, *The Secret Springs*. He read these three books and probably several more in tandem with GMAC president Curtis Cooper who was becoming one of his closest friends.[3] How and why Raskob and Cooper took on these specific tomes or who recommended the texts to the men remains a mystery. Cooper, the president of GMAC, was one of the GM executives who regularly commuted by train from New York to Detroit and back again. He and Raskob must have idled away the hours on board the train discussing these books and others between business discussions and group meetings with the other GM men.

For a faithful Catholic, Raskob's choice of readings was intriguing. None of the works fit comfortably with traditional Catholicism. Both James and Hocking, though in different ways, argued against the principle of religious doctrine as fixed truth, and Hocking challenged the right and power of a religious hierarchy—e.g., the Church—to establish the boundaries of personal religious belief and the meaning of individual spirituality. Both philosophers were sympathetic to religious belief and faith, but the philosophical pragmatist William James, in particular, believed that faith was best proved in its utility in an individual's life and that utility had little to do with established orthodoxies or even the relationship between belief and historically established fact. An individual, James argued, was best capable of supervising and defining his or her own spiritual life. James was not one for religious dogma or blind faith.

No record exists of Raskob's reactions to these works or of his conversations with Cooper about Hocking and James or of what he made of psychoanalysis. Possibly, Raskob argued against the texts, embracing the Church's authority to establish religious dogma for Catholics based on God's eternal and revealed truths. As a younger man, Raskob had enjoyed jousting with his old friend

Elias Ahuja, a religious skeptic, about the validity of the Church's teachings. But more likely Raskob was reading such serious and heterodox books about faith, religion, and the power of the unconscious mind because he had become interested in probing the workings of his own faith and his relationship to his Church.

These sophisticated secular investigations into the realm of religious belief did not, in the end, undermine Raskob's core convictions. His readings did not move Raskob to religious doubt, let alone the unbelief of the empirically minded Pierre du Pont. His church attendance did not falter, and he repeated the most basic and reassuring aspects of his religious beliefs in letters of condolence sent to close friends during these months. Soon after the death of Charles Stewart Mott's wife in late 1924, for example, Raskob wrote his old friend and GM colleague: "I sincerely hope this first Christmas without Mrs. Mott will not prove too trying and that you and children will get great comfort and much enjoyment out of having each other and good health and knowing that an excellent wife and good mother is happy in the eternity that we all are taught knows no trouble but is blessed with nothing but joy after one finishes the perilous and troublous voyage through life on this earth."[4]

Raskob meant every word of these conventional religious sentiments and he fully expected them to reassure and cheer his friend just as such sentiments reassured and cheered him. That Raskob could in perfect sincerity issue such blandishments at roughly the same time he was chewing his way through William James's tough-minded analysis of how and why faith worked in human societies is an example of Raskob's gift for taking what he found useful and applying it where he thought necessary without any sense of contradiction or concern. Raskob was a flexible thinker, a doer who was most interested in finding the means by which goals of all kinds could be achieved; he was not an intellectual or theological system-builder. While his faith was not troubled by his readings or, for that matter, by anything else during these years, Raskob was beginning to rethink his role in the Church.

During the mid-1920s, Raskob became increasingly involved in Catholic affairs. In part, he was pulled into Catholic charity work by his growing wealth and reputation—requests for his assistance came from his children's Catholic schools, the Wilmington diocese, a host of other Catholic institutions in New York and Philadelphia, and by 1926 the offices of the Vatican, as well. But Raskob was also moving forward on his own as he became more interested in working with Catholic lay leaders and clergy in rethinking at least some aspects of Catholic life in the United States. In the 1920s, led by men such as John Raskob, the United States was going through a period of corporate rationalization and even the Catholic Church would be affected.

Raskob had long given money both to his Wilmington church and to the church he had attended in Lockport, to needy individuals brought to his attention by the Catholic clergy, and to a great variety of Catholic charities. From the first years of the twentieth century through the mid-1920s, when Raskob was asked by a member of the Catholic clergy for a donation he made it; he was a soft touch. Mrs. Raskob, a committed, faithful, and generous Catholic whose childhood and youth had in so many ways been sustained and enriched by the Church, played a major role in the Raskobs' many contributions. The Irish fund, the coal fund, the school trip fund, the band equipment fund, the Catholic Orphans fund, the Catholic hospital fund, and many other worthy Church-related causes, all received major and minor gifts year after year. He and Helena gave numerous donations, often in the tens of thousands of dollars, to their children's Catholic schools. In addition, the Raskobs opened up their own estate, Archmere, to Catholic fundraising efforts, serving as hosts and benefactors for an array of causes. One such effort on behalf of the Catholic University of America in 1923 was brought to the attention of the shrewd and worldly Pietro Gasparri, the Cardinal Secretary of State, who was one of several figures at the financially beleaguered Vatican interested in the fast-growing wealth of the Catholic community in the United States.[5] He arranged for the Raskobs to receive "the Apostolic Benediction with a plenary indulgence at the hour of death." In secular terms, the fundraising effort on behalf of Catholic University—and almost certainly his other donations—drew the Vatican's attention to Mr. Raskob's financial position.[6] The Catholic Church in the United States was no longer the refuge and sanctuary of a struggling immigrant community; a number of Catholic Americans had become extremely wealthy men.

In the mid-1920s, most of all, the Raskobs were becoming the financial mainstays of St. Peter's Cathedral in Wilmington where the members of his family were communicants. At first, the Raskobs followed the pattern they had long established; when asked for money in support of St. Peters and their diocese they gave it. Mr. and Mrs. Raskob made many multi-thousand dollar donations and John became quite close both to the parish rector, Father John Dougherty, and to Wilmington Bishop Edmund J. FitzMaurice. For several years, John had supplied his priest with a GM auto and he provided Bishop FitzMaurice with a brand new Cadillac Custom Imperial upon his consecration.[7]

In late 1923, as the Raskobs' financial resources began to skyrocket, John began to think about his charitable and religious gifts and his duties as a Catholic man in a more systemic and purposeful way.[8] When Father Dougherty, the rector of St. Peters in Wilmington, asked Raskob in 1924 to look at the financing of a new parochial school, he took the opportunity to begin carving out his new role as a leading Catholic layman. Having Raskob scrutinize the school's proposed finances and construction costs was like having Babe Ruth pinch-hit at the local sandlot game. Raskob thought the construction plans and costs looked fine but he was, not surprisingly, underwhelmed by Father Dougherty's approach to soliciting donations to finance the school. Raskob, the inveterate risk-taker, urged the Father to engage in a bit of leveraged fund-raising. Rather than issue a general call for donations and then wait until all the money had been raised before beginning construction, Raskob proposed, Father Dougherty should green-light the project immediately relying mostly on money Raskob would quietly provide. Then as construction progressed and the money appeared to be running out Father Dougherty should raise a cry and publicly ask him and a few other wealthy Catholic men to save the new school project. That, Raskob explained, would allow them to "make our contributions in a way that will help make the pot boil, thus stirring up enthusiasm and having good psychological reaction among the parishioners encouraging them to come aboard in a substan-tial way."[9] Dougherty seems to have followed Raskob's unorthodox plan.

Raskob had been involved in secular philanthropic causes, including fund-raising, for several years already. He had been a party to the greatest profes-sional fund-raising effort ever launched in the United States, the World War I bond drives. He had worked closely with Pierre du Pont on his massive philan-thropic efforts on behalf of Delaware's schools. He had more than a little experi-ence raising private-sector capital. Thus, after a couple of decades of dutifully contributing to his Church at the bequest of the clergy, Raskob had begun to think that as a committed member of the laity he could offer his Church some advice, as well as his money. He began to become much more deeply involved in the financing of the Wilmington diocese.

In 1925, Raskob discussed his desire to rethink Wilmington diocesan financ-ing with Bishop FitzMaurice. The Bishop, new to his position, was intrigued but still cautious, so Raskob proceeded in stages. His first step was to organize teams of volunteers for a carefully planned fund-raising campaign to renovate St. Peters and to provide funds for the diocesan schools, the final night of which Raskob described in an emotional letter to Pierre du Pont: "The closing night (Monday) was one filled with enthusiasm and was so exciting that I experienced all the thrills I used to have when you and I and all the other good people of Delaware were working so hard in trying to do our bit in the different drives during the war.... It all seemed so worthwhile when success crowned the hearts of those two hundred people that worked so hard and faithfully in gathering in so many thousands of subscriptions from everywhere."[10]

One of those subscriptions came from the non-Catholic, religious skeptic Pierre du Pont, who gave $125,000 to the school fund. "When your subscription was announced," John wrote, "the applause was so tremendous and prolonged that I just lost control of myself and was unable to keep the tears back."[11] Pierre, once again, had touched John's heart. Raskob was not the only one overjoyed by the successful campaign. From the Vatican, now well aware of Raskob's value to the Church, came high praise. John was made a Knight Commander of the Order of St. Gregory the Great, the highest honor then awarded to an American Catholic layperson.

In the months that followed this successful effort, Raskob began thinking about how to create a more stable form of support for diocesan finances. To better leverage his own donations, Raskob proposed matching gift formulas. So in 1926, when Bishop FitzMaurice asked him to donate money for yet another repair at St. Peters, John demurred slightly; he gave $4,500 but only on the condition that the congregation provided another $1,500, noting "it is unwise to have the people get something for nothing."[12]

Raskob had already laid out his feelings about giving people "something for nothing" at greater length in a private letter to Pierre du Pont, who was pondering another huge gift for Delaware's schools. In his reply to Pierre's request for advice, John lavished praise on Pierre's continuing commitment to improving Delaware's schools. In essence, however, John told Pierre that he had a good heart, but he urged him to reconsider his approach to philanthropy: "You know how strongly I feel about the danger of spoiling people exactly as one can spoil a man with gifts," he wrote. "I think it would be distinctly harmful to the people of Delaware if an individual were to build and equip all the schools necessary for the State to have and present these schools to the State at no cost to the people," he continued. "The people usually value things at what they cost and certainly no work of a public or charitable nature a man does can be successful unless it is helping the people to help themselves or teaching the people to help themselves," he concluded. Raskob proposed that du Pont make a major gift but only on condition that the state legislature simultaneously pass a ten million dollar school bond issue. Raskob's advice reflected his growing concern about how increasingly expansive and expensive government services were to be paid off in the years ahead. He warned that "there will be great danger of an attempt to levy taxes on those best able to pay via the surtax and inheritance tax route" and urged Pierre, personally or through proxies, to educate the "people of Delaware to the dangers of surtaxes and inheritance taxes and thus secure a tax plan for the purpose of meeting the expenses of the State which will be economically sound."[13] Raskob would become ever more agitated about what he increasingly saw as the demotic desire of the people to take what they wanted from men such as himself and Pierre du Pont, but in the mid-1920s, Raskob was mostly focused on thinking through how he could best contribute to the Church that had always been a fundamental part of the life of his family.

Raskob intended to invent a new means of support for diocesan affairs. In 1926 he told Bishop FitzMaurice that he wanted to establish a large endowment for the diocese that would enable it to have a growing and predictable source of

income. An endowment, he explained, would allow the Church to plan rationally and make long-term financial decisions. Bishop FitzMaurice, by this time,
trusted Raskob; he urged him to proceed.

Raskob moved efficiently forward, seeking out philanthropic models for his
plan, just as he had long before studied corporate debentures. He knew of no
religious foundations to secure as models so he looked for a suitable analogue
and came up with the community trusts that were then just springing up all
over the United States. He contacted business colleagues in Cleveland who had
helped to organize the Cleveland Foundation, the first community trust in the
United States. Similarly, he sought out legal advice from businessmen he knew
who were associated with the recently established New York Community Trust.
Raskob was methodically plotting out how to structure what a later generation
would call a not-for-profit corporation dedicated to the Wilmington diocese.

In January 1927, to prepare for the financial restructuring, Raskob studied the
Wilmington diocese's balance sheet. In typical Raskob fashion, he scrutinized the
accounts personally. Then he asked one of his friends, the executive in charge of
managing GMAC's multimillion dollar capital pool, to check his work and offer
investment advice. Raskob, the risk-taker, thought he had better confer with a
money manager more accustomed to prudent, income-generating investment
practices than to the kind of gambles he tended to take, even with the money he
invested for his friends and family. He also pulled in a bevy of local Wilmington
lawyers, accountants, marketing men, and other executives, all of them Catholic,
to help him structure the legal and financial instruments, while making clear they
would be expected to contribute to the yet unannounced fund-raising campaign
that would be needed to endow the pathbreaking Wilmington diocesan trust
they were helping to construct. While capable and well-to-do Catholics had long
supported their Church, Raskob was dramatically increasing and systematizing
the role and responsibility of the laity in diocesan affairs, as well as insuring a
more sustainable and dependable funding source.

In February 1927, Raskob suggested to his Bishop—to whom he was always
uncharacteristically deferential—that the time had come to set the Trust plan
in motion. Raskob wrote: "If the matter is now in shape satisfactory to you, my
recommendation is that we arrange an informal dinner of some fifty or sixty
men at the Hotel DuPont....I think you should preside at the dinner and my
suggestion would be that you outline the deplorable conditions existing in the
Diocese...what you have in mind doing to build up the spiritual end and then
presenting this plan as an outline of what you are arranging to do to finance and
handle the temporal side."[14] Raskob would be the lead agent of that "temporal
side" but he also wanted to bring in as many other wealthy, committed Catholic
men as he could to assure that the Fund would be not just well-supported but
well-accepted.

Bishop FitzMaurice did as Raskob suggested and the grand project to secure an endowed trust began to take form. The Bishop wrote John: "The idea so happily conceived and sponsored by you promises life, development—everything in fact that we now lack and which hitherto there seemed no particular prospect of obtaining. May God bless you for the interest you are taking in religion! I know He will do so for you are displaying a very generous zeal in furthering his kingdom." The Bishop continued: "I cannot indeed help feeling that you are in a very special sense his agent and instrument in respect to this diocese .... I have come to realize that you are for all practical purposes our sole prop and support, and I have no doubt you have been providentially raised up by God for this very purpose."[15] Raskob rarely looked for approval from others; how he felt about his Bishop's encomium is unrecorded.

In February 1928, Raskob's plan for the Wilmington Diocese was made public. The *New York Times* heralded: "Raskob Gives $1,000,000 to Wilmington Catholics."[16] Bishop FitzMaurice sent out a pastoral letter to all parishioners announcing the Diocesan Fund and giving full praise to Raskob: "The success of the movement is to a certain extent assured through the munificence of one man—Mr. John J. Raskob." Raskob would be, the Bishop wrote, "the first donor to the Fund with an initial contribution of $500,000. This sum he will give outright." Then, following Raskob's advice, the Bishop continued, "In addition, to the limit of another $500,000, he will give one dollar for every dollar secured from other sources. If therefore $500,000 be subscribed by the other members of the diocese, the total contribution of Mr. Raskob will be $1,000,000."[17]

A sizable portion of the sought after $500,000 in matching funds had already been promised by other wealthy Catholics but at Raskob's urging those subscriptions were not yet announced. Raskob believed that it was essential for people of modest means to understand that their donations were needed so that they would contribute to the cause and feel equally committed to the financial well-being of their Church. Bishop FitzMaurice stated the matter eloquently in his public praise of Raskob: "Few can do what he has done, but all can be equally generous in proportion to their means.... Our appeal is directed not alone to the wealthy, but also to those of modest or even slender means." The Bishop asked every member of the diocese to contribute and asked for "the widow's mite no less than the rich man's gift." He ended his request with a passage from Matthew 6:19-20: "Lay not up to yourselves treasures on earth...but lay up to yourselves treasures in heaven: where neither the rust nor the moth doth consume, and where thieves do not break through, nor steal."[18] These words would stay with John Raskob.

Raskob ended up donating even more than the full million he had promised—about $12 million in current dollars. When the matching grant portion of the campaign fell just short, Raskob quietly made up the difference. John served on the board of the new Catholic Foundation of the Diocese of Wilmington, as did two other members of the laity, three priests, and the foundation's head, Bishop FitzMaurice. Raskob had insisted, with respect, that the laity play this major, though not determinative, role in overseeing the Foundation. Skilled laypersons, Raskob gently insisted, were best suited for the legal, financial, and managerial aspects of overseeing a modern, multifaceted diocese.

Raskob made his case to the American Catholic community-at-large in a long feature story in *Columbia*, the monthly magazine of the Knights of Columbus and the largest circulation Catholic periodical in the United States: "We take our young men inspired for the priesthood and train them to be theologians. Then when they come to us to teach us our theology and its social and religious consequences, we ask them to become financiers, to plan for and administer capital investment in the material necessities of the church often of a size to require the most highly developed business and financial judgment."[19] In Wilmington, Raskob continued, expert members of the laity were going to remove that burden from the clergy. The Bishop, he continued, would have final "ultimate responsibility. But we do ask the laymen to assume function for which their character and training must be presumed to fit them better than those primarily concerned with the spiritual affairs of the Church."[20] Raskob concluded by urging parishes and dioceses around the nation to look at this new model of laymen involvement and financial oversight; if it was a success, and he was confident it would be, he hoped it would become a model. This formal role by the laity in Church financial affairs was unprecedented.

Raskob wanted the Catholic Church throughout the United States to accept a far more active and critical role for the laity in Church affairs. In a letter to the Right Reverend Francis C. Kelley, the Bishop of Oklahoma, who had written to Raskob for financial help, he carefully spelled out his vision: "Personally I am a great believer in the church working out some scheme under which the clergy and the laity will work together in those things having to do with the temporal side of the church. In other words, I feel that it is important to have the lay people actively interested in the problems of the church in order that they can and may assume responsibilities in an intelligent fashion." Raskob warned that in the Church Catholics are trained not "to speak out, make suggestions and advocate plans, particularly if it happens to meet the opposition of the parish priest. This kind of policy could not work in business. In business every effort is made to get everyone to speak out openly and frankly and honestly and criticize what is being done without fear or favor."[21]

In Wilmington, Raskob's foundation allowed for a successful model of expert lay involvement in financial governance. While the financial troubles of the next few years would delay the Foundation's ability to fund the diocese, over the next several decades Raskob's trust performed as he had expected, providing some

$62 million for the good works and capital needs of the diocese. Still, even in Wilmington, Raskob's efforts never produced the kind of transparency that could have allowed a strong and informed laity to stop the diocese from covering up terrible misdeeds by a small number of clergymen.[22] Then, too, Raskob never imagined a scenario in which the laity would need to step into Church affairs so directly for so dire a reason. Raskob's reformist energies always took place within a framework of certain faith and trust in his Church. That faith and trust were magnified by Raskob's deep involvement with the Vatican. From the mid-1920s onward, even as Raskob was building this unprecedented fund for his diocese, he had also entered into a rewarding relationship with Pope Pius XI and several of the Vatican's leading officials.

Raskob's relationship with the Vatican was directly related to the changing financial fortunes of the Church. In the early 1920s, the Vatican was in an uncomfortable economic position. Postwar bond failures and bank crises in Europe had hit the Church's investments hard, and the "Peter's Pence" donations that Catholic churches around the world contributed to the Vatican were down as well. Only the American Church was sending along increased funds. Thus, financially minded Vatican leaders were looking across the Atlantic for support.

In the December 13, 1926, issue of *Time* magazine, John read that he and nine other American Catholic millionaires had been appointed by the Vatican to the Knights of Malta, the venerable and aristocratic order that had begun during the eleventh-century Crusades. It came as a surprise to John. The head of the brand new American chapter, according to *Time*, was the prominent Boston banker and well-known philanthropist James J. Phelan. Raskob fired off a polite letter to Phelan. *Time*, Raskob wrote, must have confused his August 1925 honor as a Knight Commander of the Order of St. Gregory the Great with the Knight of Malta business.[23]

Phelan seems to have phoned Raskob upon receipt of the letter: Raskob had been named a Knight of Malta. The Vatican had also bestowed knighthoods upon eight other wealthy and prominent Catholic men: Nicholas Brady, Patrick Crowley, James Farrell, James Fayne, Morgan O'Brien, John Ryan, Edward Carry, and Edward Hurley. They were to be the founding members of the first American chapter of the Knights of Malta. Phelan had sent Raskob a letter in September, he said, explaining the honor and requesting a meeting with him so that he could formally present Raskob with the Papal Bull that named him a Knight. The letter must have, somewhat mysteriously, gone missing. Why Phelan had not followed up after not hearing from Raskob for some three months remains unexplained.[24]

Phelan and Raskob met a few days later in New York and John received his Papal Bull. That night he wrote Phelan: "Words cannot express my appreciation of the great honor conferred upon me being made a Knight of the Malta." Two days later, John wrote a formal letter to Prince Galeas de Thun-Hohenstein, the head of the Knights of Malta, promising to support "such works as the newly created American chapter of this world known, old and illustrious order may dedicate itself."[25] Forthwith, Raskob sent the Prince a check for $2,000. Raskob also arranged to travel to Rome in the early spring to meet with Pope Pius XI, the head of the Knights of Malta, and other dignitaries of the Church.

In May 1927 John and Helena had their papal audience. Pope Pius XI thanked the Raskobs for their service to the Church with promises of "holy relics," including a piece of the "true cross." The Raskobs would have, over the years, several more papal audiences. Raskob did not discuss Church business directly with the Pope. But with others, he most certainly did.

Shepherding the Raskobs around the Vatican was a charming, energetic, American priest named Francis Joseph Spellman. In 1925, Spellman had been the first American assigned to the Vatican State Secretariat, which was charged with looking after the Vatican's international or foreign relationships. Spellman was at the same time the assistant to Edward Hearn, the Knights of Columbus's highly capable representative to the Vatican. Among Hearn's primary responsibilities was the solicitation of donations from wealthy Catholics. Raskob had been a dutiful though not particularly active member of the KOC, which had been founded in the United States in 1881, all his adult life.

Raskob took an immediate and powerful liking to Spellman, who in turn, did everything in his considerable power to reciprocate and foster that affection. A man of fierce ambition and prodigious charm, Spellman was a doer who relished making things happen. "Theologians spend much time talking about the Church," he famously quipped, "but they could better use the time building a church."[26] In Raskob, Spellman saw a man who could help him build the Church and his place in it.

Spellman had proved his worth to his superiors at the Vatican in numerous ways not least his ability and willingness to induce rich American Catholics to come to the aid of the Church and its leaders. Spellman's first conquests were Nicholas and Genevieve Brady, who had a spectacular estate overlooking St. Peter's in Rome. In reward for generous denotations to the Church and to important Church officials, Spellman arranged for Mr. Brady to be made a Knight of the Supreme Order of Christ and Mrs. Brady a papal duchess. The creation of the American chapter of the Knights of Malta and Raskob's membership therein was of a piece with this New World campaign.

Immediately following Raskob's return to the United States he received a long, flattering, almost syrupy letter from Monsignor Spellman. "I have thought of you and your party many times since you left Rome," Spellman wrote. "And I have talked of you frequently with Monsignor Pizzardo [leading figure of the Vatican

State Secretariat].... The recollection of your audience with the Holy Father will always be one of my cherished Roman memories." Spellman then turned practical: "I have now secured relics for you and Mrs. Raskob and the children. The relic of the true cross is also ready and it is placed in a silver crucifix in such a way that the relic may be seen." Spellman had arranged for an American-bound priest to hand deliver the items to Raskob at his New York City office. Then Spellman got down to business. Would Raskob discuss with the other nine members of the American chapter of the Knights of Malta the funding of a 350-bed hospital for children in Rome? "Will you give me confidentially your advice on this point at your convenience," he wrote, "or give me any other suggestions you may have to make in the future?"[27] Soon thereafter, Raskob and his fellow Knights funded the construction of the hospital. Thus began a long and expensive relationship between Spellman and Raskob.

In September 1927, Spellman let Raskob know that the Pope had a special project in mind that needed some assistance: "Yesterday the Holy Father called me and asked if I thought it would be convenient to ask you if you could help out in a work which is very close to his heart and a work which if the Holy Father succeeds in accomplishing or rather in having accomplished he will regard as one of the outstanding works of his Pontificate." Pope Pius XI wanted to bring together the world's leading scholars on early Christendom so that they might devote several years to creating the "authoritative classic work of Christian history and Christian archeology and of illustrated Christian dogma."[28] Raskob immediately arranged for a bank draft of 800,000 lire, a sum he carefully noted for his records as having a worth of $43,560, to be sent to the Vatican. Upon being thanked for his generosity, he wrote Spellman, "I wish you would extend to his Holiness my sincere thanks for the opportunity he has given me to assist in making possible the accomplishment of the work in which he is so vitally interested."[29] That same year, Raskob arranged for several luxury autos to be given to Vatican officials; he would continue to provide autos for the next several years. He also gave detailed investment advice to Monsignor Pizzardo and, undoubtedly, to others in the Vatican, as well.[30] In his correspondence with Spellman and other Vatican officials, Raskob requested that unless for some reason His Holiness saw it as useful, he did not want any of his donations to be publicized. While the Vatican did not publicize Raskob's gifts, he was rewarded again and again. In January 1928 the Holy See added another title to Raskob's list, appointing him Private Chamberlain to the Pope.

In a letter to Monsignor Spellman, Raskob summed up his feelings about his relationship with the Holy Father and the Vatican: "One is indeed fortunate to be blessed not only with the ability to be helpful but with a mind broad enough to appreciate the great joys of giving. I really feel embarrassed to be showered with such wonderful expressions of good will and kindness to say nothing of the great honors conferred upon me."[31] A few weeks after this letter, in direct appreciation for his help in building the Infant Jesus Hospital and contributions to other charities of the Holy Father, Raskob received a Knights of Malta uniform directly from Rome. The regalia included trousers with gold stripe, a swashbuckling hat, golden spurs and buttons, epaulettes, embroidered waist of black velvet, mantle with black velvet neck, and a gilt sword. At approximately the same time, Helena Raskob was named Lady of the Sovereign Order of Malta and received a gold medal from His Holiness. John appears to have worn his entire Knights of Malta ensemble sparingly. His only public expression of his Church status was the lapel button that James Phelan had sent him to mark his membership in the American Knights. He wore it regularly, but as it was small and modest only a very people would recognize its significance. Raskob felt deeply rewarded by his relationship with his Church but he never sought public recognition. Raskob was an amazingly self-contained man whose lack of need for public recognition was remarkable. He just very much liked to do things according to his own standards and goals.

Raskob would continue to give generously to his Church and Catholic causes throughout the late 1920s and even into the 1930s when the Great Depression changed many aspects of his life and fortune. In March 1928, John became one of the major backers of the Catholic intellectual weekly, *Commonweal*. While by no means a radical publication (indeed founder Michael Williams established *Commonweal* to "counteract the influence of the radical and socialistic reviews and magazines now so numerous"), it was unconventional and, in line with Raskob's other key initiatives, it was run independently of the Church by lay Catholic intellectuals and writers.[32] Raskob had initially begged off supporting the magazine when it was launched in 1924, promising only to become a $100 a year member of the magazine's Calvert Associates; he even refused to take a meeting with Williams in 1925. In early 1928, however, Raskob accepted the tenacious Williams's request to lead the effort to establish an endowment for *Commonweal*. Raskob hosted and paid for a fund-raising dinner at the Metropolitan Club attended by a who's who of wealthy American Catholics, including many of his fellow Knights of Malta. At the lavish dinner, Raskob helped raise over $140,000 for the *Commonweal* endowment, including a personal donation of $25,000. He also "lent" the magazine about $125,000 more which was supposed to be paid back as new donations come in; that loan, much to Raskob's frustration, even anger, eventually turned almost completely into a gift, as well. Raskob, not for the first or last time, was appalled at the lack of focus and discipline he found in some of the men upon whom he had placed his trust and to whom he had given his money. He wrote the *Commonweal* editor, Michael Williams: "Would advise that I still feel that sufficient follow-up work has not been done in the matter of gaining support for the Commonweal guaranty find. The raising of funds is a hard, arduous task and requires the most persistent, insistent and consistent work. It cannot be done spasmodically."[33] Raskob, despite his range of experiences, was still constantly surprised and quite often infuriated when others could not or would not do as he would have done in their position.

Raskob's last major gift to his Church in the final year of the Jazz Age is worth noting insomuch as it marked one of the few times when Raskob felt he could not handle a financial management problem on his own. In 1928 and 1929, despite his donation of more than $1 million to the Wilmington Foundation, Raskob continued to give a great deal of money locally to his Church, in part because the Foundation's trust account was not yet spinning off much revenue. So among many multi-thousand dollar gifts, Raskob gave $11,000 for a new floor for the Wilmington cathedral, $6,500 for land to expand a Catholic school, and another $65,000 to the Foundation. Most generously, he pledged a major donation for new housing for the Ursuline Sisters, the order that ran his daughters' Catholic school in Wilmington.

Raskob knew he was being asked to donate a great deal of money but apparently, and almost uniquely, he had not set out the exact amount he was willing to give in his initial conversations with Mother Gertrude, who was in charge of the nuns' housing project. Quickly enough, Raskob was informed by Mother Gertrude that he needed to provide her with a check for $250,000. Raskob felt that he was not being asked politely for this sum but was being told to supply it forthwith. Even before he had responded to this surprisingly huge and blunt request, Mother Gertrude wrote again to inform Raskob that, actually, an additional sum was going to be necessary to account for all costs associated with the project. Raskob wrote Father Dougherty of St. Peters and asked him what was going on, noting that Mother Gertrude's tone "really displeases me very much." He enclosed the nun's letter so that Father Dougherty could see for himself how he was being addressed and, so, provide him with advice as to how to proceed. The Father wrote back: "The letter was not fair play to you; it is hardly decent. In spite of anything said or written to the contrary, you are being jockeyed into a hold-up position. Nuns are proverbially hard to handle."

Raskob took Dougherty's response as permission to tell Mother Gertrude off and he did so though at some point he was embarrassed enough by his tone to remove the copy of this letter from his files. But he did tell Dougherty the gist of his remarks. In turn, Dougherty wrote to the diocese's greatest benefactor: "The good lady is certainly doing her best to tangle you up in her fishing line.... Unfortunately there is no Man to whom your correspondent will listen.... I am sorry you have been subjected to what is akin to real abuse." Raskob appreciated the advice and his priest's support. He did not give Mother Gertrude everything she wanted; he did, however, provide a sum well into six figures in support of the project, one of his largest single gifts to a specific philanthropic project. Mother Gertrude might have actually gotten the best of Raskob who, with the exception of Helena's Aunt Varina, was not at all accustomed to wrangling with a woman over money, let alone a Mother Superior.[34]

Raskob played one other significant role in Catholic affairs in the late 1920s. This role demonstrated the reach he had into the intertwined financial, religious, and political worlds of the American Jazz Age elite. It also revealed the limits that Raskob placed on his obeisance to the Church, especially when it involved his personal and political relationships within the United States. In early 1928, Raskob became involved, as an intermediary, in the struggle over the fate of the Catholic Church in Mexico. He did so in large part because he had close and trusted relations both with the Vatican and with the Morgan banker Dwight W. Morrow, who had been appointed Ambassador to Mexico by President Calvin Coolidge, with whom Raskob also had a good relationship.

In the 1920s, the Mexican government had launched a forthright attack on the power and autonomy of the Catholic Church in Mexico. There were ideological reasons, but the government also wanted control of the Church's material resources. By1926 this conflict had reached a boiling point and at the end of July of that year the Mexican government ordered the closing of all Catholic Churches in Mexico. The American government chose to tread lightly over this religious repression. President Coolidge refused to even meet with a delegation from the Knights of Columbus to discuss the matter, believing that he had a more important duty to the American oilmen in Mexico who were also facing a fierce nationalization campaign by Mexico's revolutionary government. Morrow, who had been the Morgan bank's most adept international negotiator, was made ambassador in late 1927 to manage the oil problem and other contentious subjects. He was sensitive, indeed sympathetic, to the concern of Catholics and he introduced the subject to his Mexican negotiating partners but he did so cautiously. Morgan kept key American Catholic leaders apprised of his efforts on the Mexican situation and he earned their trust. The Vatican, however, worried not simply about the Mexican crisis but about the position of the Church throughout Latin American, believed that Morrow could and must do more to use the power of the United States to protect the Catholic Church.

Raskob was asked by the high-ranking Vatican official Monsignor Giuseppe Pizzardo (recipient of both a Raskob-supplied black custom Cadillac and stock market advice) to use his influence to persuade Morrow to do more. Raskob did as he was asked but did so cautiously. He communicated his personal concerns and, more importantly, the Church's concerns directly to Ambassador Morrow. He carefully pressed Morrow and asked him to keep him continuously informed as to the negotiations. While he did not say as much (at least in any written documents that remain), Morrow undoubtedly knew that anything he conveyed to Raskob would be communicated to the Vatican. Nonetheless, Morrow kept Raskob appraised and Raskob passed along what he had been told to the Vatican.[35]

Morrow was one of Raskob's good friends. During the Durant debacle in 1920, they had gotten to know each other well and subsequently they saw each other frequently, usually over business but also at the various New York private elite men's clubs that Raskob had joined since taking up regular residence in the city. The Morgan bank had become deeply enmeshed in GM financial affairs and Raskob remained the point man on their various deals, including a $50 million loan package arranged to provide capital for GMAC in 1926. All the Morgan partners were Raskob's intimates but Morrow was one of his favorites. The two men had been deeply involved, along with GE president Owen Young, in a campaign organized by Secretary of Commerce Herbert Hoover to induce American industry to stamp out—voluntarily—the twelve-hour work day. They shared a number of interests. At some point, Raskob must have mentioned that relationship to Monsignor Pizzardo or perhaps Frank Spellman, who was always interested in networks of power. In the midst of the troubles in Mexico, Raskob did tell Monsignor Pizzardo directly that Ambassador Morrow "is a close personal friend and there are few things in life which I value and appreciate more than that of enjoying his confidence, love and affection."[36]

At this point Raskob was laying it on a bit thick—Morrow was a close friend but not one of the men with whom Raskob shared an intimate and informal relationship. Morrow had never, for example, visited Raskob in Archmere. But Raskob was playing up his friendship with Morrow because he wanted Pizzardo to understand that Morrow was to be trusted and that if he said he was doing his best to support the Church in Mexico then he had to be taken at his word: "Mr. Morrow than whom there is no better or fairer man in the United States is not a Roman Catholic but is a sincere friend and admirer of our Church. He has worked arduously in an effort to solve Mexico's most vexing problem."[37] Raskob, who was being urged by his Vatican contacts to push Morrow hard, was making his own statement. Raskob was not the Vatican's man; he would make his own judgments when it came to matters temporal.

For Raskob, this independence from the Church was by no means an academic or purely personal matter. Just days after Raskob wrote this letter to the Vatican he would announce to the world that he was going to head the campaign to elect New York Governor Al Smith to the presidency of the United States. Raskob would be the first Catholic to direct a national presidential run and to take on the leadership of a national political party. Then, too, Smith would be the first Catholic to run on a major party ticket for the presidency.

13

John and Al

Raskob had not planned to become Governor Al Smith's campaign director, head fund-raiser, and chairman of the Democratic Party National Committee. Up until that time Raskob had not been a member, let alone a major supporter, of the Democratic Party. A few years earlier, prior to the 1920 presidential campaign, he had written an indignant letter to Democratic National Committee Director of Finance, W. D. Jamieson, who had solicited Raskob for a large donation: "I do not understand how you secured my name as a Democrat. I am a thoroughly independent voter taking no interest whatever in politics except to vote in such way as the issues of such campaign dictate to me as being most desirable."[1] Subsequently, Raskob had given a big campaign donation to Calvin Coolidge's campaign in 1924 and had supported several Republican candidates for the Senate. But Raskob was not and had never been a partisan Republican. He was, as he had told W. D. Jamieson, a true political independent—which was a rare species in 1920s America. Even in early 1928 Raskob was still firmly resisting entreaties to become more deeply involved in party politics. When Frank du Pont, son of Raskob's old boss Coleman du Pont, asked John to take over the leadership of the Republican Party in Delaware, Raskob replied: "I am not a politician and I am such a strong believer in voting for good men regardless of party that it would be unfair for me to be aligned too closely with any party."[2] Clearly, Raskob had not come to Smith's side via traditional party politics.

Raskob signed up with Smith because he had become good friends with the governor and the crowd of predominately Irish Catholic New York businessmen who surrounded him. But Raskob had also become increasingly interested in federal tax and economic policy, as well as the Prohibition question, enough so that the idea of putting Smith into the White House and thus becoming a major player in Washington, preferably as Secretary of the Treasury, seemed like an excellent new chapter in his life.

Raskob's path to Smith's campaign and chairmanship of the Democratic National Committee was somewhat circuitous. It began as a social journey.[3] In the mid-1920s, Raskob had become increasingly interested in expanding his network of friends, driven in large part by his simple desire to have more fun. Raskob had many good friends, by then, among his business peers at GM, DuPont, Morgan, and a slew of other corporate and financial bastions. He traded quips with the hard-drinking womanizer Walter Chrysler at Palm Beach as they both egged on Alfred Sloan, a far more temperate soul who received most of his pleasures vicariously. Raskob went regularly to the Kentucky Derby with a train-load of card-playing businessmen buddies. He had taken up golf and had joined exclusive clubs in both New York and Delaware—no round went by without money on the line amid his changing crew of wealthy foursomes. And beginning in the mid-1920s Raskob had begun traveling to Europe for weeks at a time with one of his closest friends, Walter Butler, a Wilmington millionaire and one of several people whose seven-figure stock portfolio Raskob managed as a hobby. Butler no longer worked; he specialized in high times. Raskob's friendship with Butler was demonstrative of his increased hunt for new experiences.

Butler was more than a decade older than Raskob and a confirmed bachelor who knew women in every port of call. In the mid-1920s, Raskob and Butler took several extended trips through Europe, sans Helena. Butler made it his priority to introduce Raskob to a great many of the women he knew, most but not all of them unmarried American expatriates. The slippery language of 1920s correspondence—"a certain friend of yours named Marie," "another of your girls called yesterday," "Tell Noel to stop working so hard or I will come over and spank her," "I go out to her villa on Friday and stay till Tuesday"—makes certainty about the nature of either man's relationship with these women friends in Paris, London, Tuscany, Nice, and the many other spots frequented by rich Americans impossible to define. What is certain is that in their regular correspondence Butler and Raskob wrote about women they both know and these letters suggest a level of intimacy about some of these women that bears no resemblance to the chaste communiqués between Raskob and his Lockport friends in the years before Raskob's marriage. On the other hand, Raskob's European adventures with the ladies were known to at least some of his intimates back home, suggesting that his escapades were probably less risqué than they might appear. His young cousin Peggy Sandell, with whom Raskob enjoyed a merry and quite flirtatious correspondence, wrote John in September 1925, soon after he returned from a long trip with Butler: "I'm afraid you two little rascals ought to have a chaperon" and she nominated herself.[4] At a minimum, Raskob and Butler had a great deal of fun with a number of women in their fast-paced jaunts across Europe on these strictly-for-pleasure bachelor vacations.[5]

In New York City, Raskob pursued his pleasures and new friendships with equal ardor. During this time, John and Pierre kept their shared apartment at the Carlton House but John also leased at an initial cost of $10,000 a year a much larger, well-appointed apartment in the building for himself beginning in 1921, which he kept staffed with a cook and other servants. At the end of 1926 he arranged to combine 4 large units on the 8th floor into one spectacular, luxuriously decorated apartment, complete with early eighteenth-century Flemish and French tapestries, rare Persian rugs, and other non-children friendly furnishings that cost well over $100,000 (per capita consumption in the United States in the mid-1920s was around $625).[6] Raskob had friends in an increasing number of social circles. He had become close friends with the Manhattan-based Charles Keck, the sculptor who had fashioned the fountain piece and bas-relief portraits of the Raskob children at Archmere. Studio dinners with a range of Keck's highly successful artist compatriots and wealthy client friends were a regular part of Raskob's city social life. Even more regular were Raskob's theater evenings. Already good friends with Broadway impresario William Brady, Raskob soon knew several of the major figures in New York's theater world and spent many of his free evenings in the city hobnobbing backstage.

Among his closest friends in New York by the mid-1920s was the singer, composer, writer, actor, producer, musical comedy star, and general man-about-town Eddie Dowling. A decade younger than Raskob, Dowling knew not just everybody in the theatrical world but also everybody who counted in Democratic politics in New York City. Dowling was also an inveterate stock market player and he picked Raskob's brain and joined in on Raskob's various market syndicates whenever he could. Dowling was a half-Irish, fully Catholic, third-grade dropout, one-time cabin boy who had made his way to the top of the heap in New York. He was irresistible to John and, according to Dowling, John provided financial backing to several of Dowling's Broadway productions.[7] Dowling was also one of the men who brought Raskob into Governor Smith's inner circle.

In late October 1926, Raskob was, as he often did mid-week, hanging around Dowling's dressing room at the Knickerbocker Theatre a couple of hours before curtain time. Dowling was starring in the musical comedy "Honeymoon Lane"; he had also written the book for this successful bit of fluff. While Dowling went through his pre-show rituals, Raskob, according to Dowling's dramatic account, threw a hot-off-the-press edition of the *New York Evening Sun* on Dowling's make-up shelf. The headline in the Hearst-owned paper blared "MAYOR'S ACCUSERS SAY AL SMITH IS IN LEAGUE WITH WATERED MILK SELLERS." Raskob was appalled and, knowing that Dowling was an ardent supporter of Governor Smith, who was running for re-election against the silk stocking candidate Ogden Mills, demanded that Dowling explain: "Would this man Smith do anything like that? How could he do it? You know the value of decent milk. My God, how low can these men get?" While Dowling's many stories of Raskob are never to be trusted in every detail or even in every instance, this one rings true. Raskob hated political corruption, which he reasonably enough saw as nearly endemic in New York City at the time, and he was especially likely to explode over a charge of corruption that involved the safety and health of children. The story also speaks convincingly to Raskob's naiveté when it came to the inner workings of New York politics.

Although Raskob had been living primarily in New York City since 1919, he had never taken much interest in local or New York state politics. He was still much more familiar with the Delaware scene and with national policies. He simply did not know that the Machiavellian publisher Hearst had turned against Smith years earlier and was using his newspaper to shill for Mills. Hearst had first used the milk canard against Smith in 1919 and any politically savvy New Yorker would have known that the recycled "watered milk" charge was a campaign attack ad masquerading as news.[8]

Dowling figured it was time to give his friend a political education. Spying that he still had an hour and forty five minutes before the curtain rose, he sprung into action: "John get your hat and cane. I'll take care of this for you right now. We'll go over to the Biltmore Hotel, where Al's headquarters are and we'll go right up to Al's suite with this paper and let him answer it."[9] Off they went. According to Dowling, when they arrived at the 22nd floor offices of Smith's headquarters, they were greeted by James Riordan, one of Smith's oldest friends and a wealthy supporter: "Eddie, don't come now. Al is on the phone with the editor of the *New York Evening Sun* and all hell has broken loose." Dowling and Raskob went in anyway and listened to Smith tear into the editor for his calumny. Raskob was impressed. Once off the phone, Smith and Raskob were introduced and John took out his checkbook and wrote the governor a $5,000 campaign donation.[10]

Soon thereafter, the Bronx political boss and Smith crony Ed Flynn brought Raskob to the inner sanctum of New York's ruling Democrats, the Tiger Room, named in honor of the Tammany Hall tiger. The idea was to have Raskob get to know the governor and the men who ran the city. Flynn, a lawyer as well as a politician, had a prior in with Raskob; a few years earlier he had done a minor business deal in Wilmington that had involved him. But it was not Flynn who thought to cast the hook Raskob's way; he was just the able messenger. Flynn arranged the invitation at the request of construction magnate William F. Kenny, owner of some thirty buildings in the city and one of New York's biggest behind-the-scenes operators and Democratic Party campaign contributors. Kenny was also Smith's closest friend and benefactor.

The Tiger Room was on the top floor of one of Kenny's buildings at 23rd and Fourth. In honor of the old Tammany Hall symbol, Kenny had the place filled with tigers: stuffed, bronzed and whatever else his decorator could find. Photographs of old Tammany Hall bosses lined the walls. A bar and grill, shower, baths, and a barber shop were always available. Regardless of Prohibition, drinks were poured freely and a poker game was usually on tap. A stage ran across one end of the room and Kenny had Broadway performers and all-girl revues up for the occasional show. As the night went on, men sang and told tales out of school. Kenny, an able judge of what made a man tick, thought Raskob would enjoy himself. He saw an opportunity to bring Raskob into Smith's circle of supporters and he took it.[11]

Kenny had judged right. Raskob was interested. By late 1926, John Raskob had been in a lot of elite private clubs, corporate boardrooms, and most every other kind of gathering place for the rich and powerful. But the Tiger Room was a new experience. First of all, almost everyone who walked into the Tiger Room was Irish Catholic. Most were also self-made and self-created men like Raskob. Also, like Raskob, these were men who knew how to get things done. Their realm of expertise, however, was not corporate finance or management. These men knew big-city politics and inhabited a world in which public policy, public works, city and state contracts, election campaigns, patronage, and economic opportunity were all intertwined. They were all-stars in a different game than the one Raskob had mastered. Ten years earlier, Raskob might have found these Irish American pols and their business cronies too disreputable and too much of a distraction from his corporate missions. But by late 1926, Raskob the New York boulevardier felt like he had found a new home. Here was another kind of adventure among men who had, in the main and with a few more curves along the way, followed a path not unlike his own.

Kenny made sure that during Raskob's first visit to the Tiger Room he had plenty of time to talk privately with Governor Smith. The two men, devout Catholics who had made it to the top of their respective professions without benefit of formal education or family connections—both, in fact, had lost their fathers at a an early age—hit it off from the start. Different in so many ways, they saw each other as equals. Raskob got a kick out of the governor's effervescent, "sidewalks of New York," brown-derby-sporting manner. Like Raskob, Smith loved the theater and he had long been an amateur actor and singer. While Raskob was at his ease with the restrained Protestant men who ran GM and DuPont, he had always been far more of a fun-lover than Pierre or his staid corporate compatriot Alfred Sloan. Al Smith's circle promised access to a very different sort of action and from the beginning Smith's crowd looked to be a perfect combination of serious purpose and irrepressible entertainment.

Raskob immediately thereafter became a member of what Ed Flynn called Smith's "Golfing Cabinet." He, Kenny, Riordan, Tim Mara, who owned the New York Giants, the shipbuilder William Todd, and a few other wealthy backers made sure that Smith had the money he needed to take care of his political business. These self-made men vied for influence over Smith with his other set of key advisors, the so-called "Kitchen Cabinet," a group of deeply Progressive activists and intellectuals, many of whom had been working with and in some cases for Smith for years.[12]

Surprisingly, given the times, two women were critical members of this Kitchen Cabinet. When Raskob entered Smith's orbit, Belle Moskowitz was the most important of them. A one-time settlement worker, labor activist, and all around social welfare advocate, Mrs. M as Al called her, helped develop the social justice policies that made Smith a beloved figure among New York's immigrant, working-class voters. She was, in the words of one of Smith's biographers, "his strong right hand."[13] Although never officially a member of his staff—Smith got her a paid position as publicity director of the Democratic State Committee— she kept Smith on schedule and set up many of his meetings with people she felt he needed to see.[14] Another key advisor was Frances Perkins, likewise a leading New York Progressive. Perkins, in the words of one of Smith's Tammany Hall cronies, was Al's "book," the source for what he needed to know about tenement, labor, and factory reform. While the governor's brilliant fix-it man, legal advisor and speechwriter Joe Proskauer could move back and forth between Smith's two, quite different advisory camps, Moskowitz and especially Perkins were deeply suspicious of the wealthy men who often had Smith's ear. Both women were hostile, in particular, to the newest, richest, best connected, and most intellectually powerful of these wealthy men: Raskob. They saw him as a narrow-minded plutocrat with neither interest in or knowledge of the kind of social reform they championed. Perkins later described Raskob as "a measly little man," a snake in Smith's Progressive Garden of Eden.[15]

Smith saw a different Raskob. He saw a brilliant financier who understood Big Business and Wall Street, realms that intimidated him. More importantly, Smith was a bootstrapper like Raskob. The governor respected and admired people who had made their own way in the world. He had never seen himself as an enemy of business or of those businessmen who pursued wealth in honest ways. Raskob raised no red flags for Smith. Not to say that Raskob and Smith were, even in the late 1920s, ideological twins.

Smith had come of political age in New York state politics at the height of the Progressive Era. In his first years in the state assembly he was a reformer, though a Tammany Hall Democratic Party reformer; most of his efforts were aimed at fighting corrupt Republican control of the state government and their exploitative power over New York City. Smith's political education and Progressive tilt took on a new urgency after the Triangle Shirtwaist Company fire of 1911. The fire had trapped workers, almost all of them women and girls, on the factory building's higher floors. Exit doors in some areas of the building had been locked; the flimsy fire escape had collapsed; and the fire department had no ladders tall enough to reach the women. To escape the flames sixty-two women were forced to jump. Crowds of New Yorkers watched them die. Altogether 146 workers were killed. Labor activists stated the matter in blunter terms: the women had been murdered by their bosses and an indifferent political system.

Smith was vice chairman of the Factory Investigating Commission that arose out of the tragedy. While Smith had grown up in a working-class neighborhood, he had never paid much attention to the actual conditions of industrial work in his city. Guided by commission investigator Frances Perkins, Smith learned. Perkins later wrote about both Smith and commissioner chair Robert Wagner, "[They] got a firsthand look at industrial and labor conditions, and from that look they never recovered."[16] Smith became a strong and effective advocate of worker safety laws and championed, then and for years after, legislation aimed at giving workers more rights and protections against economic exploitation. He supported labor unions. As New York governor in the 1920s and then as a nationally prominent politician, Smith continued to press for protective legislation for workers, though most of his efforts were aimed at working women. Despite the waning of the Progressive movement and the national turn toward limited government during the "New Era," Governor Smith continued to press for more state and local government funded hospitals, parks, schools, and other facilities and services that he knew his working-class supporters needed. In a 1927 speech, Smith championed a strong government that worked on behalf of all of its citizens: "The State is a living force.... It must have the ability to clothe itself with human understanding of the daily, living needs of those whom it is created to serve."[17]

Raskob did not wholly agree with this Progressive litany. But he disagreed with less of it than Smith's policy advisor Frances Perkins might have thought. Yes, he opposed closed shop labor unions. He certainly was opposed, as a rule, to government interference in the industrial workplace. But Perkins would have been surprised by Raskob's indifference to or even approval of almost all of the particularities of Smith's support of government regulation of industry. Specifically at the state level, Raskob never voiced disapproval of industrial safety legislation—by the late 1910s both General Motors and DuPont, like most giant corporations, exercised safety rules above the minimum set by Progressive legislation—the laws, as executives at those companies saw it, were not aimed at them. The same held true for maximum hours and minimum wages legislation. Raskob thought little about women's position on the shop floor, but he would have approved of the paternalistic efforts that aimed to protect women from the dangers of industrial work. As the New York tainted milk scandal demonstrated, Raskob saw a role for government in protecting people from bad producers of all kinds.

Mostly, Raskob and Smith differed on these sorts of issues less on substance than on saliency and degree. Raskob just did not think that much about such issues—his approach to resolving class conflict in the United States focused on making workers stakeholders in capitalism. He also believed that few major employers had any reason to be predatory in their business relations, whether with their workers or with consumers—it was bad business. Raskob did believe in the sanctity of private property and he certainly did not believe that government at any level had the right to control, takeover, selectively punish, or ban any reasonable, legitimate business. But then, so did Smith who had great respect for his self-made friends in New York's hard-nosed business world.

At a political level, what directly linked the two men together was the issue of Prohibition. Both Raskob and Smith believed that the Eighteenth Amendment to the Constitution had been passed because of the fervent support of anti-Catholic, anti-immigrant bigots who used the excuse of temperance to attack the rights and equal citizenship of Irish and German Americans. While neither Smith nor Raskob had been active participants during the great debate over the Amendment, both found it wrong, even indefensible. Both men, in their personal lives, completely ignored it. For political reasons, during the first years after Prohibition's passage, Smith did his best to tread carefully around the divisive issue. He was far more interested in reforming state government and passing social legislation. But in 1923 he had signed—though not happily given the political risks it entailed and the amount of political capital it would cost him—an Act that ended New York state enforcement of the Volstead Act.

As Smith expected, Prohibitionists went after him with a vengeance. William Jennings Bryan, the old war horse of the populist wing of the Democratic Party and the nation's best known defender of the traditional religious verities, led the charge. He declared, "When the Governor of the largest State in the Union boldly raises the black flag and offers to lead the representatives of the outlawed liquor traffic in their assault upon the nation's honor and the people's welfare, he must expect resistance from the defenders of the home, the school, and the Church."[18] Smith had become a nationally polarizing figure, particularly within the confines of his own political party. He would be, forever after, bound to the politics of Prohibition.[19]

Raskob cheered on Smith's opposition to Prohibition. He saw in the passage of the Eighteenth Amendment religious and ethnic bigotry but he also believed Prohibition represented something that was to him even more threatening. Raskob saw in Prohibition a dictatorial grab by demagogic politicians and an inflamed majority against the rights of an entire industry. What the government had done to the alcohol beverage industry, it could do to others who made controversial products, including the manufacturers of explosives.

In the run-up to the 1928 election, Smith had not thought much about the larger implications of what might be called the tyranny of the majority, especially in regard to endangered industrialists. But Smith had long taken political stands on behalf of persecuted minorities and underdogs of one kind or another. He was conscious of the threat a powerful majority could have on others. Raskob's focus on the individual rights of industrialists to pursue a just course of action independent of what he considered populist federal usurpation and coercion would, over time, have its impact on Smith's thinking.

Smith was also prepared to understand Raskob's political economy argument more directly. Smith believed that Prohibition was a prime example of the limits of a one-size-fits-all national policy. What was good for one part of the country, Smith believed, was not always right for another part of the country. Smith had spent much of his political career battling upstate New York political interests who wanted to mandate how New York City residents could live and how local city officials could run their town. Prohibition was a national version of the dictatorial New York state politics Smith abhorred. While Smith was a firm believer in the use of government to right wrongs, he was ambivalent about the reach and power distant political powers should have over specific locales and communities.

While Smith had not applied that federalist perspective before 1928 to industrial policy, especially to the relationship between corporate autonomy and federal power, Raskob had. The federal government, Raskob believed, had neither the right nor the wisdom to control the de-centralized, complex workings of the free market. The relationship between New York City's right to local control and, say, the DuPont Company's right to corporate self-determination were not identical but they were not completely separate either. Smith was a Progressive and by the standards of the 1920s he was a liberal but that did not mean that he was a firm advocate of direct federal intervention into the workings of the national economy or of a strong federal role in the regulating of America's corporate interests. On those big political economy questions, he was ambivalent, even uncertain.

While Raskob would, as Frances Perkins feared, help move Smith away from some of the pro-labor, social welfare policies which had long played an integral part of his politics and toward a greater concern for property rights and corporate autonomy, Smith was not being manipulated or somehow tricked. He was following his own sometimes contradictory instincts.[20]

Then, too, Raskob was nurturing not just those instincts but also Smith's economic position. Beginning in March 1928 during the rise of the great Bull Market, Raskob bought Smith 1,000 shares of RCA, one of the boom stocks of the time, at a price of over $100,000. Raskob arranged for his major broker to establish an account in Smith's name that Raskob then managed. Thereafter, Raskob did his best to make his new friend a wealthy man. While Smith's policy and political evolution was not directly—or corruptly—affected by his changing economic status and participation in Raskob's financial plays, it is hard to believe his changing fortunes had no impact on his political views.[21]

Between Raskob's introduction to Smith in late 1926 and the great political turns of events of the summer of 1928, Raskob moved on his own deeper into the political life of the nation. Early in 1928, he had led a coalition of auto and auto-related businessmen fighting against a British effort to raise the world commodity price on rubber by limiting supply. Indicative of Raskob's public reputation and the esteem with which the other big men in the American auto and tire industries held him, Raskob became the chairman of the US industry campaign to use the federal government to counter the British. Specifically, Raskob wanted the government to exempt American manufacturers from antitrust laws so they could legally pool their efforts to buy massive amounts of crude rubber on the world market and break the British attempt at cartelization. American industry had already begun this effort in 1927 without benefit of legal protection.

Raskob pursued a multipronged strategy. First, he lobbied the Justice Department to waive antitrust restrictions. Since the British crude rubber squeeze threatened the viability of American industry, Raskob argued, antitrust exemption was in the best interests of the economic security of the United States. Raskob worked this angle on Assistant Attorney General William Donovan, who would later become the head of the wartime Office of Strategic Services. Donovan became another of Raskob's influential friends. More directly, Raskob lobbied a passel of senators and congressmen across party lines seeking legislative protection. In one-on-one negotiations, Raskob convinced Secretary of Commerce Herbert Hoover, on behalf of the Coolidge Administration, to support this legislation. In the end, the bill failed to pass Congress, defeated by a bevy of old Progressives and others, including most rural representatives, who remained deeply suspicious of the big businessmen behind the antitrust exemption. Even during the Coolidge Administration, when plutocrats supposedly had their way with the federal government, a strong faction in Congress kept the antitrust faith alive. Raskob did not mind the legislative failure as the American industrialists had by early 1928 already used their market muscle to push the Dutch into producing more rubber in their colonial holdings, thus breaking the Brits attempt to cartelize the commodity. For Raskob, the rubber lobbying effort had not produced policy—though it had deferred antitrust action—but it had introduced him for the first time to a great number of influential politicians, especially Democrats in the Northeast and the industrial Midwest who had supported the American industry position.

Far more publicly, Raskob had also become involved in the hot-button issue of Prohibition. Raskob had long opposed Prohibition but for several years his opposition was almost completely done in private. He had joined the major repeal organization, the Association Against the Prohibition Amendment (AAPA), in 1922 but his financial contributions were minimal. He had not become active in the anti-Prohibition campaign until 1926, and then only modestly, when Pierre, Irénée, and Lammot du Pont all began to put their money and their time into the repeal effort; Pierre became the primary backer of the AAPA.

The du Pont brothers were particularly vexed at the coercive democratic power Prohibition revealed; such majoritarian tyranny, they feared, could be directed at anyone—including themselves. The du Ponts were still haunted by the federal government's antitrust action and the special wartime tax that had singled out their company and their industry. Pierre argued that the key issue regarding Prohibition was "the right of the majority to interfere with the liberties of a minority." He conceded that alcoholism was a real problem but the "welfare" of a few alcoholics, he stated, "is not as important as the security of the American ideal, by which I mean the right to choose one's course."[22] Du Pont, usually so reserved, was a passionate advocate for the repeal of the Eighteenth Amendment.

In early 1928, in large part at Pierre's request, Raskob joined the board of the AAPA. He began using his considerable public profile to speak out against Prohibition. The AAPA began to feature the renowned Raskob and his pro-repeal statements in its publicity campaigns.[23] When John announced his commitment to Smith's campaign he was well known as an anti-Prohibitionist. During the campaign and after it, as well, Raskob would become a major voice and force on the "Wet" side of the great Prohibition fight. But Raskob did not join Smith's campaign to advocate narrowly for Prohibition. He joined Smith's campaign because of his relationship with Smith, because he believed that Smith and he shared a pro-business perspective on policy, and because he thought it would be fascinating to play politics at the highest level of the game.

Raskob and the rest of the "Golf Cabinet" went to Houston for the Democratic Party Convention at the end of June 1928. Eddie Dowling, Tim Mara, Raskob, and several other men rode down in Bill Kenny's private rail car, the St. Nicholas. Raskob who had never been to a party convention before enjoyed the pageantry. From a distance he watched Smith's political operators counting votes and keeping Smith's many delegates in line. Raskob had no duties at the convention; he was still just an interested party to the great events unfolding. But prior to the convention he had had a private, heart-to-heart conversation with Smith. Raskob had told Smith that he would like to play a major role in his presidential campaign and not just as a cash cow. Smith had made no promises in return and he seems not to have discussed Raskob's request with any of his key political advisors, but a seed had been planted.[24]

Smith had been the front runner for the nomination since mid-1927 and no one had risen up since then to seriously challenge him. Within the nearly ruinous, fractious inner workings of the Democratic Party, Smith's path to the nomination had been set after the disastrous 1924 Democratic nominating convention and subsequent national election. Primary elections did not yet play a relevant part in the nominating process; the nomination was won through backroom deals made by party bosses.

In 1924, Smith the underdog had tried to line up enough of those pols to take the nomination. As the popular governor of New York, the most populous state in the union, he had instant credibility and solid support in the Northeast and the industrial Midwest. He also had numerous instant enemies. For decades, Democratic leaders from the East intent on winning the party nomination had attacked New York City's Tammany Hall—a symbol of corruption in much of the United States—to prove themselves to the party's powerful rural, Southern and Western wing. Wilson and Cleveland, the only two Democrats to win both the nomination and the presidency since 1856, had used that strategy. Smith, obviously, could not. Instead he stood as the proud champion of the party's booming immigrant, Catholic and Jewish, urban working-class voters.

Smith had made a serious run in 1924. His main rival was William McAdoo who had been secretary of the treasury under Wilson and who had won national acclaim for keeping the railroads running during World War I. McAdoo aimed to unify the Democrats behind a tricky platform of economic progressivism and social conservatism. He would continue, he said, to pursue the national reform politics of Woodrow Wilson to fight the growing power of Big Business in the United States. At the same time, he promised to rigorously enforce Prohibition. On the polarizing issue of the Ku Klux Klan, whose four million members were waging an open war against Catholic and Jewish Americans, as well as "modern" women, African Americans, and secular influences, McAdoo simply remained silent, refusing to endorse a proposed Democratic Party plank that condemned the Klan's politics of hate. McAdoo was simultaneously on the left and the right of Smith. Caught between the crosscutting appeal of Smith and McAdoo, the Democrats had deadlocked. Smith won 80.2 percent of eastern delegates but just 0.6 percent of the southern and border state votes. It took a two-thirds majority to clinch the nomination and neither candidate could secure it. Finally on the 103rd ballot, a dark horse candidate swooped in and took the nomination. The exhausted delegates had thrown over their ideological differences and given the nod to John H. Davis, a true believer in the oldest, Jeffersonian precepts of the Democratic Party. Davis had begun his life in humble circumstance in West Virginia and through sheer brilliance and hard work had become one of the nation's preeminent corporate lawyers and public servants. He was a liberal... but of the nineteenth-century variety. The Democrats had endorsed a man who opposed almost every Progressive Era Act, including Prohibition but also the panoply of legislation that had been made to rein in monopolies and trusts and that used federal power to make industrial work safer and industrial workers better protected against exploitation.

Calvin Coolidge crushed Davis in the general election 15 million votes to 8 million (with the independent Progressive candidate Robert Lafollette taking 4.8 million). After the defeat, the Democratic leadership vowed they would not go into the 1928 election a party divided. A sufficient number also believed that the fight over the Ku Klux Klan had been disastrous. With the Klan's influence in free fall after a series of scandals, many thought the timing was right to tilt the national party in a new direction. So, while many Democrats in the South and West were anything but excited about the "wet," Catholic, New York governor as their party nominee the Party felt like 1928 was the year to give the Northeastern Democratic bloc their turn. Even "Dry" Democrats were willing to give Smith his shot, especially given the likelihood that the "Republican prosperity" of the 1920s, which was reaching its apogee in 1928, made a Democratic presidential victory extremely unlikely, regardless of the nominee. To maintain the always precarious relationship between northern and southern Democrats, many in the party felt that the immigrant-backed, Catholic, big-city-based Al Smith supporters had to be appeased.[25]

Belle Moskowitz, the brains behind Smith's march to the nomination, saw it that way. As early as 1925 she realized that the southern wing of the Party was willing to cede the nomination in order, she wrote, to "appeal to the powerful northern and eastern states with large blocks of voters in the Electoral College. I began to think about the votes needed to secure the nomination and to figure roughly where our strength might lie. Suddenly I realized that there was a certain inevitability about the situation and felt sure we could do the trick."[26] She was right. To smooth over southern delegates' concerns, Arkansas Senator Joseph Robinson was pre-chosen as Smith's running mate. Franklin Roosevelt gave the convention nominating speech for Smith, branding him "the happy warrior."[27]

Raskob had been largely a bystander at the convention, as well as during the pre-convention delegate round-up but his national reputation brought him press attention. In steamy Houston he told reporters: "Alfred E. Smith, as President, would give the country a constructive business administration. Business, big or little, has nothing to fear from Governor Smith."[28] It was a bit of a left-handed compliment but it did the trick; the stock markets closed higher the next day, creating a "Smith market."[29] Investors, at least, trusted Raskob's judgment. In 1928 both the Republican Party and the Democratic Party—which had rattled the business community during the Progressive Era by three times running "the Great Commoner" William Jennings Bryan for president—would offer the American people a pro-business candidate.

Immediately after Smith won the nomination, Raskob, Kenny, and the rest of the "Golf cabinet" crew rushed back to their hotel to telephone Smith. According to Eddie Dowling, right before the call, he, Tim Mara, Kenny, and Raskob talked about the campaign chairmanship. Dowling, John's closest friend in the Smith crowd, asked Raskob if he would serve as chairman. Dowling tells us that John replied: "I'd lay down my life for the Governor." In his account of these events,

Dowling suggests that Raskob had no idea that Dowling would promote him for the job. Maybe—but more likely Dowling and Raskob had already plotted out the conversation. Kenny, Mara, and the others jumped on board and when they were connected to Governor Smith, after much cheering and congratulating, Dowling told Smith: "Governor, we're all hoping that John will become the national chairman." Raskob then got on the phone and told Smith that he was serious about taking on the job and that he was more than willing to put aside his corporate work to serve Smith: "There's nothing I'd rather do."[30]

A few days later, in New York, Smith met with his political advisors to select his campaign chairman. Some pushed for the US senator from Rhode Island, Peter Goelet Gerry. He was rich, generally well regarded, and an old-line Protestant. His religion and lineage would help balance Smith's Irish-Catholic background. Smith was not interested. They considered Owen Young, one-time Morgan banker, president of General Electric, founder of RCA, and a long-time Democrat who had been a mover and shaker in Washington, as well as in international financial circles. But Young had recently been a target of a highly publicized congressional investigation into the "Power Trust," which some blamed, with good reason, for rising electricity costs. Smith was dubious (and some have argued that Young was not interested). The governor then announced that he wanted to go with his friend John J. Raskob. He knew that John would be thrilled. He also knew that John Raskob had access to more campaign money than any other man he could ever find.

Smith's closest political advisors, Belle Moskowitz and Joe Proskauer, begged their boss not to make the offer. Raskob was too "wet," too Catholic, and too inexperienced. They made their case for somebody—anybody—else. Already, they reminded Smith, "dry" Democrats had been threatening to bolt from the party because of Smith's support of the New York anti-enforcement bill and public calls for local determination of alcohol policy. Smith had to know the white Protestant South had already been vocal in its concerns about electing a Papist to the presidency. Raskob, they warned, would be salt in the wound. Finally, Moskowitz complained, Raskob wasn't even a Democrat. Franklin Roosevelt, though not part of Smith's inner circle, appealed to Smith's political instincts, arguing that Raskob would cost the Democratic ticket far more votes than his money and business credentials could win it.[31] But Smith had decided and he also felt that he owed Raskob: "It's the only thing Raskob has ever asked of me, and I've got to give it to him."[32] Belle Moskowitz and the rest of Smith's New York Progressive supporters were disgusted but Smith could not be moved. The job was Raskob's. The chief financial officer of DuPont and then GM was now the campaign chairman of the Al Smith presidential campaign. At Smith's request, Raskob would also become the chairman of the Democratic National Committee—beginning immediately. The announcement would be made official on July 11 when the DNC would meet in New York City but the die had been cast: John Raskob was to become the Democratic Party chieftain.

John had received many titles since becoming secretary to Pierre du Pont in 1900, ranging from the corporate to the Papal. Without exception, he had made no personal or family ceremony of his rise to these various offices. But perhaps because of the very public nature of his new positions, John decided to call his entire family together and announce the news to them before it became official. Raskob requested that the family gather for a weekend just after July 4 at their new summer home, a vast estate outside Centreville, Maryland, that the family called Pioneer Point. John would come from New York, where he had gone to check in at GM after his week in Houston and subsequent time with the governor in Albany. Skipper was already at Pioneer Point, as were most of the children. John had hoped that, in a year of many achievements, he could bring his family together in celebration of his newest triumph. It was not to be.

The Raskobs' second son, twenty-year-old Bill, was a student at Yale University. He had still been up at New Haven when he got the call to join his brothers and sisters at Pioneer Point. On the drive down, he stopped at Eddie Dowling's place outside New York where, somewhat star struck, he had visited with Eddie and his wife, also a famous Broadway player. He was driving a magnificent new LaSalle Phaeton, a sporty, open car made by Cadillac, a gift from his parents.

Bill, like all of Raskob's older sons, had a complicated relationship with his father. John was, in general, rarely satisfied with his boys' progress. Bob, for example, who may well have had a learning disability, constantly disappointed his father. John wrote him at the very end of 1927: "It is absolutely senseless for you to do so poorly.... Now if you do not want a good horsewhipping you had better knuckle down and study, because if we cannot talk sense into you we will have to beat it into you."[33] Bill, more than any of the others, had begun to perform at the level his father expected. After a rocky start, he had become a solid student at Yale and had charmed many of Raskob's friends. By 1928, father and son had developed a strong, affectionate relationship and John wrote Bill regularly with praise: "I enjoyed hearing the many nice things Mr. Kuser and his family says about you [he] thinks there are few boys like you. I guess some of the rest of us feel pretty much the same way too."[34] Bill wrote his father in a similar vein. In late March 1928, he told his father that his economics professors at Yale "are coming up and asking me what I think of the situation the stock market is in. I lean back and tell them I don't want to be quoted and that any statements I make aren't for the press but the inside dope is that many of the stocks are selling under value and that GM is worth '250.' They say, 'Do you really think so'— and I say 'Sure there's no doubt about it.' Ha! Ha!"[35] John pinned his hopes for a family successor on this bright, lively, and sweet boy.

On July 5, just a few miles from Centreville on his way to his father's celebration, Bill ran off the road. A driver a few hundred yards behind him could not tell exactly what happened, but he suddenly saw a cloud of dust. When he came to the scene of the accident, he found Bill, ejected from the open car, "lying in a field with his head against a stone." He was dead.[36]

John and Helena buried their son on July 10, 1928. They held the funeral at the Mother of Sorrows Church in Centreville, Maryland. Monsignor Dougherty, from St. Peters, led the requiem mass. Many came, including Governor Smith. Then Bill's body was transported to the Cathedral Cemetery in Wilmington where it was interred at the family mausoleum. More than 300 friends and family had gathered. Hundreds of letters and telegrams flooded in.

In reply to Dwight Morrow's letter of condolence, John wrote his most emotional response. After thanking Morrow, John wrote: "Bill's death was a terrible tragedy.... Helena and I have nothing but the happiest memories of his life, which helps us tremendously in our great bereavement." Those memories and the support of his friends, John continued, "give one a great deal of strength and fortitude to bear up and carry on and this coupled with the fact that Helena, his mother, is a wonderful and brave character, makes my lot much easier than it otherwise would be."[37] John was helping to invent modern American society with its facile ad-man language and easy credit terms, but in his grief he reached back, for shield and armor, to the formal rhetoric and the stiff emotional posture of the late Victorians.

John and Helena found particular solace in condolences from Bill's professors, coaches, and the president of Yale University who told the Raskobs that their son "represented everything fine and noble that Yale stood for and exemplified in every way the Yale spirit."[38] John and Helena decided to memorialize their son by creating a foundation in his name that would help poor and orphaned young men and women pay for college. John used Bill's estate of some $85,000 and sold nearly a million dollars in stock to endow the Bill Raskob Foundation. He and Helena wrote: "Ever since he was a child his heart responded to every appeal from those in need and he gave to his utmost ability of giving. And so we have made this foundation, for we know, if Bill were living, nothing would be more pleasing to him than to give some poor child a fair start in life, as will be done with this foundation."[39] To a close friend, John later wrote that his heart ached but "we have to carry on and do the best we can."[40] The Foundation was, at least for John, a way to make something good from something terrible.

Raskob, as always, pushed on. His boy's death had come just before the world would learn that he was to run Al Smith's campaign and head the Democratic National Committee. The official announcement came less than a week after Bill's death and the day after the funeral. Between his son's death and the funeral John had not found the opportunity to tell his family, including his brother, that he was to be named Smith's campaign chair. He left Wilmington for New York almost immediately after the funeral, leaving Helena alone with the children and her grief. It is not clear that even Helena knew, before the news was made public, of the course John had chosen. The first that the children and John's brother heard of Raskob's new position was when they read about in the newspaper.[41]

John never considered not taking up his campaign duties. On July 11 Smith and Raskob appeared together in New York City where Raskob formally accepted the chairmanship of the DNC. After a brief ceremony in which Raskob received a gavel from the outgoing chairman, John gave his first partisan political speech to a large crowd of reporters. The polished hand of Smith's speechwriter, Joe Proskauer, appeared evident in Raskob's carefully modulated remarks: "My relations with Gov. Smith are most intimate, and no one could have higher or finer ideals with respect to the relations between government and business—big and little—than he.... Gov. Smith is a strong advocate of less government in business and of more business in government. He believes in no disturbance of honest businessmen and his career demonstrates his fairness to labor." On the hot button issue of Prohibition, Raskob walked a careful line: "If, as a result of careful study, he can evolve a plan for the regulation and control of the liquor question, in a way that will absolutely prevent the return of the saloon, eliminate bootlegging, with its accompanying evils—graft, corruption, and murder—and restore temperate life in our country, then all fair-minded men must admit his right, if not his duty, as President, to promulgate such plan.... This is leadership—not pussy-footing." Raskob hinted at the Catholic issue when he called for a clean campaign in which all parties avoided "mud-slinging."[42] Raskob was never a great speaker and he read the speech, not written with his own cadence in mind, haltingly and with hesitation. No emotion marked his presentation. For many of the political reporters, this encounter with Raskob was their first and they took away a notion that he was a rather quiet and shy man, uncomfortable on center stage, not the usual type associated with politics. Few, if any, registered where Raskob had been the day before. Neither he nor the governor took any questions, allowing Raskob's prepared remarks to carry the news.

Raskob's appointment as head of both Smith's campaign and the Democratic National Committee ignited a firestorm of interest around the nation. Almost every pundit and editorial page weighed in. The *New York World*, long associated with Progressive causes and edited by the Smith-supporting Herbert Bayard Swope, headlined, "Smith Out to Win Big Business Vote."[43] That was the headline Smith and his team hoped to see. The *New York Times* took the same position, more or less, on its editorial page. In a long piece titled "Big Business and Politics," the *Times* cautiously observed: "It is a departure from the precedent which Governor Smith has made in selecting John J. Raskob, Chairman of the Finance Committee of the General Motors Corporation, as National Chairman.

No man who combines his business experience and prominence with his complete lack of political background has ever been chosen for this position." The *Times* then concurred with the *World*: Smith chose Raskob to demonstrate "that business, large and small, has nothing to fear from Democratic success."[44] Raskob had used nearly the exact same words when he had talked to the press at the Democratic Convention.

Numerous Democratic-leaning papers followed the party line, emphasizing that Smith's selection of Raskob proved Smith's pro-business allegiances: "Aside from his ability Raskob will bring to the job of managing Smith's campaign, his appointment serves notice that the Democratic Party, if successful this fall, will be a sane and responsible instrument of Government. Gov. Smith has broken utterly with the Bryan tradition" (*St. Louis Post-Dispatch*); and "the naming of Raskob already has many people saying the backing of Raskob and his powerful interests means a Smith Administration would be 'good for business'" (*Cleveland Plain Dealer*).[45] The *Baltimore Evening Sun* offered a slightly different but still positive spin: "Raskob's appointment means that the Democratic Party will be relieved of one of the handicaps under which it has almost invariably suffered. There will be no amateurism in this campaign, no Clem Shaverism [the much criticized management style of the prior chairman of the DNC]. There will be rather the same sort of efficiency which one associates with Republican Party agreement."[46] Most, though not all, of the newspaper editorials praising Smith's selection of Raskob came from big city newspapers in the Northeast.

Outside of Smith's East Coast home turf, the governor's selection of Raskob faced a good deal more criticism. A very few newspapers attacked Raskob's appointment from the Progressive Left. The *Portland Oregonian* feared the worst, noting that not only had Smith selected Raskob to run his campaign, he had also made investment banker Herbert Lehman a key member of his election team: "Democracy is making one of its periodical overtures for the friendship of big business.... If Al Smith should be elected President by the efforts of these men big business would have nothing to fear and bond dealers have everything to hope."[47] Blunter still was the national campaign manager for Socialist presidential candidate Norman Thomas: "The Democratic Party under the leadership of Gov. Smith... has served notice that it is out to serve 'big business' first and last. The issue between the Republicans and the Democrats seems to be the question of which can prove itself most sycophantic toward the business and banking interests."[48] Norman Thomas hammered home this point of view, denouncing both Smith and Raskob for using the cultural politics of Prohibition to mask their true economic agenda: "It is clear that the Democrats mean to catch the workers by dangling before them an elusive beer bottle, while they deliver themselves over body and soul to the Raskobs of Wall Street.... Not only is John Raskob Chairman of the open shop General Motors, he is bound up with the Du Pont interest which grow rich with wars, big and little."[49] The Socialists had a case, but they also had a much diminished constituency for such an argument in 1928.

The *Chicago Tribune*, perhaps the most influential Republican-aligned newspaper in the nation, attacked Smith and Raskob from a very different angle. "Smith Picks Militant Wet to Lead Fight," announced the *Tribune's* front-page headline. In much smaller type, the column head did read, "Raskob Chosen Chairman; Big Business Man," but the article, like many others from around the country, focused much less on Raskob's pro-business credentials and much more on what they knew would make Raskob a politically polarizing figure.[50] Everything Belle Moskowitz had feared about Raskob's appointment became immediately clear.

The *Tribune's* top writer, James O'Donnell Bennett, had a field day covering the story. Smith, wrote Bennett, "dictator of the northern machinery of the Democratic party...made John J. Raskob of Claymont, Del., a militant Catholic, a militant wet, and the personification of big business, chairman of the Democratic committee." Gleefully, Bennett continued, "The governor's choice plunged some of the southern notables into deep meditation, if not acute apprehension." The *Tribune* then listed every Papal award Raskob had received and the large sums he had given "for the preservation and advancement of the Catholic faith."[51] In an era when the rabidly anti-Catholic Ku Klux Klan had enrolled, just a few years earlier, millions of members and many a Protestant minister still made a living out of castigating Catholicism and the power of the Pope, the Republican newspaper's intense focus on Raskob's "militant" Catholic faith was no accident.

In the immediate aftermath of his appointment, Raskob had little time to focus on newspaper coverage, positive or negative. His decision to lead the Smith campaign and the DNC had also ignited a firestorm at General Motors. Alfred Sloan was beside himself with anger. Like Raskob's family, Sloan had first learned of Raskob's decision only after John made his public announcement in New York City. Sloan felt blindsided. His chief financial officer, a man who had thrust himself into the public eye repeatedly as the most visible face of General Motors with his various financial plans and pronouncements and his near-constant comments on the stock market, in general, and General Motors share price, in particular, was suddenly a very prominent, very public Democratic Party big-wig. What, Sloan bellowed, would Republican consumers make of a car company so intimately linked to the leader of the Democratic Party? Many years later, a cooler and calmer Sloan testified as to his thinking: "The management of General Motors, particularly myself, felt that it would be very unsound for an individual who was managing a political campaign to continue as spokesman of General

Motors. We felt that it put General Motors in politics, and we had worked very hard to get General Motors where it was."[52]

Sloan had long been extraordinarily focused on GM's image in the mind of car buyers and had worked with typical intensity to assure that the corporation was seen positively by as many potential customers as possible. Well before image advertising and public relations campaigns became a normal part of doing business, Sloan had hired the nascent field's leading practitioners to reduce Americans' concerns about General Motors immense size and market power and, instead, to give GM what ad-man Bruce Barton called a corporate "soul."[53] Anything that darkened GM's carefully constructed image was anathema to Sloan and Raskob's many, often well-publicized forays outside of the GM building had long worried him.

Only a few months before the Smith debacle, an unhappy GM shareholder—"some old gal," in the words of a junior GM executive privy to the event—had sent Sloan a photo of Raskob "in a rolling chair with a beautiful woman" that had appeared in the Atlantic City *Boardwalk News*. Sloan was not a prude or a particularly judgmental man; his dear friend Walter Chrysler was a philanderer of the first order. But Sloan could not stand for anything that, in his mind, brought uncertainty about the virtues of General Motors to the mind of the auto consumer or even one of his shareholders. Sloan demanded that Raskob come to his office. According to the office gossip spread by Sloan's executive secretary, Sloan yelled, "John, we can't have that kind of publicity, that's very bad. Indeed, I wish you would be more careful." A nonplussed Raskob yelled right back: "Listen, what I do when I'm not on duty here is nobody's damned business."[54] That incident blew over. But Sloan's concerns about Raskob's dedication to the image and reputation of GM had not been put to rest. Sloan was a corporate man above all else and he was right to think that Raskob was not.

Raskob had meant to let Sloan know about the Smith business before the news became public. But Bill's death had confused everything. He had found the time to tell Pierre but that was different. Raskob knew that not discussing the issue in advance with Sloan, who was at least nominally his boss, had been a mistake. Still, he was surprised by Sloan's outrage and he got angry in return. What, after all, was the big deal? In various ways ranging from major political donations to congressional testimony to lobbying to leadership roles in a great many different public organizations, all of the big men at DuPont and GM, including Sloan, had been involved in the great political and policy issues of the day. Nothing Raskob was planning to do in association with Governor Smith or the DNC would in any way, Raskob believed, work against the interests of General Motors. Governor Smith, Raskob explained, was not anti-business; were he to become a president he would be a supporter of the GM-DuPont point of view. Raskob's position with Smith's campaign would help not hinder General Motors.

As a result, he saw no reason to leave his position at General Motors and he had made that position known to a few Wall Street insiders the day he announced his role in the Smith campaign.[55] However, if Sloan thought it best, Raskob said he would take a leave of absence from his GM vice presidency, at least during the fall campaign. There was no cause for alarm.

For a week, the Sloan-Raskob imbroglio engulfed the leading executives and board members at DuPont and GM. Sloan insisted that Raskob must resign. Raskob thought that Sloan was being ridiculous. Pierre du Pont, of course, sided with John. He explained his point of view to his cousin Coleman: "The only way that we can improve political service is to get better men. We cannot get the best from corporations if we impose the penalty of resignation from corporate work at the same time."[56] Not surprisingly, Coleman agreed; he had become the Republican Senator from Delaware in 1924 and he had served a partial term earlier in the decade. Coleman realized that Pierre, who was still GM chairman of the board, as well as the leader of the Association against the Prohibition Amendment, meant to follow Raskob out of the corporation if Sloan forced Raskob to resign over his political role. Coleman wrote his cousin: "I think that when you and John went in to help your country, the directors of the General Motors Corporation should have said, 'For you gentlemen to take on additional patriotic work and responsibility we have nothing but praise. Your salaries are doubled until after the election.' I think someone should give you both medals for patriotism."[57] Coleman and Pierre, scions of a distinguished family and one-time family firm, arguably, saw no difference between their business roles and their public duties and they honored their long-time associate with a similar status.

Although the two du Pont cousins stood by Raskob, few others in the DuPont-GM orbit did. Walter Carpenter, the highly professional vice president—and president-in-the-making—of the DuPont Company, who also served on the GM board, sided with Sloan. While well aware of Pierre's position, Carpenter nonetheless wrote DuPont president and Pierre's younger brother Irénée that Raskob's decision to put politics above his corporate duties was a "serious" mistake: "I can think of no way in which the duP-GM interests could have dissipated the good will and respect of the country in so short a time as has been done."[58] Carpenter, a principled man, spoke from the head but it need also be said that Raskob had several years earlier publicly and privately fought hard to prevent Carpenter from moving up the corporate ladder to replace Raskob's hand-picked man, Donaldson Brown, as vice president of finance at DuPont. Raskob was discovering that despite his years of corporate commitment he had fewer key allies than he had supposed. His own successful effort to force Billy Durant from GM could have and probably should have taught him this hard truth about corporate life. A confident Sloan took the matter to the GM board for a formal vote. Outnumbered and outgunned, Raskob lost the vote. He was going to have to resign from GM.

Raskob had not expected to be forced into such a dramatic decision when he signed onto the Smith campaign. Leaving GM was going to cost him a lot of money in salary and stock option bonuses. Nonetheless, Raskob did it. He wrote Sloan a formal note on July 17th, tendering his resignation and calmly acceding to Sloan's point of view: "[T]he corporation must not be put in the light of taking sides for or against political parties, personages, or questions."[59] Sloan, with Raskob's permission, made the letter public a few days later and it was printed in full in many newspapers around the country including the *New York Times* under the front-page headline, "Raskob Quits Post in General Motors to Appease Critics."[60] The *Wall Street Journal* editorial board put the financial community's imprimatur on the resignation: "The common sense as well as the proprieties of the situation dictated the resignation of Mr. Raskob as General Motors committee chairman.... The truth persists that there is no true serving of two masters."[61] In a separate commentary, run the same day, the *Journal* praised John "for the courage of the man who is willing to make a sacrifice for what he believes," and observed, "He knows there is nothing ahead but hard work and plenty of it, but he will get a great deal of fun from doing it."[62] The editorial page writers at the *Journal* knew their man.

Raskob had turned another page in his life. He quietly held onto his board memberships at both GM and DuPont. In spring 1929 he would, without fanfare, regain his seat on GM's finance committee, serving under the leadership of his one-time protégé Don Brown. But John's days as a corporate policy maker, as a Big Business brass hat, were over. Raskob would never again commit himself fully to GM or serve as a major corporate chieftain.

Characteristically, Raskob took his defeat in stride. Nothing in his private correspondence or public statements indicates anger or even frustration over the turn of events. Instead, he joked about it. In accepting a golf date, he wrote one of his good friends that he was looking forward to their upcoming match and that he was "ready to win everybody's money which I am particularly in need of since I quit work."[63] Raskob was not known for an appreciation of the ironic but he must have at least pondered the unexpected turn his relationship with Alfred Sloan had taken. Only a few years earlier, when he and Pierre had been discussing Sloan's remarkable career, Raskob had remarked: "There... is a man who should be President of the United States. He never will, because he is not colorful enough."[64] Raskob, at least as compared to "Silent Sloan," was the colorful one. Now he would have the opportunity to see what he could do outside the confines of the corporate world. Now he would know, after better than a quarter of a century as a DuPont-General Motors man, what it felt like to operate without the structure and power of his corporate position.

The Last Days of the Old Order

What John did not know, at least at the time, was the damage his near-frenzy of activity in the days, then weeks, and finally months after the death of his son had on his marriage. After Bill's funeral, John had left Helena to grieve, to cope, to recover, to find solace as she could without him. He did return briefly to Helena, who was in reclusion at the Raskobs' summer estate near Centreville, Maryland, the day after the announcement of his campaign chairmanship. Their eldest child, John, Jr., was relieved and told a sympathetic features writer at the *New York World*, one of the very few women who ever wrote about Raskob, that he was glad that his father was with his grieving mother: "He won't leave her now."[1] But John, Jr. was wrong. His father did leave his mother; he had to leave her if he meant to do his new job. If Helena needed emotional support, she would have to look elsewhere.

Helena found that support from Jack Corcoran. Corcoran supervised water-front activities at Pioneer Point and helped manage the sprawling grounds and fields. The Raskobs had hired him away from the Lake Placid Club where he had taught the Raskob children how to swim and sail in 1924. A strong, athletic, and energetic outdoorsman, Jack was just a few years older than Bill. The two young men had become close and had corresponded while Bill was at Yale. A few months before Bill died, he had written his father praising Jack and making sure that Raskob knew how important Corcoran had become in his life: "He is certainly a great fellow....He has done a great deal for me and is far from the bottom when it comes to brains."[2] After Bill's funeral, Helena had returned to Pioneer Point and there she and Jack began to talk intimately and emotionally about Bill.

At the very first, their relationship was as might be expected between a for-ty-three-year-old married woman and mother of thirteen and a young man in his mid-twenties. In August, while Skipper was spending time at Archmere, she wrote a sweet birthday note to Jack, who was still at Pioneer Point in Maryland, and enclosed a check for $100: "You will accept this letter from me without hesi-tation or comment. As I told you the other day, providence was unkind in not having made you twins [with Bill]; so, I prove hereby my utter selfishness in claiming as my son the one and only Jack. I hope you will like your new adoption as my son and will always feel free enough to come to see us all. . . . And may the children and I live long enough to enjoy the world's great gift to us—our Jack. With deep affection, I sign myself your Fostermother."[3]

Soon, however, this maternal affection shifted radically and forever as Jack made it clear to Skipper that he did not think of himself as her son. Helena did already have gray hair, worn in a bob, but there was little matronly about her. Despite her many pregnancies she was fit and athletic. She had an infectious smile and she dressed stylishly, often wearing a tailored jacket with a man's tie over a matching skirt. In late October 1928, a reporter for the New York *Evening World* gushed: "her eyes are the most winning thing about her—big deep-set eyes that look now brown, now gray, under the shadow of her felt hat; eyes that are humorous and friendly and thoughtful and warm with interest in life." Skipper was a dashing woman.[4]

In the late summer and early fall, Jack and Skipper were further drawn together in response to a series of threatening letters Skipper and, somewhat mysteriously, Jack received. The carefully crafted letters came from a man in Philadelphia. In his last letter, dated in early September, he implied that he was behind the death of Bill. He threatened to blow up Archmere with everyone in it if he did not receive $100,000. He actually apologized for his threats, stating that his personal financial situation necessitated his actions. The Raskobs and Jack had ignored the first letters but after the letter mentioning Bill arrived, Helena had become quite upset and John, while downplaying the threat, asked the head of DuPont security, Major Richard Sylvester, to stop the man. Sylvester worked closely with the Philadelphia police and, following a well executed plan involving a letter drop, the police captured the extortionist, a career criminal who quickly confessed and was sent to prison. The arrest, however, made the headlines and within days another set of threats appeared, addressed solely to Mrs. Raskob, this time from a gang of near-illiterates who demanded the more modest sum of $15,000. Mrs. Raskob did not reply and two more letters appeared. In the third and final letter, the new extortionists explained why they demanded the sum of $15,000: "you Hausbant few Yers go head pay some $15.000 for tacken girls in New York She Macke him pay or go to court . . . we want to same if you all wand live." The letter was signed by Dancio Ferdinand, who claimed he was in charge of a large gang of men who had cased Archmere and were ready to blow it up. Helena turned the letters over to John. What if anything was said between the Raskobs over Ferdinand's assertion about the payment of $15,000 to the unnamed girl is unknown. No arrests were made in this incident. The series of threats left Helena shaky and she and the younger children left Archmere and returned to Pioneer Point, where Jack helped look after the family's security.[5]

In early November, for reasons unclear, Jack left Pioneer Point and went to Pittsburgh. Soon thereafter, Skipper sent him this cryptic telegram: "Rome was not built in a day but a New World was discovered in four days STOP Although a democracy a princess was enthroned and a prince saw fit to pay homage STOP The sequel to this story is stern but comprehensive realities and they lived happily ever after = Skipper."[6] Exactly what happened next and at what speed and with what emotional consequences is also not clear but by the summer of 1929, Skipper and Jack had made a most intimate and enduring relationship.

Jack moved back to Pioneer Point. In July 1929, Skipper gave him a copy of Kahil Gibran's *The Prophet* with a lock of her hair, an oval photographic portrait, and a letter which read, in part:

> True Heart,
>
> This little oval is a companion for your hours of reading; keep it in your book and when, after the hours of toilsome work are over you turn to some loved volume for relaxation, you will find me ever with a willing ear to listen.... [T]oday my mind wandered back to the 'Heart's Sanctuary,' I found the same wonder and fearsomeness that I expressed there. Why such a great gift has been bestowed upon me, and just how I can ever prove worthy is beyond me. Anyway, I'm grateful to the Gods for last evening.... Good night! May your "dream" deserve all the sweet dreams about her!
>
> Always and ever—Your Skipper.

On the oval portrait Skipper gave to Jack that day she inked this message: "T.E., E.W.D.W.A, W.E.S.W.L.F.T.H. Y.L.H.O.T.M.W. 7/22/29."[7] Presumably Jack knew exactly what she meant.

No evidence indicates that John knew then that his wife was falling in love with the much younger man that he had employed to work at his summer estate. Certainly in the fall of 1928 he was far too busy to find the time to assess the state of his marriage. Certainly, too, that marriage had been strained for a number of years. For nearly a decade John had spent more time away from his wife and family than he had with them. Since moving to New York he had enjoyed, to put the case most delicately, a variety of relationships with women.[8] So after John left his home, his family, and his wife immediately after his son's funeral to take up his new responsibilities, it is perhaps not surprising that Helena, in response and simply in following her own separate course, had discovered her new "Heart's Sanctuary." She maintained her marriage with John, then and after. They were both devout Catholics and they were both devoted in their own way to their large family and to each other but their relationship was never again to be what it had once been. It was a price John had not expected to pay for his embrace of all the opportunities that came his way.

After Bill's funeral, John was back in New York. He was under immediate and immense pressure. He was, first of all, focused on getting Al Smith the money he needed to campaign. The election was less than four months away. His time was spent at Bill Kenny's Tiger Room and at his swank new Democratic National Committee headquarters, which he had setup just a few floors below his old offices at the General Motors Building in mid-town Manhattan (conducive to the dual role as DNC chairman and GM head of finance Raskob had, erroneously, expected to perform simultaneously). Raskob estimated that Governor Smith needed $4 million to run a strong national campaign, something the Democrats had failed to do in the previous two presidential elections. In 1920, poor James Cox had been forced to run his campaign on $1.3 million; the Republican Warren Harding had a war chest of some $5.3 million. In 1924, the Democratic nominee John W. Davis had less than a million while Calvin Coolidge spent better than $3 million.[9] Raskob would not allow Governor Smith to be so outspent. Raskob was besieged by cash-hungry Democratic county chairmen, incumbent office-holders, and candidates from around the country. Everyone wanted money, even as they wanted to offer him advice.

Meanwhile, the key members of Smith's kitchen cabinet, led by Belle Moskowitz, were doing everything they could to keep Raskob away from Smith, the major campaign issues, and the national press. Moskowitz, along with Smith's other long-time lieutenants, including Robert Moses (whose powerful role in New York politics was still at a relatively early stage), managed Smith's campaign schedule, publicity, and political organization. They tried to keep Raskob focused narrowly on fund-raising. Moskowitz, who had played a leading role in Smith's previous winning campaigns for New York governor, complained of Raskob: "I don't know how he ever got on in business. He won't believe those who know how things ought to be done."[10] Moskowitz and the other campaign professionals were right to worry. The national press and political pundits scrutinized Raskob's every move, eagerly waiting for the political novice to make a gaffe and create headlines.

Raskob had long enjoyed throwing himself into new ventures, and he had assumed the Smith campaign and his role as campaign chairman would be a challenge but far from overwhelming. Raising $4 million dollars, after all, was small change for Raskob who had arranged financing for dozens of deals worth far more. While he knew almost none of the men involved in Democratic Party politics, the Democratic National Committee and the Smith campaign were relatively intimate affairs compared to the combined organization and global interests of the DuPont and GM corporations. Raskob assumed that it would be relatively easy to put the DNC on a business-like footing and rationalize the campaign operation. A political campaign was really not much different than the car business, he believed. He told a *New York Times* reporter that in both the auto business and in the election game, "You have to sell something. It is up to us to sell the Democratic Party to the people of the country. Our platform is what we have to offer. Now as I look at it about half our population is already sold. They have either bought our line or our competitors, so no matter what we do we cannot affect their vote. The other half are prospects. When you have a prospect and you feel convinced that you have the goods the only thing to do is to send your salesmen after it."[11] Raskob quickly began to reorganize the moribund DNC into efficient, purpose-driven bureaus. His plan did not exactly match Alfred Sloan's "Organization Study," but it was a big improvement over his predecessors' chaotic efforts. In short order, the New York City campaign headquarters employed 375 people, far more than prior campaigns. Raskob approached his new work with confidence. He should have been more wary.

John had never been a part of a political operation or even participated as a volunteer in an election campaign. Nor had he ever personally dealt with an adversarial press. Reporters had always treated him cordially and with respect. Business writers for the big-circulation magazines had written dozens of fawning stories. *Time* magazine, in particular, had become one of his favorite organs. In the year prior to the campaign, *Time* had championed Raskob's vision of a new industrial-consumer age. The November 28, 1927, issue had run a long article celebrating Raskob's founding of GMAC and promotion of installment buying. That week, Raskob had hosted a dinner for 500 of the country's most influential businessmen, financiers, and economists so that they could hear Professor Edwin Robert Anderson Seligman of Columbia University present the highlights of his massive study of the economics of installment buying in the United States. Raskob, through General Motors, had funded the study. According to *Time*: "Mr. Raskob . . . believed that the installment system was good. However, said he: 'If we were wrong we wanted to know it. If we were on fundamentally solid economic ground we wanted to know that also. All agreed that no opinion would tend to give a greater sense of security than that of Professor Seligman.'"[12] *Time* assured readers that Seligman and his team of twenty leading economists, John Raskob, and General Motors—as well as *Time* magazine—were completely confident that installment selling was producing a great boon for the American economy and the American people. This positive, even adoring press coverage was the sort to which Raskob had grown accustomed. He had never held a press conference before his appointment as Smith's campaign director. He had controlled the flow of information. Raskob, naively, saw the press as a useful and manageable tool in getting out important and necessary information.

The very first campaign press treatment John received was the very best he was ever going to have as a political operator. Governor Smith and John stopped off at Lockport, where they were greeted by a crowd of over a thousand people. John's old newspaper gave the visit an entire page of coverage and quoted Raskob's emotional remarks to his well-wishers who greeted him with a chant of "Welcome Home, John." With a smile "as deep as the locks" of his hometown, John told his old friends and neighbors, "Few people have the opportunity to enjoy the thrill that comes to a lad in being so loyally received by the people of his nativity. This is, and always will be home to me for the reason that it was here at my mother's knee I received the training fitting me to meet the battles of life which have been most happy largely by reason of the hard work required to keep pace with our strenuous times." Classic Raskob both in style and substance. Governor Smith spoke briefly, praising John, and then they were off. John's hometown newspaper reported that people shouted "Godspeed" to Raskob and Smith and "all through the city the railroad embankments were lined with enthusiastic, cheering crowds."[13]

Raskob held his first formal press conference on August 1 and it was a disaster. The political reporters threw a barrage of questions at him. Several of the questions stumped him but that did not stop him from trying to supply answers. Belle Moskowitz, who—given the ubiquitous prejudice that still existed against women mixing among men over political affairs—almost never took a visible public role in the Smith campaign, tried to throw herself between Raskob and the journalistic pack. She was too late. Raskob had already made a muddle of Governor Smith's farm policy position, which most pundits believed to be a make or break issue west of the Mississippi where declining agricultural prices were a desperate matter. Worse, Raskob stirred up a hornets' nest of trouble when he made an offhand remark about anti-Catholicism in the South.

Raskob had been asked about Smith's support in the usually solid-Democratic South. Raskob thought he was being clever by denying that Smith's known anti-Prohibition views were harming his southern support. So he began by downplaying the "wet" versus "dry" issue in the region: "I think there is nothing in the South that need give us cause for alarm," he said rather temperately. That answer was fine, even useful but then he made a colossal mistake by blundering into the Catholic issue: "From the analysis we make they show more religious prejudice than anything else, the sort of bigotry that can be easily dispelled." Raskob should have, the professionals knew, dodged the anti-Catholic issue altogether. Still, his remark, even with the words "religious prejudice" and "bigotry" foregrounded, was at least shaded by his casual assertion that such anti-Catholic feelings could be "easily dispelled." But Raskob kept going: "Some of the [wealthier] Methodists are serving notice upon the Church, its officials and others who are trying to inject the religious issues into the campaign that they must stop or they will cease to contribute to the Church."[14] Where Raskob got his information about wealthy Protestants and their unwillingness to support pastors who spouted anti-Catholicism is not clear, and it is doubtful that Raskob actually had evidence to support such a claim other than a second-hand anecdote someone had told him. He had only meant to imply that he had faith and hope that anti-Catholicism was not going to be a powerful force in the election.

Whatever Raskob had intended, his remarks gave Smith's anti-Catholic enemies an opening which they took. Among major elected officials, Alabama's junior US Senator Tom Heflin led the way. A proud white supremacist and a man who had no problem lambasting Catholics, in general, and Al Smith's Catholicism, in particular, Heflin feigned great and near-continuous outrage over Raskob's statement. Heflin told all who would listen that the rich, "wet," Catholic New Yorker Raskob had made "a bold and brazen effort to muzzle the Protestant preachers of the South."[15] Heflin assured his fellow Protestants that neither he nor the good people of the South would be silenced by the rich, "wet," Catholic New Yorker. Heflin, a self-proclaimed "yellow dog" Democrat, threw his support behind the Republican—and "dry," Protestant, Iowan—Herbert Hoover. Such vitriol continued throughout the campaign and whenever Raskob attempted to answer it he only seemed to make things worse. After he wrote his Republican Party counterpart, Hubert Work, asking him to repudiate anti-Catholic literature being distributed by a leading Hoover advocate, North Carolina Senator George Moses, Raskob was publicly accused by the Republicans, inexplicably, of trying to start a "holy war." Hoover's campaign chair denounced Raskob for "dragging in the issue of religious tolerance," as if it were Raskob and not Senator Moses and others who had introduced the subject and made the religious attacks.[16]

Anti-Catholicism was already well established in the United States and religious bigots would certainly have acted without Raskob's misguided intervention or prominent campaign position. Michael Williams, the editor of the Raskob-supported Catholic *Commonweal* magazine, reported that nearly one hundred explicitly anti-Catholic publications appeared every week in the United States with a circulation of well over three million.[17] The zealously anti-Catholic and pro-Prohibition Ku Klux Klan was still an influential presence in many states, particularly in the Midwest. Klansmen distributed anti-Smith flyers that targeted, as they conflated, Smith's Catholic faith and his "wet" position. "When Smith was a boy he was being carefully inculcated in St. James Catholic Church to regard all Protestants as hellish heretics," read one of these flyers; this one distributed in Indiana. "Smith was conniving with all the forces of evil that would transform our Golden Grain into liquid damnation to destroy health, homes, and happiness.... Choosing between Hoover and Smith is like choosing between Jesus and Barabbas," it concluded.[18] Fighting religious bigotry in 1928 was not easy and Raskob certainly had nothing to do with creating anti-Catholicism in the United States. Still, his comments did not help keep a lid on it, either.

Less than two months after Raskob took on his party duties, the *New York Times* spoke for many political pundits and powerful insiders when it urged him "to say much less." The editorial page was blunt: "The Democratic Chairman is an eminent businessman, a financier and industrialist of high caliber, but there are many things about public life which are strange to him, and the kind of limelight he now is in has the effect of making the tongue wag unless it is carefully curbed." The editorial went on to chastise Raskob for making "ridiculous" electoral claims for Smith and for needlessly bragging about how much money he would raise for his candidate. Worse, the editorial concluded, was Raskob's seemingly irresistible desire to tangle himself up in Smith's farm policy, an issue which "seems to tantalize his tongue." The *Times* lectured: "[I]t is a cardinal rule of a campaign management to let the candidate speak for himself, and this Democratic National Chairman seems unable to do."[19] The *Times* editorialist offered sensible advice but it ran up against Raskob's well-tested self-confidence—he believed that he almost always had something useful to bring to any situation—and his reason for taking the campaign position in the first place. He did not want to hide in the back office with a green eyeshade perched on his brow, studying columns of figures. Raskob, while dedicated to serving his friend Al Smith's campaign, very much wanted to have fun playing his new game.Raskob's political learning curve was steep. While he never shut up or shut himself in the DNC headquarters, he did take more care in his public remarks. In the campaign's last few weeks he made no gaffes and he even gave a few well-received radio speeches. After one of them, his old Lockport friend Tom Feeley wrote: "I want to congratulate you on your address last night. You had more confidence in yourself and your talk had a 'kick' which carried weight and will bring results."[20] That even Feeley believed he could offer John such a patronizing comment indicates the limit of Raskob's improvement at the microphone. Nonetheless, with a month or so to go before the election, Raskob's press coverage and public image was improving.

At the very end of September, the *New York Times* ran a long feature story on Raskob.[21] It was a puff piece: "Here was a genius at organization with a breadth of vision and a gift for seeing into the future.... In his office which overlooks Broadway, in his shirt sleeves he receives politicians from all over the country, and one gets the impression that here is a man who is deeply engrossed in the job ahead of him." More important to Raskob, he was also able to get the writer to spread his new, carefully spun message: the 1928 election was a referendum on Prohibition. Yes, farm policy was important, Raskob stated for the benefit of any pundits or politicians who might try to use his words against Smith in the rural counties—Raskob was learning—but really the great question of the day was Prohibition.Raskob insisted that the Prohibition issue should not be seen as a moral crusade between "wets" and "drys" but as a battle to restore Americans' respect for law and order and to stop the growth of tyrannical federal power. Prohibition, Raskob observed, had turned millions of Americans into criminals and co-conspirators of gangsters. "Feeling as I do about this growing disregard for law and order," Raskob continued, "you can readily see why I have taken up arms to help a man who has the courage of his convictions and who has not been afraid to 'talk out,' as he says." Raskob argued, "Prohibition is a purely local subject that should be passed upon and enforced by small sections of the country as each locality sees fit, and not by the country at large."[22] Having a national policy on alcohol, he insisted, was like allowing ranchers in Montana to have the right to mandate traffic patterns in Manhattan. It makes no sense. Towns and counties that wanted to be "dry" should surely have the right to do so; so, too, Raskob argued, should other areas of the nation have the right to be "wet." Local decision making, not national tyranny, was the American way. Here was an issue about which Raskob felt comfortable talking and in the last weeks of the campaign almost all of his policy-oriented statements focused on Prohibition.

Raskob even refined a kind of class-warfare attack on Prohibition. To the gaggle of campaign reporters who hung out at the DNC headquarters he argued: "Prohibition is just a scheme to prohibit those without money from having something that those with money have.... That is causing this lack of respect for our laws. The workingmen, too, are getting tired of this sort of thing."[23] Raskob even drew his old, if estranged, friend Alfred Sloan, as well as Walter Chrysler into the argument, gently chiding the auto bosses for ignoring the feelings of their assembly-line workers and publicly supporting Prohibition. John did write Chrysler right after his remarks made the papers. After first pointedly thanking Chrysler for vouching for him at a private club that served cocktails, Raskob half-apologized: "Everything seems fair in politics as well as love and war so I am having a lot of fun taking a crack at you and Alfred every now and then about denying the workingman his glass of beer, with your lockers filled with vintage champagnes, rare old wines and selected brands of old whiskey, liqueurs, etc.... Anyway I love you and nothing else much matters."[24] Being a public man, Raskob noted, was sometimes quite amusing.

Raskob was confident that a carefully articulated "wet" position would win votes for Smith. Despite tremendous misgivings by Moskowitz, Franklin Roosevelt (who became the Democrat's nominee for New York governor as of October 1), and many others in the party, most especially southern and western politicians, Raskob kept pushing the issue. Smith, while more careful than Raskob in how he discussed Prohibition, sided with his campaign chairman.

As the presidential election of 1928 drew close, *The World's Work*, the business and society magazine that had first championed Raskob in 1920, reminded readers of the power Raskob had given up: "For several years his judgment has been regarded as canny. Whatever he said has found his world listening as it listens to few men in this time. A few of his words, last March 24th, were worth $47,850,000. That represented the difference in value of outstanding General Motors stock before a prediction he made, and its value afterward."[25] This is what had happened: Raskob's words had moved almost 2 million shares of stock in exactly two hours after he told a few reporters who accompanied him as he prepared to sail to Europe that GM was about to have a banner year in 1928 and suggested that by his estimation GM, like all stocks, should sell for about fifteen times its earnings. Raskob's ratio of 15-1 became a standard share price calculation for years. "Such may be the weight of one man's words," the magazine reported, "And this, in short, was the height to which Raskob had climbed in such brief years. He stood among the foremost figures of his day and nation."[26]

The magazine noted that Raskob had made a great gamble in leaving behind his corporate throne and throwing himself into Alfred Smith's bid for the presidency: "These two men are the sum of this new Democracy so long as the campaign lasts. Should victory come, a party built on new lines will be the result. Should the war of ballots bring defeat, the new element will have difficulty in asserting its claim to power." The article ended on a gentle but foreboding note: "Whatever the result will be, Raskob is the most interesting personality to enter upon the political stage in many campaigns....But regardless of any and all results, the Democratic Party has a new kind of chairman, who risked much to stand up for the cause he believes is right. Whether the country will agree with him we shall not know until a frosty night next November."[27]

The election came fast. Just four months had passed since Smith had won the nomination, appointed Raskob, and begun his campaign. Smith, the pundits observed, had not had an easy time connecting with the national electorate. Smith specialized in retail politics, meeting voters one-on-one. He could also deliver humorous, barnburner speeches in packed halls. He could not do either effectively in a national election, and he had difficulty breaking down the barriers that separated him from the majority of the electorate. The 1928 presidential election was one of the very first that depended on the new medium of radio and Smith's animated and highly inflected style of public speaking played poorly over the available audio technology; it better suited Hoover's flat, calm articulation. Smith's New York accent, idiosyncratic pronunciations, and casual grammar also sounded odd and off-putting to many who lived on the other side of the Hudson River. On the campaign trail, Smith had a hard time relating to voters who had not spent their lives in crowded streets filled with raucous and diverse people. A number of Protestants were simply not ready for a Catholic president and Smith found no answer to their prejudice. A majority of voters, especially in the South and much of the West, did not want to end the great experiment in mandatory temperance. And a great majority of voters saw no need to make a political change: Republican prosperity had been a boon to much of the nation. During the campaign, Smith spoke very little of the economic progressive vision he had pursued as governor; instead he (and Raskob) promised to maintain pro-business policies. In that case, voters wondered, why not just stay the course with the Republican Party that had already delivered such policies. Hoover made that argument stick.[28]

Smith was badly beaten. He lost by more than six million votes, winning just 41 percent of the electorate. Still, his overall vote total was much better than Cox had done in 1920 or Davis in 1924, a fact that Raskob highlighted in his post-mortem with the press. But Smith had taken a terrible shellacking in the Electoral College, winning only eight states and their eighty-seven votes. Surprising many of the Democrat's political professionals, who believed that white southerners could not bring themselves to vote for the Party of Lincoln, regardless of Smith's religion and position on Prohibition, Hoover took five of the old Confederate states: "Hoovercrats" ruled in Texas, the Carolinas, Virginia, and Florida. Smith lost every border state. Republican National Committee chair Hubert Work had specifically targeted the South to take advantage of Smith's "Rum and Rome" vulnerability. Sadly, Smith's few victories in the Deep South were fueled by white racists' scorn for Hoover, who had been attacked by Mississippi Senator Theodore Bilbo and other racist demagogues for "making white women work with negroes," to quote one of the least offensively worded charges.[29] Outside of the South, Smith won only Massachusetts and Rhode Island. He even lost his home state of New York.

Republican prosperity explained Hoover's victory in the northeast—an area Smith counted on carrying—and several other areas of the nation. But anti-Catholicism played a fundamental role elsewhere. While Raskob refused to believe it, a majority of voters still preferred the "dry" position when it came to Prohibition. One leading "dry" Democrat who had become a prominent anti-Smith "Hoovercrat," the Methodist Bishop James Cannon of Virginia, blamed Raskob and not Smith for the loss, stating that he could not countenance Smith's appointment of Raskob, who was a notorious "wet": "When Governor Smith had John J. Raskob...appointed chairman of the National Democratic Committee he drove the nails into his own coffin." But even as Cannon denied he was anti-Catholic, his additional remarks indicated that he would have had a very difficult time supporting "one who follows Pope Pius XI...I stated from the beginning that there was no question but what if Governor Smith was nominated it would be impossible to keep the religious question out of the campaign."[30]

Raskob had not expected religious bigotry to play such a powerful role in the campaign and he had been surprised by the margin of the loss. The night before the election he told the press that Smith would win 402 electoral votes.

He seems to have actually meant it. There were no reliable polls or voter surveys to go by and Smith had been greeted by large, enthusiastic crowds in the last days of the campaign. If Raskob was embarrassed by the inaccuracy of his prediction, he hid his feelings well. If he was upset by Smith's defeat, he showed no signs of that either. Shortly after midnight, just a few hours after the polls had closed in California, Raskob issued a statement acknowledging Hoover's victory: "In accordance with Democratic principles, we cheerfully accept the will of the majority."[31] He told the press that he was proud of Smith's accomplishments, calling the Democratic vote tally "quite encouraging" and then quite ably ran off a series of numbers from Ohio and New York to make his case.[32]

Raskob had accepted Smith's offer to run his campaign because he was Smith's friend, because he was ready to do something different with his life, and because he had become increasingly interested in politics and public policy. Smith's defeat was a sad personal note and a very real disappointment. On the other hand, he had only given four months of his time to candidate Smith. Raskob knew, too, that he had succeeded in the main job he had been asked to perform. He raised a lot of money for the DNC, much of it his own. He had, through one form or another, donated $230,000 to the campaign and had lent another $150,000. He had raised more than the $4 million he had targeted and at the national committee level he out-raised the Republicans. It was the first time the DNC had more money to spend than the RNC. Even Frances Perkins, Smith's Progressive domestic policy advisor and no friend to Raskob later admitted: "This was the only time that I've ever known the Democratic Party when it seemed to have plenty of money."[33] Many of Raskob's wealthy friends, most of whom had traditionally supported Republicans, chipped in. Pierre du Pont, relishing John's anti-Prohibition stance, gave $50,000 to the DNC. Smith's "Golf Cabinet" had made big donations, too, led by Bill Kenny's $100,000. Almost three-quarters of Smith's campaign money came from New York State and almost 30 percent of all donations came in checks of $25,000 or more. All told, Raskob had provided the campaign with around $6 million. Raskob had proven to be one of the greatest campaign fundraisers the Democratic Party had ever seen.

Raskob knew, however, that his fundraising success had not come without some complications. As usual, he had introduced a little leverage into his efforts. The last $1.5 million, or so, of the campaign funds had come in the form of bank loans that Raskob and many of the "Golf Cabinet" cronies had guaranteed. Following Smith's defeat, the DNC was in a big financial hole and Raskob's first job was to try to raise the money needed to pay off the bank loans.[34] That debt became far more of a burden than Raskob had ever expected, especially since he had agreed, unhappily, to personally guarantee an additional $270,000 of the outstanding amount due from Smith's circle of rich friends.

While beating the bushes for money and haranguing everyone who had pledged it, including longtime Democratic eminence Barnard Baruch and most of the men with whom he had become friends at the Tiger Room, John decided to do something prior Democratic chairs had talked about but had never accomplished: make the DNC a permanent, ongoing, policy-making operation. In prior election cycles, the campaign chairman had slipped away and the DNC had quietly folded its tents and disappeared until the next presidential candidate was selected and a new national campaign was launched. Raskob argued for an institutional presence that could work as a counterpoint to the Hoover Administration. Many state party chairs and powerbrokers, most especially those in the South who wished to be rid of Raskob, had serious misgivings: "This is not time to parade Raskob," snarled South Carolina Senator Coleman Livingston Blease. John simply moved forward.[35] After taking time off to recuperate in Palm Beach with Al Smith and Bill Kenny, Raskob convened a meeting of the somewhat moribund DNC in April. Showing his growing political skills, Raskob maneuvered to gain support from Smith loyalists and a number of powerful northeast Senators with whom he had established good relations. John laid out plans to establish a new national headquarters in Washington, D.C. and with sufficient allies already on board, he was able to get majority approval from the party's chieftains. As chairman, Raskob intended to commit the Democratic Party to the business interests and capitalist principles that, he believed, gave opportunity to the American people.

Forthwith, John began hiring professional political operatives to run the new, permanent DNC. As his chief administrator he brought on the savvy old hand Jouett Shouse, a spats-wearing, pince-nez sporting, Kentucky-born former congressman from Kansas who had served on the DNC's 1928 advisory committee. Raskob made it very clear to the debonair and charming Shouse to whom he owed his loyalty, his job, and his impressive paycheck of $50,000 a year. Those funds came directly from Raskob who capitalized a sizeble stock market investment portfolio for Shouse that was intended to provide him with his DNC remuneration (the subsequent stock market crash would mean that Raskob would end up paying Shouse $232,000 out of his own pocket). John was also supplying the new permanent DNC in Washington with essentially all of its money, a "loan" of $10,000 a month and a direct donation of at least another $5,000; sometimes he chipped in an additional $20,000.

Shouse, after conferring with Raskob, in turn hired Charles Michelson to head the DNC's publicity bureau, effectively the anti-Hoover propaganda division. Michelson had been the star Washington correspondent for the *New York World* and his flood of well-informed and often humorous attacks on the Republican president would, in the words of pundit Frank Kent, "more than any other...mould the public mind in regard to Mr. Hoover."[36] Raskob paid

Michelson's $25,000 a year salary. In just a few months' time, Raskob had completely reinvented the DNC and established it as a permanent institution of American political life. The new DNC, with its vital and accomplished staff, gave Raskob a powerful and influential presence in Democratic politics. While he backed away from the day-to-day operations of the DNC and spoke much less often to the press, he was far from done playing in this new high stakes and expensive game.

Raskob's political maneuverings hardly took up all of his energies. After putting the DNC on operational footing, he still had lots of spare time. For the first time in more than thirty years he did not have a full-time job. But he did have a couple of big ideas that he wanted to pursue.

The first of these was something John had been kicking around since mid-1928. He called it the Equities Securities Company and it would be modeled, loosely, after GMAC. Raskob wanted to create a company that allowed working people to buy stocks the way nearly 60 percent of people bought new cars, through installment buying or what he was calling "intelligent debt." Not only would his imagined Equities Security Company extend credit directly or in coordination with local banks so that people could leverage a small amount of their savings to make regular and substantial investments in the market, the company would also pick the stocks for its investors, creating a working-man's investment trust.

Just as auto finance companies had existed before Raskob had developed GMAC, others had already pioneered investment trusts in the 1920s as a means of bringing small investors into the stock market. Many of these trusts, however, suffered from shaky foundations and uncertain reputations. Raskob, nationally renowned for his role in creating GMAC, intended to bring far greater integrity to the new retail investment business and to market his trust using his own good name and national reputation for wealth production. Raskob also believed that he could bring massive scale to his investment trust by targeting people of modest means. They would be able to buy shares in the investment trust through a combination of a cash down payment and regular installment payments. The loan portion of the investment would be guaranteed by the very same purchased equities. Raskob was hoping to offer millions of Americans the chance to do what he had done back in 1904 when Levi L. Rue, the president of the Philadelphia National Bank, had loaned him the money to buy his first substantial block of corporate stock.[37]

Raskob talked to economists, Wall Street financiers, businessmen, and politicians about the idea. He had already brought it up in the spring of 1928 with President Coolidge and others when he had been invited to the White House to talk about economic policy over dinner. Columbia economist Edward Seligman had conferred with Raskob. John had discussed the idea with Pierre du Pont and many of his friends. He had asked Julius Rosenwald, president of Sears, Roebuck and Company, for advice. John was excited by the wealth-creating possibilities of a workingman's investment trust and he wanted to do it right.

In early May 1929, somebody leaked Raskob's still inchoate plan to a reporter at the *New York Post*. The reporter ran with it. The reporter was less interested in the investment trust than he was in speculating on what Raskob and Smith would do with themselves, since they had both given up their old jobs and had nothing to show for it. There had been a lot of stories like that in the papers post-election. The gist of the story, that Raskob was contemplating a new kind of stock investment company, was true. But the reporter had gotten some things wrong, including the notion that ex-President Calvin Coolidge would play a sub-stantial role in the new enterprise. John decided he had better get his own ver-sion out to the public as soon as possible, even though he would have to make clear that he was not yet prepared to move forward with the idea.

Typically, Raskob was not completely unhappy about the leak. He wrote Calvin Coolidge the very night the story came out in the *Post* to apologize for the errant use of his name but he also noted, "I am not at all provoked about the publicity, as this perhaps will be helpful in developing public opinion." He did note, too, that he had delayed moving forward with the plan "for the reason that the prices of equity investments, as generally represented by common stocks, seem to me to be very high."[38] Nonetheless, Raskob figured he had best publi-cize the investment idea while the opportunity existed. He had enough expe-rience with the press by then to understand how these things worked. What he did not anticipate was that the scheme would produce so much national attention.

Raskob called the editor of the *New York Times* and asked him to send a busi-ness reporter over to his new offices at 230 Park Avenue. The result of that inter-view appeared on the front page of the *Times* under the title, "Raskob Will Help Workers to Invest: Plans Large Company to Hold Stock and Let Small Buyers Share Profits." Raskob laid out his scheme in general terms. For too long, Raskob noted, working people had few options for investing their savings. They could turn to low interest bank accounts or home mortgages. Those who wanted more risked "taking the advice of stock swindlers." Raskob wanted to give those small investors a better choice. His plan was to line up the best financial experts so that all Americans could have access to the best equity investment advice. A "factory mechanic in Detroit with $200" to invest, he told the reporter, would be able to secure a strong financial future for his family.

Raskob emphasized that he was not yet ready to move forward with the investment plan but because it had been revealed in the previous day's news-paper story he wanted Americans to know that he "was actually working on it." Anticipating concerns about the current high prices of equities, Raskob argued that while "it was true that some stock may be selling at 20 percent less in another year ... in my judgment many stocks are not too high even at their present levels." "If the investor has any belief in America," Raskob claimed, he should trust that American industry will continue to prosper and "common stocks, wisely chosen, of course" will, then, be a sound investment. Sounding a bit like a pitchman, Raskob concluded, "I now have all the money I want and now I want to help a lot of other people make some."[39] Several other reporters were intrigued. Raskob held a press conference. The story just took off.

Raskob's workers' investment trust became the talk of the nation. Virtually every major paper in the country ran a story on it. Pundits and editorial writers weighed in on the plan's merits. The *Literary Digest* quoted a prominent New York banker: "This is the greatest vision of Wall Street's greatest mind." The *Ashville Times* declared, "It is apparently a splendid idea for the common welfare, well based upon a solid rock of this country's material prosperity." The Philadelphia *Evening Public Ledger* concurred, suggesting that Raskob's invention "might prove to be the most modern and the most useful of all the numerous humanitarian enterprises founded at various times by rich Americans." "What Raskob has in mind," stated the Newark *News*, "might well be called the ultimate step in industrial socialization, the most outstanding development and most rapidly moving trend of big business today."

Doubters did exist. The *New York World* wondered what effect "the storm and stress of a bear market" would have on Raskob's leveraged investment trust. Along similar lines, the *New York Evening World* told of "a woman reporter" who challenged Raskob at his New York press conference; she wanted to know how Raskob could be so confident that the investment trust "would be profitable?" Raskob replied, "Young lady, if this goes through I shall have the advice and counsel of many men who know a darn sight more about finance and industry than I ever could hope to know, and my individual judgment wasn't so bad. It will be a matter of mutual trust.... Invest your money with us, under proper legal safeguards and we will make money for you." While the quoted words do not sound quite like Raskob, the argument does—Raskob was confident that a well-managed trust could make money for its humble investors just as Raskob had been making money through stock investments for himself, his family, and friends for better than a quarter of a century.[40]

John wholeheartedly believed in the merits of his plan. But as he hinted at publicly and as he stated privately, he was worried that the timing was not right. He believed that the market, in general, was overpriced with the Dow-Jones Industrial Average having doubled in just five years and he was being careful with his own investments. He did not trust the big run-up in stock prices in 1928 and early 1929, and the press had quoted him urging investors to be cautious several times in late 1928.

Raskob was not a stock market bull in the summer and fall of 1929. But he could not control what the press published about him. On August 29, 1929 the *New York World* ran a front-page story that proclaimed Raskob to be one of the four "New Kings of Wall Street"; the others were the "plungers" Arthur Cutten and Billy Durant, who had ridden his massively leveraged plays in the Bull Market to new—if short-lived—fame, as well as the slightly more careful Fisher brothers of GM prominence. Raskob was pointedly described as an "industrialist" and not a speculator and he made the list primarily for his huge holdings in GM and for his frequent announcements about the wonders of equity investments. Still, Raskob was not pleased about this particular bit of publicity. The newspaper had reported that Raskob "has been consistently bullish" about GM's stock price. In fact, he was not; throughout much of 1928 and all of 1929 he was shorting the stock.[41] Without ever mentioning his GM position, Raskob did try to make it clear that he was not, in fact, bullish about the market. In early October 1928 he made his bluntest statement to the *Wall Street Journal*: "[I]t is my opinion that security prices have so far outrun demonstrated values, earning power and dividend returns, that a material readjustment is necessary before they will again be attractive to the prudent investor."[42] Raskob feared that the market was facing a correction.

To protect his major holdings in GM, Raskob had engineered a complex hedge. He had largely matched his "long" position on GM shares (shares Raskob owned outright and held in expectation of increased value) with a "short" position (GM shares Raskob borrowed from different sources that he sold on the open market in expectation that the share price would drop in the near term, allowing Raskob to pay back at a later date the borrowed shares with lower prices shares and thus make a profit through the stock's decline in value). He was betting, in other words, that GM's shares would not increase much, if at all, in value; and if they fell dramatically, he might make a lot of money. Raskob actually was expecting GM shares to trade in a narrow range assuring that he would, in an uncertain market, neither lose nor gain much money either way. He was being cautious while leaning toward a downturn in the general market and in GM's share price, in particular.

Raskob's strategy actually had caused him a good deal of consternation shortly after he began shorting GM. In March 1928 GM's shares shot upwards in the bull market, in part due to Raskob's well-quoted remarks about GM's earning prospects that year, and Raskob chose to buy, on margin, additional shares "long" in order to cover his "short" position (without having to sell any of the GM shares he already owned outright). Throughout 1929, however, Raskob bet that the market, in general, and GM stock, in particular, was overvalued. He maintained a massive short position on GM. If GM's share value had continued to increase dramatically through the end of 1929 Raskob would have lost a good deal of money.[43] He did not lose that bet.

Despite Raskob's cautious position during the great Bull market of 1928 and most of 1929, he did see opportunity in the speculative tidal wave that was flooding the stock exchanges with new investors. To take advantage of these less savvy investors, Raskob joined an investment pool that aimed to manipulate the share price of RCA. Some sixty-three other men participated in the pool, many of them the extremely wealthy Irish-American New Yorkers with whom John had become good friends. Walter Chrysler and Billy Durant were also involved. Mike Meehan, one of New York's most swashbuckling brokers, led the pool. John was the single biggest investor, placing a million dollars in Meehan's hands.

Meehan, with over $12 million available to manipulate the market, used the "pump and dump" method to jack the share price of RCA all over the place— creating flurries of excitement and then fear—to buy and sell and buy and sell for large profits in a short period of time. Raskob made $291,710.86 in less than a month. Many much smaller stock market investors, who bought late in the "pump" stage and then sold at the end of the "dump" stage, took a terrible beating. They were the chumps who provided the profits for pool operators such as Meehan and pool participants such as Raskob.[44]

Even as Raskob was working the financial angles with his long and short GM strategy and his major play in the RCA pool, he was also doing his best to find growth stocks in a market he felt was generally overvalued. After missing much of the big Bull market of 1928 and early 1929, Raskob decided to take some of the cash he had salted away to invest in a few stocks he thought still had some upside. In June 1929, John arranged for his one-time secretary on the GM finance committee, C. D. Hartman, Jr. and Robert Young, who had also worked under John in the treasurer's office at GM, to create Equishares Company, a small investment trust. Young, who would go on to a storied career investing in railroads, had looked after much of John's stock portfolio while he had been in the thick of the Smith campaign. Pierre put a million dollars into the trust; Hartman and Young came up with another $600,000 and John made up almost all of the rest of the $5 million dollar kitty (equivalent to some $63 million in current dollars). Of that amount, $820,000 came directly from John's own accounts, another $1.2 million was invested in Helena's name; and another million came from cash that had been socked away for tax purposes in the Archmere account John had originally set up to pay for the Claymont mansion expenses. John invested $100,000 from the Bill Raskob Foundation and he lent money to several of his employees so that they could invest in the trust, too. His secretary Frank Garey was in for $100,000 in borrowed money; interestingly Jack Corcoran was also lent $50,000 by the Raskobs so that he could participate. The investment trust took no short positions.[45]

Raskob was particularly excited about the growth possibilities of Warner Brothers Pictures stock and even as the trust bet heavily on it so, too, did John invest a pile of his own money in the stock, as did Pierre du Pont at John's sug-gestion, creating a good deal of publicity as the business pages speculated that Raskob was looking to take a controlling interest in the movie company, just as he had done with GM a decade earlier. John visited the Warner studios in Southern California several times in 1929; he was enthralled by the possibilities of "the talkies" that Warner Brothers had promoted with the release of *The Jazz Singer* in 1928. Raskob stated publicly that he had no intention of taking a direct interest in the movie studio but that did not stop press speculation. When asked by a *New York Times* reporter about the rumors that he was going to take over the studio, perhaps in association with Al Smith, he replied, "Every day they have the Governor and myself entering some new industry. The movies were certain to be reached sooner or later."[46] Nothing in Raskob's private correspondence indicates anything different; in all likelihood he just got a huge kick out of hanging out with the movie stars and watching the filmmaking in sunny Southern California, a locale he begin to frequent.

So Raskob was promoting his investment trust for the working man with some admitted concerns about the near and mid-term future of the stock market but with faith, too, that even in mid-1929 money could still be made investing wisely in stocks.[47] Raskob was also pitching his working man's trust with an encyclope-dic understanding of just how the "little man" could be toyed with by the mar-ket's biggest investors. For most of his life, John had used equity investments to grow rich. He had bought stock for his friends and family. He had set up com-pany stock option plans for workers and executives at DuPont and GM. Raskob believed in what he was doing.

In July 1929, Raskob prepared to launch his trust with a bold publicity campaign. He teamed up with his well-placed business writer friend, Samuel Crowther, to pen an article on the investment trust plan aimed at exciting read-ers across Middle America. The lengthy piece was published in the August edi-tion of the *Ladies Home Journal*. The title given to the article would make Raskob infamous. The title was taken directly from a phrase Raskob used in explaining why he wanted to start a workingman's investment trust: "Everybody Ought to be Rich."

In the article, John mostly just repeated the statements he had been making in the newspapers for several months but with a greater degree of specificity and, it need be said, hype.

First, John defined what he meant by rich: "a man is rich when he has an income from invested capital which is sufficient to support him and his fam-ily in a decent and comfortable manner—to give as much support, let us say, as has ever been given by his earnings. That amount of prosperity ought to be attainable by anyone." Raskob then argued that the current level of economic inequality in the United States was a problem—too many Americans were poor or lacked economic security—but that this inequality could be remedied by providing far more Americans with investment opportunities. He reminded his intended audience of economically unsophisticated readers that a person who had invested just ten thousand dollars in General Motors common stock ten years earlier and reinvested all dividend payments would "now be worth more than one and a half million dollars." While issuing a few gentle caveats, Raskob then declared: "In my opinion the wealth of the country is bound to increase at a very rapid rate. The rapidity of the rate will be determined by the increase in consumption, and under wise investment plans the consumption will steadily increase." Everyone should be given the opportunity to use installment buying techniques—"beneficial borrowing"—to invest in the stock market so that they, too, could enjoy the wealth American capitalism provided the investing class. Raskob stated that he expected soon to create a company led by "men of outstanding character, reputation and integrity" to provide millions of Americans the opportunity to invest in the stock market the same way they bought their autos, through an installment plan. Raskob concluded: "The way to wealth is to get into the profit end of wealth production in this country."[48]

Raskob was about to be proved a very poor prognosticator of near-term American economic growth. Raskob's August 1929 prophesy of "rapid" economic growth was exactly the opposite of what was about to happen. The fall of 1929 was not the time to get into the stock market and John recognized that his timing was spectacularly bad. Samuel Crowther wanted to follow up on the great publicity the *Ladies Home Journal* article generated with a big book promoting the investment trust. John could not believe that Crowther failed to understand what was happening to the stock market. By early October, Raskob knew that the workingman's investment trust had been a time-consuming bust and, worse, that the hoopla surrounding it would be a badge of infamy his enemies would use against him in the dark times ahead.

15

Higher and Lower at the Same Time

No one or nearly no one saw the Great Depression coming in 1929, not even after the stock market plunged in October. Raskob had understood the market bubble was going to pop. He did not think the US economy was in any serious danger and he still had a lot of money looking for a home. The market was down but real estate, he believed, was still going up.

In the late 1920s, several of Raskob's friends and acquaintances had gone skyscraper crazy. Coleman du Pont, who had sold his stake in his family's company so he could become a New York real estate operator, was in the thick of several major building projects. A thirty-four-year-old investment banker with a Midas touch, George Ohrstrom, was doing his best to build the tallest skyscraper in the world on Wall Street. Out to beat everyone, as he so often did, was John's ever-aggressive friend Walter Chrysler, who had decided in 1928 to build the tallest building in the world and name it after himself.

Involved in every aspect of the building, even as he ran his auto empire, Chrysler was having a grand time as real estate magnate and he made sure all his friends knew about it. As he later recounted: "I had all kinds of fun: spent lots of hours down on my hands and knees creeping about the floor of my office ... carpeted with blueprints and other drawings of the architects; made the final choice for the marbles in the corridors; chose the veneers that make the interior of each elevator cab seem to be the work of some extraordinarily gifted cabinetmaker."[1] A big, impossible-to-miss building sited in the most dynamic city in the world was a monument like no other.

Ego was a part of the equation in the skyscraper game, but commercial real estate also seemed to be a solid investment, especially at a time when the equities markets appeared to be overly carbonated. In 1928, New York City developers changed the skyline, putting up 760 buildings at a cost of over $258 million dollars. In 1929, they had plans to spend another $472 million. "Large scale real estate development in New York City," assured one promoter hunting for investors, "has established a record for generous and consistent profits not equaled by any other type of investment. Certainly you should consider New York real estate with its inevitable increase in value as the first field in which your dollar should be put to work for you." While such ballyhoo might have served as a warning to a sophisticated investor such as John J. Raskob, especially given the upward creeping vacancy rates in New York commercial buildings even before the stock market crash, John was drawn to the high-stakes game. He meant to join the skyscraper competition and he believed that he could make good money doing it.[2]

Raskob was no real estate expert but he did have some experience in the field. He had worked on the Du Pont Hotel and Playhouse years earlier and then he had put up the county and municipal building in Wilmington during the same period. His work with Wilmington diocese on its various construction projects and his own private real estate deals, including the half million dollar Archmere project and the huge purchase and development of more than nine miles of water-front property in Maryland—Pioneer Point—all contributed to his sense of confidence. For better and for worse, Raskob had been a prime player in the financing of the General Motors Building in Detroit in 1920. Raskob believed that he knew his way around the financial end of real estate development.

The record remains unclear as to when John decided to get into the sky-scraper business. His pal Eddie Dowling claims that not long after the 1928 election, Raskob entered the men's room at the elegant Lotos Club in New York where he spotted Dowling and Governor Smith at adjoining urinals. Smith, with only a modest guaranteed state pension to support his family, was bemoaning his uncertain economic future. Raskob sidled up to Smith and declared: "Don't worry, Al, I'm going to build a new skyscraper—biggest in the world—and you're going to be president of the company."[3] Other than Dowling's tale no other evidence indicates that Raskob in very late 1928 or early 1929 planned to build a skyscraper, let alone the tallest one in the world. As with many of Dowling's undocumented and almost always overdramatized claims about the famous men he knew in Jazz Age New York, however, the events might have actually happened as he described them. The men who first set up the Empire State deal were all part of Raskob's inner circle.

Coleman du Pont owned the site upon which, eventually, the Empire State Building was to be built on the west side of Fifth Avenue between 33rd and 34th Streets. On that site sat the Waldorf-Astoria. Built in 1897, the Waldorf-Astoria had for a time reigned as city's most luxurious hotel. In the faddish frenzy of the Jazz Age, it had become an outdated Victorian relic. The newest and glitziest hotels had moved further uptown. Coleman du Pont put the property up for sale in late 1928. John and Coleman were intimate friends who stayed in close contact. Raskob would have known about Coleman's decision.[4]

John was, however, still very much focused on the presidential election when the Waldorf-Astoria was first put on the market. In December 1928, Bethlehem Engineering Company, led by longtime developer Floyd de L. Brown, moved first; he intended to tear down the old hotel and put up a commercial sky-scraper. To buy the hotel and site, Brown arranged primary financing through the Chatham Phenix Bank.

Chatham Phenix was well inside John's orbit. Raskob was a longtime friend and trusted business associate of the bank's president, Louis Kaufman.[5] They had met in 1915 when Kaufman needed Pierre and John to help salvage GM. Kaufman, with millions on the table, had introduced du Pont and Raskob to Billy Durant. Two years later, Kaufman invited John to join Chatham Phenix's board, where he served for six years, only stepping down in 1923 when John engineered a merger between two other New York banks—one of Raskob's innumerable side business deals. Raskob remained one of Kaufman's go-to-guys, especially if the banker needed to find a lot of money quickly. Raskob, who spoke regularly with Kaufman, must have heard about the deal between Coleman du Pont and Bethlehem Engineering, which was only possible because of the loan negotiated by Louis Kaufman.

The plot, so to speak, thickened when Brown turned to Metropolitan Life Insurance in February 1929, looking for a huge construction loan. How and why Brown approached the insurance company or who steered him there and not to another bank or syndicate of banks for the money is undocumented. What is known is that less than a year earlier, while John Raskob was still in charge of GM's finances, Metropolitan Life and General Motors had contracted for the largest group insurance policy ever written, some $400 million. Brown may well have approached Met Life on his own power but Raskob did have a recent and direct relationship with Met Life's big men.

The insurance giant was a reasonable enough place to try for such a gargan-tuan loan; it had avoided risking capital in the equities markets and was flush with cash with total assets of well over $2 billion. Some of that money was being channeled into building loans; Met Life was becoming a prominent player in New York real estate. Brown did get the money, $24 million, contingent on his ability to stay current with his Chatham Phenix loan and to arrange additional secondary funding, estimated to be another $10 or $12 million. Despite imme-diate signals of a weakening commercial real estate market, Met Life was betting a very large sum on Manhattan property's long-term profitability in an expand-ing American economy. If Raskob was involved at this early stage, he was deep in the shadows.

Shortly after Brown secured backing from Met Life, Al Smith returned from his Florida sojourn with Raskob and took over his modest but remunerative duties as a brand new member of Met Life's corporate board. Bill Kenny and

Raskob had likely worked out Smith's appointment. As board member, Smith was made privy to the details of the company's recent spectacular New York City real estate investments. From every angle, then, Raskob was almost surely aware of the unfolding drama of the Fifth Avenue and Thirty-Third Street development and the finances of the project's instigator, Floyd de L. Brown.

Those finances were shaky. By mid-1929, Brown was desperately short of cash to meet his debt obligations. Despite the promise of Met Life's big construction loan, Brown could not secure secondary financing from other sources. On June 1, 1929, Brown needed to make a $1 million dollar loan payment to Kaufman's bank. He could not raise the money and Kaufman would not budge on the payment schedule. Brown had no other choice but to sell his rights to purchase the Waldorf-Astoria Hotel and site to the bank. Kaufman was in control.

John Raskob may well have been waiting in the wings for this very moment. How often Kaufman and Raskob had conferred up until this point is difficult to determine. For sure, almost immediately after the June 1 default, Raskob had a couple of his associates banging out revenue figures on a very big commercial building, in part by gathering data on the GM building in Detroit and the Du Pont building in Wilmington.[6] Raskob liked the numbers. He conferred with Pierre du Pont who, as usual, promised that he was ready to back John's play. Raskob, with Kaufman's eager cooperation, was ready to negotiate.

After a flurry of letters and phone calls in July 1929, Raskob began to stitch up the deal with Kaufman and his associates to take over the project. Raskob worked out a new price for the Waldorf, around $16 million. Kaufman remained a key player in the development. Pierre du Pont was named to the newly created Empire State Inc. board, assuring that John and Pierre would again be partners. Finally, Raskob was able to make good on his assurances to Al Smith that he would stand by him. The three-term governor of New York was named president—front man—of the Empire State Building, the very name reflective of Smith's role and status in the project. Smith gladly stepped down from his board directorship at Metropolitan Life to avoid any conflict of interest and Raskob went to work securing the money Empire State Inc. needed to get building. John immediately began dickering with Frederick Ecker, president of Metropolitan Life, to work out a new financing deal. Before becoming president of the company in March 1929, Ecker had long served as company treasurer. He and John spoke the same language and quickly came to terms. Met Life would back the project to the hilt.[7] Raskob had all the money he needed to begin. The exact particulars, as to exactly when Raskob decided to build the Empire State Building, remain a mystery but he almost surely was watching the project's development from its very beginnings. New York's financial elite lived in a little village.

As always, John had multiple motives in throwing himself into his newest big project. Certainly, he expected to make money. Equally, he saw the Empire

State Building as a perfect place to secure a publicly prominent and lucrative staging ground for Smith. Raskob was not sure what political future the governor still had but, if Smith chose to go back into the political arena, being the front man for the world's tallest building was not a bad calling card. Finally, John saw the Empire State Building as a bold challenge that would be made squarely in the public eye. He was confident that the whole business would be a hugely entertaining undertaking. Immediately after Raskob secured the deal, he began a headlong rush to get his building in the air. He wrote his favorite sister Gertrude: "We have started demolishing the old Waldorf Hotel preparatory to building the new Empire State Building which I think will go about ninety stories in the air. It is going to be a beautiful structure and, of course, the largest office building in the world. The Governor and I are having a lot of fun building it."[8] Raskob sunk, up front, $2.5 million into the deal. More of Raskob's personal fortune would follow as "other people's money" would become ever more difficult to secure in the dismal economic days—and years—that were on the horizon.

From the first Raskob did more than make the financial numbers add up. As with most of his more recent adventures, he did his best to put his stamp on all aspects of the project. First and foremost, he massively upped the building's scale. Floyd Brown had imagined a skyscraper of only fifty or so floors. John had a very different idea in mind. He was the one who pushed for much more height. He meant to best Walter Chrysler, who was already working hard to beat out his downtown rival, the banker George Ohrstrom, for the honor of building the highest structure in the world. Both men had a considerable head start but that gave Raskob the advantage. He would build the last—and tallest—building in the game.

The Empire State Building was announced to the world on August 29, 1929. John handed the story to Al Smith who assembled his press loyalists at his old Hotel Biltmore headquarters. "I'm to be an Irish landlord," Smith quipped. The Empire State Building would cost $60 million and be a thousand feet high. The building would be open for business May 1, 1931. "There are no pikers in this organization," Smith continued in his inimitable style. He named Raskob, Pierre du Pont, and Louis Kauffman as the principal figures on the board of directors. "This building we're going to put up," he bragged, "will be wonderful. It's going to be the largest office building in the world and the largest single real estate undertaking in the country." [9]

Smith's Empire State Building announcement made headlines around the nation. With Raskob handling the finances and Smith the publicity, demolition of the Waldorf-Astoria began soon thereafter. John and Al, with photographers in tow, took the first ceremonial swipes at the grand hotel. Smith stole the show. Grabbing a long cable connected to a long section of copper ornament along the roofline, Smith declaimed: "Gentleman, stand back while I start the real work of demolition."[10] John was pleased to watch his friend, confident and back in the limelight. For a few short weeks, Raskob was, nearly, on top of the world.

The Great Bull Market of the 1920s reached its peak in September 1929. The decline John had long predicted began. The Dow Jones Industrial average fell some seventeen percent over the next few weeks. Briefly, the market bounced back, regaining almost half its losses. But then, for no exact reason, all hell broke loose. The first blow came on October 23 when investors dumped 6 million shares. High-flying stocks that had been pumped up by speculators deflated and brokers began to close out margin accounts. Those who had run up not-so "intelligent debt" had to liquidate their holdings, putting sharp pressure on stock prices. The next day was nastier as panic set in. Tens of thousands of investors demanded that their brokers sell at market before their margin accounts, too, were liquidated. On "Black Thursday" shareholders traded in frenzy and the market dropped over $9 billion in a couple of hours.

Winston Churchill, on a lecture tour in the United States, was in the visitor's gallery of the New York Stock Exchange that day and witnessed the meltdown. Since Exchange rules did not allow brokers to run or shout, the crash happened almost in pantomime: "So there they were, walking to and fro like a slow-motion picture of a disturbed ant heap, offering each other enormous blocks of securities...and for many minutes together finding no one strong enough to pick up the sure fortune they were compelled to offer."[11] Morgan bankers and a few carefully chosen compatriots held an emergency lunchtime meeting and decided that they had best lead an effort to prop up the market through a visible show of confidence. The suave Morgan partner Thomas Lamont, backed by a pool of nearly a quarter of a billion dollars, began buying blue chips. Back in 1907, the Morgan men had turned a panicked herd of investors with a similar, well-capitalized show of faith, and at the first, their play seemed to work again; the market stabilized and then held on Friday. But when the markets opened up Monday morning and no additional market-sustaining buy orders came in, shareholders panicked again. Or maybe it was not panic. Raskob had argued almost a year earlier, when the market had been priced far lower, that share price and corporate valuations had taken a leap of faith that could only be explained by speculative fervor. RCA, for example, had sold as high as seventy-three times its annual earnings, far above Raskob's oft-quoted remark that a reasonable price for corporate stock valuations was fifteen times annual earnings. Suddenly, no one wanted to be the last person holding a share of stock that had been bid up to prices difficult, if not impossible, to justify based on corporate earnings. For years, the stock market had been seen by many investors as a money-making machine. Suddenly, it appeared to be more like a casino in which the house odds had caught up with the gamblers.

Raskob was not caught in the immediate undertow of the Crash. He did not have to sell into the big bear market. His massive shorting of his GM stock paid off. He made millions from GM's drop in price, netting for the year some $6 million (which included his RCA pool profits and other well-chosen speculative trades, including a $400,000 profit in Cosden Oil, another of the high-flying stocks of 1929).[12] Of course, that profit only masked the steep decline in value of John's long-term holdings in GM and DuPont. At the end of 1929 John's stock portfolio, like most everyone else's, had plummeted in value.

To zero out the $6 million in profits so as to avoid paying capital gains taxes at a time when his net worth had declined sharply, Raskob decided to balance that gain with a portion of his unrealized losses. John and Pierre du Pont engaged in a complex paper swap of GM shares. The two men, in other words, sold an equal number of shares to each other at end-of-1929 market price so the "loss" could be applied to their respective tax liabilities. They made a similar swap in January 1930, as well, creating several million more dollars in capital losses without any loss of actual stock holdings. Both men were confident that the arrangement was legal—they had engaged in similar operations before and no one had ever raised a legal challenge—but the cool maneuver would be seen quite differently by their political enemies down the road. Some of those enemies, though not the same ones who would seize on the profit-loss swap, came at Raskob immediately after the Crash.

Republican Senator Arthur Robinson of Indiana rose on the floor of the Senate on November 1, 1929, to lay the blame for the Crash squarely on John Raskob, head of the Democratic Party. Raskob, he fulminated, was a "lucky plunger" who had advised everyone, "even people of small means," to throw their money into the stock market. Raskob, he declared, was "responsible for veritably thousands of Americans plunging into the sea of finance."[13] What would have happened to the American people if the Democrat Al Smith had somehow won the presidency and made Raskob the Secretary of the Treasury, he asked, "Would he have plunged into the market? Would he have undertaken to uphold these fictitious values against which the American people have been warned?" Robinson took obvious pleasure in filling the Senate chambers with variations on the doomful-sounding word "plunge" attached to the name of the DNC chairman.

Raskob calmly fought back. He wrote a long letter to his ally and friend Senator Pat Harrison of Nevada defending his good name and asked the Senator to read it into the *Congressional Record*. Raskob pointed out that he had repeatedly warned the American people against inflated stock prices. Raskob did not mention the great publicity that had swirled around his investment trust idea for the "little man" in the weeks just prior to the crash.[14]

Raskob did not believe that the Crash portended a long-term decline in stock valuations. He saw "panic" and, like many other wealthy investors, he went public, urging investors to stay calm and to buy into the bear market. The *New York Times* quoted Raskob at length: "The present decline in the stock markets of this country has carried prices, in many instances, to levels ridiculously low.... In a panic, whether in a theatre fire or the stock market, people lose their heads and go too far, which always results in needless and unnecessary suffering." Raskob claimed: "Prudent investors are now buying stocks in huge quantities and will profit handsomely when this hysteria is over and our people have opportunity to appreciate the great stability of business by reason of the sound fundamental economic conditions existing in this great country."[15]

Raskob was operating only partially in good faith. In early October, right before the Crash, John was still buying and selling stock; he had made big purchases of Warner Brothers and Checker Cab. At the same time he did dump a huge block of the high-flying Anaconda, making a nice gain. In the weeks immediately after the Crash, Raskob was more manipulative. After his comments about "prudent investors" coming back into the market had appeared in all the newspapers, John bought 50,000 shares of GM valued at over $2 million. But John's well-publicized purchase was a ploy. After his buy order had the desired effect on GM's share price, John quietly dumped the lot the very next day, making a tidy sum on the transaction. However, by late December 1929, John believed the bear market was bottoming out and he began to reinvest in value-oriented stocks. As the market ticked up in the early months of 1930 he appeared to be right.

Raskob was, of course, very wrong. With an occasional misleading uptick, the market just kept dropping. In September 1929 GM sold for over $91 a share; after the first big drop in October the share price fell to $40; on July 28, 1932, GM sold for a fraction over $10. DuPont fared slightly better, falling from a high of over $166 to a July 1932 low of $28 and change. Raskob's other holdings took similar and even worse falls; Cosden Oil, for example, fell from a high of $135 in 1929 to a low of just over a $1 in November 1931 before the company declared bankruptcy and reorganized, wiping out its shareholders' investment. From the high in 1929 to the low in 1932, the Dow Jones Industrial Average dropped 89 percent.

The bear market cost Raskob tens of millions. Equishares, Raskob's family-and-friends investment trust, fell by roughly the same percentage as the Dow. In 1932 Raskob liquidated the trust and ate the all the losses connected to his investments and those of his family, the Bill Raskob Foundation, and his employees. He did not ask his secretary or Jack Corcoran to pay back the money he had lent them to enter the trust. Nor did Raskob ask Al Smith or DNC director Jouett Shouse or many others friends and family members to pay back the capital he had loaned them to enter the market. At the tip-top of the market, Raskob was, on paper, worth around $100 million (though Raskob's sometimes highly leveraged stock holdings make that number hard to calculate) or well over a billion dollars when corrected for inflation. Never again would he command anywhere near that kind of fortune.

John was hurt by the Crash but his wounds were relatively minor—he was very, very rich before the Crash and very rich after it, though during the Great Depression his assets, including the Empire State Building and his GM and DuPont holdings, were often in a far from liquid state. Many of his friends fared far worse. The hardest hit was his Smith "Golf Cabinet" crony, James Riordan, who ran the County Trust Company of New York. Riordan had started the bank at Eighth Avenue near 14th Street to serve the needs of his fellow Irish American businessmen, many of whom made their living as small-time beef and poultry dealers at nearby Gansevoort Market. Riordan's political connections turned the little bank into a seemingly well-capitalized operation; its stock traded for as much as $1,000 a share. The Crash hit County Trust's share price hard and worried investors and depositors feared for the worse. In a panic, they began pulling their money out of the bank. Riordan's own highly leveraged financial position was in tatters. To raise cash to save his bank, he believed that he needed to call in as many loans as he could as fast as he could. He knew that calling in those loans would destroy the lives of a good many Irish American businessmen, almost all of whom he counted as his friends. Riordan could not do it and he could not face not doing it. On November 8, he pulled a .38-caliber revolver out of a drawer at the bank, went home, and killed himself.[16]

Al Smith and Bill Kenny had learned of their friend's state of mind and rushed to his house, but they were too late to help Riordan. All they could do was to try to save his bank and for that they needed Raskob. They called John and he rushed over. Together they came up with a plan. They agreed that news of Riordan's suicide might cause a full-out run on the bank. So Smith and Kenny convinced the medical examiner to hold off on reporting Riordan's death to the police or the public until the bank closed for the weekend. Simultaneously, Raskob ordered a rush audit of the bank and an emergency meeting of the bank's board. He was elected temporary chairman. On Sunday, Riordan's death was made public but so, too, were the results of the audit. Raskob announced—accurately—to friendly reporters that County Trust's finances were "unusually strong."[17] As backup, Raskob had also arranged for the Federal Reserve to provide County Trust with a large supply of currency to stave off any shortfall in the event of a bank run. Raskob made sure newspaper photographers were present for the delivery of the cash to the bank. Just to make sure that all would be well, Raskob told reporters that he and other wealthy supporters of the bank, Jim Riordan's friends, guaranteed the bank depositors' holdings. When the bank opened Monday, no run materialized. Instead, the bank ended the day with a net increase in deposits. Smith, Kenny, and Raskob had saved the bank. Smith wept over the death of his friend; if only Riordan had called upon him before he discharged his gun. John, ever attuned to the practical, especially at a time of crisis, shed no tears. He took charge of the bank for the next several weeks, making sure that all was well before he turned over the chairmanship—and then presidency—to New York City's beloved and trusted Al Smith.[18]

Raskob had helped to save County Trust and stemmed, at that time, a potential bank run in New York City. The men who took over the bank's day-to-day management returned the favor by insisting that Raskob make good on the million-dollar-plus loan that he had arranged with Riordan for the DNC in the fall of 1928. They needed the money to run the bank and told Raskob they could not extend the terms of the loan. John, Pierre, Bill Kenny, and many of Smith's businessmen cronies had guaranteed that loan. The DNC, led by John, was trying to raise donations to pay off the campaign's debts but given the fury of the economic downturn it was having little success. Raskob, du Pont, and Kenny paid their substantial guaranteed amounts. No one else did. The rest of the men complained that Riordan himself had told them that the loan would never be called and that their guarantees were a mere formality. Raskob had to confront the men and explain, in ever less polite terms, that they were legally required to pay what they had promised. Most pled that they simply did not have the money; the market downturn had sapped them. John ended up paying off most of the called loan. Even through most of 1930 and 1931, Raskob looked at the financial troubles some of his friends were having, most of it due to bad stock market investments, and saw only personal failure that was rebounding on to him.

Despite Raskob's financial acumen, he had surprisingly little to say and no serious analysis of the unfolding economic hurricane that was tearing up America by early 1931. The banks runs of October 1930 had caught him by surprise. He had no ill words for the Federal Reserve Bank's disastrously restrictive credit policies, and he had long supported the relatively unregulated states of America's financial sector. As he had shown during the 1928 election, he had little knowledge or understanding of American agriculture and thus had little to say about the collapse of crop prices, which was ruining millions of farmers who could not therefore pay back the small-town banks that had lent them money during good times. Raskob offered up public words of encouragement but during the early 1930s mostly Raskob just watched, offering the occasional bromide about the need for confidence or a call for government budget-balancing, as the economy came undone. Long accustomed to making history, Raskob was like almost all other Americans suddenly its victim. Bankers began asking him not for his business but for large sums of money; they were calling in loans.

Many of Raskob's business partners were in far worse shape than he was. Even after some bad reinvestments in the market, his stock shorts and profit taking in 1929 had given him a generous cash cushion. As a result, he was in several cases forced to carry his business partners' debt load. Raskob was particularly annoyed and eventually infuriated by the actions of George Crabb, a Cincinnati industrialist with whom he had teamed up to build a large factory in Wilmington to manufacture asbestos and asphalt. To build the factory they had together borrowed $350,000 from the Wilmington Trust. By October 1931 the bank was in trouble and called in the loan. Raskob, not happily, came up with his $175,000. Crabb said he could not. The bank, politely but firmly, insisted that under the terms of the loan Raskob had to pay Crabb's share. He did. The factory went under. For the next seventeen years, until Crabb's death, Raskob kept trying unsuccessfully to get Crabb to make good on his debt or at least to show Raskob exactly why his financial position did not allow him to pay Raskob back.[19] Such personal financial unpleasantness became a regular and costly part of Raskob's life throughout the Great Depression. Raskob still had rich assets but he was, throughout the 1930s, never sure what creditors would demand of him or what financial obligations might necessitate large cash payouts. Raskob never had less than ten million dollars in assets (corrected for inflation that is around $170 million in 1933) and plenty of available cash even at the nadir of the Great Depression. Nonetheless, he was never sure during those years how solid that wealth would remain.

As a result of Raskob's far tighter economic position, he could not be the benefactor to church, charity, or friends the way he had been for more than a decade. Raskob hated having to say no. He was especially discomforted when the ever solicitous Frank Spellman wrote him in 1931 asking for a large donation: Would John please provide the Vatican with two private railroad carriages? Raskob had bought himself just such a Pullman car, which he jauntily named the "Skipaway," during the flush times of the late 1920s. His custom car had a parlor, dining room, observation deck, and three separate bedrooms, each with its own full bathroom; the fully outfitted car weighed, according to John, "twenty tons" more than a conventional Pullman (John bragged to Coleman du Pont, it "rides much more comfortably").[20] As a result of his own indulgence in rail-car luxury, Raskob knew that two, well-appointed Pullman cars would cost well over $150,000. For the first time, Raskob had to say no to the Vatican's request, explaining that "bad times and the condition of the security market" made it impossible for him to supply the cars. Perhaps, he added optimistically, if the markets improved he could meet the request later in the year.[21] He could not.

Raskob had not anticipated the depths of the Depression. Even in late 1930 he had believed the economy would soon turn around. As a sign of that faith, he and Helena had donated some $250,000 to build a beautiful new stone church and rectory near their estate in Queen Anne's County, Maryland. But that gift was his last major one for many years. In 1931 John began to cut back. With his secretary, he went through his dozens of private club memberships and resigned from those he rarely if ever visited. He sold his private railroad car. Other pleasures went, too. Most Morgan bankers had bought spectacular yachts in the 1920s, following the lead of J. P. Morgan's earlier leap into ultra-luxurious nautical pursuits and John, having mostly overcome his problem with seasickness by learning to stare at a fixed point, had gotten into the game in a big way. He had several yachts, launches, and sloops by 1930 including a 10-meter beauty he captained himself in races. He bragged to friends about taking home the first-place cup in the 1930 Chesapeake Bay race. But in February 1932 he decided not to put his boats in the water that summer, and he told his longtime, well-paid professional captain that he had better look for another job. When his valet asked for a $600 loan to help out his mother, John inexplicably turned his loyal retainer down—something he had never done in the past for a deserving friend or trusted employee. He told others the same. Although he could still easily afford such assistance, he was showing a symptom of the panic and tunnel vision that was affecting his class.

Raskob certainly still had money enough to insure good times for himself. In 1930 he went to Havana for several weeks, where he met up with friends to drink legally, play golf and gamble. In both 1930 and 1931 he traveled to Europe, sparing no expense. In mid-1931 Raskob moved into a brand new luxury apartment building developed by Vincent Astor, who had in 1912 at age 20 inherited some $60 million in city real estate after his father went down with the *Titanic*. Raskob was one of many well-known and well-heeled figures who chose to lease at the then out of the way but opulent building at 120 East End Avenue. The huge apartment rented for $22,000 a year, a princely sum at the time.

Raskob's move was of a piece with the family's more general domestic reorganization and separation. The Raskobs sold Archmere in 1932 to the Norbertine Order for a relatively modest sum so that a Catholic school for boys could be established on the estate. Archmere, the home of their dreams, had lost its charms for the Raskobs. John, though still a director at DuPont was ever less in Wilmington. Helena, too, had become increasingly unmoored from Archmere and life in Wilmington. Her time was spent at Pioneer Point, first purchased as a summer retreat.

At Pioneer Point, Helena had developed her own rich life. She, and not John, had decided that the family would buy the property in Queen Anne's County, the very place where the Green family had long farmed and where she had been born and raised until tragedy had forced her move away when she was seven. While John worked out the contracts and costs, it was Helena who had named the holdings and led in developing the Raskobs' estate, which claimed nearly 1,600 acres and more than nine miles of waterfront bounded by the Corsica and Chester Rivers.

She made Pioneer Point a working, forward-looking farm. She put in a substantial crop of flax, the first in the region for more than a century, and then invested heavily, with John's support, in a textile company that hoped to develop an economic means for commercializing flax production (a costly failure). She and John built state-of-the-art hygienic, glaze-tiled dairy barns for her prized Guernsey cows and a well-appointed facility for raising hogs. In the late 1920s, Helena began buying and racing thoroughbreds. At Pioneer Point she built a spacious, mirrored indoor riding arena, complete with a clubhouse, paddocks, tack rooms, and stables for 36 horses. Like many other wealthy families at the time, the Raskobs had become horse-racing enthusiasts.

Together, Helena and John made Pioneer Point the family's main gathering place. By 1932 the children had a separate, dormitory-like residence, neatly divided by a giant central hall into two wings, one for boys and one for girls. One of the Raskob children, upon first seeing their new home, declared that it was "mostly" hall—and so it was designated in mock Olde English as Mostley Hall, complete with a faux portrait of Sir Mostley, dated 1627. By the early 1930s almost all of the children were in Catholic boarding schools or college, but nearly all of them returned to Pioneer Point on weekends and holidays and for the summer.

Skipper gave her children the run of the estate and expected them to thrive largely on their own. "I have read all the books on child psychology...but it seems to me they must be written by people who have either no children or only one or two," she told a reporter writing about her approach to child-rearing. "They are so impractical." She continued: "It seems to me that children, if they're given a chance, are mostly healthy little animals. They're decent naturally." They did not need ceaseless "nagging."[22] The Raskob children from an early age took full advantage of the waterfront and the many opportunities for adventure the estate promised. In the summer the children were expected to swim 25 long laps in the river every morning. All were diligently taught by Jack Corcoran and other members of the staff to master the big Adirondack canoes and to sail everything from tiny Wee Scots to the racy Star Boats to the big 10- and 12-meter vessels. Joined by a constant stream of visiting school friends, young relatives, and the sons and daughters of the Raskobs' social circle, the Raskob children put on musicals and plays for the grownups and crafted elaborate pranks and late-night raids. The Great Depression did not touch them.

The Raskobs also built a comfortable nineteen-room mansion for themselves and their adult guests. John and Helena had separate wings on the second floor. John certainly visited Pioneer Point on a regular basis and conferred with Helena about operational and financial issues. He took full advantage of the waterfront and the estate's other opportunities for recreation. He often started his day with a speed walk down to the estate's entrance and back, a roundtrip distance of some four miles, sometimes with a child or two in tow. But during John's visits, he and Helena were rarely alone. A steady stream of overnight guests attended innumerable weekend parties. To their wide circle of friends, the marriage appeared strong, and John and Helena were committed to maintaining not just that appearance but the continued importance of their marriage to the family. Despite all the complications, they did still love each other.[23] As John's life was primarily in New York while Helena's was 200 miles away on the Eastern Shore of Maryland, the stresses on their relationship were manageable.[24]

Archmere had marked the Raskobs' ascent to great wealth. Pioneer Point was something quite different. It was even more extravagant, costing upwards of $3 million to buy and develop.[25] But Pioneer Point was not a showcase for the Raskobs' wealth so much as it was Helena's creative domain; it was a place to do and to work and to have adventures and experiences. At Pioneer Point, Helena was the Skipper. Dozens of employees worked the land, ran the barns, maintained the grounds, and kept the household operating. John set up yet another corporation to finance the estate's operations but Helena was the majority stockholder. That the Raskobs were able to keep Pioneer Point fully staffed and operational throughout the Great Depression, even at the nadir of the stock market crash, demonstrates the solidity of their economic position. It also marked the separate spheres they had carved out a quarter of a century after they had married.

In 1931 and 1932, as the economy broke down, John remained fully committed to his two major ongoing undertakings: the Empire State Building and the Democratic Party. Each was a costly struggle. Both were proving to be more difficult to control than John had anticipated. In particular, the Empire State Building was fast becoming a major drain on John's finances.

Construction of the building had gone better than anyone could have expected. Outsiders saw a task of daunting challenges. But one of the architects, William F. Lamb, explained to his fellow professionals: "The logic of the plan was very simple.... In essence there is a pyramid of non-rentable space surrounded by a greater pyramid of rentable space." True enough, but Lamb was overly modest. A leading architectural journal studied the plans and judged the building to be "transcendentally well designed as to mass, ornament, relation of its parts."[26] The construction company of Starrett Bros. and Eken, which had made its reputation by building skyscrapers fast and well, appreciated the architects' work. The company's partners understood what needed to be done and got busy. Paul Starrett observed that his job was one of efficient repetition in the application of labor to material based on impeccable organization. Some three thousand men tore into the task of erecting the world's tallest building. Raskob was impressed and so was much of Manhattan as its residents watched Starretts's crews dance along the girders as the Empire State Building raced into the air.[27]

Construction of the Empire State Building was finished under-budget and a couple of weeks ahead of its scheduled May 1, 1931 opening. Raskob had contributed to the final product in ways large and small. Most importantly, in the days after the market crash, he had refused to give up. According to one account, perhaps apocryphal, in early October 1929—after stocks had taken their first big hit after peaking a month earlier—John had gathered a few of the market's biggest investors (or speculators, depending on your point of view) and displayed to them a scale model of the yet-to-be-built Empire State Building. "Gentleman," he announced, "this is a part of what I have at stake. A monument to the future." Architect William Lamb described the scale and scope of the building to the men and Raskob concluded: "Gentlemen, a country which can provide the vision, the resources, the money and the people to build such an edifice as this, surely, cannot be allowed to crash through lack of support from the likes of you and me."[28]

Over the next year and a half, John had kept the faith. Even as the economy worsened, Raskob refused to cut corners and pushed instead to make the Empire State Building bigger and more spectacular. He gave the builders the go-ahead to use limestone for the entire façade of the building despite the extra cost, and he and Pierre had a delightful time debating the color of the marble that would be used at the building's base. Raskob, working with the building's board, commissioned photographer Lewis Hine to publicize and memorialize the "poet builders" and "sky boys" who constructed the Empire State Building.[29] Most importantly, Raskob, from the beginning and unwaveringly, pushed the Empire State Building higher and higher. At an early meeting with the architects, John took a new, sharpened pencil and held it at arm's length. With the pencil jutting straight up towards the ceiling, he told them, this is what I want the building to look like. When real estate experts told Raskob that his building would maximize revenues at 75 floors, he simply rejected the advice. He wanted more height; it was up to the architects' to figure out how to make it pay. Raskob meant to have the tallest building in the world.

So when Walter Chrysler pulled his last gambit in the race to the sky, Raskob and his team were ready. Chrysler's men had built a 185-foot tall steel vertex that had been constructed and chambered in secret within the Chrysler Building's fire tower. Chrysler had ordered the vertex to defeat his downtown rival, George Ohrstrom, who had topped out his building at 40 Wall Street at 927 feet in April 1930. In May 1930, the Chrysler vertex was hoisted from its secret chamber and affixed to the top of the art deco masterpiece. Chrysler's skyscraper stood 1,048 feet high, a compelling 60 feet more than the old record holder, the Eiffel Tower, and 118 feet higher than 40 Wall Street. With the Empire State building still in an early state of construction, Raskob knew the exact number he had to beat.

Raskob, Smith, and company had originally announced that their building would rise to 1,050 feet; the Empire State Building would have 85 floors of commercial and office space and an observatory deck on the 86th floor. But Raskob doubted that his good friend Walter Chrysler would settle for losing the skyscraper stakes by a few feet and insisted that his team of architects and builders give the Empire State Building a sure height advantage that no clever move by Chrysler could defeat. "What this building needs is a hat!" he told them.[30] The architects added a narrow 158-foot tall, windowed column atop the 86th floor, giving the Empire State building a proclaimed 102 floors and a height of 1,250 feet, surpassing Chrysler by a safe margin of some two hundred feet. Both the 101st and 102nd floors would be set up as observation decks. Governor Smith assured the public that Raskob's "hat" was not just an adornment or artificial height-enhancer but was a useful structure "built for the future." The building's uppermost floor, he explained, would also serve as a waiting room for the mighty 1,000-foot long dirigibles that would moor above the building on a steel mast. This mast, not insignificantly, gave the Empire State Building another 204 feet. Dirigibles, Smith predicted, would be the great commercial aviation wonder of tomorrow and the Empire State Building would be their New York City air-site.[31] John had not been exaggerating when he told his sister that he and the governor were having a lot of fun with the Empire State Building.

Constructing the Empire State Building had been fun. Leasing out space was not. By the time the world's largest and tallest building opened its doors May 1, 1931, the Great Depression had turned even mighty New York City's commercial real estate market upside down. Property values plummeted as commercial vacancies climbed. In the 1920s, owners of a new, first-class office building could count on pre-leasing more than half of its space before it opened and averaged better than 90 percent occupancy at the end of five years. Despite all the ballyhoo during construction, front-page newspaper coverage and a successful publicity campaign managed by Belle Moskowitz, the Empire State Building had barely 20 percent of its space rented out when Al Smith and his two grandchildren cut the red ribbon that ceremoniously opened the building for business.

A professional staff pushed hard to find tenants, and both Smith and Raskob pressured friends, business acquaintances, and connections to rent space. Smith tried to convince Governor Roosevelt to bring state government business to the building but with no success. John had better luck with the DuPont Company. He and Pierre had double-teamed President Lammot du Pont. Lammot had at first resisted their pitch, making the practical argument that the company's scattered New York offices were already in suitable locations and no compelling business reason mandated their movement. But he eventually folded and agreed to take over three lower floors for DuPont businesses, making DuPont the building's single largest tenant.[32] A number of the companies that had profited from constructing the building took big spaces, too, including Starrett Bros. and Eken, as well as the key supplier US Steel. Very few other major tenants were found. Soon enough New Yorkers in the know were mocking the building as the "Empty State Building."[33]

At least in 1931 and 1932, John was not panicking, even as revenues far from kept up with the building's financing and operating costs. Besides Raskob's initial investment of around $2.5 million, Raskob and Pierre du Pont were also directly and equally responsible for payments on second mortgage debentures of some $6.75 million.[34] In just the first six months of operations, the Empire State Building's costs exceeded revenues by about $1.2 million. In 1932 the building remained deep in the red, meaning that Raskob and du Pont were on the hook for the entire payment on those second mortgage debentures.[35] But despite the cash outflow, John still had faith in the building's success.

John and Pierre decided once again to share offices; they leased over half of the 80th floor of the Empire State Building for themselves. Pierre, only episodically in New York, would use his office suit at the Empire State Building sparingly but John set up shop; it would be his business headquarters for the rest of his life. John and Pierre both spent lavishly. The *New York Times*, alerted to their plan by Mrs. Moskowitz, was impressed: "Featured by rare imported paneling, the decorative scheme of private offices of John J. Raskob and Pierre S. du Pont in the Empire State Building will be carried out on an elaborate scale.... The paneling, elaborately hand carved in Georgian Period style, will cost more than $120,000 exclusive of other furnishings." The office suits had custom-built furniture, bespoke drapes and rugs. Mrs. Moskowitz made sure the reporter also noted the "open fireplaces"; the Empire State Building, the *Times* printed, "is the only office building equipped for the installation" of such an amenity.[36] The availability of fireplaces was not enough to turn around the Empire State Building vacancy rates.

The main business John conducted in his new elegant office during 1931 and 1932 was preparing the Democratic National Committee to take on President Herbert Hoover. The Democratic Party had already enjoyed a very good mid-term election in 1930 and many pundits gave Raskob and the DNC substantial credit for the success. The DNC had, at Chairman Raskob's expense, rented out an entire floor of the National Press Building in Washington. From their well-equipped and deep-staffed headquarters, the DNC publicity bureau had churned out some 500 press releases before the 1930 election, almost every one of them hammering the same theme: the Party of Herbert Hoover was responsible for the nation's darkening economy. The DNC had nationalized the election, confounding the usual local, incumbent-protecting nature of mid-term congressional elections. The Republicans had called the DNC's unrelenting national campaign dirty pool and argued that the DNC should be ashamed for attacking the president at a time of national crisis. The prominent political writer Will Irwin later decried the rise and success of the DNC publicity bureau, claiming that Raskob and his minions had deployed "the propaganda of hate" developed during World War I and turned it inward against America's elected leader.[37] Whether that was true or not, the DNC's campaign had worked. That success, combined with Raskob's financial contribution to the party—he was paying for almost the entirety of the DNC's operations—seemed to have strengthened his position as chairman as he laid the groundwork for the June 1932 Democratic presidential nomination.

Raskob wanted the Democrats to renominate Governor Smith. He knew, too, that that might not happen and he maneuvered to find a backup candidate, especially since throughout 1931 Smith remained ambivalent about running. Right after the 1928 election Smith had vowed never to return to politics. But he was certainly wavering in 1931. Even as Raskob continued to hope that Smith would run and could win the nomination, he put most of his energies into pushing the Democratic Party to support the wet position on Prohibition. As the economy worsened, Raskob single-mindedly drove the Party to make Prohibition the major campaign issue of 1932. Many of the party's biggest men, most assuredly including New York Governor Franklin D. Roosevelt, were appalled and angered by Raskob's nearly frenetic campaign to turn the 1932 presidential race into a referendum on Prohibition.

By 1932, Raskob had been an active "wet" for half a dozen years. His reasons remained the same. Most fundamentally, Raskob believed that a government that could take away a person's right to buy a drink legally was capable of taking away a man's private property just as easily. Raskob believed wholeheartedly that the American government should be restricted, not enlarged, in its ability to interfere, as he would see it, in the lives and livelihoods of the American people. Individual liberty, he felt, was the bedrock principle upon which the American system was built. Raskob also wanted to end Prohibition so that Congress could lower the federal income tax on the wealthy by using an excise tax on legalized alcoholic beverages to bring in revenue. These beliefs structured his approach to Prohibition and they explained his concerns about the upcoming election.

Raskob was well aware that the ongoing economic contraction that was setting the stage for the 1932 presidential election might lead some politicians, including the flag bearer of his own party, to insist that the answer to America's problems was outright and full-scale intervention in the capitalist system by the federal government. Raskob was certain that such intervention could destroy the liberty-loving American way of life to which his long and storied career gave brilliant testimony. The near consensus among prominent politicians of both parties in the late 1920s on the right of Big Business common sense to rule America's political economy was breaking up as more Americans lost their jobs, their savings, their homes, and their hope.

By keeping the issue of Prohibition front and center in the 1932 national election, Raskob believed he could keep talk of radical economic policy offstage. When Raskob had first been named head of the DNC in 1928, Socialist leader Norman Thomas had predicted Raskob's tactics when he had told reporters that Raskob would use a beer battle to lure workers to his political side. Now, in the nation's days of crisis, Raskob worked even harder to make the cultural politics of Prohibition, and not economic reform policies, the Democrat's electoral trump card in the unhappy election year of 1932.

As the election neared, Raskob marshaled his forces. The DNC publicity bureau, which Raskob funded singlehandedly, turned out a steady stream of anti-Prohibition pieces. Raskob commissioned polls and surveys showing that Democratic supporters overwhelmingly favored making Prohibition the number one campaign issue, though doubters pointed out that Raskob had paid to poll only campaign contributors to Smith's 1928 election, people who were most likely to be predisposed to the wet issue. Raskob also worked with sympathetic politicians to work out a policy position that called not for outright repeal of the Prohibition measure but only for the right of each individual state to hold a referendum in which its own citizens would determine state policy on the great question of Prohibition. Raskob kept up a relentless campaign of letter writing and personal meetings with influential politicians on the subject, including southern politicians who had long been among his detractors. Especially after the successful 1930 mid-term election, Raskob was taking his position as head of the DNC very seriously.

Raskob's campaign was modestly successful. In courting southern politicians, he found a strong ally in Maryland Governor Albert Ritchie, long an ardent "wet," as well as an advocate of state's rights. Ritchie worked with Raskob, in part, because he wanted Raskob's support for the Democratic presidential nomination in the event that Al Smith's efforts flagged, and Raskob stoked Ritchie's ambitions all through 1931 and into 1932. Raskob had some success, too, with Virginia power broker Harry Byrd. After their meetings, Byrd had been impressed and privately, at least, he had come to agree with Raskob on Prohibition as he admitted in a letter to University of Virginia President Edwin A. Alderman, "I enjoyed greatly meeting Mr. Raskob . . . and was greatly impressed by the clarity of his vision and understanding. I sincerely hope that he and I will not be placed in a position of hostility."[38] Raskob maintained his strong relations with Byrd, hinting in his correspondence with him that Byrd might make an excellent presidential candidate and that the American people might well need a southerner as their president. Southerners, Raskob wrote Byrd, are "much more temperate and conservative people than the average in this country . . . a much older people

in experience and in American tradition and... understand American government, principles and doctrine, better than the average, and particularly younger
sections of our country."[39] In part, Raskob was sweet-talking Byrd to keep him
from endorsing Roosevelt who was pursuing southern politicians with a vengeance. Even as Raskob courted Ritchie, Byrd, and others, Al Smith remained
his greatest hope and Franklin Roosevelt had become his strongest enemy.

The two-term New York governor, who had already run once on the party's
national ticket as vice presidential candidate in 1920, had his sights set on the
nomination and he did not intend to run on a narrow "wet" platform. Roosevelt,
though opposed to Prohibition, planned to reunify the southern and northern
wings of the party by sidestepping the Prohibition question and instead waging
war against the incumbent president of the United States and his failed economic
policies. He was ready to battle anyone who tried to tie his hands in that fight.

The first battle between Roosevelt and Raskob over the direction of the party
came in 1931, a year before the election. Raskob had called a special meeting of
the DNC to try to jam through a binding "wet" party platform. The meeting was
a disaster for Raskob. Most Southern Democrats picked up where they had left
off in 1928 in their attacks on Rum, Rome, and Raskob: "You cannot inscribe
on the banner of the Democratic party the skull and cross bones of an outlawed
trade," yelled Smith's former running mate, the ever-excitable Arkansas Senator
Joe Robinson.[40] Governor Roosevelt, angling to win over the Democrat's powerful southern wing, sided with the anti-Prohibition forces at the meeting and
helped lead the successful fight against Raskob's maneuver.

Raskob and Roosevelt, then, were already squared off against one another
by early 1932. Al Smith, naturally, stood with Raskob. During much of the
1920s, Smith, like many career New York politicians, had been unimpressed by
Roosevelt. Following Smith's defeat and Roosevelt's win in 1928, Smith had been
disappointed, even embittered when Roosevelt would not hire Belle Moskowitz
or other Smith loyalists and by Roosevelt's general disregard for Smith's advice
on how to run the state. While Smith conceded that Roosevelt had become by
1932 an effective governor, the "Happy Warrior" did not want to see him become
the party's 1932 presidential nominee.

Raskob, unlike Smith, did not know Roosevelt well. They had only first met
during the Smith campaign when Roosevelt had taken charge of the effort to
reach out to the business community. But Raskob, with far greater connections to Big Business, had sidelined him. Roosevelt felt slighted. At the same
time, once Smith decided in September 1928 with reluctance that Roosevelt
was the best man to fill his shoes, Raskob had been instrumental in convincing
Roosevelt to accept the New York gubernatorial nomination. Roosevelt had at
first turned Smith down, explaining that his financial obligations to the Warm
Springs Institute in Georgia, where Roosevelt had gone earlier in the decade to

recuperate from polio, prevented him from running. Roosevelt explained that he had bought the Warm Springs property in 1926 and had incorporated his holdings there in 1927 in order to build a first-rate polio treatment center and resort. Roosevelt had to look after his interests, he told Smith, and so could not run for governor. Smith turned the matter over to Raskob. Raskob quickly ascertained that in his terms relatively little money was involved. He assured Roosevelt that he would privately provide the needed funds to keep Roosevelt's financial concerns satisfied. He immediately sent a check for $250,000. Raskob wanted a portion of that money, however, to be treated as a loan which would be paid back when fundraising efforts had proven successful. Roosevelt—or individuals associated with the project—found Raskob's approach too complicated and sent back the check. Raskob then sent a straightforward donation of $50,000 and assured Roosevelt that he would help with further fundraising. When additional donations were slow to come in, Raskob sent four additional checks for $12,500 each, in the name of his children, to the Warm Springs Foundation.[41] Raskob's gift did not bring the two men closer but only seemed to inspire a mutual sense of mild distrust. Raskob, on his part, was not impressed by Roosevelt's money management skills. In taking Roosevelt's political measure, Raskob listened to Smith who downplayed FDR's merits. Raskob, well aware too of Roosevelt's battle with polio, doubted that Governor Roosevelt had the strength of body and mind, to take on the nation's problems in 1932.[42]

Raskob's doubts about Roosevelt were more than matched by FDR's feelings about Raskob. Roosevelt looked at Raskob almost completely through a political lens. He was among those Democrats who suspected from the beginning that Raskob was more of a hindrance than a help, even with all his money, to the Smith campaign and to the long-term fortunes of the Democratic Party. By 1931, Roosevelt was privately telling his supporters that he rejected Raskobism: "I think you will feel that the Democratic Party is still the party of progress and that there is no danger of being made over into a poor imitation of the conservative Republican group which had only the interests of big industry at heart."[43] Roosevelt's political strategy had no room for Raskob or Raskobism and from 1928 onward Roosevelt had been assiduously going around the DNC by creating his own loyal political team. That team was led by two men: his longtime political strategist Louis Howe and Jim Farley, an Irish Catholic New Yorker. Farley, like Bill Kenny, had used his deep political connections, which included a strong relationship with Al Smith, to build a successful construction business; he even had several lucrative contracts supplying the Empire State Building. But by 1928, Farley committed himself to Roosevelt, and in 1932 Howe and Farley were steeling Roosevelt to do what it took to win the nomination. None of them would allow any one-time sympathy or gratitude to the old "Happy Warrior" to get in their way.

Roosevelt did his best to run a campaign long on attacks on Hoover and short on details. He did, however, make it clear in his public pronouncements, as he had previously in his private communications, that Hoover's unwaveringly pro-business economic policies would not be his. In April 1932, Roosevelt gave a brief but memorable address on the radio show *The Lucky Strike Hour*. FDR blasted Hoover for helping bankers but not homeowners and said that if he was president he would come to the aid of "the forgotten man at the bottom of the economic pyramid." Smith, indicative of his growing sympathy with the wealthy men at the top of the economic pyramid, was enraged by Roosevelt's rhetoric: "This is no time for demagogues," he roared in public response.[44] In an ugly-sounding, if perhaps inadvertent swipe at his polio-stricken adversary, he went on to say, "I will take off my coat and fight to the end against any candidate who persists in demagogic appeals to the masses of the working people of this country to destroy themselves by setting class against class, rich against poor."[45]

Smith and Roosevelt were the front-runners for the nomination, with FDR well ahead in pledged delegates. Roosevelt had captured the South and had scattered strength all around the country. Smith had a big delegate lead in the Northeast. No one, however, had a lock on the nomination and a number of other candidates did their best to keep their chances alive. In 1932 the party nominee still needed to receive the votes of two-thirds of the convention delegates a great majority of whom were chosen not in open primaries but in the proverbial smoke-filled rooms. As a result, anything might happen if the delegates, usually pledged to a candidate only for the first nominating ballot, began horse-trading in subsequent ballots.

As Raskob counted down the days to the June 27 convention in Chicago he still had hopes that Smith could pull off an upset victory, but he was also looking for any favorable candidate who could head off Roosevelt. John was just too good at math to feel confident of Smith's chances. Smith had just over 200 delegates and as far as Raskob could tell no path to securing the roughly 570 additional votes he needed to win the nomination. A few days before he boarded the train for Chicago an increasingly pessimistic Raskob wrote Curtis Cooper, his old friend from GMAC, and admitted that Smith's chances were poor. In the letter he pondered another possibility, their mutual friend Owen Young, chairman of General Electric and a man praised across the partisan line for his various and many public services. Young, a Democrat since his days supporting Woodrow Wilson, had been floated as a compromise candidate and despite his claim that he was not interested, Raskob wrote to Cooper, "There is no better candidate and should we be able to nominate him I am certain the country would concede his election and immediately start to pull itself out of the Depression." Raskob had been touting Young for months with little success and had to know that he was a very dark horse. Raskob forlornly declared to Cooper: "I am [still] very hopeful that we will nominate a strong candidate and that our platform will be a courageous determination to return to the good old fashioned Jeffersonian doctrines of government which will lead us back to happiness and prosperity."[46] Raskob's hopes for such a candidate and such a doctrine of limited government were dashed at the Democratic Party Convention.

Raskob met with Shouse and his other loyalists in Chicago as the convention opened. Raskob and Shouse were quietly but directly doing what they could to stop Roosevelt. Shortly before the convention, Raskob had told Virginia's Byrd that, after Smith, he was his first choice for the nomination. Raskob, his hopes of nominating Smith fast waning, was trying to keep other plausible nominees in the game as long as possible. Raskob's problem was that he and the other anti-Roosevelt forces had no single strong unifying candidate to defeat Roosevelt and his efficient delegate-gathering team led by Jim Farley. Their weakness became apparent almost immediately when pro-Roosevelt forces easily defeated a measure that would have made Shouse permanent chairman of the convention; Shouse and Raskob had hoped that the chairmanship would give their forces a sharp procedural edge in the jousting that was sure to come. Raskob took some pleasure from the platform committee's strong vote in favor of repealing Prohibition as he had personally spoken in favor of the plank in his opening remarks to the convention delegates.[47] But that was small comfort. It was all too obvious to Raskob, given the convention's general enthusiasm for some sort of economic reform to combat Hoover's failures to end the Depression, that his hold on the party, despite all the money he had spent, was fast slipping away.

The delegates took four ballots to nominate Roosevelt. The first three ballots had taken all night and the convention had adjourned at 9:15 A.M. with no winner. Amid the frantic maneuvering that followed, Raskob found there was little he could do to alter or even influence events. The old pols and party professionals had taken over. Smith was frenetic, holding meeting after meeting, but he could not move his vote totals nor was he willing to throw his supporters to any of the other anti-Roosevelt candidates. That evening, the party war horse William McAdoo, who had himself lost twice before in the battle for the Democratic presidential nomination, took up the podium and broke the deadlock by announcing that California's entire delegation had swung to Roosevelt. Jim Farley had easily outmaneuvered Raskob.[48]

Angry and dejected, Smith could not let go. He was furious that McAdoo, the man who had stood with the Ku Klux Klan in 1924, had become Roosevelt's champion. In a break with tradition, he refused to release his remaining delegates so that the Democratic nominee could emerge from the convention with a unanimous vote: "I won't do it. I won't do it. I won't do it."[49] Smith's pique won him no friends.

Roosevelt wasted no time in taking over the party. In one of his very first acts as nominee, he announced Jim Farley as the new chairman of the Democratic National Committee. Raskob had been fired.

Raskob expected to be removed. He was ready to leave but before departing from Chicago he had to go through a little show with Farley. At a public meeting in the Gold Room of the Congress Hotel, Raskob formally turned over the party gavel to his successor. Roosevelt managed to enter the room just after Raskob had done his duty. Raskob had to listen to Roosevelt give one of his typical quips, "This is the second time I have been late today." Roosevelt's plane had been late earlier, delaying his tradition-breaking appearance before the delegates to accept their nomination. "I had hoped to get here while my old friend, John Raskob, was presiding," said Roosevelt.[50] Raskob took the casual slight in stride. A reporter noted that Raskob listened to Roosevelt's "curt words of thanks... quietly and without a word of protest."[51] Another chapter in Raskob's life was over.

Raskob knew that Roosevelt's ascent and his removal from the party was more than just a change in personnel, personalities, and status. Raskob had listened carefully to Roosevelt's acceptance speech earlier in the day. He had heard Roosevelt condemn the kind of government policy that "sees to it that a favored few are helped and hopes that some of their prosperity will leak through, sift through, to labor, to the farmer, to the small businessman." He had heard Roosevelt inform "those nominal Democrats who squint at the future with their faces turned toward the past, and who feel no responsibility to the demands of the new time, that they are out of step with their Party." He had sat there while Roosevelt solemnly declared to his audience in the hall and the millions who listened on the radio: "I pledge you, I pledge myself, to a new deal for the American people.... This is more than a political campaign; it is a call to arms. Give me your help, not to win votes alone, but to win in this crusade to restore America to its own people."[52] Raskob had lost more than his post. The business-celebrating Jazz Age was finished. Raskob's time on top was over.

16

Money to Burn

For the first time in his life, John Raskob was on the wrong side of history. The slim, dynamic young man who had refused to accept a limit on his ambitions and who had rushed from the dim reaches of upstate New York to the midnight glow of Manhattan was suddenly a portly older man standing on the outside of a fast-changing world. He had no position of authority. He had no day-to-day responsibilities. No newspapermen were camped outside his offices, waiting to report his latest pronouncements on politics or the economy to an avid public. Even his family life was in disarray. Raskob was neither in public life nor in financial terms the man he had long been. Although he could not know it in the summer of 1932, John Raskob would never again take center stage in American life.

Raskob did not go down quietly. In the middle of the decade he fought one last big battle. With his closest business allies, Raskob took on the New Deal. He lost that fight. The modern, antistatist, economic-liberty-based conservative political movement, however, had been sparked into life by the efforts of Raskob and his like-minded industrialist compatriots.

In early July 1932 Raskob returned to New York unsure of what came next. Friends and colleagues commiserated with him over how the Democratic Convention had turned out. James Cox, who had been the Democrat's presidential nominee in 1920 and had become one of John's new political friends, was one of several who gave the ex-chairman of the DNC the praise they felt Roosevelt, Farley, and the rest of the new crowd had denied him. Raskob thanked each of his correspondents for their well wishes, but he also told them, in no uncertain terms, that he was done with politics. To his New York friend and political ally Elizabeth Marbury he was blunt: "I am now definitely out of politics—a field in which I really do not belong."[1] Marbury, onetime literary agent for Oscar Wilde and George Bernard Shaw, Broadway powerhouse and champion of Cole Porter and Jerome Kern, as well as a Democratic Party activist, devout Catholic and longtime companion of the great style-setter Elsie de Wolfe, did her best to cheer Raskob up.[2] Bessy, as her wide circle knew her, despite her own failing health, promised to keep him entertained. Marbury was one of many friends who offered restless Raskob nights out on the town. Raskob would not be bored as he worked out his future.

Immediately, Raskob decided to take care of what was under his immediate control. Since his youth, John had prided himself on being trim and fit. But beginning in the late 1920s he had let himself go. He had ballooned to over 170 pounds on his 5′ 6″ frame and looked pudgy and older than his fifty-three years. He vowed to get back in shape. Two years earlier, Raskob had joined Artie McGovern's celebrity gym at 41 E. 42nd Street whose regulars included Babe Ruth, Jack Dempsey, the golfer Gene Sarazen, and several of John's Wall Street friends. Raskob had infrequently taken advantage of the "scientific body building and reducing through individual treatment."[3] In mid-1932, he wrote McGovern that he wanted to pay him $1,000 a year—double the going rate—if McGovern would give him regular individual training sessions of one and a half to two hours. Raskob believed that if he committed that kind of money he would oblige himself to actually workout. McGovern agreed and Raskob used some of his freed-up time to go regularly to the gym. Also, he walked everywhere, always at a fast clip, weaving around the masses of slower pedestrians. Raskob steadily lost weight. While he would never regain the wiry build of his youth, he kept at his gym and fast-walking regiment for the next several years and his energy level remained high.

All through the remainder of 1932, when not traveling, Raskob went almost daily to his Empire State office, mostly to clear up loose ends or attend to his troubled finances. Unfortunately, he still had much too much of the Empire State Building to himself. Raskob worried over the empty space, numbers, and financing arrangements, but he left management to the building's professional staff. Concerns about his stock investments, too, gnawed at him as he tried to salvage what he could. He sold off many of his speculative stocks and reorganized the many corporations he had created for investment purposes to maximize tax advantages. Raskob was also in the middle of the lawsuit brought by the County Trust to recoup the outstanding loan the bank was still owned from the Al Smith campaign in 1928. Raskob testified against a couple of the men who had been part of Smith's inner circle and who still had not made good on their loan guarantees. It was unpleasant and earned Raskob the undying enmity of several of the old Smith circle, including his Broadway pal, Eddie Dowling. Raskob had always known that friends found through financial relationships rarely lasted through the inevitable ups and downs of money matters, which is why, at least in part, he had always held on to his boyhood chums from Lockport.

Raskob had to contend as well with the large amount of money he was still owed by the DNC for the 1928 Smith campaign. Between July and October, Raskob and the DNC's new chair Jim Farley fenced over the money, with each side leaking nasty bits to the newspapers. Raskob agreed to forgive most of the money after Farley agreed in principle to pay him back a few hundred thousand dollars. To cement the deal, Raskob very publicly donated $25,000 to FDR's campaign. Days before the election, after nearly four months of silence, Raskob gave an uninspired radio speech on Roosevelt's behalf aimed at the business community, and the campaign team reached out to him in hopes he would lure a few big donors to the cause. But Raskob's role as capitalist front man for the Democrats had been taken over by the party's old standby, the financier Bernard Baruch, making Raskob redundant. So once Raskob had been at least symbolically brought on board, Farley slipped away from the seeming financial commitment to Raskob. John would spend a good deal of time trying to collect on the money he had been, he believed, promised. After John sent a great many reminders, Farley eventually—nearly four years later—forked over $100,000.

Raskob had a very long list of such debtors. He wrote all of them with near-metronomic regularity seeking payment. It was not fun work. Many of Raskob's correspondents told him that they had no money, or at least none to spare.

Roosevelt's landslide victory in the November election left Raskob largely unmoved. Right before the election, despite his claims that he was done with politics, Raskob had gone public with a list of suggested economic policies that closely followed the business community's conventional wisdom. Above all he insisted that Roosevelt, who he fully expected to win the election, must balance the federal budget to restore business confidence. He also called for "radical reductions in the high surtaxes on income."[4] To make up for these lost revenues, he suggested that a national sales tax be imposed, as well as an excise tax on alcoholic beverages, following the immediate repeal of Prohibition. He also called for major reductions in federal spending. Raskob had no pipeline to Roosevelt and while his ideas made the front page of the *New York Times* they went no further.

John was on the outside. He knew it and he accepted it. He feared the worst from President Roosevelt and in a moment of uncharacteristic bitterness, soon after the DNC nominating convention, he had expressed those feelings to his friend and political ally Governor Albert Ritchie: "It seems almost unbelievable that the Democratic Party has been delivered into the leadership of such radicals as Roosevelt, Huey Long, Hearst, McAdoo and Senators Wheeler and Dill and out of the hands of such a fine body of men as yourself, Governor Byrd, Carter Glass, John W. Davis, Governor Smith, Governor Ely, Governor Cox, and Pierre S. du Pont."[5] Given that assessment, not surprisingly, Raskob had nothing to do with Roosevelt in the months leading up to the election. He and Governor Smith, who had given a few desultory speeches on Roosevelt's behalf, did show up together at Roosevelt's headquarters at the Biltmore Hotel on election night. They stood together, watching as a beaming Franklin Roosevelt and his campaign manager Jim Farley accepted the accolades that Smith and Raskob had hoped would be theirs.

During the long interregnum between Roosevelt's election and his inauguration on March 4, 1933, Raskob had nothing but doubts about Roosevelt and his New Deal. But FDR's first actions in office, especially his handling of the bank crisis that had nearly paralyzed the American economy, won his approval. Raskob found himself cheering, as well, when the Administration sought to reduce government red-ink by cutting veterans' benefits and government workers' wages. Most of all, FDR's embrace of the Prohibition repeal effort led by the overwhelmingly Democratic Congress thrilled Raskob. Most of Roosevelt's other early efforts to stabilize the economy, including the creation of the pro-Big Business National Recovery Administration, earned FDR Raskob's respect. Raskob, like almost all of his friends still running industrial concerns, worried about the New Deal's growing support of organized labor but overall he was surprised to find himself, actually, a Roosevelt man.

In the late spring of 1933, Raskob admitted to his friends that he seemed to have been wrong about FDR. He wrote to Gretchen Dau Cunningham, a business writer and Democratic Party activist to whom he had taken a shine, that Roosevelt's leadership and his skillful handling of the economy was electrifying: "Never in my whole life have I been so mistaken about a man and his ability as I was about Franklin Roosevelt. I always liked him for his courage and grit in overcoming the tremendous handicap of his infantile paralysis. But I felt, because of this great affliction and the great problems to be solved not only in this country but in the world that it would be a mistake to nominate and elect him. As I said, never has anyone been so wrong as I in that conclusion."[6] Raskob telegraphed the president in April to let him know how appreciative he was of his leadership and his seeming lean toward business interests: "The people of the whole nation are back of you and are showing their respect for a man who knows how to respect them."[7]

Soon after writing the president, John accepted an invitation from Roosevelt's Secretary of Commerce to join the Business Advisory and Planning Council. Pierre du Pont and several dozen other leading businessmen, including Alfred Sloan, joined as well. The appointment was largely ceremonial and Raskob had little to do with the Council, but its creation demonstrated to Raskob that Roosevelt understood the role that business had to play in the economic recovery. Raskob spoke favorably about Roosevelt to his many friends at the DuPont Company, unsettling many of them who were far more suspicious of the president's motives and direction.

Despite such niceties, Raskob just did not care that much. He was tired of politics. He had also told Gretchen Cunningham, "Under no circumstances could anyone ever get me into politics again. It is a thankless job and one which holds not the slightest interest for me."[8] Cunningham did not believe him, "Your letter gave me a chuckle don't you know we can never stop 'politicing' when once we start."[9] In 1933, John would have sworn that she was wrong. She was not.

Raskob spent months at a time in the first year of the New Deal traveling, taking off to places near and far solely for purposes of recreation and pleasure. He had stuck around to attend Roosevelt's inauguration but soon after embarked on a long trip to Europe. He went, as was usual, without Helena. She and Jack Corcoran, accompanied by at least a couple of the children, took a more humble vacation to a hunting reserve Corcoran owned, Camp Melody Pine in Carthage, North Carolina. She and Corcoran, for the next several years, always with Raskob children in tow, would go to the lodge twice a year. There they would hunt wild turkeys and other game, camp, and take long hikes through the forest. Raskob knew all about their trips and blandly wrote a friend at one point about them, noting nothing unusual about the arrangement.[10]

In Europe, John held to a pattern that he repeated almost annually through the 1930s, at least until Europe's troubles made his trips impossible. He would cross the Atlantic on one of the faster ocean liners—his favorites, when going to Italy, his usual point of disembarkation, were the "Savoia" or the "Rex" because they took seven days to reach Naples instead of the usual nine. Then he would get hold of a car through his General Motors connections and begin an epic motor trip. He loved to drive himself around Europe and he became expert on the roadways throughout France, Italy, and Switzerland. He usually spent at least a month and sometimes more than two months on the continent, "motoring," as he always said, from place to place, taking in the sites.

Raskob was the kind of traveler who remembered the name of every town, church, monument, museum, and ruin that he visited. Just as he once used to share his vast knowledge of the business world and the stock market with his friends, he did likewise with his travels. He loved to give travel advice and would do so with Raskobian thoroughness: "Take the Mafia drive to Sorento and on this drive visit the island of Capri, which is very quaint and most interesting, staying overnight there if at all possible.... Motor around Sicily, through Syracuse and Gigent, to see the ruins of the old temple standing there since 500 B.C., arriving at Terramina." On and on he would go, specifying amount of time to stay at each place, the best mode of transportation, optional side trips, and places not to be missed. To his old GM friend and onetime protégé Don Brown, he indicated his own travel bias: "Personally, I keenly enjoy motoring and would rather spend ten days over there taking such a trip than I would lounging about the Riviera."[11]

Even as he grew older, Raskob insisted on a strong pace and a firm sense of purpose and direction when traveling. Often, he would only stay for a single day and night at any particular spot, taking in the best of what was on offer and then moving on. Exceptions were made for special purposes, such as gambling.

Raskob generally spent several days playing blackjack and other games of skill in Monte Carlo. He seems to have always come out on top.

At the end of 1933 Raskob was still without clear focus but at the least he seemed to have patched things up with Roosevelt and Farley. In mid-November, Governor Smith and Raskob went to the White House for the first time and sipped tea with the president in an upstairs sitting room. The tea party was assiduously nonpolitical, a tone assured by the presence of Roosevelt's daughter and several of his grandchildren. Reporters had been alerted to the meeting and a photo of Raskob and Smith in front of the White House, though not with President Roosevelt, duly appeared in the papers. Smith, well aware that Roosevelt had maneuvered him into a strictly ceremonial visit, and a second-tier one at that, wistfully commented in reporters' hearing, "The last time I was here, we were talking law enforcement with President Hoover."[12]

Ten days later, the rapprochement between Raskob and Roosevelt continued. A Smith-less Raskob again visited with the president at his invitation, this time at Warm Springs where Roosevelt was celebrating the opening of a new facility, paid for in part with Raskob's money. The *Times* ran a large photo of the two men in close conversation, smiling.[13] Raskob and Roosevelt spent private time together as well and had a friendly conversation on the unemployment problem. Whether the ever politically adept president was keeping a potential enemy close or if, in fact, Roosevelt felt that Raskob was genuinely onboard is not clear.

As 1933 drew to a close, John had made not a single negative public statement about Roosevelt or the New Deal and his private correspondence indicates only positive feelings, though he was worried about members of Congress who were agitating for higher corporate and personal taxes—"they are losing all sense of morality," he fumed.[14] Right after the Warm Springs visit, Raskob wrote the president an effusive handwritten thank-you note in his still impeccable copperplate script, noting that his thank you "sounds terribly formal after the thoroughly informal and homelike manner in which you received and entertained me on my most happy and interesting visit to the Little White House over the weekend." Raskob complimented the president, as many others would over the years, on his extraordinary ability to appear amidst so many pressing problems to be without a care in the world.[15] Raskob was a big believer in emotional equanimity, a trait he associated with Pierre and for which he strived but did not always succeed.

Raskob followed up on his visit, two weeks later, with a more formal letter to Roosevelt. During their Warm Springs conversation, the president had asked Raskob about Albert Deane and his plan for economic recovery, which both Secretary of Labor Frances Perkins and Secretary of Commerce Don Roper had drawn to the president's attention. Deane had been the key man at GM in turning Raskob's general ideas about installment automobile buying into GMAC and he had eventually become GMAC's chief executive. In 1932, Deane had published a book outlining an elaborate plan to tackle what he called the "under consumption" problem caused by overproduction and excessive unemployment that included a countercyclical job-sharing and wage-increasing program based on a complex employment tax scheme. During the Warm Springs tête-à-tête Roosevelt had asked Raskob about the plan. Raskob pled only a passing acquaintance with the multitiered proposal but he did his best to explain it. Roosevelt had ended their chat by asking Raskob to bring Deane to the White House for a talk. At the end of 1933, Roosevelt was still courting businessmen, and businessmen, as a block, were not sure where Roosevelt intended to take the country.

On returning to New York, Raskob set up a block of meetings with Deane, grilled him on his plan, ran it by some of his friends, and then wrote the president: "I think the plan which, when understood is most simple, is quite the biggest thing that I have ever heard of and I doubt that there is any one thing that will do more to promote, secure and insure the permanency of your New Deal policies than will this plan." Raskob asked the president to give him and Deane two hours at the White House to present the plan: "Please realize that I fully appreciate how valuable your time is and the number of crazy ideas put up to you. Let me assure you that there is not the slightest doubt in my mind that you will count the time you give to this as time well spent." Raskob added a heartfelt note: "Except as it may be helpful to you in carrying out your New Deal and reorganizing our entire economic structure, I have not the slightest interest, directly or indirectly, in any way, shape or form in this plan. My only desire is to be helpful if I can." Roosevelt agreed to see Dean and Raskob, and in early January they spent two hours at the White House briefing the president.[16] Throughout 1934 the Deane Plan enjoyed a vogue among a number of New Dealers and various job-sharing plans were floated in Congress though none became law.[17]

Raskob was pleased to be of service but even after this bit of peripheral policy-advising chose to make no effort to get closer to the White House. While many of his closest friends in the business world fought to influence New Deal policies, Raskob had not. Quietly, out of the limelight, he had instead offered Roosevelt his general support and encouragement. Raskob had told everybody that he wanted to steer clear of politics and he meant it. But in March 1934 his separate peace with the New Deal came to an end, changing the course of Raskob's last years.

In February 1934 Franklin Roosevelt called for major regulation of the stock market and securities underwriting. For close to two years Congress had been investigating Wall Street. With the indomitable legal counsel Ferdinand Pecora in the lead, the Senate Banking and Currency Committee had forced Wall Street's biggest names to explain the workings of the securities markets to the American people. Pecora, a $255 a month employee of the federal government, took on J. P. Morgan, Winthrop Aldrich, Thomas W. Lamont, Richard Whitney, and other Jazz Age giants in public hearings, under oath, and made them bleed. Americans learned about the pools, syndicates, and other schemes insiders used to take advantage of small-time investors. In May 1933, Pecora forced the release of the Morgan bank's "preferred list," which was a roster of well-to-do and influential men, ranging from President Calvin Coolidge to Charles Lindbergh, who were allowed during the Great Bull Market to purchase new stock offerings from Morgan at below-market rates, almost certainly assuring them easy profits. John Raskob's name appeared on that list. Pecora's investigations also revealed that John, ever polite, had thanked his friends at Morgan, in writing, for putting him on the list and that he hoped that there would soon be "opportunities for me to reciprocate."[18] Pecora explained that putting influential men, such as Raskob, under obligation to the House of Morgan was the very point of the "preferred list."

Raskob shrugged off the Pecora revelations, including his quoted remark, but Roosevelt's embrace of serious government regulation of the securities markets rankled. Roosevelt's top legislative draftsmen Tommy Corcoran and Ben Cohen cranked out a fifty-page bill that outlawed such stock market practices as pools and wash sales, and placed strict limits on leveraged stock purchases. Both the Senate and the House immediately took up the legislation. Raskob was appalled: many of the practices specified in the proposed legislation were ones he had used. As he saw it, at a time when the economy desperately needed capital investment, the Roosevelt Administration planned to treat investors as if they were all potential criminals. Raskob was not alone. James Rand, who ran the largest office supply company in the United States, spoke for many big businessmen when he accused the Roosevelt Administration of willfully driving America "along the road from Democracy to Communism." This overblown charge, made in response to the New Deal's foray into stock market regulation, was suddenly everywhere. The Hearst papers, which only a few years earlier had blasted big businessmen as treacherous oligopolists—and the DuPont Company as the "traitor trust"—now warned that "much of the Administration is more communistic than the Communists themselves."[19] Roosevelt's long anticipated efforts to rein in the speculative abuses that had contributed to the Stock Market bubble had touched a nerve in the capitalist class.

After the stock exchange bill appeared, Raskob used similar, emotionally charged language in his private correspondence but to make a different point about the New Deal. In a March 30, 1934, letter to his old DuPont colleague and Pierre's brother-in-law, the fixedly anti–New Deal Ruly Carpenter, Raskob

wrote a nuanced assessment of the Roosevelt Administration. He was responding to Carpenter's politely phrased but nonetheless clear charge that Raskob, in
his defense of FDR at a DuPont board of directors meeting at the end of 1933,
had shown himself to be a wrong-headed dupe. Carpenter, who had recently
retired from his corporate duties, was particularly exercised by the Roosevelt
Administration's public works programs. He informed Raskob that the "negroes
on my place in South Carolina refused work this Spring...saying they had easy
jobs with the Government."[20] Carpenter's vitriol was not just directed at the New
Deal's supposed effect on African American labor patterns. Although Raskob
was not aware of it, Carpenter also had nasty things to say about what he called
the "fanatical and communist Jew professors," who Carpenter believed had
taken over New Deal policy making.[21] Carpenter believed that the Roosevelt's
New Deal was upending the normal, long-standing social, economic, and political hierarchies that had effectively ruled the United States.

In response, Raskob chose to ignore Carpenter's particular gripes about the
impact the New Deal was having on the cost of "negro" labor and instead spoke
more generally about New Deal public policy debates. He argued that Roosevelt
was not anti-business and that, generally, he supported good economic policy.
At the end of 1933, Raskob insisted to Carpenter, Roosevelt had promoted
"sound-money policy" and had sworn to maintain "the credit structure and good
faith of the United States." But the New Deal, Raskob knew, was not monolithic
and New Dealers were not all pulling in the same direction. Like Carpenter,
Raskob was wary of the new proposed stock market regulations and like
Carpenter he blamed the restrictions on the influential Harvard law professor
Felix Frankfurter and his Progressive acolytes, who included Tommy Corcoran
and Ben Cohen. Raskob believed that some of Roosevelt's people were seeping
poisonous anticapitalist rhetoric into public discourse. In his letter to Carpenter,
Raskob for the first time used the word "communist" to refer to aspects of the
New Deal. He suspected that the New Deal was approaching a critical juncture
and that factions within the New Deal were trying to push Roosevelt down the
wrong path. A battle, he believed, had begun over the direction of American
economic policy. Someone, Raskob wrote Carpenter, needed to organize sound
men who had the steel and the stature to stand tall against the kind of radical
ideas that could destroy the United States. They had to keep Roosevelt on the
straight and narrow free market path that led to restored economic prosperity.

Raskob insisted that he was not the man to lead such a charge: "I have been
entirely out of politics since July, 1932, and I am anxious to keep out," noting
that Carpenter, on the other hand, would be a terrific leader of such a movement.
"You haven't much to do," Raskob wrote bluntly, "and I know no one that could
better take the lead in trying to induce the du Pont and General Motors groups,
followed by other big industries, to defiantly organize to protect society from

the suffering which it is bound to endure if we allow communistic elements to lead the people to believe that all business men are crooks, not to be trusted and that...[no] one should be allowed to get rich." Raskob, his brain fully engaged, gained enthusiasm as he wrote: "There should be some very definite organization that would come out openly with some plan for educating the people to the value of encouraging people to work, encouraging people to get rich, showing the fallacy of Communism in its efforts to tear down our capital structure, etc." Raskob urged Carpenter to take up the challenge: "you are in a particularly good position to do this...you are young enough to undertake the work, you have the time, you are wealthy enough to not have to depend upon a job or salary for a living and you are in a position to talk directly with a group that controls a larger share of industry through common stock holding than any other group in the United States."[22] John genuinely did not appear to see that he was describing not Ruly Carpenter, who had never shown interest in such political organizing, but himself. Pierre du Pont would help him to understand.

Raskob, as was not unusual when he found himself intervening in du Pont family business, passed along a copy of this letter to Pierre du Pont. Pierre, perhaps much more than John expected, embraced the offhand notion of setting up an organization dedicated to promoting sound economic policy. Predictably, Pierre wanted John and not Ruly to take the lead.

By the spring of 1934, Pierre had had enough of the New Deal. Against his better judgment, Pierre had accepted in late 1933 a seat on the newly created National Labor Board as one of five employer representatives. The NLB was one of the many semi-governmental agencies created as a part of the National Recovery Administration, the New Deal's monumentally unwieldy attempt to restore economic stability through voluntary industrial regulation and cooperation between workers and employers. Du Pont, who also served on the NRA's Industrial Advisory Board, watched the NLB move toward protecting unionization and collective bargaining in American industries. Pierre did his best to fight this unexpected turn but his voice—and vote—was drowned out by his enemies. The New Dealers' increasing support of organized labor was a potentially expensive problem for labor-intensive industries such as General Motors and would lead the men who ran and profited from those industries, as a rule, to turn against the New Deal.[23]

Du Pont had thought for a while that his role inside the NRA had given him some political influence, especially over the boss of the NRA, Hugh Johnson. Du Pont had urged Johnson to direct more financial and rhetorical support to the private sector, cut back on expensive public works that took away opportunities from the business community, and instead stimulate the economy and employment by subsidizing skilled vocational training for millions of young people and by increasing the size of and spending on the armed forces, an idea that would have led directly to government contracts for the DuPont Company. Du Pont's suggestions went nowhere.[24] Pierre had numerous other gripes over New Deal interventions into private economic concerns, several of which directly affected his own investments and interests. In early April 1934, when du Pont received his copy of John's letter to Ruly, he was fully primed to do what he could to stem what he felt was a rising anti-business, pro-labor tide. That President Roosevelt had simply ducked out of sight during the NLB battles only intensified Pierre's belief that something had to be done to pull the New Deal back from its collectivist turn.

Additionally, and not inconsequentially, the Democratic Senate's decision in April 1934 to investigate the role munitions companies, particularly DuPont, had played in pushing the United States into the Great War back nearly twenty years earlier, greatly increased Pierre's growing suspicions about the course of the New Deal. Pierre found the very premise of the Special Committee on Investigation of the Munitions Industry to be ludicrous; nonetheless, the committee only gained momentum throughout 1934. He and his brothers would end up testifying before a passel of hostile Senators, needled constantly by the committee's lead investigator, Alger Hiss. The committee did not succeed in proving that the du Ponts had angled to bring America into the Great War or in starting any other war. The committee did force the du Ponts to explain publicly their role in supplying their deadly wares to belligerents around the world, not just during World War I but in subsequent conflicts in Latin America and elsewhere. The DuPont Company, the committee demonstrated, was literally, as charged, "a merchant of death," though the term could be equally applied to a great many other companies in the United States and around the world involved in the "defense industry."

The committee chair Prairie Populist Senator Gerald Nye of North Dakota made his contempt for the du Ponts and their company clear: "The world is going to see the need for curbing these merchants of death and their business."[25] Such language and governmental intent was part and parcel of why Pierre had so adamantly opposed Prohibition, which had so spectacularly outlawed the alcoholic beverage industry. While President Roosevelt gave no encouragement to the investigation, neither did he make any attempt to rein in the committee's Democratic senators. Pierre, Irénée, and Lammot du Pont could barely contain themselves as the Nye Committee's investigators zeroed in on their company during the late spring and summer.[26] The du Pont brothers were ready to launch a war of their own against the New Deal.

Over the spring and summer of 1934, almost as if by accident, Raskob began organizing the capitalist class's major foray against the New Deal. Pierre, Irénée, and Lammot du Pont propelled John forward and supplied much of the funding, as well as the political passion. Once Pierre and his brothers had signed on to the general idea of forming an organization to promote a "sound economic policy," John contacted his old friends at General Motors about joining the effort. Don Brown was the first to commit. Alfred Sloan, John Pratt, and others agreed, with varying levels of enthusiasm, to support the project. In their early conversations the GM and DuPont men talked about focusing their organizations around the ideal of economic liberty and the right of every American to control his own private property without government interference. While John would have had a hard time admitting it, after a year of drift and relative exclusion from the front table of American public life, he was having fun meeting with his old friends and taking yet another project from little more than talk to an up-and-running, big-time operation. He was so good at it.

At the same time, even as he helped to organize the operation, Raskob never really embraced the actual cause. Despite the du Ponts' urgent desire to stem the New Deal tide, Raskob never quite took the campaign seriously, even as he spent buckets of money and, episodically, hundreds of hours on it. The whole affair was like a fun-house mirror version of Raskob's Empire State building venture. He knew everybody involved; he had friends who needed jobs; his pent-up energies needed an outlet. Willy-nilly, Raskob became the lead organizer of the major conservative uprising of the New Deal years. So much for staying out of politics.

At least during 1934 and even into 1935, Raskob genuinely believed that he was not fighting Roosevelt and the New Deal. He was just trying to move the president back toward the temperate, pro-business, pro-sound currency policies that Raskob believed had once characterized the Roosevelt Administration. Probably because he saw no direct personal attack in the doings or tactical silences of FDR, his anti–New Deal passion never matched that of Pierre or Irénée, the leading firebrand in the crew. Raskob, like many others, desperately wanted to believe that he knew where Roosevelt really wanted to lead the nation. He seemed to think that the aspect of the protean, shape-shifting New Deal that he had fixed his gaze on back in the first months of 1933 was the real and true New Deal. Everything else done in the name of the New Deal—what Raskob saw as the anti-business, pro-labor, market-regulating, anticapitalist aspects— were dangerous deviations. The right mixture of political pressure and public education, Raskob hoped, would bring the Roosevelt Administration around. For a man who had run the DNC, it was a remarkably naïve understanding of the politics of the New Deal and of the desires of the American electorate.[27]

Raskob's first step in getting the organization off the ground was to ask his friends to give it a name and a focused purpose. John primed the pump by suggesting that the organization be formed around a simple and general call to arms: Americans needed to resist government's attempts to take private property from its rightful owners through regulation, government edict, and anticapitalist policy. Americans must remember, he asserted, that the right to property is the first Constitutional right of them all. Thus, the organization's name should efficiently remind Americans of the need to respect property rights.

In response to this sort of property-rights-and-property-owners talk, one of GM's more politically astute and ideologically conservative executives, the in-house economist S. M. DuBrul, wrote a memo that made the rounds of both corporations' upper echelons in mid-June 1934. He warned his colleagues against organizing too narrowly around "some sort of property owner's protective league." He tried to remind his colleagues that the New Deal had turned against the capitalist class for political reasons—"the majority of voters are not directly interested in the preservation of property rights." As a result, "no open organization of property owners can be effective." DuBrul feared that "public morality has broken down" in response to economic downturn. New Dealers' offer of "doles, benefit payment, and so on," he argued, had won over a majority of fearful voters. In that climate, DuBrul concluded, they would need to make a case not just for property rights but a grander more politically enticing campaign "for the preservation of constitutional liberties" in order to win the public back. "The whole point," he explained, "is that by preserving the principles of the Constitution, property rights will be thoroughly and adequately protected." DuBrul, several of the men agreed, had struck rhetorical gold.[28]

Raskob kept herding his team of capitalists. Alfred Sloan, the du Ponts, and several other leading executives met several times in June and July at Raskob's wood-paneled office suite at the Empire State Building. They batted around ideas and at a July 23rd meeting Raskob offered up a draft proposal. He suggested a name, "Union Asserting the Integrity of Persons and Property" and a slogan, "Integrity is the foundation of all social order." The first sentence of his cri de coeur ran 125 words and was full of carefully spelled out definitions and specifications of classes of property and property owners. The whole thing read a good deal more like a stock debenture or corporate contract than a political document. Even Alfred Sloan, by no means a prose master, wondered if they could not do better with fewer words. He also suggested—"I am simply trying to be helpful"—that they might want to refrain from listing jewelry and works of art as categories of property that needed protection from government marauders. Maybe, said Sloan, they should call their group the Association Asserting the Rights of Property? It was an incremental improvement.[29]

More professional wordsmithing came from John W. Davis, the silver-haired Democratic presidential nominee of 1924 and an unreconstructed Jeffersonian—though Jefferson would not have shared Davis's fierce loyalty to Wall Street and America's largest corporations. Davis despised the New Deal. He was Big Business's favorite corporate counsel, and he had repeatedly appeared before the Supreme Court to challenge the constitutionality of key New Deal legislation.

He was a gifted advocate, writer, and speaker with a prodigious memory; he could not only quote Shakespeare and the Bible at length but also the Koran. In response to Raskob's request for rhetorical advice, Davis offered up a list of alternative names for the property holders' organization: the League for American Rights, League for Constitutional Rights, League for Individual Rights, Liberal Union, Constitutional Union, Union for Personal and Property Rights, and then the elegant consensus choice: the American Liberty League.[30]

Raskob pulled together the rest of his old political crew to give the Liberty League organizational panache and, he hoped, political legitimacy. Al Smith stepped forward as a charter member of the League and agreed to serve on the small executive committee. Walter Chrysler joined, as did several of John's other well-heeled friends. Raskob's erstwhile right-hand man at the DNC, Jouett Shouse, was hired to run the organization. Poor Shouse had been largely unemployed since Jim Farley had let him go back in the summer of 1932; he had tried to set up as a Washington lobbyist, but since neither Roosevelt Democrats nor his old Republican enemies would have anything to do with him that venture was a bust. He had been living, in large part, on loans he had received from Raskob. Pierre du Pont also arranged for the top men at the now redundant Association Against the Prohibition Amendment, the group he had chaired and to which he had given great sums of money, to take on positions at the League. The Liberty League was a full employment program for old Raskob and du Pont political operatives.

Raskob privately launched the Liberty League on August 21, 1934, at the exclusive Metropolitan Club in New York. He put together a posh dinner attended by John Davis, Irénée du Pont, Al Smith, the broker E. F. Hutton, the Wall Street lawyer R. E. Desuernnine, and a half a dozen other leading financiers and industrialists. Pierre and Alfred Sloan were traveling and unable to attend but both pledged $25,000 to the League, as did Walter Chrysler. Altogether Raskob had lined up $775,000 to get the Liberty League off the ground. Much of that money came from the GM–DuPont crowd. Leaked stories of the wealthy men's meeting in their ritzy club made their way into the newspapers. It was not an auspicious beginning but Raskob, operating as if the Jazz Age were still roaring, appeared to be deaf to the political signals he was sending.

Raskob had, as always, moved with extraordinary speed and efficiency. In less than five months Raskob had turned his casual remarks about the need for a pro-capitalist force into a formidable-appearing political organization. Working with Shouse, Raskob had arranged for the Liberty League to take up spacious digs on the tenth floor of the National Press Club in Washington, DC, the same building in which they had housed the DNC between 1928 and 1932. Focused on the many logistical steps it had taken to interest his powerful friends and colleagues into supporting the organization, to write up the many necessary legal and financial documents, to line up a professional staff, and to set up an impressive shop for his association, Raskob had spent almost no time thinking about what exactly the Liberty League was to do and how it would operate in the cut-throat world of American politics in the midst of the Great Depression. Raskob had been so busy creating the League that he had never come to terms with how his fellow Democrats, especially Franklin Roosevelt, would view him and his new creation.

With word of the League already percolating in political circles, Raskob and Shouse knew they had to move quickly. At least recognizing that the White House might not be fully appreciative of their efforts, Shouse called in a favor from his erstwhile Democratic Party colleagues and arranged a last minute meeting with President Roosevelt. Shouse and Raskob wanted the president to understand that the League intended only to educate the public on economic policy and Constitutional principles. At the brief meeting, Shouse presented the League's statement of purpose to Roosevelt. The president glanced at it. When Shouse asked what he thought, Roosevelt gave a typically ambiguous answer: protecting private property was something "subscribed to by every American citizen." When Shouse pushed the president, asking him if he objected to the formation of the League, Roosevelt said "that he did not consider it any of his business and that he had no objection anyway."[31]

With that ringing endorsement from the man in the White House, Raskob and Shouse released an official statement to the press. In the still-wordy document, the League's founders had taken great pains to establish the Liberty League as a "nonpartisan" association. The Liberty League was not anti-Roosevelt, the press release emphasized, and certainly not an anti–Democratic Party organization. It was only "formed to defend and uphold the Constitution of the United States and to gather and disseminate information." The press release made national headlines, as had been hoped. The New York Times ran the Liberty League's press release word for word. At a Washington press conference held the same day, the politically astute Shouse held forth, explaining that the League "is definitely not anti-Roosevelt.... We want to try to help the administration." The wealthy funders and founders were nowhere to be seen. To reporters' questions about his old boss's role in the new organization, Shouse allowed that "Mr. Raskob was among those who had discussed the necessity of an educational campaign" to oppose "the destruction of property rights."[32] Shouse tried to keep the reporters focused on the issues, not the League's backers.

John believed that the launch had gone well. The New York Times editorial page gave its establishmentarian blessing to the League, opining that "the great majority of this country" stood with the Liberty League in its Constitutional mission and that "all save the Socialists, the Communists and the wilder radical fringe of the two great parties" should support its efforts.[33]

The very next day, a self-confident Irénée du Pont attempted to build on the League's first-day success. At the DuPont building in Wilmington, he came forward as a spokesman for the League, offering a far more impolitic message. He began by reminding the press that he had supported and voted for President Roosevelt in 1932. But those were the last carefully couched words of the day. He then went on the attack. The president, he proclaimed, must repudiate the National Industrial Recovery Act, which included the labor union protection clause that so frustrated Pierre. The Constitution forbade it. Perhaps straining credulity, he then backtracked, stating that he wanted only to be of service to Roosevelt. However, he concluded, the League would not and could not "condone any unconstitutional act, regardless of the politics of the transgressor."[34] Irénée du Pont, one of the nation's relatively few mega-millionaires, had abruptly ended the one-day honeymoon between the Liberty League and the New Deal.

New Dealers were quick to go on the offensive. Several, including Secretary of the Interior Harold Ickes, welcomed the Liberty League's attack on the New Deal from the political right. Ickes, a highly skilled political operator, told reporters: "I've been hoping ever since 1912 that we'd have political parties divided on real issues. It looks as if it's working out that way at last. Today we have different groups in each party. I'd like to see all the progressives together and all the conservatives together. Then you'd always be facing your enemy and not wondering about what is happening behind your back."[35] Ickes's desire for a clear ideological divide between Democrats and Republicans was exactly the scenario Raskob had been fighting during his four years as DNC chairman.

Raskob had wanted to blur the lines between the two parties, at least when it came to questions of economic policy—both parties, Raskob believed, should be pro-business. Raskob did not want the Liberty League to be a Republican-aligned organization. He intended it to be nonpartisan. John still hoped that the Liberty League's appeal to the propertied class—both the wealthy and the respectable middle class—might gently push Roosevelt and at least some New Deal Democrats back into the business fold. He soon learned from FDR just how badly he had misunderstood the president's politics.

President Roosevelt weighed in on the Liberty League just a day after Ickes's comments appeared in the newspapers. He called in the White House press corps. Breaking all presidential precedent, Roosevelt often met with reporters in the Oval Office. He would hold forth, puffing on his long cigarette holder while he fiddled with things on his desk. More often than not, what he said was not for attribution. But when it came to the Liberty League, Roosevelt assured the press, they could report fully and directly. The Liberty League, the president mused, "is good as far as it goes." But he wondered if the League "laid too much stress on the protection of property and too little on protection of the average citizen." The Liberty League, he said, reminded him of a religious group that demanded a higher morality but then spoke up for only two of the Ten Commandments, ignoring the rest. Warming up, he wondered if the founders of the League had perhaps forgotten other parts of the Bible. "Someone had said to him," he reported, "that the tenets of the organization appeared to be to 'love thy God but forget thy neighbor,' and that this person had added that 'God,' in this case, appeared to be property." The president noted that early that morning while still in bed he had read in the papers that "Wall Street indicated that the announcement of the American Liberty League was little short of an answer to a prayer." The president told the press corps that after that gem he "laughed for ten minutes."[36] The president was clearly enjoying himself. His deft hatchet job made the front page of newspapers across the country.

Raskob was not happy but, as was typical, shrugged off what he called "the President's attitude."[37] Letters poured in from Raskob's friends and colleagues, most of whom were supportive. Samuel Harden Church, president of the Carnegie Institute and one of Raskob's strongest allies in the anti-Prohibition campaign, felt that Roosevelt's comments could only help the cause: "The fact that President Roosevelt is making sarcastic comments upon the purposes of the League is the very best thing that could happen to it." Church assured Raskob that the best people summering at Cape Cod were all against Roosevelt's "policy for the redistribution of wealth" and were already rallying around the Liberty League.[38]

While Raskob received many such letters over the next months he also discovered far more political friction than he had anticipated. He had hoped to work closely with the Chamber of Commerce in promoting sound economic policy. The Chamber President Henry Harriman gave Raskob his heartiest personal support but then told him that he feared that some of his members, at least, might consider the League to be "merely an instrument of big business."[39] Harriman also wondered what policies, exactly, the League would support in promoting employment and economic recovery. Similar demurrals came in from other organized business and finance groups. By the end of 1934 Alfred Sloan, impatient with the League's slow rollout of specific criticisms of the New Deal, had begun working closely with the National Association of Manufacturers on its own anti–New Deal educational outfit: the National Industrial Information Council. Other early enthusiasts who had pledged large sums to the Liberty League were slow in sending in their promised checks. In late December, E. F. Hutton complained to John that he had arranged to meet with several hundred businessmen to talk up the League and had no idea exactly what he was supposed to tell them. Howard Pew of Sun Oil, another major backer, wrote John complaining that "because of the vagueness in the public mind about the real aims of the League," some people had begun to imagine the worst. He urged John to take strong stands both for and against specific New Deal legislation.

"The sort of leadership that takes no chances of getting out in front where the shooting is going on," he insisted, "is not likely to make much contribution to the victory."[40] Raskob was increasingly annoyed by all the second guessing. He pushed at Shouse to get cracking and he hired legendary public relations maestro Edward Bernays to help with the Liberty League's increasing image problems. Bernays, as always, was glad to take his client's money but privately he was struck by the political blinders Raskob and the other men seemed to be wearing: "They had no idea that a broad ideological revolution was taking place under their noses."[41]

Bernays was wrong, at least when it came to Raskob; he was well aware that he was living through a time of political upheaval. He just did not like it. But that did not mean that he was unaware of the balancing act he believed the Liberty League needed to perform. Given the charged political atmosphere, he understood that the League could not block the New Deal at every turn. Nonetheless, he believed the New Deal seemed to be moving ever leftward, pressured by the demotic fury of men such as "Share-the-Wealth" Huey Long and the embarrassing—to Raskob—Catholic radio priest, Father Charles Coughlin, who blasted Wall Street bankers, Jewish financiers, and President Roosevelt in the same breath. By the end of 1934, the political atmosphere of the United States was soupy with red-hot rhetoric and Raskob felt as though he could barely breathe.

John decided he had had enough. He told Pierre and Shouse that he had not intended to spend anymore of his life in the political playpen. He needed to get away.

On January 10, 1935, John set off on an around the world tour. He took along his son Bob, who had recently graduated from Yale, and two of his daughters, nineteen-year-old Jo and Marcy who was almost twenty-one. Raskob also sailed with his long-time valet Mike Valdez; it was a working trip for Valdez but mostly Raskob had him along so he could, at long last, visit his mother in the Philippines. For Raskob it was a way to make amends for his uncharacteristic thoughtlessness three years earlier when, cutting financial corners, he had turned down Valdez when he had asked for a loan to help out his mother.

They traveled first-class on the *Empress of Britain*, which would take them from New York to Europe to the Holy Land across the Suez Canal and onward to the "East" before heading back to New York via Hawaii, California, and the Panama Canal. They were gone for 128 days. Raskob showed no regard for the effect his luxury voyage might have on the image of the Liberty League at a time when one in five Americans was desperately looking for work.

Raskob was not as rich as he once was, but he still had plenty to spare. Every port of call was an opportunity for a new adventure, and John threw the family headfirst into every place they visited. The first landing in the Canary Islands set the trip's tone. Raskob had lined up a quick-stepping mountain hike that included "native girls carrying flower-filled baskets on their heads."[42] Soon they were in Monaco where everyone, especially John, gambled. Jo won $500 at the chemin de fer table—like father, like daughter. After stops in Italy and Greece, they sailed to Palestine. On board, John insisted that after every dinner the family in unison had to walk at a solid clip at least five times around the ship (not so easy for the girls who wore high heels).

Just before landing in Haifa, John received word that his long-suffering daughter Yvonne, just twenty-two years old, had died. Yvonne's lungs had been growing weaker for years but no one had known she was so close to the end. Jo wrote about her sister's death many years later, "In the bitter cold winter of five degrees below zero, she died with her dear mother at her side and a burning candle to light her way to her real love, Jesus."[43] John and the children did mourn but all of them, fortified by their faith and in Raskob fashion, pushed on.

In Egypt they rode camels into the desert. They saw pyramids and the King Tut excavation and the tombs of the sacred bulls, and they had a festive picnic complete with snake charmers. Then it was the Suez Canal, the Red Sea, the Indian Ocean, and, after many more laps around the ship, Bombay. In a little over a week in India, the Raskob family covered thousands of miles. There was the requisite trip to the holy city of Banaras where John had the troupe up at sunrise to attend to a host of cremations. They stood before the Taj Mahal, which, all agreed, lived up to its reputation. Over to Ceylon where a towering white elephant in a Buddhist procession at Kandy left the Raskobs in awe. Then it was off to Indonesia and the Malay Archipelago. Well before hordes of tourists littered the grounds, the Raskobs wandered through the haunted ruins of Angkor Wat. In Thailand, John posed atop a giant elephant. They went to Bali, which had been, so to speak, discovered by foreign travelers only a few years earlier. Still, in the mid-1930s only 100 or so tourists a month visited the island. John and the children were spellbound by the Kecak dance and the accompanying gamelan orchestra. Jo, at least, said she was ready to stay forever. But on they moved.

Next was the Philippines where the Raskobs watched Mike reunited with his extended family. Raskob celebrated his birthday in Zamboanga on Mindanao Island. Then they made their way to Hong Kong, where tailored clothes were duly purchased, and then to mainland China. They took trains and donkeys and elaborate walks with stops in Canton, Shanghai, and Peking. John's favorite daughter-in-law, Minerva, who had married John, Jr. in 1930, had friends in Peking—an adventurous young Jewish couple—and much to John's delight they took the Raskobs on an insider's tour. Jo reports: "They took us to a real Chinese restaurant.... All told there were about twelve that sat around the table with a dirty dish and tiny, dirty wine cup in front of each of us. Under these were several sheets of toilet paper." Fifteen dishes were served, including shark fins, buried eggs, and duck brains. Everyone, including John, loved it. Then it was off to a cacophonous Chinese theatre followed by a trip to an opium den—the Raskobs skipped the opium. Back on board the ship steamed to Japan just in time for cherry blossom season. In Japan, the Raskobs did register one sour note: the Japanese government, at the last minute, refused to allow American visitors to tour certain areas; though softly, the winds of war had begun to blow across the Pacific.

After the long crossing, John and his children arrived home on May 20, 1935. Al Smith was waiting for him at the pier, as were several reporters. John had done his best for 128 days to avoid both business and politics, but the reporters immediately began plying him with questions. What did he think of Roosevelt's newest maneuvers? What were his plans for the Liberty League? Was he supporting Smith for president in 1936? Raskob told the reporters that he had not kept up with the political situation in the United States while he was traveling. He seemed to be speaking from the heart when he said: "I hope that I am out of touch with politics for all times."[44]

Raskob actually had heard from Shouse about the League's difficulties. Shouse wrote him May 8th, warning that the League was rudderless. Irénée had taken off to his Cuban estate not long after John had left, leaving the League without a leader. Pierre had eventually dressed down his younger brother and insisted he come home and speak for the League and Irénée did so but not, according to Shouse, happily. Meanwhile, many of the GM group, led by Chevrolet president William Knudsen, had backed off their pledged financial support. Shouse believed they had been affected by Roosevelt's continuous sniping at the Liberty League. Shouse did have some good news: the League had distributed weekly studies of New Deal legislation, put on several radio speeches criticizing specific aspects of the New Deal, and received a great deal of editorial support in major newspapers, especially the *Chicago Tribune*. Shouse made it clear that he and the rest of the staff, as well as the du Ponts, were eagerly awaiting Raskob's return.[45]

Despite his best resolutions, Raskob was sucked back into the League's affairs. While he generally avoided the limelight over the next several months, he organized the League's fundraising, vetted their communications, and occasionally lashed out at the New Deal. Raskob, like almost all of his industrialist friends, was shaken when the president signed the National Labor Relations Act on July 5, 1935. The White House, in the minds of the big men at the Liberty League, had just given its imprimatur to the most radical labor unionists by guaranteeing their organizing campaigns full federal protection. From that day forward, the League was no longer engaged in a balancing act, weighing the good and the bad in New Deal legislation; it was in open revolt. Raoul Desvernine, chairman of the National Lawyers' Committee of the Liberty League, led the fight by rounding up several dozen prominent lawyers, many of them corporate counsels, all of whom declared the Labor Act to be an unconstitutional usurpation of American's economic liberty. Raskob agreed but he was not really ready for the final break with Roosevelt, though it was fast coming.

Thus, Raskob felt betrayed when an SEC report came out in August 1935 accusing him of having used insider knowledge of GM's dividend policy to buy a bloc of GM shares earlier in the year ahead of the public announcement. Raskob believed, with reason, that the report had no basis in fact. He further believed that the report was politically motivated and was an attack not just on him but on all the backers of the Liberty League. Raskob called a press conference to defend himself personally against the particulars of the charges made by the SEC. He also made what the *Wall Street Journal* called, in a front page, headline story, "a sweeping defense of the ideals and integrity of the nation's industrial and banking leaders and an equally vigorous attack on attempts to destroy confidence in those leaders."[46] Without naming names, Raskob lambasted "political demagogues" and "unscrupulous members of Congress in and out of investigating committees." He called upon "every leader in industry and finance to rise to the defense of the form of government which the Fathers established in America."[47] Despite his anger, Raskob still held out hope that Roosevelt was not involved in the personal attack and that the president had not, as Raskob understood it, turned against the business community.

Raskob sought out common ground with Roosevelt. He wanted the president to know that he still believed that the Liberty League, speaking for responsible businessmen, could make a contribution to Roosevelt's Administration. John contacted his successor as DNC chairman, Jim Farley, and asked him to set up a private meeting with the president.

Raskob got his White House visit with Roosevelt and Farley. The meeting had been fairly short but John had thought it had gone well. They talked cordially and Roosevelt appeared to listen attentively to Raskob's defense of the business community. Raskob left the White House thinking that Roosevelt had appreciated his thoughts and that they had parted on good terms.

Soon enough, John heard what the president really thought of his appeal. John was still close friends with the California Democratic activist Gretchen Dau Cunningham, who had good White House contacts. One of them, a DNC senior staffer, had sat in on the FDR–Raskob meeting. He told her what happened right after Raskob left the White House. Cunningham passed his words right to Raskob: "About Raskob's talk with the President, you imply that the President acquiesced. In fact, the President told me of Raskob's advice. Roosevelt likes Raskob, but cited this [advice] as an illustration of how the long time, privileged crowd failed to understand the social crises in America." Farley's man then told Cunningham that Roosevelt was only worried about the political threat from the Left and that "a rightist third party would not hurt, in truth it might even help" in the 1936 election. "Thus has spoken the Master," wrote Cunningham to Raskob. She tried to soften the bad news by urging Raskob to come out to California for a visit. "The Santa Anita race track is opening Christmas day," she chirped.[48]

Raskob wrote her right back. He was agitated, as Cunningham must have known he would be: "What the President said about me sounds funny, particularly when I am used as an illumination of how the long-time privileged crowd failed to understand the social crises in America. That is a lot of bunk! It is silly to class a man, who, starting as a poor boy, worked hard and acquired a comfortable fortune, as one of the long-time privileged crowd. It is really too silly to discuss."[49] Despite having been one of the richest and most powerful men in the country during the 1920s, and a wealthy man for better than twenty years, John could not imagine anyone could see him as a longtime member of the elite. John still looked in the mirror and saw the boy from Lockport who had made good through pluck, talent, and hard work. Long-term privilege, he knew, had played no part in his success. That Roosevelt was not talking about Raskob's climb to success but about his longtime position atop the economic ladder flew right by Raskob. He felt the sting of a personal insult.

Raskob rededicated himself to the Liberty League. Under his whip hand, the League distributed millions of anti–New Deal pamphlets. With a staff of fifty operating out of thirty-one rooms in Washington's National Press Building, as compared to the Republican National Committee's seventeen paid workers housed in twelve, relatively humble offices, the League carried the opposition message in the run-up to the 1936 election, railing against public works programs, farm subsidy programs, the Tennessee Valley Authority, Roosevelt's embrace of organized labor, and, above all, the New Deal's budget-busting, profligate government spending. Well-managed by Shouse, the League focused on one issue a week, beginning a sustained media blitz each Sunday to take advantage of newspaper editors' need to fill the news-starved Monday morning papers. William Murphy, head of the League's publicity corps, claimed that by December 1935 some 200,000 articles and editorials had been published promoting the League's political message.[50] The League had become a professional organization, a kind of Super PAC before such non-party aligned, Big Money groups formally existed.

In early 1936, Raskob became the public face of the Liberty League. John used his industrial contacts to help the League's staffers put together a mailing list of the shareholders in many of America's large corporations. John then wrote a letter that targeted this list of 150,000 people for League membership. John's letter to these shareholders was personal and direct. In what could only have been a response to Roosevelt's private remarks about his "long-term privileged" existence, Raskob started his appeal with a bit of self-mythologizing: "Beginning life as a poor boy with splendid health, the finest heritage which a good father and mother can leave any child, I was able to acquire a good grammar and commercial school education before starting work at $5 a week, at the age of nineteen years to make my way in the world." Journalists had often told John's life story this way but that did not make it true. Perhaps by this time Raskob perceived the solidly middle-class existence that he had enjoyed as a youth in Lockport as humble enough to count him among the ranks of the "poor." At any rate, after that move John got down to business, pointing out "his good fortune to be born a citizen of the United States of America—a country whose government is founded on a Constitution which respects the rights of persons and property as fundamental." That Constitution, John asserted, was under attack by New Deal radicals. The Liberty League existed only to "defend our charter of liberty" and "to root out the vicious radical elements that threaten the destruction of our government."[51] Please, John implored, join the Liberty League so as to preserve the American way of life.

Over the next several weeks, Raskob received a great many personal replies to his letter. Some commended him for his efforts to restore common sense to American politics; a great many others did not. The writer Elmer Rice mocked Raskob's effort: "To the hungry, the maimed, the disinherited of this land of ours, your phrases about liberty and freedom must seem as empty as the Empire State Building."[52] John Frederick, the chairman of the board of the Continental Steel Corporation, which had employed some 3,000 people just before the Great Depression hit, wrote a powerful critique of Raskob's attack on the New Deal from a business perspective. It was a gem of a letter: "I dislike a strong central government that interferes too much with the individual. I like democracy because it rests upon self restraint, but I think you will agree with me that in the past the business interests and their dominant leadership have not very effectively restrained themselves.... What we need is human justice, fair play, a willingness to help and be our neighbor's keeper in all matters pertaining to service. Surely the wealthy man of this country is better off surrounded by a populace that is prosperous than he is by a mass of people who are unable to secure employment and a decent living."[53] John was surprised and disappointed by how many people, including many in the corporate community, felt as Frederick did.

By April, Raskob understood that the Liberty League was not going to have the impact he had hoped. Membership and fund-raising drives had badly faltered despite his personal appeals. Rather than concede that his attack on the New Deal was failing because too many Americans, even wealthy ones, rejected the Liberty League's ardent defense of unfettered property rights, Raskob chose to believe that many of his peers in the financial and industrial world were just too cowardly to stand up for what they believed. He complained to Alfred Sloan, who was equally appalled by the New Deal's continuing popularity, about "the lack of courage shown by men who ought to be leaders in the effort to rescue our people and their government from the dangers of the disaster that will surely be visited upon this glorious country of ours.... I say again, the most discouraging thing to me is the way men in our walk of life, who should stand fearlessly and lead, are being cowed down by threats of being cracked down if they stick their necks out."[54] Raskob had lost faith in his own class of wealthy men.

In the run-up to the presidential election, Raskob and his fellow Liberty Leaguers made desultory attempts to counter Roosevelt's near-certain road to victory. Al Smith made numerous speeches attacking Roosevelt in an attempt to split off urban voters from the New Deal coalition. Building upon some of the conversations during the 1928 election about the fragile unity of the Democratic Party, Raskob and Pierre du Pont pondered the possibility of splitting the Democratic vote by supporting a southern, third-party candidate. Sloan, Raskob, Irénée and Pierre du Pont sent large checks to the Southern Committee to Uphold the Constitution, which was a front group for the presidential aspirations of Georgia Governor Eugene Talmadge, an economic conservative who castigated the New Deal for its pro-African American policies. The third-party Talmadge campaign became infamous, at least in Progressive circles, for circulating photos of Eleanor Roosevelt with black Americans in order to fan racist flames in the Deep South. Raskob sent donations to a variety of other fringe groups, including openly anti-Semitic organizations, which attacked Roosevelt and his "Jew Deal." Driven by personal and political passion, Raskob had sunk low.[55]

Roosevelt relished the Liberty League's attacks. As Gretchen Cunningham had reported months earlier, Roosevelt was confident that attacks by the Liberty League's wealthy backers would only harden his support on the Left and inspire voter turn-out. In his last major address before Election Day, Roosevelt spoke to an adoring crowd at Madison Square Garden: "We know that Government by organized money is just as dangerous as Government by organized mob. Never before in all our history have these forces been so united against one candidate as they are today. They are unanimous in their hate for me—and I welcome their hatred. I should like to have it said of my first Administration that in it the forces of selfishness and of lust for power met their match. I should like to have it said of my second administration that in it these forces have met their master."[56] Raskob and the Liberty League had no answer for that kind of rhetoric. FDR had turned the Liberty League into a sideshow. But Raskob and his colleagues by ignoring real suffering and by joining forces—for political advantage—with those who trucked in hatred, had turned themselves into a carnival attraction not fit for the large majority of respectable voters.

Well before Roosevelt's Madison Square Garden address, John had drifted away from the Liberty League. He still kept in communication and he still sent checks, but his heart was not in it. Increasingly, he came to wish that he had stuck to his repeated promise to stay out of politics. He did ardently believe that the New Deal was dangerous and that Roosevelt had allowed himself to become a demagogue trading in class warfare. But he also believed that his effort to fight the New Deal had resulted in too little success for the effort expended.

Raskob's mental fatigue over the Liberty League and politics was overshadowed the summer of 1936 by a serious physical ailment. Raskob took off in July for an extended trip through the American West. The plan was to travel for several weeks, including long sojourns in Yellowstone and Glacier National Park. On the train westward, just before stopping in Omaha, Raskob felt a pain in his knee. He figured it was just stiff from sitting too long, so he got off the train and took a fast walk around the station. Two hours later, back on the train, he was in agony. After a night of fitful sleep, he woke up feverish. He was so weak he could barely sit up. He was taken off the train in a wheelchair and brought to the closest hospital in Idaho Falls.

For the next three weeks, he was bedridden while the doctors tried to figure out what was wrong with him. He grew increasingly worse. Finally his doctor in New York, William Sullivan, was able to convince the local doctors that Raskob was suffering from a severe staph infection that had spread to his knee, which he must have injured somehow on the train trip. Raskob had been treated for a very mild staph infection by Sullivan in March. Sullivan deduced that the infection had not been killed, as he had thought, but had only gone into hiding. With no antibiotics yet available to treat the bacterial infection, Raskob was in serious danger of sepsis. At least according to Raskob's reports to friends, Doctor Sullivan "had made a serum from the previous infection" and had this serum shipped to Idaho Falls. The doctors then started a series of injections, which Sullivan, at least, "thinks perhaps saved my life."[57] Raskob did start recovering in late August and, accompanied by a nurse, was able to return to New York, where he went directly to St. Vincent's Hospital. He spent several more weeks in bed where he was visited regularly by his children and many of his friends including Francis Spellman. Spellman reported Raskob's troubles to the Vatican and then wrote Raskob that "the Holy Father was grieved by your illness and was praying for your speedy recovery."[58] No doubt cheered by the Pope's well wishes, John began a long process of physical therapy to regain his strength and flexibility in his knee.

Raskob had never before been confined to bed. He told everyone that he was immeasurably impatient with the process. In early November, despite a disciplined approach to his physical therapy, he was still in recovery, making his way around only with crutches. He had yet to return to his Empire State Building office. Nor had he rejoined the Liberty League election-year attack on Roosevelt and the New Deal, though he did foot the bill for Al Smith's vitriolic anti-Roosevelt national radio speech made right before the election.

Instead, Raskob went up to the Mayo Clinic in Minnesota and spent more time getting checked out from top to bottom.

John hated his months of illness and recovery, but he showed no displeasure about missing the last months of the presidential campaign. Almost from the start of the fall campaign few political pros doubted Roosevelt's reelection. Raskob knew what was coming. Roosevelt won nearly 61 percent of the popular vote and 523 electoral votes; the best election showing since 1820 when James Monroe had essentially run unopposed. Raskob actually claimed to be pleased with the outcome. To his old GMAC compatriot Curtis Cooper, who had just left the hurly-burly of both business and politics to start an idyllic life ranching in Sulpher Springs Valley in Arizona, on the western edge of the Coronado National Forest, John wrote, "While I was against him [FDR], I think God was good to us in causing the election of Roosevelt for another term, for the reason that if the things he is doing are economically unsound, their unsoundness is bound to demonstrate itself and, if this demonstration occurs with him in power, the people will place the blame where it properly belongs and the New Deal will be dead forever." Raskob concluded, "If however he had been defeated, and after his defeat, the fallacies of the things he has done were demonstrated via the route of another depression or whatnot, the people would blame the whole thing on the Republican Party and say that when Roosevelt was in he made his plans work."[59] Raskob believed what he wrote; he had no reason to spin an upbeat version for Cooper who was living far from the political storm. While Raskob, by late 1936, had no affection left for Franklin Roosevelt and the New Deal, he really was going to keep his distance from the political stage. The Liberty League would limp along for a few more years and Raskob would send in donations and continue to serve in an advisory position, but Shouse and the professional staff would run the organization until finally John and the other funders told them that they would have to find other work. John's last political fight had ended in total defeat. Now, he really would step off the public stage.

The Distant Shore

Raskob could have become depressed by his change in status. In the long hours with which he suddenly had to contend he could have obsessed about his finances, become bitter over his political failure, agonized over his banishment from the inner chambers of General Motors, ruminated over what had gone wrong in his marriage. Characteristically, he did not. Mostly, Raskob felt freed. He was free to come out from under many, if not all, of the organizational pressures and responsibilities he had long shouldered. He was free to be a private man. He was free to reinvent himself one more time. Starting in the late 1920s, when asked to give his occupation, Raskob simply called himself a capitalist. And a capitalist, Raskob believed, had to know that there were no straight lines in business or in life.

While the economic travails the Empire State Building put him through, even into the early 1940s, were not welcome, Raskob managed them calmly and remained rightly optimistic about the value, financial and personal, of his grand adventure in the skyscraper business. Although his fortunes would go up and down and personal and policy attacks from his political enemies would on occasion enrage him and drive him back briefly into the public arena, in his final years of life Raskob would find peace and pleasure and reward in the challenges he created for himself. Up until the end, Raskob kept doing things. He kept imagining that his next enterprise or his newest investment would produce another fortune and that his latest project would prove rewarding for everyone he had invited to the game.

Raskob was not lying around idly during the last half of the 1930s. The Empire State Building needed constant financial attention. He and Pierre worked out a complicated arrangement to keep the building solvent while also allowing du Pont to walk away whole from the still precarious state of the building's finances. That Pierre and John were able to work out the complex buyout of du Pont's interest with almost no friction was a testimony to the undying strength of their bond. Raskob remained on the boards of both GM and the DuPont Company, and he took his duties at both companies seriously, though he no longer sought to make corporate policy or engineer financial deals. He had instead thrown himself into several new business ventures, though instead of investing millions, he risked only hundreds of thousands in each.

Most significantly, beginning in 1934, he began buying up mines in the West. Anticipating inflationary pressure due to New Deal spending, and gambling that new technologies would allow the old silver mines to become productive again, Raskob started investing. In these mining ventures he also saw an opportunity to find useful and potentially lucrative work for his oldest sons who were having difficulties finding their own way economically. His oldest two sons would be put in charge of the mining ventures. The mines never made money nor did the work experience lead directly to economic self-sufficiency for his sons but Raskob, at least, thought he had done what he could in that direction. His eldest son and his namesake, known as Jun for Junior, would be a source of some continuing consternation for Raskob. Jun had inherited not his father's business genius but his eye for good-looking women.

John's western tilt also included some serious land speculation. In New York in 1930, Bessy Marbury, who knew everybody who was anybody, had introduced John to Tom Campbell, the "wheat king" of Montana. The two men hit it off. In the mid-1930s, Campbell interested Raskob in bargain-priced scrub lands in the West that new federal agricultural subsidy and conservation plans were making potentially profitable. Together they began buying up hundreds of thousands of acres of land on the east flank of the Sandia Mountains, near Albuquerque in New Mexico. This venture turned out financially no better than the silver mines, though Raskob did mostly enjoy the experience. Campbell was a world-class can-do character, a Raskob kind of man. During World War I, Campbell had first convinced the federal government to turn over 200,000 acres of Montana land to him and then the Morgan bankers to lend him $2 million so that he could create the most productive wheat farm the world had ever seen. Campbell spent over $1 million on machinery, some of which he devised, and then made his fortune growing wheat on this mechanized wonderland. He became, as a result, internationally famous, a kind of agricultural Henry Ford.[1] Raskob's business operation with Campbell never quite got off the ground, mostly because the land was so arid but also because local *Hispanos* had long used the area to graze their livestock and had no interest in stopping, nor did local authorities intend to help Campbell or Raskob police their holdings. Campbell had never fully figured out how to make any money out of the land beyond applying for federal subsidy payments of one kind or another, and these did not add up sufficiently to justify the cost of the land.

While Raskob and Campbell had numerous friendly and only occasionally testy communications about getting a reasonable return on their investment, mostly they seemed to just enjoy the opportunity to spend time together. In the summer of 1937 both men excused themselves from their other responsibilities and took off for an extended motor trip that took them to Bryce and Zion National Parks and the Grand Canyon. With a sense of high adventure the two men drove through unpaved Navajo country all the way to Mesa Verde. John wrote gleefully to his favorite new Westerner, Curtis Cooper: "Fortunately it did not rain and we got through without any trouble but it certainly is not a road to advise any tenderfoot to take."[2]

John's mining and land investments were meant to make money—and in the case of the mining ventures to provide employment for his sons—but mostly they were just his way to justify spending time roaming through the great American West, a part of the world he had fallen in love with back in the early years of the twentieth century during his cross-country railroad trip with Pierre du Pont. By the summer of 1937, Raskob's knee was fine and he loved taking long walks through America's national parks and reveling in the wonder of the landscape. Having a business destination made the sightseeing even more pleasurable as he could take time off from one kind fun for another, looking over accounts, playing with columns of numbers, and giving his various underlings, including his sons, advice on what needed to be done. Given the relatively low cost of the western investments, the stakes were not that high and he really did not have to sweat the bottom line.

Raskob loved motoring and he thought nothing of driving hundreds of miles a day along his ever-carefully plotted itineraries. He also got to play the big man at the local cafes, especially when a pretty waitress caught his fancy. The newspapers got wind of one of these occasions when in god-forsaken Sonora, Texas, probably with Campbell, a western-bound Raskob stopped at the local café for a 25 cent lunch. They were served by the attractive young Eleanor Hanson. Raskob introduced himself and upon leaving placed a twenty dollar bill under his plate. She was thrilled and told the local papers whereupon the tale went national.[3] Along the same lines, Raskob loved surprising his favorite daughter-in-law Minerva at her home in New Mexico and asking her to bake his favorite pie. Raskob, the man who had worked so hard for so long to become a Big Man in the East spent much of the latter part of the 1930s and into the early 1940s wandering the West, usually with a friend in tow, enjoying the lonely landscapes, and the occasional pretty woman.

Throughout these years and well into the 1940s, Raskob also wintered in the West. Beginning in the early 1930s he had switched allegiance from Palm Beach, Florida, to Palm Springs, California. That Palm Beach was where he had always traveled with Helena must have played a major role in John's decision to go somewhere else after their trips together came to an end. John always stayed at the luxurious El Mirador, hotspot for Hollywood types and other racy sorts, and he became a winter regular, year-after-year, in the thick of the action, wearing oversized cowboy hats and long walking shorts, dancing, drinking silly cock-tails, and playing cards and plenty of golf for modest stakes. In the late 1930s he bought several thousand acres of land outside Palm Springs with vague plans of developing a residential community. Such investments were almost habit; he did little to move the project forward. The investment did, however, provide John with a bit of casually enticing business activity to break up his comfortable daily recreational routine.

At the end of the 1930s, Raskob was at peace. He had not come to that peace without setbacks. In 1937 he, along with Pierre du Pont, suffered some serious attacks from the Roosevelt Administration. In particular the Treasury Department had come after him and Pierre for the wash trades they had engineered in 1929 and 1930 to safeguard their long-term stock portfolios from tax liability after the Crash. The government had accused them of an illegal attempt to defraud the government of capital gains taxes. Government bureaucrats demanded that Raskob fork over more than a million dollars in back taxes and threatened seri-ous penalties, as well. The matter made headlines across the nation and then wound its way through the courts. John felt the matter was entirely political and his enmity toward Roosevelt and the New Deal became undying. Still, even as John bitterly organized his holdings to assure that he could come up with more than a million in cash, he largely compartmentalized his feelings toward the gov-ernment. Mostly, he just felt good as he turned sixty.

Shortly before his sixtieth birthday, John got in touch with Bill Kenny, who had retired to Florida. Kenny was really the only member of the old Golf Cabinet with whom he had stayed close. Kenny, a decade older than John, told Raskob he was still doing just fine. John was cheered that his old friend was healthy and that he had begun a daily constitutional. John gave his own report: "Yesterday I walked down to the office, four miles, walked back at night, four miles, and took a five mile walk in the evening. I merely tell this to you so you can appreciate what a 'piker' you are." Kenny, a New Yorker to the bone, must have known that Raskob was exaggerating the distance from his apartment on East End to the Empire State Building. Raskob then let Kenny know that he was eating "any-thing that comes my way" and, in sum, enjoying perfect health.[4]

The advent of World War II largely left Raskob unmoved. Even as all of his sons joined the military—with his youngest boy, Ben, eventually seeing action in Guadalcanal—Raskob seemed untouched by both the horror of the war and the patriotic fervor that affected most Americans. Unlike during the World War I, when he had played a vital role in bond drives and wartime fund-raising, he kept his distance. His few public comments on the war revealed both his anti-Nazi feelings and an uncharacteristic unwillingness to take action. In late 1938, just after *Kristallnacht*, reporters asked Raskob, as he disembarked from a train that had taken him from New York to Los Angeles on his way to Palm Springs, what he thought of deteriorating events in Europe and he told them, "The German situation is atrocious and seems like a bad dream."[5] However, the man who had spent decades using his once prodigious energy to turn his own dreams into reality chose to do nothing about this nightmare.

Raskob never explained his reticence in joining the great prewar debate about American intervention or his unwillingness to aid in the actual war effort. Perhaps it was the fierce divisions between his closest friends that disinclined him to become involved in the prewar debates. Al Smith became an early and outspoken anti-Nazi and a public champion of American intervention. Pierre and Irénée du Pont, along with Alfred Sloan, remained firmly opposed to American involvement. Before the Pearl Harbor attack, Irénée wrote privately to Pierre: "Mr. Roosevelt is capable of trying to embroil this country in war for the purpose of having himself made dictator by force."[6] Even after Pearl Harbor, Pierre, Irénée, and Sloan never became strong supporters of the war effort—mostly out of their animosity toward Franklin Roosevelt. John shared their anti-Roosevelt animus, though characteristically he was at least slightly more optimistic that American voters would repudiate Roosevelt before it was too late. In 1940 he wrote Pierre, "Personally, I am beginning to feel that the people of the United States are appreciating the dangers of various New Deal 'isms' to the extent that there will be a rapid change in laws in evolution that will almost amount to a revolution, thus avoiding the actual revolution that otherwise would come in the course of a few more years."[7] That same year, Raskob did become financially involved in an airplane company that made gliders for the war effort—mainly because one of his sons-in-law held a major executive role in the company—but John let the war against fascism go on without him. Although anti-Roosevelt politics probably played a role in that decision, mostly John had just fundamentally pulled back from public affairs of all kinds.

Instead, after years of only intermittent concern, John focused more on his family life. He relished visits from his daughters, who began to spend more time with him in his New York apartment. He demonstrated a less affectionate side to his sons as he continued to pay close attention to their often less-than-successful business affairs. He also began to attend to his increasing number of sons-in-law, most of whom proved to be better suited to the business world John knew so well. As ever, John was blunt about any shortcomings he perceived. Joseph Geuting, his son-in-law involved in the airplane company in which Raskob had invested, drew his most direct scrutiny.

In his pointed letters to Geuting, Raskob revealed how he saw his own life in business and what he had learned after more than four decades. Don't be a prima donna, Raskob wrote, and stop complaining so much. No one wants to hear it. The trick to advancing yourself is to become indispensable to the men around you. Raskob then told his son-in-law not to "sulk" after reading his hard-nosed advice. He should buck up and do what Raskob said he should do. Raskob assured Geuting that he knew what he was talking about. For the first time in any of his letters to his hundreds of correspondents Raskob made a blunt appraisal of his own achievements and experience: "There are few men who have had a broader or vaster experience in corporate affairs and management, that have keener appreciation and realization of the necessity of swallowing pride and being humble and working with the team, than I." Raskob went on, explaining that a businessman, especially a highly placed one, should "not sit in meetings, chewing the rug and wasting valuable time instead of crystallizing your views." To get your point of view across, he told his son-in-law, write clear and compelling reports. Distribute them to the people that matter; get or hold a meeting; make your case; and then resolve the matter without delay. Then, win or lose, live by the decision made. That's how it's done, Raskob concluded, "That is the way the du Pont Company and General Motors Corporation and every other company of which I have been a director have always run their business."[8] John rarely gave such direct advice but when he did he made it loud and clear.

In the early 1940s Raskob worried some about his expansive family's varied life courses but he worried more about money. He feared that the IRS was going to finally win their large tax case against him and that he would need at least one million in cash to satisfy its demands. He was right. In 1941 the Supreme Court refused to hear Raskob's appeal and he was forced to pay $1,450,000; the government was not interested in creative financing, either—the money had to be paid in cash immediately. Despite spirited efforts by Raskob and Al Smith, still president of the Empire State Building, to find tenants for what people still mocked as the Empty State Building, Raskob's investment in the building remained deep in the red. In 1938, Raskob had taken over Pierre's investment to the tune of $8.5 million—using much of his GM stock as collateral for the deal. Most of Raskob's remaining wealth was tied up in the building's fortunes. Beginning in early 1942 and continuing into 1944, Raskob and Smith were trying, without success, to sell the building. Money was not that tight, at least not in the sense that the non-rich would understand, but Raskob pared down his expenses in the first half of the 1940s. A small example: in 1929 John spent $3,225.25 on flowers and $2,129 on books. In 1942, the fresh flower account, meticulously kept as always, shows a total of just $229 and the book receipts added up to only $224.[9] Raskob had no certainty during the war years that his fortune would remain intact and he spent accordingly.

Due to rationing and other restrictions, Raskob curtailed his travels and began to spend most of his time in New York, with regular weekend sojourns to Pioneer Point. While he and Helena were sometimes together in Maryland, increasingly Helena was living out West in Tucson. Helena had long suffered from asthma and the dry air of Arizona was a curative. She and Jack spent longer and longer periods of time together there. In early 1942, Jack sold his hunting lodge in North Carolina and bought 4,600 acres of land near Tucson to set up a new Camp Melody Pine. Helena used her holdings in Archmere, Inc. to lend Jack the money. She also established a home in Tucson. Together Jack and Helena went horseback riding and spent long stretches outdoors enjoying the mountain air. Increasingly, Helena focused her philanthropic efforts on the Arizona Catholic community. Somehow, John and Helena seemed to have had no major difficulties in maintaining a cordial and affectionate relationship when they were together, even as Jack Corcoran's role in Helena's life became obvious if never openly stated. Helena even arranged to send John fresh cut flowers every other week to brighten his offices at the Empire State Building.

In 1945, John's old friend Frank Spellman urged Raskob, who was now sixty-five years old, to throw himself into one more venture. Spellman was by this time a powerful force in American life. His role in the Church had taken a spectacular turn since he and John had first become friends in the late 1920s. After his time at the Vatican, Spellman had spent some uneasy years in the Boston archdiocese. Then Spellman's patron, Eugenio Maria Giuseppe Giovanni Pacelli, who had been Vatican Cardinal Secretary of State, became Pope Pius XII in March 1939. Weeks later, Spellman was named Archbishop of New York. During the war, Spellman found even more use for his abundant talents; President Roosevelt, well aware of Spellman's work for the Vatican Secretary of State, asked the Archbishop to undertake an array of diplomatic missions in Europe and elsewhere for the Administration. By war's end Spellman was the nation's preeminent Catholic powerbroker. Raskob was proud of his friend's rise. Despite the different trajectories of the two men's lives, they remained close. Raskob was eager to serve his bishop, especially given the nature of Spellman's request. He wanted John to help the Church memorialize Al Smith who had died October 4, 1944, at the age of seventy.

Smith's last six months of life had been rough. He had been deeply depressed since his wife's death in May. John and Al's other good friends had been as attentive during Al's months of grief. In early August, John decided that something more was wrong with Smith than depression. From the Empire State Building, John wrote Smith's old lieutenant, Robert Moses: "I am really worried about Governor Smith. He feels miserable and is home today."[10] A few days after that letter was posted, Smith was in the hospital; he would never go home again. John, often accompanied by Pierre du Pont, went at least once a week to sit at Governor Smith's bedside. This routine went on for nearly two months as the doctors debated over his condition and Smith's health deteriorated. The evening of October 2, John was with Al and watched over him as he lapsed in and out of consciousness; during his lucid moments, he prayed. Two days later Governor Smith died.

Archbishop Spellman had then taken charge. Smith's body lay in state at St. Patrick's Cathedral, where more than 150,000 people filed by to pay their last respects to the "Happy Warrior." Despite his turn against Roosevelt and the New Deal, New Yorkers still loved Governor Smith. The next day John was one of the 7,000 mourners who gathered inside the Cathedral to attend a memorial mass, while another 35,000 stood outside. Cardinal Spellman, never a man to waste an opportunity, soon thereafter began to organize the Alfred E. Smith Memorial Foundation to raise money for Catholic causes in the Archdiocese of New York. Spellman's first goal was to renovate St. Vincent's Hospital, founded by the Sisters of Charity in 1849 to help New York's poor Catholic immigrants. Spellman planned to build a new wing for the hospital to be named after Smith; he asked John to help him. Raskob went to work raising money for a cause that could not have been dearer to his heart. In 1945, John spent hours with Spellman working out the $3 million dollar hospital project's financing and construction. He also met regularly with his old friends John Davis, Bernard Baruch, Thomas Lamont, and even Herbert Hoover, all of whom had signed on to the effort.

Raskob's work with Spellman and the Smith Foundation seems to have focused his mind on his own legacy. In late 1945, John began talking with Helena about setting up a family Catholic charitable foundation. Here was a subject where their hearts were still in the same place. Helena was enthusiastic and John moved quickly forward, working out the legal and financial issues. The Raskob Foundation for Catholic Activities (RFCA) was established in December 1945 with John as president and Helena and John's secretary as the only two other trustees. The new foundation's first meeting was held the day after Christmas 1945 at the du Pont Building in Wilmington; Helena was in Arizona.

In setting up the foundation, Raskob hoped to put into practice several of his long-held beliefs. Building on his work with the trust he had set up for the Wilmington archdiocese nearly twenty years earlier, Raskob went much further in insulating this charitable organization, as well as its grant-making process from the Church. No member of the clergy could directly serve the Foundation. Raskob established that only laymen of either sex who professed the Roman Catholic faith were eligible for membership or could serve as trustees of the RFCA.[11]

John wrote a long letter to Helena in early 1946 spelling out his views on the foundation. It was imperative, he noted, "to find an experienced man who could take hold of this [foundation] and operate it in an intelligent way" and "make a study of the manner in which funds could be best used for building up the Catholic religion." John then reiterated—as if for the record—the views on charity he had long held and that he had preached on more than one occasion to Pierre du Pont. "The great difficulty in work of this kind," he wrote his wife, "is to avoid making donations and contributions to things which could be secured from small contributions among Catholic people had not some large contribution been received. The way to be successful in anything is to get people so interested in it that they are willing to make contributions and thus half of the effort [should?] cost them something." He then complained, probably not for the first time, that he and Helena (and by that he really meant Helena) had erred in giving too much money to the parish in Centreville, Maryland; they should have used matching grants or some other tool to leverage local donations and thus the local priest's and the local parishioners' commitment to their own church. "A test of real charity," he continued, "is whether one is teaching people to help themselves or helping people to help themselves. Thus one is on guard every minute less things done may be the reverse of charity."[12] Helena, at least in writing, voiced no objections to John's views. Later that year, she donated over $1 million of her money—in the form of about 10 percent of her shares in Archmere Inc. Helena specified that the money should be used to aid the Roman Catholic Church in its religious, educational, charitable, and other works. John also added an Empire State Building interest-bearing bond worth more than $1 million to the RFCA's assets. These gifts were just the beginning.

That same year John attached to his will a new statement "To the Present and Future Trustees of Raskob Foundation for Catholic Activities (Inc.)," further spelling out his wishes. Raskob stated that he would leave almost his entire estate to the RFCA. In doing so, he was not rejecting his family. Helena and the children had already been well provided for; their share of the Empire State Building, for example, almost equaled his. John provided bequests for each of his grandchildren, as well as for his longtime valet Mike Valdez and his loyal assistant Frank Gehrey. But John had decided that he wanted the Foundation's philanthropic mission and not his money to be the tie that bound together his family. He wrote in his statement that he wanted his descendents to manage the Foundation: "As of the present time a majority of the Trustees of the Foundation are members of the Raskob family and I hope that this condition will continue."[13] Raskob hoped that the RFCA could offer his many descendents a common purpose that would bring them together across the generations in commitment to each other and to the Catholic faith that had always been John's anchor in his turbulent life. As John looked back at his life, he chose his Catholic faith and his family, not his conservative politics or his capitalist endeavors, as the focal point for his final legacy.

In 1946, at the age of sixty-seven, John was thinking about death but he was not yet finished. He did admit to his close friends that he was slowing down, that year he resigned from the boards of both General Motors and DuPont. He had thought it prudent to wait until the war ended, he wrote Pierre, but the time had now come: "I am so out of the atmosphere of the company's operations that I can contribute little or nothing and should not burden myself with the serious responsibilities which directors assume nowadays." It was not easy for John to give up his long, if attenuated corporate connections.

In his last years, John wrote his friends, particularly Pierre, several letters reminiscing about their shared corporate adventures, especially the triumphant takeover and makeover of General Motors. In the end he could laugh at the zeal he had brought to all things GM but, above all, he was proud of his reasoned faith in a car company that others, again and again, had written off. In 1947, he sent Pierre a newspaper clipping that listed the top manufacturing companies in the United States. GM was on top, followed by US Steel, and in third place was the DuPont Company. How different things had looked before John and Pierre had gone to work at the advent of the twentieth century. In a letter, accompanying the clipping, John reminded Pierre about the time in early 1925 when he and the Morgan men Tom Cochran and George Whitney had gone to Detroit to acquire the Dodge Company for GM. They had lost out—"fortunately," John noted—in a bidding war with Dillon Read, which soon after sold Dodge to Walter Chrysler. On the train ride back to New York, John remembered, "Tom knowing I was bubbling over with enthusiasm for General Motors started kidding me trying to make believe it was a third or fourth rate concern. I remember George Whitney warned him that he was playing with fire and I just laughed but after we got home I wrote Tom a long letter supported by a great deal of statistical data. I headed the letter 'HAVE FAITH IN GENERAL MOTORS.'" John recounted the rest of the story, how he had then distributed the data he had first sent Tom Cochran in a formal report internally at GM and then to useful outside interests. "That report," John recalled, "resulted in General Motors, as an investment, jumping over pretty near everything else in the eyes of the Morgan, First National, Bankers Trust and Guaranty Trust groups and soon permeated Wall Street generally. It was like a lot of men suddenly discovering or realizing that they had a fine looking girl in their midst, which fact they had not appreciated before."[14] John had never been the kind of man who ignored a "fine looking girl." He had spotted GM well before most and he still remembered how the company had first looked to him in all its statistical glory back in 1915; the numbers still dazzled him.

Even as he closed down some parts of his life, John did not just look backward. It was not his way. He had gotten wind of speculative gold, silver, and copper operations in Mexcala, some 250 miles south of Mexico City. The Mexican owners were looking for American capital. In 1946 Raskob began to invest heavily—though again in amounts of hundreds of thousands and not millions. Soon John took over the mining venture. He refinanced and reorganized the newly established Compania Minera de Mexcala. John named himself president of this new venture. Once again his desk at the Empire State Building was covered in financial statements, operating budgets, and reports. Unfortunately, Compania

Minera de Mexcala was plagued with labor actions, squabbles between investors, Mexican government difficulties, and, worst of all, a lack of rich claims. John was frustrated by the troubles but he was also, suddenly, busy again. Now he had to visit Mexico regularly, as well as the American West. It was good to be on the move, solving problems and looking to make new money. It was an expensive hobby but he loved it. And as he wrote Pierre in the summer of 1948, grumpy as ever about the political situation in the United States and worried that Truman might just pull off his presidential bid, it was good to have property in Mexico, for that way "we still can go down there to live if everything goes to pot in this country." He added, "I can see you smile as you read all of the above."[15] The two men had been friends for nearly half a century.

In early 1950, at the age of seventy, John decided he wanted to see Europe again. He began making elaborate plans for a grand motor trip with his brother and sister-in-law, three of his daughters, and one of his granddaughters. John also included his faithful valet Mike Valdez. Everything would be done first-class from the voyage on the SS America to the two private chauffeur-driven autos he arranged.

They left March 14, 1950, just a few days before John's 71st birthday. In France, after resting up at the Hotel Crillon in Paris, Raskob took everyone to the Folies Bergère. Once they departed Paris, Raskob decreed that, as a rule, they would stay in no place longer than one day. Most days included a good deal of fast marching between sites and frantic driving. A particularly Raskobian day had the following stops: Maintenon, Chartres, Bonneval, Fontaine, Vendome, Tours, St. Maure, Chateauroux, and Poitier. While the visit to Lourdes was quick, it was memorable. They all prayed at the shrine where Mary appeared to the child Bernadette and then they silently studied the "ex-votos" left by people who had been miraculously cured of their ailments (Raskob's granddaughter Patsy would later become a nun). Soon after, they gambled in Monaco (Raskob bribed the doormen so his granddaughter could accompany them). In Italy they saw Florence and Venice—one day each. Rome got three days—possibly the family rebelled against John's pace. In Switzerland they relaxed at the Hotel Schweizerhof in Lucerne and then back to Paris, then London and the SS America home. It was John's last whirlwind extravaganza.[16]

In the fall of 1950, John's thoughts turned more and more to the past. On October 13, 1950, John wrote his old friend Rodney Sharp from his desk at the Empire State Building: "It seems only yesterday that Pierre and I, sitting at the table we always occupied in the DuPont Hotel dining room, discussed plans to purchase Coleman's stock which Pierre told me about." Two days later, John was entertaining his oldest friend, Will Bewley, at Pioneer Point. John and Will had never lost touch with one another but over the previous two years they had become once again intimate friends, passing the time together remembering their old crowd in Lockport and revisiting their boyhood days. That night, Will and John were sitting comfortably, reminiscing, when John suddenly collapsed and crumpled to the floor. His oldest friend gathered him in his arms.

John's funeral service was held at the church in Centerville that he and Helena had built. Bishop FitzMaurice, John's old friend and beneficiary, presided. He told John's friends and family that, as the Raskobs had requested, no eulogy would be given. The Bishop agreed, "This, too, I feel, would be the wish of Mr. Raskob, could he express himself on the subject, for he was ever the most modest, unassuming, and self effacing of men."[17] Just after the service ended, as people gathered outside the church, they saw a strange and wonderful sight. Behind a broken-down auto—not a General Motors car, everyone noted—being slowly pushed along the road by its chauffeur walked eighty-one-year-old Pierre du Pont and his two younger brothers, Lammot and Irénée. Tired but unbeaten they had come to pay their last respects to their friend.

In December 1951 a real estate syndicate bought out the Raskobs' interest in the Empire State Building for some $51 million, the largest sum ever paid for a building. John's estate owned 44 percent of the building and his family had another 36 percent. John's last great capitalist adventure had, after years in the red, finally begun making money—netting around $5 million the prior fiscal year (decades later, in the twenty-first century, the Empire State Building's observation deck and antenna alone generated about $65 million in annual profits and in 2012 the skyscraper's appraised value was $2.52 billion). The sale of the building guaranteed the Raskob Foundation for Catholic Activities a sizable endowment. John would have loved the final deal-signing ceremony. It was so complicated and involved so many people that a dress rehearsal had been staged the day before the actual transaction to be sure it would go smoothly. Some seventy-five buyers, sellers, attorneys, bankers, real estate men, insurance executives, brokers, and other sundry experts gathered at the Bankers Trust Company in Wall Street to sign off on the sale. *Life* magazine ran a picture of the assemblage with an article titled "104 Steps, 600 Documents—And a Skyscraper is Sold."[18] John, of course, had pulled off the original deal almost entirely on his own.

On July 15, 1952, Helena Raskob married John Corcoran. John and Helena's family, their ten surviving children, and their growing number of grandchildren, were by that time scattered across the country. Some had settled near Skipper in New Mexico and Arizona, while others had settled in John's old northeastern turf. Every year, ever since, this ever larger family, across the generations, gathers together as John had hoped to debate how best to give away the money John and Helena had bequeathed to the Raskob Foundation for Catholic Activities. Together they have distributed more than $150 million in grants to Catholic organizations around the world.

Raskob had never sought fame, and in history books and popular memory he never received it. But in his quiet, almost always behind the scenes way, he had forever changed America's political, religious, and economic landscape. From his home behind his father's little cigar business in Lockport to his wood paneled offices high above Manhattan, John had made for himself an extraordinary American adventure. And he had fun doing it.

NOTES

Introduction

1. "A New Captain of Industry: A Rising Luminary of Industry and His Vast Orbit," *Current Opinion* 69 (November 1920), 627.

2. Alan Temple, "The Finance Chief of General Motors," *Commerce and Finance* 16 (January 5, 1927), 11.

3. The phrase "ill-timed words" is used by Rob Wherry in his pithy profile "Rethinking Raskob," *Forbes* 166:10 (October 9, 2000), 64. Wherry's article, one of the very few recent assessments of Raskob, greatly contributed to my thinking about Raskob's legacy. The best put-down of Raskob in a recently published book because of his five-word declaration is by Steve Fraser in *Every Man a Speculator* (New York: HarperCollins, 2005), his tour de force historical critique of Wall Street speculators and the political economy they generated. After describing the great fall of several of the Wall Street kings of the 1920s, he writes, "The fall of these men . . . became more than an object lesson in greed and hubris. They were the living refutation of 'new era' hype, of John Jakob Raskob's 'Everybody Ought to Be Rich' fairy tale, of Wall Street as the yellow brick road to fun, fame, and fortune" (422).

4. Edwin C. Hill, "First Got Pierre S. du Pont to Buy Its Stock, Then Induced Company Executives to Load Up with It," *New York Sun*, n.d. [1919?], 1–2, Clippings, John J. Raskob Archive (JR), Hagley Library, Wilmington, Delaware.

5. The social and cultural journey of Americans from the economic backwaters to the new corporate economic centers is deftly explored in Alan Trachtenberg's *The Incorporation of America* (New York: Hill and Wang, 1982) and in Olivier Zunz, *Making America Corporate, 1870–1920* (Chicago: University of Chicago Press, 1992).

6. Samuel Crowther, "John J. Raskob, and the World's Largest Business," *The World's Work* 40:6 (October 1920), 612.

7. Such books do exist, for example the celebratory accounts given by John Steele Gordon in *An Empire of Wealth: The Epic Story of American Economic Power* (New York: Harper, 2004) and the more analytic work by Maury Klein, *The Change Makers: From Carnegie to Gates* (New York: Times Books, 2003), Charles Morris, *The Tycoons* (New York: Times Books, 2005), Robert E. Wright and David J. Cowen, *Financial Founding Fathers* (Chicago: University of Chicago Press, 2006), and my more narrow account, *Sloan Rules* (Chicago: University of Chicago Press, 2003), but they have not gained much currency in academic historical scholarship or, especially, in the textbooks that guide the teaching of American history. A new turn, however, among academic historians toward the writing of the history of capitalism has begun in earnest. Many of these new histories of capitalism focus on the transnational history of capitalism and look more at the flow of commodities and structure of markets than they do at the particular reach of individual capitalists and entrepreneurs.

Sven Beckert has written several major works in the field including: *The Monied Metropolis: New York City and the Consolidation of the American Bourgeoisie* (New York: Cambridge University Press, 2001) and "Emancipation and Empire: Reconstructing the Worldwide Web of Cotton Production in the Age of the American Civil War" in *American Historical Review* 109 (December 2004), 1405–38. Another important work focused on the role of businessmen in the making of the modern conservative movement is by Kim Phillips-Fein, *Invisible Hands* (New York: Norton, 2009). Also important in exploring the rise of mass ownership of equities in the United States is Julia Ott, *When Wall Street Met Main Street* (Cambridge, Mass.: Harvard University Press, 2011). An older work that figures importantly in my study is Robert F. Burk's *The Corporate State and the Broker State* (Cambridge, Mass.: Harvard University Press, 1990). I draw heavily on Burk's pathbreaking work on the du Pont group's attempts to influence politics in the 1920s and 1930s. While he and I agree on many things, he sees their anti-Prohibition effort as a stalking-horse for a more general attempt to assert a powerful control over the federal government; whereas, I see a far less purposeful and well-conceived struggle. I see Raskob and the du Ponts as engaged in a struggle to understand democratic practice and find useful tools both to influence and participate in a political system that often baffled and frustrated them as it countered their goals and interests. Burk sees this process, too, but is more focused on arguing that they meant to construct an alternative to the Progressive and then New Deal state. We disagree more on emphasis and process than in a fundamentally substantive way about their political efforts in the 1925 to 1936 period. I am simply more interested in exploring how a particular capitalist, John Raskob, learned to use his power in elite circles and how, where, and why he failed and succeeded. Like Burk and unlike some others who have argued that corporate interests fundamentally had their way in the New Deal, e.g., Colin Gordon, *New Deals* (New York: Cambridge University Press, 1994), I see the efforts of Raskob and his close circle as having mainly failed to sway New Dealers even as he and his corporate allies had great success in shaping the consumer capitalist system that so powerfully structured economic, social, and cultural life in modern American history. I made a related argument in *Sloan Rules* when looking at the life and work of Alfred P. Sloan and the rise of General Motors.

8. The framed sign now hangs in the Raskob Foundation for Catholic Activities building just outside Wilmington, Delaware.

9. Surprisingly little has been written about Raskob's role in the forging of the credit revolution, in general, or even in the making of the General Motors Acceptance Corporation. Raskob does appear in a significant role in Louis Hyman, *Debtor Nation: The History of America in Red Ink* (Princeton: Princeton University Press, 2011).

10. I am influenced in this formulation by the work of Jennifer Klein, *For All These Rights: Business, Labor and the Shaping of America's Public–Private Welfare State* (Princeton: Princeton University Press, 2003); Klein explains how "the ideology of security" launched by the New Deal structured a public–private competition to provide various forms of social insurance and provision. Raskob hated not just the specific New Deal welfare state programs but this entire social construct.

Chapter 1

1. The material on the Morans and Raskobs comes from sleuthing among a variety of sources including the 1870 federal census, federal tax records, and Lockport business directories. JJR wrote a letter to his old friend Thomas E. Spalding on August 24, 1917, recounting some family lore, file 2148, JR; also invaluable is the *Raskob–Green Record Book* (Claymont, Del.: Archmere, 1921), a family genealogy and history commissioned by JJR.

2. Some information on the Raskob's family life, including the description of John Raskob, is found in the correspondence between JJR and his cousin Mamie Sandel in file 2034, JR.

3. Carol Sherriff, *The Artificial River* (New York: Hill and Wang, 1996), 117. Throughout my history of the Erie Canal, I rely on Sherriff's superb account.

4. George E. Condon, *Stars in the Water: The Story of the Erie Canal* (Garden City, N.Y.: Doubleday, 1974), 89–90. I have borrowed heavily from Condon's wonderfully written popular history.

5. Sherriff, *The Artificial River*, 35.

6. Richard G. Garruty, *Recollections of the Erie Canal* (Tonawanda, N.Y.: Historical Society of the Tonawandas, Inc., 1966); a priceless testimony of life on the Canal.

7. Gertrude Sanders to John Jakob Raskob (JJR), January 21, 1932, JJR to Gertrude Sanders, February 9, 1932, file 2106, JR; John J. Roberts, "Judge Praises Youth His Brother Employed," *Courier-Express*, July 14, 1914, clippings, JR.

8. Here is a good place to explain how I can confidently write a great deal about John Raskob's life. Raskob, from the age of eighteen onward kept copies of the letters he sent and collected the letters he received. Despite moving around a great deal, he kept these letters and a great many other documents besides, all of which are collected at the Hagley Library. He wrote and received a great many letters, especially to and from his Lockport friends, some of whom he corresponded with all his life. Much of what I wrote about Raskob's early life is drawn from hundreds of such letters.

9. "New York Association of YMCAs," *Christian Advocate*, March 3, 1892, 141.

10. "Catholics Must Hold Aloof," *New York Times*, April 20, 1902. My source is a few years off from JJR's YMCA days in Lockport, but all evidence indicates that the Church's opposition to the Y was in effect earlier and would, indeed, continue for several decades.

11. David A. Lassos, "Catholic Central Union of America," http://genealogyinstlouis.access-genealogy.com/ccua.htm.

12. The account of Raskob working as a candy butcher is drawn from a problematic source, the oral history of the well-known Broadway producer, composer, and actor Eddie Dowling. Dowling and Raskob were very close friends in the 1920s, part of the Governor Al Smith circle, but that friendship ended badly, and Dowling uses his oral history to blast Raskob for a variety of sins. Separating fact from fiction in Dowling's account is not easy. But he does get a lot right and the candy butcher business fits the timeline of Raskob's teenage years. Eddie Dowling, "The Reminiscences of Eddie Dowling," Columbia University Oral History Collection.

13. David Nasaw, *Children of the City* (Garden City, N.Y.: Anchor Press, 1985), 51–52.

14. I am indebted to Patricia A. Cooper, *Once a Cigar Maker: Men, Women, and Work Culture in American Cigar Factories, 1900–1919* (Champagne-Urbana: University of Illinois Press, 1987) and to Tony Hyman, "Cigar History, 1860–1910," http://www.nationalcigarmuseum.com/Cigar_History/History_1860–1910.html, a web page on the essential cigar history website, "National Cigar Museum," created by Hyman, http://www.nationalcigarmuseum.com/Site/NCM_HOME.html.

15. JJR to Frank Dole, January 23, 1901, file 630, JR.

16. Raskob recalls the event in two different letters: JJR to Hazel Thomson, July 21, 1937, file 2258, JR and JJR to Pierre du Pont (PdP), file 303, box 216, Pierre du Pont Papers (PDP), Hagley Library (HL), Wilmington, Delaware.

17. Trentwill M. White, *Famous Leaders of Industry* (Boston: L. C. Page and Company, 1931), 250–52.

18. "John Rascob" [*sic*], *Lockport Daily Union*, June 4, 1898, 5; and "John Rascob" [*sic*], *Lockport Daily Union*, June 6, 1898, 5.

19. JJR to Roy Flagler, January 24, 1902, file 820, JR.

20. J. Roberts, "Judge Praises Youth His Brother Employed."

21. White, *Famous Leaders of Industry*, 253.

22. JJR to S. H. Bunnell, January 12, 1900, file 1849, JR.

23. John E. Pound to Pierre du Pont (PdP), January 23, 1900, file 1849, JR.

24. JJR to PdP, February 10, 1900, file 303, box 216, Pierre du Pont Papers (PDP), Hagley Library.

25. PdP to JJR, February 16, 1900, file 303, box 216, PDP.

26. JRR to PdP, February 17, 1900, file 1849, JR.

27. Alfred D. Chandler, Jr. and Stephen Salisbury, *Pierre S. du Pont and the Making of the Modern Corporation* (New York: Harper & Row, 1971), 23. I draw heavily on this path-breaking biography throughout the rest of this chapter. I also spoke at length with Alfred Chandler in his Cambridge apartment before his death in 2007 about Pierre du Pont and John Raskob. His thoughts on their relationship figure here, as well.

28. Ibid., 37.
29. JJR to Frank Dole, March 15, 1901, file 630, JR.
30. JJR to Roy Flagler, January 24, 1902, file 820, JR.
31. Ibid.

Chapter 2

1. The history of the second industrial revolution is a complex and contested one. For a tour de force historical critique of the big railroad operators' role in the process of consolidation—and predation—see Richard White, *Railroaded: The Transcontinentals and the Making of Modern America* (New York: Norton, 2011). For the classic and laudatory treatment of the role of managers on the making of the new industrial corporations, Alfred Chandler, *The Visible Hand: The Managerial Revolution in American Business* (Cambridge, Mass.: Belknap Press, 1977). For an instructive work on the role of finance, Ron Chernow, *The House of Morgan* (Boston: Atlantic Monthly Press, 1990). The era of incorporation was not driving all producers toward consolidation and mass production as is cogently explained in Phillip Scranton, *Endless Novelty* (Princeton: Princeton University Press, 2000).

2. David F. Hawkins, "The Development of Modern Financial Reporting Practices among American Manufacturing Corporations," in *The History of American Management*, ed. James Baughman (Englewood Cliffs, N.J.: Prentice Hall, 1969), 106 n. 16.

3. Thomas R. Navin and Marian V. Sears, "The Rise of a Market for Industrial Securities, 1887–1902," *Business History Review* 29:2 (June 1955), 105–38.

4. Moxham alludes to this in a letter to Pierre du Pont (PdP), July 31, 1900, file 681, JR.

5. All based on JJR's correspondence with Sydney DeWitt, file 612, JR.

6. Moxham to PdP, July 31, 1900.

7. From the several letters between PdP and JJR for the summer of 1900, file 681.

8. JJR to Joseph A. Moran, July 10, 1905, file 1586, JR.

9. A. Rae Du Bell, memo of conversation, March 22, 1954, 3, file 303, box 216, Pierre du Pont Papers (PDP), Hagley Library. Du Bell was Raskob's secretary from 1911 to 1919. In February 1954 he began to write a biography of Raskob with the assistance of Pierre du Pont but after du Pont's death in April he gave up the project leaving behind only a frustratingly thin record of the three interviews he had with du Pont about his relationship with Raskob.

10. Ibid., 2.

11. Raskob and du Pont almost always referred to each other by their first names and I shall do likewise in those sections that trace their relationship.

12. Stephen A. Zeff, "How the U.S. Accounting Profession Got Where It Is Today: Part I," *Accounting Horizons* 17:3 (September 2003), 190–91. See also Paul Maranti, *Accounting Comes of Age* (Chapel Hill: University of North Carolina Press, 1990).

13. Quoted in John D. Gates, *The du Pont Family* (Garden City, N.Y.: Doubleday, 1979), 114.

14. The entire story comes from a troublesome source, the oral history of Eddie Dowling, 269–72. Several of the facts are clearly wrong in Dowling's long-winded version and so I corrected to what I knew to be more accurate, for example, the one million dollar investment figure he recalls seems too high so I did not use it; I know that Johnson still owned a controlling interest in the railway as late as 1905. Dowling, a great storyteller with an amazing memory, swears: "John told me this story himself" (271). And it does so perfectly capture the relationship between Raskob and du Pont. For more on the Lorain Street Railway, see Herbert H. Harwood and Robert S. Korach, *The Lake Shore Electric Railway Story* (Bloomington: University of Indiana Press, 2000), 172–74.

15. JJR to John E. Pound, December 18, 1900, file 1849, JR.

16. Sterling Bunnell to JJR, July 9, 1901, file 297, JR.

17. JJR to Robert Allen, February 16, 1901, file 34, JR.

18. JJR to Thomas Spalding, March 15, 1901, and JJR to Tom Spalding, April 24, 1901, file 2148, JR.

19. JR to Roy Flagler, March 16, 1903, file 820, JR. I have slipped a slightly later account in here. Raskob would make similar efforts for most of his life, eventually providing his Lockport friends' children and, alas, widows, assistance, as well.

20. JJR to Frank Dole, March 15, 1901, file 630, JR.
21. Frank Dole to JR, November 5, 1900, file 630, JR.
22. JJR to Frank Kent, October 2, 1934, file 1250, JR.
23. JJR to Frank Dole, February 21, 1901, file 630, JR.
24. JJR to Frank Dole, February 28, 1901, file 603, JR.
25. JJR to Frank Dole, April 13, 1901, file 630, JR.
26. Ibid.
27. T. F. McGuire, file 1499, JR. It is not clear if JJR paid the entire cost of the chalice. The Church of the Sacred Heart was located in nearby Oberlin, Ohio; the Raskobs lived in South Lorain and had no local parish.
28. JJR to Frank Dole, March 15, 1901.
29. Condon, *Stars in the Water*, 246.
30. Quoted in Chandler and Salisbury, *Pierre S. du Pont*, 41.
31. Chandler and Salisbury lay out du Pont's plan, 40–46, and I follow their narrative. I also studied the original documents they used in file 240, box 200, PDP.
32. Brown Brothers to PdP, April 13, 1902, file 303, box 216, PDP.
33. I am drawing on the correspondence in file 240, box 200, PDP.
34. JJR to Frank Dole, May 3, 1901, file 630, JR.
35. JJR to Anna Raskob, June 16, 1901, file 1904, JR.
36. PdP to George T. Bishop, January 21, 1901, file 240, box 200, PDP.
37. Chandler and Salisbury, *Pierre S. du Pont*, 42–44, and file 240, box 200, PDP.

Chapter 3

1. Biographical details taken from the official company history, Adrian Kinnane, *DuPont: From the Banks of the Brandywine to Miracles of Science* (Wilmington, Del.: E. I. d Pont de Nemours and Company, 2002), 50–51. While not the place to read a critical account of the du Pont family or the Company, the book is spectacularly well researched and is an excellent source for family and company lore.
2. The biographical material is drawn from the encyclopedic Gerard Colby, *Du Pont Dynasty* (Secaucus, N.J.: Lyle Stuart Inc., 1984), 133–36. Here is the place to read a critical account of family and Company; it accentuates the negative though it is admirably researched and written with verve.
3. The DuPont tale is straight from Chandler and Salisbury, *Pierre S. du Pont*, ch. 3. The quoted passage is taken from p. 48.
4. All drawn from Chandler and Salisbury, *Pierre S. du Pont*, ch. 3.
5. Telegram from R. S. Penniman to JJR, January 3, 1905; at the bottom of the telegram is a typed decoding and the entire document is stamped with the date January 8, 1905, file 1799, JR. So, for example, the list at the bottom of the page reads: "SNIFFED = 18,000." I cannot exactly figure out how the code works; my guess is that a preselected set of words were encoded, which is why a few of the words in the message, not preselected for coding, are in plain text. I have no idea how often Raskob and the others used such coded messages; this is the only one I found.
6. JJR to L. L. Rue, October 7, 1925, file 2006, JR.
7. This figure is drawn from Kinnane, *DuPont*, 71.
8. Ibid., 65.
9. From an internal DuPont report made in 1910 quoted in H. Thompson Johnson, "Management Accounting in an Early Integrated Industrial: E. I. DuPont de Nemours Powder Company, 1903–1912," originally published in *Business History Review* 69:2 (Summer 1975), reprinted as ch. 1 in *Systems and Profits: Early Management Accounting at DuPont and General Motors*, ed. H. Thomas Johnson (New York: Arno Press, 1980), 187 [page number is the reprinted number from the original article].
10. The complex story of the invention of the modern DuPont Company is told in brilliant detail by Chandler and Salisbury, *Pierre S. du Pont*, chs. 3 and 4. I follow their account. The statistics are noted on p. 104. In writing of Raskob's role I rely, in part, on the December 2004 conversation I had with Mr. Chandler about the relationship between PdP and JR.

11. From Appendix I in the seminal work by David A. Hounshell and John Kenly Smith, Jr., *Science and Corporate Strategy: Du Pont R&D, 1902–1980* (New York: Cambridge University Press, 1988), 601.

12. JJR to Will Bewley, April 1, 1903, file 199, JR.

13. JR to Rob Moore, March 17, 1903, file 1580, JR.

14. Elias Ahuja to JJR, January 28, 1909, file 15, JR.

15. See Chandler and Salisbury, *Pierre S. du Pont*, ch. 7.

16. JJR to Anna F. Raskob, March 1, 1905, file 1904, JR.

17. JJR to Frank Dole, April 12, 1905, file 630, JR.

18. Ibid.

19. The quoted passages are all drawn from Elias Ahuja to JJR, June 9, 1905, file 15, JR.

20. See the 1905 and 1906 Ahuja letters in file 15, JR.

21. JJR to Anna F. Raskob, April 18, 1905, file 1904, JR.

22. This early account of Helena Springer Green is drawn from several sources. The genealogical information, as well as details on Helena's early years, is drawn from the *Raskob–Green Record Book* (Clayton, Del.: Archmere, 1921), which was authored by Varina Corbaley. From 1905 onward, Corbaley was, to put it bluntly, constantly after JJR for financial support and the genealogy project was, at her suggestion, a means for her to earn some of it. Corbaley had all kinds of money trouble, including some serious issues in 1905 with her trusteeship of the inherited money; see file 488, JJR. I also found brief mentions of Corbaley relating to her musical positions and vacation plans in the Philadelphia newspapers in the 1880s and 1890s; e.g., "Delaware Water Gap," *Philadelphia Inquirer*, September 6, 1908, 22. I also drew on Anthony F. Dorley, *Historical Sketch of St. Anthony's Church together with a History of Sacred Heart Academy and St. Anthony's Parochial School* (Lancaster, Pa.: Lancaster Lithographing Company, 1895). I admit to making some informed guesses and taking some interpretive liberties with these various scraps, but I think I have things close to right.

23. The story is given in the sound and informative "Biographical Note," written by Richard James, that introduces the Hagley Library on-line material on John Raskob, http://www.hagley.lib.de.us/raskob/raskob-bio.pdf.

24. JJR to William Raskob, May 2, 1905, file 1925, JR.

25. Elias Ahuja to JJR, March 14, 1906, file 15, JR. Ahuja explains that he first sent a letter of congratulations in October after receiving word of the engagement from John's September 12, 1905, letter but that he learned that it had not been properly posted, thus the late response.

26. Helena Springer Green to PdP, February 15, 1906, file 303, box 216, PDP.

27. Wedding Invitation to PdP, n.d., file 303, box 216, PDP.

28. JJR to Thomas Feeley, June 4, 1906, file 791, JR.

29. JJR to PdP, June 20, 1906, file 303, box 216, PDP.

Chapter 4

1. The People's Party Platform, 1892, http://historymatters.gmu.edu/d/5361/.

2. See Charles Postel, *The Populist Vision* (New York: Oxford University Press, 2007).

3. Chandler and Salisbury, *Pierre S. du Pont*, 261. Throughout this section I rely on Chandler and Salisbury, ch. 10. The authors believe Waddell's charges to be largely without merit.

4. Quoted in Henry F. Pringle, *The Life and Times of William Howard Taft*, Vol. 2 (Hamden, Conn.: Archon Books, 1964), 655.

5. Theodore Roosevelt, "First Annual Message," December 3, 1901, Miller Center website, http://millercenter.org/scripps/archive/speeches/detail/3773.

6. Theodore Roosevelt, State of the Union Address, December 5, 1905, TeachingAmerican History.org, http://teachingamericanhistory.org/library/index.asp?document=1312.

7. Theodore Roosevelt, "Fifth Annual Message," December 5, 1905, Miller Center website, http://millercenter.org/scripps/archive/speeches/detail/3777.

8. Richard Hofstadter, *The American Political Tradition and the Men Who Made It* (New York: Alfred Knopf, 1967), 224.

9. For a balanced account, see Lewis Gould, *The Presidency of Theodore Roosevelt* (Lawrence: University Press of Kansas, 1991).

10. Quoted in Chandler and Salisbury, *Pierre S. du Pont*, 261.

11. JJR to Tom Feeley, March 14, 1906, file 791, JR.

12. Drawn from "Southern Trust Company," file 2144, JR.

13. Colby, *Du Pont Dynasty*, 227.

14. For the Bee Hive, see folder 174, JR.

15. The correspondence is located in file 667, JR, with the key letter from JJR to Alfred du Pont, dated January 7, 1909.

16. Again, the correspondence is found in file 667, JR; the key letter from which the quotes are taken is from JJR to Alfred du Pont, October 13, 1910. For the specifics on Alfred du Pont's position, see Kinnane, *DuPont*, 72–73.

17. This story is told by Chandler and Salisbury in a related way in which Pierre is the major player: *Pierre S. du Pont*, 290–91. Pierre du Pont explains in his own report on the matter that Raskob, and not he, did the deal and provides some different details about the arrangement; Pierre du Pont to President's Committee of Awards, November 29, 1909, file 681, JR.

18. PdP to JJR, March 14, 1910, JR.

19. Though to become Delaware's senator, Henry du Pont engineered a long corrupt campaign in the state legislature that resulted in no senator being seated from the state for several years; his re-election effort in 1912 was not much better: see Colby, *Du Pont Dynasty*, 146–50 and 159–60.

20. The quote and the narrative of the events are drawn directly from Chandler and Salisbury, *Pierre S. du Pont*, 264.

21. JJR to Andrew Carnegie, December 31, 1908, file 345, JR.

22. Ibid.

23. Ibid.

24. Andrew Carnegie to JJR, January 4, 1909, file 345, JR.

25. Intriguingly, John did not keep copies of the letters in his own obsessively comprehensive files. Pierre did; see especially JJR to Tom Feeley, February 5, 1909; O. Field to Tom Feeley, February 18, 1909; JJR to Tom Feeley, March 5, 1909; and O. Field to Tom Feeley, March 9, 1909; all are in file 303, box 216 PDP.

26. Quoted in Chandler and Salisbury, *Pierre S. du Pont*, 277.

27. Ibid., 287.

28. Ibid., 278.

29. Both Taft quotes are drawn from Colby, *Du Pont Dynasty*, 164.

30. See the correspondence between W. A. Donaldson and JJR in July 1911, file 635, JR.

31. JJR to Joe Moran, n.d., (1909?), file 1586, JR.

32. I studied much of the documentation on this complex affair, but in the end I relied in this section completely on the lucid and detailed account given by Chandler and Salisbury, *Pierre S. du Pont*, ch. 10.

Chapter 5

1. Doug Rossinow states the matter succinctly: "The new liberals were part of progressivism; only a minority of progressives were new liberals." In *Visions of Progress* (Philadelphia: University of Pennsylvania Press, 2005), 40.

2. JJR to Arthur Moxham, December 28, 1911, file 1604, JR.

3. E. G. Buckner to JJR, November 1, 1913, file 265, JR.

4. The Wilmington Club, just around the corner from the Hotel Du Pont, served local elites.

5. Richard F. Snow, "William A. Brady," *American Heritage Magazine* 31:3 (April/May, 1980), http://www.americanheritage.com/articles/magazine/ah/1980/3/1980_3_74.shtml.

6. JJR to William A. Brady, December 1, 1916, file 251, JR.

7. John's Playhouse adventures and the quoted passage can be found in file 1838; also of use is file 251 (William A. Brady), JR.

8. "Businessmen are Planning for a Greater Wilmington," *Philadelphia Inquirer*, March 2, 1913, 19.
9. "Delaware Waits for Adjournment," *Philadelphia Inquirer*, March 10, 1913, 9.
10. JJR to H. Rodney Sharp, October 13, 1950, file 2075, JR.
11. Chandler and Salisbury, *Pierre S. du Pont*, 335.
12. Henry Loos, "The Great Powder Romance: A True Story of Strong Men and Their Millions," *Philadelphia Evening Public Ledger*, January 28, 1916, 1, 5.
13. "The Story of Raskob," *Philadelphia Evening Public Ledger*, January 28, 1916, 5.
14. Quotes are taken from Chandler and Salisbury, *Pierre S. du Pont*, 348.
15. JJR to William Raskob, April 13, 1917, file 1925, JR.
16. As reported in a memo written by Edward Stettinius who oversaw the Allied purchasing program for the Morgan bank. The memo appears in the highly sympathetic, but useful, document-driven biography written by John Douglas Forbes, *Stettinius, Sr.: Portrait of a Morgan Partner* (Charlottesville: University of Virginia Press, 1974), 64.

Chapter 6

1. Henry A. Rudkin to JJR, February 9, 1914, file 1469, JR.
2. This analysis is drawn from Bernard Weisberger, *The Dream Maker* (Boston: Little Brown and Company, 1979), 176. Chandler and Salisbury say on p. 435 that JR bought 500 shares initially but JJR writes William A. Brady on February 28, 1914, file 251, that he had already made a GM stock purchase before his 500 share buy order. Pierre du Pont's secretary claims that Raskob made an initial purchase of 50 shares for $3,500 but Thompson does not mention his certain purchase of 500 shares in late February 1914. Probably he bought 50 shares and then 500 shares soon thereafter. Despite Raskob's meticulous record keeping, I could not track his early GM purchases through his stock records, which may have been taken out of his files in the 1940s when the DuPont–GM antitrust suit caused Raskob a great deal of concern but this is only speculation on my part. See George E. Thompson, "Memoirs, ca, 1954–1982," n.d. (1982?), 9; a copy of this document is kept in the Soda House archive of the Hagley Library, call number 2025.
3. JJR to Brady, February 28, 1914.
4. Quoted in Weisberger, *Dream Maker*, 176.
5. H. Rodney Sharp to JJR, October 12, 1950, file 2075, JR.
6. Du Pont's remarks are from the May 1951 transcript of the testimony of Pierre du Pont made in a pretrial rehearsal for the DuPont–GM antitrust suit as quoted in the George Thompson, "Memoir," 10.
7. Thompson, "Memoir," 10.
8. Weisberger, *Dream Maker*, 27.
9. W. A. P. John, "That Man, Durant," clipping from *Motor*, January 1923, box 57 87–11.2–144b, Durant Collection (DC), Scharchburg Archives (SA), Kettering University, Flint, Michigan.
10. Ibid., 97.
11. Quoted in Lawrence R. Gustin, *Billy Durant: Creator of General Motors* (Grand Rapids, Mi.: William B. Eerdmans Publishing Company, 1973), 87.
12. For the general narrative, I am relying on Durant's own account; see William C. Durant, "The True Story of General Motors," 75-page typescript, The True Story of General Motors folder, DC. The memoir is told in separate sections, each with its own page numbering, and kept in the Durant Collection in several sequential folders. Only 75 pages, it is obviously not a complete or objective account of Durant's life. An excellent, more comprehensive and balanced account of Durant's creation of GM, also based in part on Durant's version, can be found in Weisberger, *Dream Maker*, ch. 5. I also rely on the undocumented article by James Flink and Glenn Niemeyer, "The General of General Motors," *American Heritage* 24:5 (August 1973), http://www.americanheritage.com/articles/magazine/ah/1973/5/1973_5_10.shtml. Flink and Niemeyer provide an insightful character study of Durant, but their facts about the investments of PdP, JJR, and the DuPont Company in GM are inaccurate.

13. Quoted in Weisberger, *Dream Maker*, 139.
14. Quoted in Gustin, *Billy Durant*, 137.
15. Weisberger, *Dream Maker*, 147.
16. R. S. McLaughlin, Part Three, "My Eighty Years on Wheels," Our Company, General Motors of Canada, http://www.gm.ca/inm/gmcanada/english/about/OverviewHist/RSbioPart3.html.
17. "Helen Storrow," Wikipedia, http://en.wikipedia.org/wiki/Helen_Storrow. Scholars are not comfortable using Wikipedia as a source for obvious reasons but this biography of Helen Storrow and the material on her husband is well researched, professionally cited, and elegantly written. So I have used it! For the Storrows' Swiss meeting, see Henry Greenleaf Pearson, *Son of New England: James Jackson Storrow* (Boston: Thomas Todd Company, 1932), 11.
18. Durant, "The True Story of General Motors," 4. Chevrolet Folder, DC.
19. "Tentative Statement of F. Donaldson Brown," 5, June 15, 1952, 1976.005.057, John Pratt Papers (JP), SA. Brown sent this overview of his involvement with GM to former DuPont and then GM executive John Pratt for his comments. The statement was made in preparation for Brown's involvement with the DuPont–GM antitrust case.
20. Here is a useful place to note that I am relying in this section and what will follow on the material gathered for the *U.S. v. Du Pont G. M. et al.*, antitrust action. Here, in particular I am drawing on the *U.S. v. Du Pont G.M. Et al.* (USDP), Second Series, 1–2, 1910–1919 set of documents. The case records I used are located at the Hagley Library (HL), Wilmington, Del. I am guided here by the account given in Chandler and Salisbury, *Pierre S. du Pont*, ch. 16.
21. Quoted in Weisberger, *Dream Maker*, 187.
22. Chandler and Salisbury, *Pierre S. du Pont*, 441.
23. James J. Storrow to Pierre S. du Pont, September 20, 1915, (PS) 60, p. 281, USDP, Second Series.
24. "DuPont Makes Financial Reorganization," *Wall Street Journal*, August 20, 1915, 1, 7.
25. I am indebted to Chandler and Salisbury, *Pierre S. du Pont*, ch. 13 and I am following the USDP, Second Series documents.
26. The question of Pierre du Pont's sexuality is obviously not central to a biography of John Raskob, but it is an intriguing one given the intimate and enduring relationship between the two men. Anyone who does research on PdP runs into the issue given du Pont's well-known relationship with Lewes A. Mason. Gerard Colby, in *DuPont Dynasty*, suggests carefully that Pierre had a romantic relationship with Lewes, pp. 189–90. I talked to Alfred Chandler about the issue and he said that he thought Pierre probably was what we would today call "gay" but that he did not think the issue was relevant to his study of du Pont's business career and that answering the question would be difficult and, from his perspective, more trouble than it was worth. I understood him to mean that the issue might have upset members of the du Pont family. I interviewed one of Pierre du Pont's relatives about her recollections of the man and she became quite angry with me when I raised the question.
27. "Tentative Statement of F. Donaldson Brown," 5–6.
28. Ibid., 6.

Chapter 7

1. JJR to Robert Moore, July 6, 1908, file 1580, JR.
2. JJR to Tom Feeley, April 12, 1907, file 791, JR.
3. JJR to Frank Reynolds, March 23, 1915, file 265, JR.
4. JJR to Elias Ahuja, November 14, 1907, file 15, JR.
5. Elias Ahuja to JJR, November 22, 1910, file 15, JR.
6. All quotes are from, "'On with the Dance' Cry of Wilmington Party Here to Burn up Money," *The Evening-Telegram*, November 26, 1915, clipping, file 1224, JR. Also in this folder are JJR's attempts to keep the unwanted newspaper coverage from spreading.
7. A. G. Saylor to JJR, November 29, 1915, file 1224.

8. JJR to Varina Corbaley, November 28, 1916, file 488, JR.
9. Inez Yvonne Raskob, file 1911, JR.
10. JJR to Frank Reynolds, January 6, 1914, file 1952, JR.
11. While that is a significant sum, around $625,000 in current dollars, between the Civil War and World War I housing prices in Delaware had not much increased; in the early 1870s Archmere with the same acreage and the same house sold for $22,000. The financial information is included in an essay on Archmere written by Helena Raskob in the *Raskob–Green Record Book*, 131–33.
12. Helena Raskob, "Archmere," in the *Raskob–Green Record Book*, 134. Mrs. Raskob is not listed as the author, but it is clearly her work.
13. Helena Raskob, "Archmere," 134.
14. Henry James, *Collected Travel Writings, Great Britain and America* (New York: Library of America, 1993), 731.
15. For Mr. Flagler and his hotel developments, see A. K. Sandoval-Strausz, *Hotel: An American History* (New Haven: Yale University Press, 2007), 117–18.
16. Helena Raskob, "Archmere," 134–35.
17. Harper provided a short autobiographical sketch in *Secretary's Fourth Report: Harvard Class of 1901* (Cambridge, Mass.: Crimson Printing Company, 1916), 200–201. See also Kirk J. Himelick, Colvin Randall, and Sandy Reber, *The Heritage of Longwood Gardens: Pierre S. du Pont and His Legacy* (Kennet Square, Pa.: Longwood Garden, Inc., 1998), 25. For more on Harper and McClure, see "Archmere's Application for a National Historic Place," 1992–1993, prepared by Stephen H. Moffson, 6, Hagley Digital Archives, http://digital.hagley.org/cdm4/item_viewer.php?CISOROOT=/p268001coll27&CISOPTR=1295. I have relied on this document for general information on Archmere. See also Stephen J. Rossey, "Estate of Archmere: A Personal View," 1984, Hagley Digital Archive, http://digital.hagley.org/cdm4/item_viewer.php?CISOROOT=/p268001coll27&CISOPTR=1296.
18. McClure and Harper to JJR, November 13, 1915, Hagley Digital Archives, http://www.hagley.lib.de.us/raskob/raskob-1468.pdf.
19. Weisberger, *Dream Maker*, 217.
20. Archmere, Inc., file 93, JJR.

Chapter 8

1. Chandler and Salisbury, *Pierre S. du Pont*, 397.
2. Daniel Okrent, *Last Call: The Rise and Fall of Prohibition* (New York: Scribner, 2010), 297.
3. "Tentative Statement of F. Donaldson Brown," 3.
4. Ibid., 2.
5. William Laird to JJR, May 22, 1916, (PS) 267, p. 347, USDP, Second Series.
6. Alfred P. Sloan, Jr., in collaboration with Boyden Sparkes, *Adventures of White Collar Man* (New York: Doubleday, 1941), 96.
7. On Sloan and Sloan's relationship with Raskob, I rely on my own work, *Sloan Rules* (Chicago: University of Chicago Press, 2002).
8. Quoted in Chandler and Salisbury, *Pierre S. du Pont*, 443.
9. Weisberger, *Dream Maker*, 215.
10. JJR to PdP, February 16, 1917, file 313, box 216, PDP.
11. Ibid.
12. JJR to W. C. Durant, March 6, 1917, file 677, JR. Raskob copied this letter to the du Ponts and this citation is to the copy in Irénée du Pont's file.
13. Weisberger, *Dream Maker*, 23–24.
14. I have tracked these developments in the Raskob papers but, in the end, I have followed the account of Chandler and Salisbury, *Pierre S. du Pont*, as their narrative and analysis is perfectly sound, see pp. 444–47.
15. JJR to T. T. Feeley, May 6, 1917, file 791, JR.
16. For those paying attention to the inflation-corrected dollar figures, note that there was a good deal of inflation between 1914 and 1917 in the United States.

17. The Red Cross donation and Raskob's role in it is well reported in "DuPont Declares a Red Cross Dividend," Philadelphia *Evening Ledger*, June 13, 1917, 1.
18. Not that the Chamber of Commerce and other business groups opposed all Progressive Era legislation. They often led the charge for good government, anticorruption measures, but they were suspicious and often opposed expensive programs that raised taxes and they guarded business prerogatives.
19. Weisberger, *Dream Maker*, 226.
20. Chandler and Salisbury offer this speculation and I am seconding it here based on part on my own discovery of Raskob's 1916 investment in GM. But I found no statement by Raskob in his papers or in Pierre du Pont's explaining why he joined Durant's syndicate.
21. Taken from Charles W. Cheape, *Strictly Business: Walter Carpenter at Du Pont and General Motors* (Baltimore: Johns Hopkins University Press, 1995), 26.
22. Thanks to the US government antitrust suit, Raskob's memo dated December 19, 1917, to the Finance Committee from the Treasurer is in the public record: Exhibit 85, *U.S. v. Du Pont, GM et al*, Defendants' Exhibits, Exs. 1 to 182, P. S. Du Pont Deposition. I used the copy located in the Hagley Library.
23. Ibid.
24. All quotes in this paragraph are from Raskob's December 19 memo.
25. Colby, *Du Pont Dynasty*, 202.
26. Chandler and Salisbury, *Pierre S. du Pont*, 454.
27. I am indebted to Chandler and Salisbury, *Pierre S. du Pont*, for the story of the DuPont meetings and debate, pp. 452–55. I have also relied in this section on materials from *U.S. v. Du Pont, GM et al*, specifically Defendants' Exhibits, 1–107.

Chapter 9

1. M. S. McLaughlin, "My Eighty Years on Wheels, Part Three" GM–Canada website, Our Company http://www.gm.ca/inm/gmcanada/english/about/OverviewHist/RSbioPart3.html.
2. McLaughlin even shared Pierre du Pont's love for horticulture and landscaping; with his wife he created the famed Parkwood gardens outside Toronto.
3. "We are Thirty Years Old," *News and Views*, February 1949, 83.12.162, GMAC, SA. In the valuable overview of the early years of the auto installment buying business, *Debtor Nation* (Princeton: Princeton University Press, 2011), 20–27, Louis Hyman gives a misleading history of GMAC. Hyman argues that GMAC's founders "concerned themselves with wholesale financing and not as GMAC would later claim, retail financing.... Only by the mid-1920s did GM begin to realize it had a relationship with the consumer as well as the dealers" (22, 25). As I shall show, from the beginning Raskob intended GMAC to lend to consumers; but to do so in large amounts he and his allies would have to prove the merits of the system to bankers so that GMAC could borrow the capital it needed to provide massive numbers of individual consumer loans. And contrary to Hyman's claim, even in 1919, GMAC's first year, GMAC lent more money to individual consumers than it did to dealers: $9,989,019 to retail customers and $7,635,777 to dealers. GMAC released regular financial information to the public and to shareholders. The numbers referenced are taken from a chart of GMAC's 1919 to June 1922 financials that shows exactly how much GMAC loaned annually to consumers and dealers, as well as to its "foreign department" distributors; "General Motors Acceptance Corp.," *Wall Street Journal*, August 9, 1922, 6.
4. Lendol Calder, *Financing the American Dream* (Princeton: Princeton University Press, 1999), 160–61. I rely throughout this section on Calder's richly researched account of installment selling.
5. Ibid., 165.
6. I am still closely following Calder's history, *Financing the American Dream*, 184–89.
7. "Guaranty Securities Co.," *New York Times*, February 26, 1918, http://query.nytimes.com/mem/archive-free/pdf?res=FB0810FA3A5B11738DDDAF0A94DA405B888DF1D3.
8. Sloan devotes a chapter to GMAC in *My Years with General Motors* (New York: Currency Doubleday, 1990), ch. 17. The book was first published in 1964. In the book he gives

Raskob full credit for promoting installment selling at GM but, reflecting their rift in 1928, he says little about Raskob's actions.

9. Calder, *Financing the American Dream*, 189. This section on Ford is drawn from Calder, 189–91.

10. "Guaranty Securities Co.," *New York Times*, February 26, 1918.

11. Quoted in Vincent Curcio, Chrysler: The Life and Times of an Automotive Genius (New York: Oxford University Press, 2000), 253.

12. Sally H. Clarke, *Trust and Power* (New York: Cambridge University Press, 2007), 218–21.

13. "To Finance Auto Dealers," *New York Times*, January 26, 1919, sec. II, p. 5.

14. Ibid.

15. See ch. 9, n. 3.

16. "That First Offering," *News and Views*, February 1949, 27, GMAC, 83.12.162, SA. The entire issue of this GMAC publication is dedicated to the 30th anniversary of GMAC.

17. T. H. Keating, "Grandfather Said It Was Wrong," *News and Views*, February 1949, 11.

18. The quoted passage is from Alfred P. Sloan, "Congratulations to GMAC," Raskob's unrecorded speech, as well as GMAC's early days, is discussed in the article "Looking Over the Long Pull," *News and Views*, February 1949, 8–10.

19. "Income Status of Buyers of Autos on Deferred Plan," *Washington Post*, April 29, 1920, 6.

20. Ibid.

21. "Tells of Financing $300,000,000 in Cars," *New York Times*, May 1, 1922, 25.

22. "The Best of Whatever We Are," *New and Views*, October 1949, 17, GMAC 83.12.162, SA.

23. Robert Moore to JJR, November 18, 1918, file 1580, JR.

24. JJR to Robert Moore, November 21, 1918, file 1580, JR.

25. JJR to S. H. Bunnel, November 22, 1918, file 297, JR.

26. JJR to T. E. Spalding, December 7, 1918, file 2148, JR.

27. Quoted in Curcio, *Chrysler*, 247.

28. JJR to Margaret Allen, April 2, 1924, file 32, JR.

29. Robert Allen, Jr., to JJR, June 8, 1933, file 32, JR.

30. "Benefactor," The Chester County Hospital History, http://www.cchosp.com/cchhist.asp?p=509. The relationship between Lewes and Pierre du Pont is not well documented, but this website provides a key account including a narrative, photos, and documents aimed at explaining how and why Pierre du Pont gave the Chester County Hospital the $1,000,000 gift.

31. JJR to William Bewley, December 21, 1918, file 199, JR.

32. The back and forth is recorded in letters between JJR and Alfred Sloan, December 1918, file 2109, JR.

33. Curcio, *Chrysler*, 247.

34. JJR to PdP, March 24, 1917, box 216, PDP.

35. Quoted in Robert J. Taggert, *Private Philanthropy and Public Education: Pierre S. du Pont and the Delaware Schools 1890–1940* (Newark: University of Delaware Press, 1988), 48. Throughout this section, I relay on Taggert's excellent work. The endnotes for ch. 3, especially n. 1, explore in depth Raskob's influential role and Pierre's other motives in creating the Service Citizens of Delaware; 179–80.

36. Quoted in Beverly Gage, *The Day Wall Street Exploded* (New York: Oxford University Press, 2009), 28.

37. Ibid., 27.

38. Ibid., 119.

39. JJR to Charles Copeland, December 22, 1914, file 135, JR.

40. JJR to C. S. Mott, November 11, 1919, file 1599, JR.

41. JJR to A. J. Moxham, February 2, 1920, file 1604, JR. For details on the plan, see Sidney Fine, *Sit-Down: The General Motors Strike of 1936–1937* (Ann Arbor: University of Michigan Press, 1969), 23–24.

42. Historians have long been intrigued by the SCC but relatively little has been written about its early days, since few records seem to be available. In the 1930s, a Senate committee investigated the SCC and a number of records from the mid-1920s on were discovered and made public. By then JJR's interest had waned, alas. So I am piecing the scraps here and the

quote comes in a letter focused on the work of the Chamber of Commerce but the paragraph right above the quoted passage references the work of many of the figures involved not in the Chamber but in the SCC so I think it is fair to use here as I have done; JJR to Lammot du Pont, March 18, 1922, file 668, JR.

43. "Who's Who at President's Conference," *New York Times*, October 5, 1919, sec. IV, p. 8.
44. Ibid.
45. "U.S. Troops Raid Gary Strikers' Homes, Seize Arms, Industrial Parley Organizes," *New York Tribune*, October 8, 1919, 3.
46. Chest Wright, "Employers Win Delay on Collective Bargaining," *New York Tribune*, October 18, 1919, 2.
47. Quoted in Margaret L. Coit, *Mr. Baruch* (New York: Beard Books, 2001), 308. I rely on Coit for the general narrative of the conference.
48. See JJR to C. S. Mott, June 4, 1920, file 1599, JR, for Raskob's enthusiasm for Cartwright's little book.

Chapter 10

1. Charles Kettering to JJR, July 25, 1919, 87-11.2-22, box 159, Kettering Archive (KA), SA.
2. The fraught relationship between Durant and Raskob is built on many sources. Immediately after the debacle of 1920, Durant did his best to defend himself and argued that Raskob was primarily at fault for GM's financial difficulties, and he corresponded with many of his friends and colleagues in seeking to make his case: many letters to and from Durant speak to this issue, see in particular the material collected in the Durant Papers, D74–2.12. Also useful in thinking about the Durant–Raskob relationship in 1919 and 1920 is W. A. P. John, "That Man, Durant," and Donaldson Brown's account, "Tentative Statement of F. Donaldson Brown," June 15, 1952.
3. Quoted in Alfred D. Chandler, *Strategy and Structure* (Cambridge, Mass.: MIT Press, 1962), 127.
4. Pratt tells the story to Alfred P. Sloan in a letter he sent him in response to a draft chapter on Durant and the early years of GM from the manuscript that would become *My Years with General Motors*; John Pratt to Alfred P. Sloan, June 8, 1956, 1976.005.037, John Pratt Papers (JP), SA. In the letter he also highlights the role of Raskob in 1919 and urges Sloan to give him more credit as well as to give Pierre du Pont more credit for the changes that took place between 1920 and 1923.
5. Weisberger, *Dream Maker*, 246–47.
6. Ibid., 242. In this section I am drawing heavily on ch. 7 of *Dream Maker*, as well as ch. 2 of *Sloan Rules*.
7. Weisberger, *Dream Maker*, 242.
8. Curcio, *Chrysler*, 251.
9. Sloan told Raskob that he was angry with Durant. Raskob pleaded with him to stay, telling him that if Durant continued to mismanage GM he would eventually be forced to leave; JJR tells the story in a letter to Lammot du Pont, March 14, 1944, file 678, JR. Raskob seems not to have known that even after their conversation Sloan had begun looking for other employment.
10. Chandler and Salisbury, *Pierre S. du Pont*, 476.
11. This argument is made by Alfred Sloan in ch. 2 of *My Years with General Motors* and based on all the primary sources I have scoured in both the Durant papers and in Raskob's own, seemingly thinned account of these years, I concur with the assessment that Raskob shared the blame with Durant for GM's financially risky strategy.
12. Durant kept a careful record of his 1920–21 correspondence with Raskob; see D74–2.49, DP. Intriguingly, as best as I can tell, many of the letters from Raskob to Durant during this period, as well as letters JJR sent to other players in the GM financial debacle and then copied to Durant, do not appear in Raskob's own records.
13. JJR to Sir Harry MacGowan, April 2, 1920, D74–2.49, DP. See also Brown, "Tentative Statement of F. Donaldson Brown" 12.

14. Ibid.
15. JJR to Durant, April 18, 1920, D74–2.49, DP.
16. JJR to Durant, April 22, 1920, D74–2.49, DP.
17. Durant offers up this quote, from an uncertain source, in his own recounting of these events, see D74–2.41A, DP.
18. Weisberger, *Dream Maker*, 261.
19. Forbes, *Stettinius*, 129; Stettinius's lengthy account of the Durant affair is included in Forbes's useful biography, which contains a great deal of documentary evidence.
20. Weisberger, *Dream Maker*, 263–64 and Chandler and Salisbury, *Pierre S. du Pont*, 482–84.
21. John, "That Man, Durant," 27.
22. JJR to Durant, October 4, 1920, D74–2.49, DP.
23. Quoted in Chandler and Salisbury, *Pierre S. du Pont*, 483.
24. JJR to Durant, October 30, 1920, D74–2.49, DP.
25. The quote is from a November 26, 1920, letter that PdP wrote to Irénée du Pont. This letter is the best and fullest contemporary record of the events that surrounded Durant's debacle. The letter can be found in full in Sloan, *My Years with General Motors*, 32–38. A copy of the letter is also included in full as an exhibit in *U.S. v. Du Pont, GM et al*, vol. 5–6, (DP) GMC-854.
26. Ibid.
27. Ibid.
28. An interesting back story: Morgan partner George Baker told Stettinius that "we should all either increase our interest in and control over the affairs of the [GM] Company or should withdraw altogether." Stettinius who had that summer overseen a fraught $100 million loan to the government of France, took, in the words of his biographer "a more relaxed position," and wrote Morgan partner Henry Davison that they could not withdrew in "justice" to the du Ponts and other critical parties nor was a buyout worth the risk; "I think that we should work along quietly and patiently and watch developments." See Forbes, *Stettinius*, 131–32.
29. Brown, "Tentative Statement of F. Donaldson Brown," 12.
30. Raskob's lead role is stated by Pierre du Pont in George Thompson, "John J. Raskob, Pierre s. Du Pont and General Motors," typescript, 18, Hagley Library.
31. For the correspondence on Raskob's culpability, see D74–2.12, DP.
32. For the Durant–Raskob fight over just compensation, see D74–2.49, DP; the quoted passage is from Raskob's angry letter to Durant, dated March 31, 1921. Again, these letters are not included in JJR's papers.
33. Forbes, *Stettinius*, 130.
34. Taken from Du Pont's preliminary antitrust testimony in regard to DuPont's relationship to GM, which is quoted at length in Thompson, "John J. Raskob, Pierre S. Du Pont and General Motors." The quoted passage appears on p. 18.
35. All the quotes are from Sloan, *My Years with General Motors*, 43–44.

Chapter 11

1. JJR to Elias Ahuja, December 13, 1920, file 15, JR.
2. JJR to IdP, November 10, 1921, file 677, JR.
3. JJR to Walter S. Carpenter, July 6, 1922, file 351, JR.
4. JJR to Jesse Cruiser, September 8, 1919, file 321, JR.
5. JJR to Anna Raskob, February 27, 1922, file 1904, JR.
6. JJR to Walter H. Johnson, December 27, 1921, file 1195, JR.
7. JJR to Walter H. Johnson, December 20, 1921, and November 23, 1921, file 1195, JR.
8. JJR to William Blatz, February 22, 1922, file 215, JR.
9. "Business: Du Pont Dividend," *Time*, July 6, 1925.
10. Samuel Crowther, "John J. Raskob, and the World's Largest Business," *The World's Work* 40:6 (October 1920), 612.
11. Alan Brinkley, *The Publisher: Henry Luce and His American Century* (New York: Knopf, 2010), 149.
12. Crowther, "John J. Raskob," 612.

13. Ibid.
14. Ibid., 617.
15. Ibid.
16. "A New Captain of Industry: A Rising Luminary of Industry and His Vast Orbit," *Current Opinion* 69:5 (November 1920), 627.
17. Ibid., 628.
18. Quoted in Ott, *When Wall Street Met Main Street*, 24. Ott's work is an important source for this section though she chose not to discuss Raskob or the publicity that surrounded his comments from 1920 through 1929 on creating widespread equity investment opportunities. Despite my parochial complaints, Ott's work is a vital contribution to the new history of capitalism being written by academic historians.
19. Ott, *When Wall Street Met Main Street*, ch. 1.
20. John J. Raskob, "How Big Should a Business Grow?" *System*, October 1920, 612.
21. Ibid., 612, 613.
22. Ibid., 750.
23. Farber, *Sloan Rules*, chs. 2 and 3; and Chandler and Salisbury, *Pierre S. du Pont*, ch 19.
24. For Sloan's strategy, see his *My Years with General Motors*, ch. 4 and also Farber, *Sloan Rules*, ch. 3. Those who know their automobile history realize that Sloan was, here, not just battling Ford. He was also fighting GM's head of research, Charles Kettering, who wanted to bet GM's future on a new "copper-cooled" engine. Sloan was, rightfully, dubious about Kett's innovation, but he also believed that GM need not ever risk its fortune on product innovation when its strategic strength and advantage lay in its multidivisional mass manufacturing and mass marketing power. Sloan was right, at least he was until the late twentieth century when GM became so weighed down by huge fixed costs and a resistance to change that it allowed foreign competitors to overtake it.
25. Based on the documents collected in the Pratt Papers, 1976.005.084.
26. JJR to PdP, May 26, 1922, box 216, PDP.
27. For a solid overview of this complex affair which focuses on Pierre du Pont's role, see Chandler and Salisbury, *Pierre S. du Pont*, 538–43. I also relied on several of the government exhibit documents collected for the *U.S. v. Du Pont, GM et al* trial, especially Government Exhibit No. 189, which includes J. J. Raskob to Finance Committees, General Motors Corporation and E. I. Du Pont de Nemours & Company, July 26, 1923, and J. J. Raskob to Finance Committee (E. I. DuPont de Nemours & Company), October 10, 1923.
28. The quote is from Donald Brown, "A Tentative Statement," 27. The debate and Raskob's retort is also from the same source.
29. Carpenter's side of the story is well told by Cheape, *Strictly Business*, 61–62.
30. Alfred P. Sloan to JJR, October 8, 1923, Defendants' Exhibit No. 335.
31. Alfred P. Sloan to JJR, December 12, 1927, file 2109, JR.
32. JJR to PdP, file 681, JR.

Chapter 12

1. The quoted passage can be found in the exchanges collected in file 641, JR.
2. Book information can also be found in file 641, JR. I am also indebted to Raskob archivist Richard James who provided me with a detailed list he compiled from multiple documents on Raskob's spending on select categories, including books, between 1918 to 1942, which includes the following years: 1918, 1923, 1928–1934, 1936, 1939, and 1942.
3. JJR to Curtis Cooper, August 6, 1923, file 481, JR.
4. JJR to Charles Stewart Mott, December 22, 1924, file 1599, JR.
5. On the Vatican finances in the 1920s, see John F. Pollard, *Money and the Rise of the Modern Papacy: Financing the Vatican, 1850–1950* (Cambridge: Cambridge University Press, 2005), chs. 5–6.
6. See file 2072, JR, which contains the correspondence between JJR and Bishop Thomas J. Shahan, the rector of Catholic University.
7. An irresistible side note: Raskob had first offered use of an auto, though only on an occasional basis, to Father John A. Lyons in Wilmington in early 1911. Father Lyons,

born in 1843 and just named Domestic Prelate of St. Peters, had rejected the offer stating that he did not ride in such "machines," which he associated with the wealthy but if Raskob provided him with a short-term leased horse and buggy he would ride out to bless Raskob's new residence. Raskob thanked him for the offer but could not stop himself from commenting: "Every year is bringing more and more machines into use among the masses.... Instead of renting a horse and carriage from a livery stable, people are now becoming accustomed to hire an automobile for two or three hours a day." Raskob's carefully worded piece of advice was his first recorded attempt to use his expertise to guide his Church, however humbly in this case, in a new direction. JJR to Father Lyons, March 27, 1911, file 1403, JR.

8. Most of this section draws on material collected in file 644, JR.
9. JJR to Father John J. Dougherty, January 9, 1925, file 644, JR.
10. JJR to PdP, May 14, 1925, file 303, box 216, PDP.
11. Ibid.
12. JJR to Bishop FitzMaurice, August 18, 1926, File 815, JR.
13. JJR to PdP, September 8, 1924, file 681, JR.
14. JJR to Edmond FitzMaurice, February 21, 1927, file 815, JR.
15. Edmond FitzMaurice to JJR, March 2, 1927, file 815, JR.
16. "Raskob Gives $1,000,000 to Wilmington Catholics," *New York Times*, February 19, 1928, 8:2.
17. Pastoral Letter of the Right Reverend Edmond J. FitzMaurice, February 15, 1928, file 815, JR.
18. Ibid.
19. John McHugh Stuart, "Faith, Works—and Raskob," *Columbia*, April 1928, 11.
20. Ibid., 39.
21. JJR to Right Reverend Francis C. Kelley, June 28, 1929, file 1236, JR.
22. The Wilmington diocese foundation was disbanded in 2011. The diocese needed its $53 million in assets to provide recompense in Church-related sexual abuse cases. See Joseph Ryan, "Settlement Plan would Mean End of Foundation's Historic Role," *The Dialog* 46:3 (January 26, 2011), 1, 9.
23. JJR to James J. Phelan, December 16, 1926, file 1226, JR.
24. Given the near endless, often bizarre speculations and conspiracy theories that surround the venerable Knights of Malta, including the American chapter, I could not resist noting the odd occurrence of Raskob's missing announcement and the odd lack of follow-up by Phelan. Neither men in their correspondence comments on the strange three-month gap between the September 16 letter and the *Time* magazine announcement. More grist for the conspiracy theorists.
25. JJR to Prince Galeas de Thun-Hohenstein, December 22, 1926, file 1226, JR.
26. John Cooney, *The American Pope: The Life and Times of Francis Cardinal Spellman* (New York: Times Books: 1984), 5.
27. Frank Spellman to JJR, May 16, 1927, file 2356, JR.
28. Frank Spellman to JJR, [n.d. but stamped as answered September 16, 1927], file 2356, JR.
29. JJR to Frank Spellman, September 16, 1927, file 2356, JR.
30. See the correspondence between Pizzardo and JJR in file 1836, JR.
31. JJR to Frank Spellman, October 29, 1927, file 2356, JR.
32. The quoted passage is from Michael Williams to JJR, April 3, 1925, file 457, JR.
33. JJR to Michael Williams, October 30, 1929, file 457, JR. More generally, see *Commonweal* materials in files 457 and 458, JR.
34. This episode occurred in July 1929 and all quotes are drawn from the correspondence with Father John Dougherty in file 644, JR.
35. This narrative draws from L. Ethan Ellis, "Dwight Morrow and the Church–State Controversy in Mexico," *The Hispanic American Historical Review* 38:4 (November 1958), 482–505, and the correspondence between Dwight Morrow and JJR, file 1594 and material in the "Vatican" file 2356, JR.
36. JJR to Monsignor Guiseppe Pizzardo, July 3, 1928, file 2356, JR. Raskob sent a copy of this letter to Morrow.

37. Ibid. Raskob wanted the Church to follow Morrow's advice and reach a compromise with the Mexican government. Throughout 1928 the Church resisted Raskob's advice but in June 1929 the Church accepted a compromise negotiated, in part, by Morrow that normalized Church–State relations in Mexico.

Chapter 13

1. JJR to W. D. Jamieson, November 15, 1919, file 602, JR.
2. JJR to Frank V. du Pont, January 20, 1928, file 681, JR.
3. Robert Burk, in *The Corporate State and the Broker State*, makes a similar argument though he suggests that there was an important element of political "cultivating" (41) on Raskob's part. Could be, of course, but I think Raskob's interest in becoming friends with Smith preceded any ideas he might have developed later about impacting national politics through his relationship with Smith.
4. Peggy Sandell to JJR, September 23, 1925, file 2034, JR.
5. Butler and Raskob wrote each other many long letters in the 1920s, see file 317, JR.
6. Raskob's New York City apartments are detailed in files 87 and 88, JR. For per capita consumption figures in the 1920s, see *The Value of a Dollar, 1860–2009*, 178.
7. Dowling, "The Reminiscences of Eddie Dowling," 115–20. According to Dowling he first met Raskob in 1924 when Dowling used his influence with New York Cardinal Hayes to keep Yvonne Raskob enrolled in her Catholic boarding school despite her health problems. In typical Dowling fashion, the story of their first meetings involves a number of dramatic events and a great deal of name-dropping and probably a bit of truth-stretching.
8. For the original Hearst attack and an incisive explanation of why Hearst made it, see Christopher Finan, *Alfred E. Smith: The Happy Warrior* (New York: Hill and Wang, 2002), 130–38.
9. Dowling, "The Reminiscences of Eddie Dowling," 105.
10. Dowling, "The Reminiscences of Eddie Dowling,", 106. Robert A. Slayton, in his excellent biography of Smith, *Empire Statesman: The Rise and Redemption of Al Smith* (New York: Free Press, 2001), gets this story wrong when he places the meeting in 1919; see p. 260. Slayton did not realize that the milk scandal issue, which did indeed take place in 1919, was reintroduced as a campaign weapon by Ogden Mills in 1926 and publicized by the Hearst papers; it is in 1926 that Dowling introduced Raskob to Smith. For the 1926 election, see the wonderfully written biography by Mathew and Hannah Josephson, *Al Smith: Hero of the Cities* (Boston: Houghton Mifflin, 1969), 335–39, which is flawed by its overreliance on the perspective of Smith's longtime advisor and Progressive champion Frances Perkins.
11. Ed Flynn, *You're the Boss* (New York: Viking Press, 1947), 64–65; Josephson and Josephson, *Al Smith*, 354–55; and Dennis Tilden Lynch, "Friends of the Governor," *The North American Review* 226:4 (October 1928), 420–28.
12. It was not so much that the business cronies opposed Smith's urban progressive vision; most thought Smith's allegiance to his working-class constituents was fine, especially since all of the men—including Raskob—came from humble backgrounds and had their own allegiances to the people who lived in New York City's Catholic immigrant neighborhoods. The business cronies just were more interested in keeping Smith fixed on expanding capital projects and bringing government contracts and economic support to well-positioned New York businessmen such as themselves. The two groups had different agendas for Smith and Smith had only so much political capital and time to expend. When it came to national politics, these different agendas would produce a more complex set of tensions, though during the 1928 election only Raskob among the business cronies figured centrally in sorting them out.
13. Slayton, *Empire Statesmen*, 129.
14. Ibid.
15. Frances Perkins, who became Franklin Roosevelt's Secretary of Labor, gives full voice to her hatred of Raskob, which was greatly magnified by Raskob's anti–New Deal behavior in her Columbia University oral history account. Full of exaggerations, factual errors, and willful mischaracterizations, she paints a wicked picture of Raskob: Frances Perkins, oral

history transcript, Columbia University Oral History, Butler Library, New York City. The quote is on 17; see also 523–24.

16. Quoted in Finan, *Alfred E. Smith*, 90. I follow Finan's analysis on the role of the fire and subsequent commission on Smith's political development. Wagner was elected to the US Senate in 1926, where he championed labor legislation during the New Deal, most famously the National Labor Relations Act in 1935.

17. Quoted in Slayton, *Empire Statesman*, 170.

18. Quoted in Slayton, *Empire Statesman*, 200–201.

19. Slayton, in *Empire Statesman*, gives an astute analysis of exactly why Smith signed the state enforcement repeal; after outlining all the factors that went into the decision, he argues that in the end, Smith "refused to be a hypocrite" (199). He opposed Prohibition and so he would take his political lumps by signing the controversial bill.

20. Smith's biographers energetically debate this point, weighing in on Smith's progressive bona fides and his conservative impulses. An excellent summary of this debate, though it precedes the two major scholarly biographies of Smith, is by Douglas Craig, *After Wilson: The Struggle for the Democratic Party, 1920–1934* (Chapel Hill: University of North Carolina Press, 1992), ch. 6, "The Problem of Al Smith," 112–30. As I state in the text, I think both Raskob and Smith wanted to make sure that workers were not exploited and that people had a fair shake and opportunities to better their lives. Raskob always emphasized the role business and capitalists played in assuring American prosperity and his perspective on capitalists' needs and prerogatives in an economically sound society increasingly influenced Smith who already had a strong interest in protecting and promoting business and the ideal of the self-made man as his friendships with Riordan, Kenny, and the other members of the Golf Cabinet showed and whose economic position changed, in large part thanks to Raskob, beginning in 1928. Finally, as Craig emphasizes, Smith, like Raskob, was in his own mind a self-made man and this self-image played a vital role in Smith's approach to business policy. Christopher Finan makes a related but different argument in the lucid opening pages of his Smith biography. He begins the book by asking how Smith went from being "the most powerful spokesman for liberalism in the United States" to an outspoken opponent of the New Deal and supporter of Raskob and the du Ponts in their battles against Franklin Roosevelt in the 1930s. Finan argues that the main reason was not Smith's changing views but his consistent fear of "arbitrary government" and "abuses of power" (302–3). I agree with Finan that Smith's old-school liberalism played a critical role, but I think he underplays Smith's evolution over time and his ambivalent feelings about economic self-making, which were affected by his growing allegiance to Raskob and by his personal feelings toward Roosevelt. Historians also emphasize that "liberalism" before the New Deal was an inchoate and developing approach to political economy issues; I think Smith was much more an urban progressive than he ever was a Big Government New Deal liberal. I discuss the tensions between early twentieth-century Progressivism and the various sometimes contradictory forms of New Deal liberalism in *The Rise and Fall of Modern American Conservatism* (Princeton: Princeton University Press, 2010). Alan Brinkley gives the most sophisticated account of the evolution of New Deal liberalism and New Dealers final embrace of macroeconomic management of a consumer-oriented capitalism in *The End of Reform* (New York: Knopf, 1995). New Deal liberalism was for both its changing array of proponents and opponents a moving target.

21. I am closely following the account and evidence laid out by Roy Haywood Lopata, "John J. Raskob: A Conservative Businessman in the Age of Roosevelt" (Ph.D. dissertation, University of Delaware, 1975), 62–63. Lopata's superbly researched dissertation is a major source for Raskob's role in the Smith campaign and his other political activities in the 1928 to 1937 period.

22. The quotes are from a letter du Pont wrote to the head of the Association Against the Prohibition Amendment in April 1926, which appears in Burk, *The Corporate State and the Broker State*, 37.

23. Robert Burk, in *The Corporate State and the Broker State*, further argues that the du Ponts, at least, wanted to "restore the hierarchical ideals of the American polity of the Founding

Fathers" (viii). They also wanted to create a "Corporate state" that would sanction "their economic hegemony" (ix). Du Pont and Raskob's support of repeal, Burk argues, was the first step in their attempt to dismantle the modern State and a democratic polity. Burk is, I think, deliberately stating his case in the bluntest terms to make a point about how reactionary the politics of the du Ponts were. I do not think that Burk makes his case though I do agree with him that the du Ponts were deeply suspicious of the public and wished it would leave economic policies to the economic elite. And I do think that he is right to argue that the du Ponts and Raskob felt that an irrational public, often blinded by prejudice, was a danger to their economic interests and that they opposed Prohibition, in part, for that very reason. But my reading of the archive convinces me that the du Ponts and Raskob were less certain of their goals and the political process, more generally; they were feeling their way into democratic practice from the late 1910s through the 1930s as they struggled to make sense of the changing face of the federal government and their place and status in US society. While the du Ponts were, as Burk argues, appalled by the power of the democratic majority to use the Constitution amendments process, as well as elections, to challenge the rights of the propertied elite, their political activities over time concentrated ever less on direct attempts to manipulate government officials than to redirect society—the electorate—through public campaigns or what might less generously be called well funded propaganda. The du Ponts and Raskob were developing the Super PAC long before the term came into existence. Finally, as I wrote (and as Burk argues, too), I think Raskob's reasons included this fear of an anti-business public but were also driven by his pro-Catholic immigrant sentiments, as was the case with Al Smith.

24. See Finan, *Alfred E. Smith*, 204–6.
25. For both the 1924 and 1928 national Democratic Party analysis I rely on Craig, *After Wilson*, chs. 3 and 5.
26. Ibid., 100–101.
27. FDR had used the same phrase, supplied by Smith speechwriter Joe Proskauer, in his 1924 Smith nominating speech.
28. Quoted in Lopata, "John J. Raskob," 60.
29. Ibid., 61.
30. Dowling, "The Reminiscences of Eddie Dowling," 108–9.
31. Frank Freidel, *Franklin Roosevelt: The Ordeal* (Boston: Little Brown, 1954), 246.
32. Josephson and Josephson, *Al Smith*, 370. The chronology of events surrounding Raskob's selection is all over the map in the various accounts by Dowling, the Josephsons, and Smith's other biographers. I have done my best to mesh the accounts into an order that makes best sense of Raskob's actions.
33. JJR to Robert Raskob, December 8, 1927, file 1682, JR.
34. JJR to William Raskob, January 20, 1928, file 1926, JR.
35. William Raskob to JJR, March 29, 1928, file 1926, JR.
36. "W. F. Raskob 2d, Son of John J. Raskob, Killed When Auto Plunges off Maryland Highway," *New York Times*, July 6, 1928, 1. Dowling also tells the story in his oral history account, 253.
37. JJR to Dwight Morrow, July 24, 1928, file 1594, JR.
38. Ibid.
39. "A Tribute from John and Helena Raskob to Bill Raskob," [n.d.], Bill Raskob Foundation website, http://www.billraskob.org/testimonials.php.
40. JJR to William Brady, December 24, 1935, file 251, JR.
41. Julia McCarthy, "Raskob as Democratic Chairman Puts Business into Fight," *New York World*, July 15, 1928, 1. McCarthy interviewed John Jacob Raskob, Jr., for the story.
42. "Text of Raskob's Acceptance Address," *New York Times*, July 12, 1928, 2.
43. Charles J. V. Murphy, "Smith Out to Win Big Business Vote," *New York World*, July 12, 1928, 1.
44. "Business and Politics," *New York Times*, July 12, 1928, 22.
45. Both quoted passages are from a summary of newspaper editorials from around the country compiled in "Editors Predict Raskob will Bring New Element to Support of Democracy," *New York World*, July 17, 1928, 2.

46. From a selection of newspaper editorials quoted in, "Smith's Choosing of Raskob Viewed by Press of Nation as Sign of New Era in Party," *New York World*, July 16, 1928, 2.
47. "Editors Predict Raskob," 2.
48. "Socialist Assails Raskob," *New York World*, July 13, 1928, 2.
49. "Socialist Leader Assails Raskob," *New York World*, July 15, 1928, 3.
50. James O'Donnell Bennett, "Smith Picks Militant Wet to Lead Fight," *Chicago Tribune*, July 12, 1928, 1.
51. Ibid.
52. Farber, *Sloan Rules*, 118–19. I should note that I cover this episode in great detail in *Sloan Rules* from Sloan's perspective and I am following my own narrative herein.
53. See Roland Marchand, *Creating the Corporate Soul* (Berkeley: University of California Press, 1998), ch. 4.
54. The quoted material is from the account given by GM executive Frederick Horner in his unpublished memoir [n.d.], 122–123, folder 3, box 70, Frederick Horner Papers, Library of Congress, Washington, D.C. Horner states that he was told the story, as quoted, from Sloan's secretary, who could hear the two men shouting through the closed office door. Horner, who expresses great admiration for Raskob, also states that JJR "was quite fond of the ladies." And that "he 'knocked around' a bit."
55. "Selection of Raskob Stirs Wall Street," *New York Times*, July 12, 1929, 2.
56. Farber, *Sloan Rules*, 120–21.
57. Coleman du Pont to Pierre du Pont, August 15, 1928, file 682, JR.
58. Farber, *Sloan Rules*, 119.
59. JJR to Alfred Sloan, July 17, 1928, box 2109, JR.
60. "Raskob Quits Post in General Motors to Appease Critics," *New York Times*, July 25, 1928, 1.
61. "The Raskob Resignation," *Wall Street Journal*, July 26, 1928, 3.
62. "Broad Street Gossip: John J. Raskob," *Wall Street Journal*, July 26, 1928, 2.
63. JJR to John Davis, September 27, 1928, file 560, JR.
64. "Autos: Mr. Sloan," *Time*, February 25, 1968, http://www.time.com/time/magazine/article/0,9171,835166-2,00.html.

Chapter 14

1. McCarthy, "Raskob as Democratic Chairman," 1.
2. Bill Raskob to JJR, February 17, 1928, file 1926, JR.
3. Helena Raskob to Jack Corcoran, August 15, 1928, copy in author's possession. This letter, the envelop in which it was sent, and several other similar items relating to the early stages of the relationship between Mrs. Raskob and Corcoran were kept by Jack Corcoran; after his death these items came into the possession of a person who wishes not to be named. This person made them available to me and I then arranged to make a copy of each relevant item. I was allowed to look at these items and make copies if I agreed not to name the source. I will refer to this collection as the Jack Corcoran collection (JC).
4. The quoted passage is from Marguerite Mooers Marshall, "Teach Children How and Why, but Don't Nag, Advises Mrs. Raskob, Model Mother of Eleven," New York *Evening World*, October 27, 1928, 3. Mrs. Raskob is also profiled in "Flax, Not Politics, Mrs. Raskob's Joy," *New York World*, July 29, 1928, 14. The paper also has a marvelous photo of Mrs. Raskob.
5. The first incident is detailed in "Raskob Blackmail and Death Threat Nipped by Arrest," *New York World*, September 21, 1928, 1–2. JJR's letter to Major Richard Sylvester, September 5, 1928, is in file 2205, as are the threats made in late September and October 1928 from the "gang," including the quoted letter, Dancio Ferdinand to Mrs. John J. Raskob, October 29/28 [1928], file 2205, JR.
6. Skipper to J. P. Corcoran, November [?], 1928, JC.
7. This book, locket of hair, oval photo with inscribed message, and letter dated July 22, 1929, are all in the JC. I have a copy of the photo with the message and the letter, as well as a copy of the inscribed first page of the Gibran book.

8. As noted earlier, I am never sure exactly what Raskob was doing with women and what he means when he refers to these women in his letters to his friends. For example, on December 28, 1927, he writes his millionaire Wall Street intimate Matt Brush to thank him for a Christmas gift of a "good luck" stuffed elephant: "outside of me the elephant is the handsomest thing in the apartment. Except, of course, when you and some of our girl friends happen to be in it." JJR to Matthew C. Brush, December 28, 1927, file 287, JR.

9. Figures taken from Slayton, *Empire Statesman*, 276.

10. Quoted in Elizabeth Israels Perry, *Belle Moskowitz* (New York: Oxford University Press, 1987), 204.

11. S. J. Woolf, "Raskob Takes Off His Coat for Smith," *New York Times*, September 10, 1928, 17.

12. "Business: Installment Buying," *Time*, November 28, 1927, http://www.time.com/time/magazine/article/0,9171,751736,00.html.

13. "City Gives Raskob and Governor Smith ... " [full title is cut off], *Lockport Union-Sun and Journal*, clipping, n.d. [June 26, 1928?], file 1914, JR. Kenny received his honorary degree June 25, 1928, and the Lockport paper notes that he had received the degree earlier in the day; the article was printed the next day.

14. I am indebted to Roy Lopata's narrative and analysis here. He quotes Raskob on p. 71.

15. Quoted in Lopata, "Raskob," 71.

16. "Raskob is Accused by Senator Moses," *New York Times*, November 2, 1928, 5.

17. Finan, *Alfred E. Smith*, 211.

18. "Hoover or Smith?" file 1249, JR. Raskob had a small collection of such flyers in his files, this one is from the Indiana KKK.

19. "Chairmen Who Talk," *New York Times*, September 3, 1928, 12.

20. Tom Feeley to JJR, September 26, 1928, file 791, JR.

21. Between 1923 and 1948, Woolf published a charcoal portrait of a person in the news in the NYT *Sunday Magazine*. The portrait was accompanied by the interview he conducted with the person while he drew. For more, see the note that accompanies the on-line inventory of the S. J. Woolf papers archived at the Archives of American Art, Smithsonian Institution, http://siris-archives.si.edu/ipac20/ipac.jsp?uri=full=3100001~!211491!0#focus.

22. Woolf, "Raskob Takes Off His Coat for Smith," 5.

23. William Woodford, "Raskob Hits Big 'Dry' Employers," *New York Times*, September 5, 1928, 2.

24. JJR to Walter Chrysler, September 27, 1928, file 342, JR.

25. James C. Young, "Raskob of General Motors: The New Generalissimo of the Democratic Party," *The World's Work*, September 1928, 489–90.

26. Ibid., 491.

27. Ibid., 492.

28. Slayton, *Empire Statesman*, 277–79.

29. Craig, *After Wilson*, 169.

30. "Raskob Defeated Smith, Says Cannon," *New York Times*, November 27, 1928, 26.

31. "Raskob 'Accepts Majority's Will, Takes Place in Ranks,'" *New York World*, November 7, 1928, 2.

32. "Raskob to Retain Democratic Post," *New York Times*, November 7, 1928, 2. Some scholars backed up Raskob's claims about the campaign's relative success, arguing that Smith had brought urban ethnic working-class voters to the polls and aligned them with the Democratic Party—a key development that portended the Democrats' future winning coalition; see Oscar Handlin, *Al Smith and His America* (Boston: Little, Brown, 1958), 134. The leading scholar on this subject, Allan Lichtman, however, does not believe that the numbers back up any claim that Smith contributed to the making of what came to be called the New Deal coalition; he states that FDR's politics not Smith's campaign created the "urban emphasis" of the national Democrats' vote. See Allan Lichtman, *Prejudice and the Old Politics: The Presidential Election of 1928* (Chapel Hill: University of North Carolina Press, 1979), 237.

33. Perkins, oral history transcript, vol. 2, p. 686.

34. The exact amounts of Raskob's contributions and the DNC's haul are the subject of debate. I have relied on Douglas Craig's careful work in *After Wilson*, 176–77 and 184 and the work

of Roy Lopata, "Raskob," 72–74. As for the campaign debt, usual practice was to launch a drive after the election to raise the money nationally. Raskob did so, but he saw little chance of the large debt being met by this method so he pushed all the guarantors of the loans to pay. None were happy; they believed that they had signed on to the campaign loans only as a legal expedient and that the money would, eventually, come from other sources, as was common.

35. The quote is in Robert Cruise McManus, "Raskob," *North American Review* 231:1 (January 1931), 13.
36. Craig, *After Wilson*, 183. I am relying on Craig's account of the new DNC here.
37. For the best overview of investment trusts and the more general effort to make Americans a nation of shareholders, see Ott, *When Wall Street Met Main Street*; for investment trusts, in particular, see ch. 8.
38. JJR to Calvin Coolidge, May 6, 1929, file 479, JR.
39. "Raskob Will Help Workers to Invest," *New York Times*, May 7, 1929, 1, 8.
40. All quotes in this section are made in "Mr. Raskob's 'Poor Man's Investment Trust,'" *The Literary Digest* 101:9 (June 1, 1929), 88–91.
41. Lawrence Stern, "Durant, Raskob, Cutten, Fishers are the New Kings of Wall Street," *New York World*, August 19, 1928, 1–2.
42. "Raskob Sounds Caution on Security Prices," *Wall Street Journal*, October 5, 1928, 5.
43. While I have done my best to make sense of JJR's complex investment strategy here, I must give immense credit to Roy Lopata, JJR's first major biographer and Rob Wherry, one of the nation's preeminent business writers who has long been deeply interested in JJR's financial career for their analysis of JJR's GM investment strategy during this time. Wherry's insights are reported in "Rethinking Raskob," *Forbes*, October 9, 2000, and Lopata reports on the GM strategy in his dissertation, 52–59.
44. *Time* reported on the RCA pool in its coverage of a famous congressional investigation of such pools that took place in 1932, "Business & Finance: Anything Can Be Done…," *Time*, May 30, 1932, http://www.time.com/time/magazine/article/0,9171,769617,00.html.
45. "Equishares Company Inc. Stockholders as of June 25, 1929," file 755, JR.
46. Quoted in Finan, *Alfred E. Smith*, 233–34.
47. I have found nothing in Raskob's papers to support the claim made by Dana Thomas in *Plungers and Peacocks* (New York: G. P. Putnam, 1967) that Raskob was willfully misleading the public in 1929 so as to advance the fortunes of stock market speculators, especially Billy Durant, who were quietly selling their stock in 1929 in advance of a bear market. Raskob did note publically in late 1928 and throughout 1929 that he thought the market was overvalued though he also did state, several times, that he thought some stocks were still good investments, even in the summer of 1929. His own substantial investments in Equishares further demonstrates JJR's faith that money could still be made in the market in the summer and fall of 1929.
48. Samuel Crowther, "Everybody Ought to be Rich: An Interview with John J. Raskob," *Ladies Home Journal* 46:8 (August 1929), 8, 36.

Chapter 15

1. Curcio, *Chrysler*, 419.
2. In this section on the Empire State Building, I rely throughout on two excellent books for context and specific narrative development: Neil Bascomb, *Higher: A Historic Race to the Sky and the Making of a City* (New York: Doubleday, 2003) and John Tauranac, *The Empire State Building* (New York: Scribner, 1995). The dollar figures for New York building are from Tauranac, 81, and the quoted passage is on 78.
3. Dowling, "The Reminiscences of Eddie Dowling," 111.
4. While no letters in Raskob's files demonstrate that Coleman du Pont and Raskob write to each other about the real estate deal prior to 1929, the extant letters in Raskob's papers indicate the closeness of their relationship; see file 682, JR. See also Tauranac, *The Empire State Building*, 114–18.
5. Bascomb does take note of Kaufman's long-standing relationship with JJR, *Higher*, 146.

6. I am speculating throughout here on the extent to which JJR was aware of unfolding events and the degree to which Kaufman was keeping JJR in the loop in anticipation of Brown's loan default. Though I place JJR much more into the early days of the story, I am in general following Tauranac's superb narrative of events in *The Empire State Building*, 120–22. Bascomb, in *Higher*, also speculates that JJR was involved from early on with the Empire State Building project, 185–86.

7. Raskob comments on the financing in "Raskob Denies Smith Got Building Loan," *New York Times*, December 1, 1933, 9.

8. JJR to Gertrude Bradley, October 10, 1929, file 219, JR.

9. Quotes are from Bascomb, *Higher*, 149–50.

10. Ibid., 188.

11. Edward Chancellor, *Devil Take the Hindmost: A History of Financial Speculation* (New York: Farrar Straus and Giroux, 1999), 215. I am following Chancellor's vividly drawn account.

12. Financial Statement, December 31, 1929, file 1916, JR.

13. "Break in Stock Debated in Senate," *New York Times*, November 2, 1929, 2.

14. JJR to Senator Pat Harrison, November 2, 1929, file 1914, JR.

15. Quoted in the *New York Times*, October 30, 1929, and then read into the Congressional Record by Senator Harrison on November 2; see JJR to Harrison.

16. I am following the account given by Finan, *Alfred Smith*, 246–27.

17. Raskob's statement was printed on the front page of New York newspapers; see "Officials Report on Audit," *New York World*, November 10, 1929, 1.

18. The quoted passage appears in Slayton, *Empire Statesman*, 344, and the general narrative comes from both Slayton, 344–45 and Finan, *Alfred E. Smith*, 246–47.

19. See file 566, JR.

20. JJR to Coleman du Pont, August 20, 1929, file 682, JR.

21. JJR to Frank Spellman, April 22, 1931, file 2356.

22. Quotes are from Marshall, "Teach Children How and Why."

23. A typical event from those days, demonstrative of the strength and complexity of their relationship: on John's 51st birthday, Helena sent him 51 red roses. He was in Florida and she was in Maryland. He telegraphed her, "Thoroughly appreciate your kindness and thoughtfulness in sending them to me STOP Red roses, of course, have always been my weakness STOP Much love John." JJR to Helena Raskob March 19, 1930, file 1910, box 1, JR.

24. One of the Raskobs' grandchildren told me, in confidence, that Mrs. Raskob had told her mother, who was upset by her husband's philandering, that maintaining a marriage involved recognition of its limits as well as its fundamental importance to family life. I am paraphrasing what I was told.

25. The dollar amount comes from an article on Pioneer Point published in the mid-1940s, Robert G. Green, "A Place to Lead the Simple Life," *The Sun*, which was reprinted and included in materials used to sell the estate; copies of this material were provide to me by the Raskob family.

26. Both quotes are taken from Tauranac, *The Empire State Building*, 156 and 157.

27. Ibid., ch. 10.

28. Quoted in Bascomb, *Higher*, 187–88.

29. Bascomb, *Higher*, 255. As Bascomb points out, JJR also wanted to counter Chrysler's use of Margaret Bourke-White to publicize his baby.

30. Bascomb, *Higher*, 235.

31. Tauranac, *The Empire State Building*, 184–85. Raskob, and almost surely Smith, knew that the dirigible mast was not practical. He and the architects for the building had planned for such a mast at least since late 1929, but as John wrote Coleman du Pont in December of that year, "the engineers doubt the feasibility of a mooring mast on our building due to the fact that apparently they have to weigh the tail down" of a zeppelin to avoid it spinning around in the air and wreaking havoc. JJR to Coleman du Pont, December 16, 1929, file 682, JR.

32. Lammot's reluctance is shown in Lammot du Pont to JJR, August 29, 1929, file 678, JR; at the top of the letter is scrawled "Answered by telephone."

33. Tauranac, *The Empire State Building*, 276. More generally, the material on tenants and leasing problems also comes from Tauranac, ch. 15.

34. Raskob's own records make his investment and obligations in the ESB difficult to deter-
    mine but a 1937 SEC investigation spelled out the situation that was reported in the news-
    papers; see "Empire State Building Financing Examined at SEC Trust Hearing," *New York
    Times*, May 14, 1937, 6.
35. Finan, *Alfred E. Smith*, 259.
36. "Raskob to Occupy Elaborate Offices," *New York Times*, August 30, 1931, sec. XI, p. 2.
37. I am closely following Craig, *After Wilson*, 184.
38. Quoted in Craig, *After Wilson*, 194. I am indebted to Craig's narrative and analysis of
    Raskob's efforts; see ch. 9, especially pp. 187–97.
39. Quoted in Craig, *After Wilson*, 241.
40. Quoted in Finan, *Alfred E. Smith*, 261.
41. JJR's gift to Warm Springs has long been a contested tale. I have not located a receipt or
    invoice of the gift in JJR's papers. According to Jim Farley, FDR told him that Raskob had
    promised to raise $200,000 and personally guaranteed $50,000 immediately but then only
    paid $37,500; Farley, February 7, 1936, private files #39, JAF, LC. A total gift of $100,000
    by JJR to the Warm Springs Foundation is documented in the newspaper story, "John
    Raskob Gives $100,000 for Warm Spring Foundation," *Chicago Daily-Tribune*, June 17,
    1930, 3. This story again became news in 1950 when New York Governor Tom Dewey dis-
    cussed the matter publicly in October 1950, quoting—actually misquoting—the version
    given by Jim Farley in his 1948 memoir, *Jim Farley's Story*. Raskob's side of the story, which
    I have used here, is told in detail in a letter JJR wrote to John T. Flynn in response to Farley's
    account in his memoir. Raskob states that as told by Farley, "the statement is untrue." JJR
    to John Flynn, March 5, 1948, file 828, JR. When it comes to remembering an amount of
    money my bet is on Raskob.
42. Raskob describes his feelings about FDR in his 1933 letters to his friend Gretchen Dau
    Cunningham, a California political operator; see file 529, JR.
43. Quoted in Craig, *After Wilson*, 217.
44. I am closely following the account given by Donald A. Ritchie, *Electing FDR* (Lawrence:
    University Press of Kansas, 2007), 86. The quoted phrase is also 86.
45. Finan, *Alfred E. Smith*, 276.
46. JJR to Curtis Cooper June 16, 1932, file 481, JR.
47. An incisive account of Raskob's efforts on behalf of repeal is given in David Kyvig, "Raskob,
    Roosevelt, and Repeal," *Historian*, May 1975, 469–87.
48. A great inside account of Farley's strategy and efforts is noted in Private File, boxes 37–38,
    James A. Farley Papers, Library of Congress, Washington, D.C. Alas, for my purposes little
    on Raskob appears in his accounts.
49. Craig, *After Wilson*, 109.
50. "Democrats Name Farley Chairman," *New York Times*, July 3, 1932, 1.4.
51. "From a Senator's Diary," *Washington Post*, November 8, 1932, 7.
52. Franklin D. Roosevelt, "The Governor Accepts the Nomination for the Presidency," July 2,
    1932, *The Public Papers and Addresses of Franklin D. Roosevelt*, Vol. 1 (New York: Random
    House, 1938), 647–59.

Chapter 16

1. JJR to Elizabeth Marbury, July 11, 1932, file 1434, JR.
2. Alfred Allan Lewis, *Ladies and Not-So-Gentle Women* (New York: Viking, 2000).
3. From Artie McGovern's letterhead; see file 1495, JR.
4. "Raskob Offers Plan to Spur Prosperity by Democratic Rule," *New York Times*, November
   5, 1932, 1.
5. JJR to Albert Ritchie, July 8, 1932, file 1966, JR.
6. JJR to Gretchen Dau Cunningham, May 29, 1933, file 529, JR.
7. I am much influenced in this section by Roy Lopata, "John J. Raskob," chs. 4 and 5. The
   quoted passage is from p. 218.
8. JJR to Gretchen Dau Cunningham, March 23, 1933, file 529, JR.
9. Cunningham to JJR, April 30, 1933, file 529, JR.

10. JJR to John Small, June 11, 1936, file 2111, JR.
11. All quotes are from JJR to Donaldson Brown, April 2, 1934, file 278, JR. The letter includes a highly detailed proposed itinerary.
12. "'Al' at 'Frank's' Tea Party," *Washington Post*, November 15, 1933, 6, for the quote; the photo appears on p. 1.
13. "President Entertains Warm Springs Visitors," *New York Times*, November 27, 1933, 3.
14. JJR to Phil Beakart, December 19, 1933, file 177, JR.
15. JJR to Franklin Roosevelt, November 28, 1933, PPF, 226, FDR. Interestingly no copy of this letter appears in Raskob's papers.
16. JJR to PdP, December 21, 1933. John matter-of-factly tells Pierre of his scheduled meeting with FDR and Deane at the White House.
17. For the first iteration of the Deane Plan: A. L. Deane and H. K. Norton, *Investing in Wages* (New York: MacMillan, 1932). For an overview of the Deane Plan and New Deal interest, including the White House meeting in January 1934, see Benjamin Hunnicutt's instructive monograph, *Work Without End* (Philadelphia: Temple University Press, 1988), 232–35. The quoted passages are from JJR to Franklin Roosevelt, December 15, 1933, PPF, 226, FDR. No copy of this letter can be found in JJR's papers.
18. I am following the narrative of Arthur M. Schlesinger, Jr., *The Coming of the New Deal* (Boston: Houghton Mifflin, 1959), ch. 27. The Raskob quote appears on 436.
19. Ibid.; the Rand quote appears on 457 and the Hearst quote is on 460.
20. R. R. M. Carpenter, March 16, 1934, file 350, JR.
21. Quoted in Burk, *The Corporate State and the Broker State*, 130.
22. JJR to Ruly Carpenter, March 30, 1934, file 350, JR.
23. Several historians have explored which members of the corporate elite turned against the New Deal and which ones did not; I explore in detail how and why Alfred Sloan of General Motors became an ardent anti–New Dealer in *Sloan Rules*. The argument generally, but not always, holds that capital-intensive industries were more likely to support or at least remain neutral toward the New Deal and labor-intensive industries, due to their intense concerns about the New Deal legislation that protected labor organizing, were most likely to oppose it; see Thomas Ferguson, *Golden Rule: The Investment Theory of Party Competition and the Logic of Money-Driven Political Systems* (Chicago: University of Chicago Press, 1995), especially ch. 2.
24. I am following, Burk, *The Corporate State and the Broker State*, 124–25.
25. Ibid., 152.
26. I rely on Kim McQuaid, *Big Business and Presidential Power* (New York: Morrow, 1982), 37–45; see also Chandler and Salisbury, *Pierre S. du Pont*, 589.
27. Here I am in some degree of dispute with Robert Burk who makes the case that Raskob was by 1934 fiercely New Deal and an advocate of a "corporate state." I think Raskob remained more ambivalent and less certain about the nature of the pro-business political regime he promoted.
28. S. M. DuBrul to Donaldson Brown, June 19, 1934, file 61B, JR. I believe this memo was widely distributed to GM and DuPont top executives as it figures in their conversation and also since Raskob had a copy in his files, which he appears to have received soon after its composition.
29. Alfred Sloan to JJR, July 24, 1934, file 61B, JR. Raskob writes of Sloan's suggested name in his letter, JJR to PdP, July 30, 1934, file 61A, JR.
30. I tell this story in *The Rise and Fall of Modern American Conservatism* (Princeton: Princeton University Press, 2010), 20–21; for the actual list, see John W. Davis to JJR, August 8, 1934, file 61C, JR.
31. "Roosevelt Twits Liberty League as Lover of Property," *New York Times*, August 25, 1934, 2.
32. "League is Formed to Scan New Deal, Protect Rights," *New York Times*, August 23, 1934, 1, 4.
33. "Unexceptionable Aims," *New York Times*, August 23, 1934, 16.
34. "End of NIRA asked by Irénée du Pont," *New York Times*, August 24, 1934, 2.
35. "Five Senators Cool to Liberty League," *New York Times*, August 24, 1934, 2.

36. "Roosevelt Twits Liberty League," 1.
37. JJR to Ellis Spreckels, August 30, 1934, file 2157, JR.
38. Samuel Harden Church to JJR, August 27, 1934, file 61c, JR.
39. Henry Harriman to JJR, August 31, 1934, file 61C, JR.
40. J. Howard Pew to JJR, January 4, 1935, file 61F, JR.
41. Edward Bernays, *biography of an idea* (New York: Simon and Schuster, 1965), 543. No caps in original title
42. The story of the trip is recounted by Josephine Raskob Robinson in the charming family history compiled and edited by Peter S. Robinson, *Robinson Remembrances* ([n.p.]: CFW Press, 1989). The quoted passage is on 89.
43. Ibid., 93.
44. "Raskob Ends World Tour," *New York Times*, May 21, 1935, 11.
45. Jouett Shouse to JJR, May 8, 1935, file 61h, JR.
46. "Raskob Praises Integrity of Business Leaders," *Wall Street Journal*, August 20, 1935, 1.
47. Ibid., 1, 3.
48. Gretchen Dau Cunningham to JJR, October 21, 1935, file 529, JR.
49. JJR to Greatchen Dau Cunningham, [n.d.], file 529, JR.
50. "Liberty League," *Newsweek*, December 7, 1935, 11–12.
51. The letter, in whole, was quoted in newspapers around the country, amplifying its reach; see, for example, the front page story, "Raskob to Expand Liberty League," *New York Times*, February 1, 1936, 1–2.
52. Slayton, *Empire Statesman*, 382.
53. J. E. Frederick to JJR, February 5, 1936, file 61L, JR.
54. JJR to Alfred P. Sloan, April 24, 1936, file 61N, JR.
55. I rely on the standard account of the Liberty League, George Wolfskill, *The Revolt of the Conservatives: A History of the American Liberty League, 1933–1940* (Boston: Houghton Mifflin, 1962), see especially 62–63.
56. Franklin D. Roosevelt, "Address at Madison Square Garden, New York City," October 31, 1936, in *The Public Papers and Addresses of Franklin D. Roosevelt*, Vol. 5 (New York: Random House, 1938), 568–69.
57. Raskob details his illness in letters to his old GMAC friend Curtis Cooper who Raskob had intended to visit at his ranch in Arizona, see the letters between the two men in the fall of 1936, file 481, JR.
58. Francis Spellman to JJR, [n.d.], file 2152, JR.
59. JJR to Curtis Cooper, November 23, 1936, file 481, JR.

Chapter 17

1. See "The Power of the Plains," Herman Drache, *Agricultural History* 51:1 (January 1977), 78–91.
2. JJR to Curtis Cooper, September 15, 1937, file 481, JR.
3. Raskob kept an undated clipping of the story in his files with the only information the article's title: "Raskob's Famous Tip Rewelds Marital Bond," and the typed caption: "one of the Brooklyn papers about two weeks ago," file 1914, JR.
4. JJR to Bill Kenny, February 2, 1939, file 1249, JR.
5. The quote was put out on the AP wires and was carried by the *Times*, "Deplore German Terror," *New York Times*, November 19, 1938, 3.
6. Slayton, *Empire Statesman*, 392.
7. JJR to PdP, January 11, 1940, file 681.
8. JJR to Joseph T. Geuting, Jr., July 21, 1942, file 889, JR.
9. The figures come from Raskob paper archivist Richard James who added up the figures for me and presented me with a bounty of such accounts.
10. Quoted in Finan, *Alfred E. Smith*, 345.
11. This policy is set out in the Minutes of the First Meeting of the RFCA, December 26, 1945, Raskob Foundation for Catholic Activities files (RFCA), Wilmington, Delaware. The Foundation kindly made numerous materials from the RFCA's early days available to me

at their headquarters at Irisbrook, which had been the longtime home of John's brother, William.

12. JJR to Helena Raskob, January 25, 1946, file 1930, JR.

13. "To the Present and Future Trustees of Raskob Foundation for Catholic Activities (Inc.)," November 21, 1946, RFCA files.

14. JJR to PdP, January 17, 1947, file 303, box 216, PDP.

15. JJR to PdP, August 31, 1948, file 303, box 216, PDP.

16. See file 678 Travel, JR and I also benefited from an email Pat Geuting sent to Richard James (JJR archivist), September 14, 2005.

17. Bishop Edmund FitzMaurice, "John J. Raskob Funeral," October 18, 1950, RFCA files.

18. "104 Steps, 600 Documents—And a Skyscraper is Sold," *Life*, June 7, 1952, 23. The contemporary figures are from Craig Karmin, "High Stakes Feud over Skyscraper," *Wall Street Journal*, March 3–4, 2012, B1–B2.

INDEX